If I'm the King of My Castle, Then Why Am I Holding a Dirty Diaper?

If I'm the King of My Castle, Then Why Am I Holding a Dirty Diaper?

Norman Moore, Ph.D.

ISBN: 1511997273
ISBN 13: 9781511997270
Library of Congress Control Number: 2015907206
CreateSpace Independent Publishing Platform
North Charleston, South Carolina

To both of my families...the one that raised me and that one that makes life worth living. Mom, Dad, and Dan...we weren't rich money-wise, but we were in every other way. Amy, Nick, Andrew, and Jason...I can't think of life without you.

Table of Contents

Section 1

The Dating Life

or

If Men Are from Mars, That Would Explain Why They Have No Clue Where Women Are From

Men and women are fundamentally different, like oil and water, fire and ice, and Michael Jackson in the Jackson 5 years and later in the Diana Ross look-alike years.[1] Men and women have vast variations in how they think, act, talk, and basically breathe, to the point where you'd think they belong to two entirely separate species. However, if you weren't able to leap to that conclusion yourself, then tying your shoes is not so much a morning ritual but a life's goal.

This section of the book doesn't serve so much to ameliorate differences, but to point them out.[2] It is to make men understand that they are not alone in their daily dealings with the opposite sex, such as when they get into trouble and have no idea how they ended up in this situation and can't find out because they are getting the silent treatment. On the flip side, if a woman realizes that the guy she is dating appears immature, she may as well get used to it, as trying to find a man who is truly mature is on par with opening Cracker Jack boxes trying to find the Hope Diamond as the prize.

---

1   It may not be considered highbrow to start this book with a Michael Jackson joke considering his untimely passing. Regardless of his talent, you have to admit that he changed looks more often than *Time* magazine changed its cover. Besides, if you were in the bookstore to pick up something intellectually challenging and came home with this particular book, it would appear that you ended up in the wrong aisle.

2   And hopefully make a few dollars in the process. The kids' college bills ain't cheap!

Most men spend their lives trying to uncover the secret of understanding a woman. The secret is this: You'll never understand them, so why bang your head against a table trying?[3] If a man ever did get close to this mythical understanding, the rules would then be arbitrarily changed to put him back to square zero, as square one may give him some hope. Women have the opposite issue—they understand the guy but also understand that he doesn't understand her and doesn't want him to...unless she does, and then he had best understand in a hurry. Understand?

Now when I mention that there are differences between the sexes, I'm not talking just about the physical differences that we all obsess about. You know, the ones on display in commercials to make men buy beer, power tools, cars, dental floss, shoe polish (even when they only own sneakers), and anything else Madison Avenue wants to spoon-feed us. And where buffed-up men make women buy, ummm, well...OK, so women aren't as pathetically gullible as men on that issue. [4]

The physical differences between men and women are not what really cause all the difficulties between the sexes. Most men feel that life wouldn't be worth living if it weren't for these differences. The only big exception to the big-difference-no-problem rule is when men try to think with their "difference," because it has certainly tallied more than a few crashes on its track record.[5] Instead, I am talking

---

3 For those men on their third-plus marriage, it is like banging your head on a table littered with broken glass and rusty nails.

4 So how do advertisers guilt women into buying things they don't need? By showing the same thin women they show the men. The models in these commercials are often so thin and malnourished that a stiff wind could snap their spines. Yet they are held as the ideal and so are used to sell shampoos, makeup, and clothes, all the while looking like they just escaped a concentration camp run by a Nazi version of Richard Simmons. Some women feel compelled to view these models as something they should aspire to for fear that anything less will get Green Peace volunteers pushing them back into the water whenever they visit a beach. Slap a "made especially for women" label on the same product, and you can even triple the price. So who's more gullible? At least men know that they are being manipulated and happily go along for the ride.

5 An epileptic driving in a NASCAR race blindfolded and inebriated in a car full of bees would have fewer crashes than when the man's little head assumes decision-making control from the big head.

about the emotional and intellectual distinctions that confound the relationships between men and women.

There are just some things that men and women will never be able to understand about each other. Women will never know what men find inherently important about ultimate fighting, flatulence, monster trucks, and anything else with an engine. Men will never understand a woman's attraction to soap operas, flowers, and spending two months' salary on a dress that is two sizes too small for her to wear as an incentive to lose weight.

Many women anguish over the belief that men's minds do little more than think about sex and sports, which would help explain men's fascination with female mud wrestling. Men get frustrated because they believe women's minds change direction about as often as a chameleon dropping acid changes color in a plaid-skirt factory. In actuality, they're both right. Rather than just accept that they are different, many men and women continue to try to change the other person to their way of thinking, when they should just throw up their hands about the whole thing and get on with life. Therefore, it may help if we take a different approach and start defining why and how men and women are different and resign ourselves to the fact that that is the way it is and always will be.

Growing Up

or

At Least Men Get Taller

When They Mature

Men and women are inherently different from birth. A lot of so-called "enlightened" people argue that this is not the case. They believe that it is only because people treat boy babies differently from girl babies that boys and girls start acting differently. Girl babies are handled as if they were made of delicate lace, whereas boy babies are quite often tossed around like drooling footballs. These same enlightened people then talk of how when they have their own children, they won't burden them by infusing them with gender stereotypes. They think they'd no more do this than perform plastic surgery on their children to install a hunchback.

Then these people have children of their own. Guns are banned from the boys, and anatomically exaggerated Barbies are removed from the sight of girls. Does this work? About as well as banning fish from drinking. Boys will take a few of their Legos, smash them together and—presto—homemade gun. Throw two boys together, and they end up mauling each other and running around like their clothes were on fire. Take all the dolls away from a little girl, and she'll end up carrying on endless conversations with Mr. Potato

Head. Throw two girls together, and they will talk incessantly without ever actually taking the time to hear what the other is saying.[6]

Boys and girls are different, and the average parents want them to be viewed as different. Some parents freak out with how their newborn babies look. Let's face it, with a diaper on, telling a girl baby from a boy baby is about as easy as flossing an alligator. They all start off looking more or less like Elmer J. Fudd.[7] If, however, you mistakenly call a she "he," then the mother starts sobbing hysterically thinking that her daughter is going to grow up to look like an inside linebacker for the New York Giants. If you call a he a "she," then the father bristles, thinking you are calling his son a wimp.

This is why parents (actually mothers) go to such great lengths to give people hints as to the baby's gender. If it is a girl, they'll usually put a bow in her hair. What if the baby doesn't have any hair? Then she'll tape it on. Why do this at all? Because they don't make fishnet stockings small enough for those chubby legs, and the baby's eyelashes aren't strong enough to take the mascara. Then the mother throws the girl into baby outfits with enough frills to make Liberace roll over in his grave. If it is a boy baby, he's lucky because the mother can't accessorize. The mother can only dress him in clothing plastered with baseballs and footballs even though the boy looks more like the actual ball than a future athlete.

In the early years, girls are usually more advanced than boys in school. While the boys look like they all have some level of attention

---

6 As a personal example, my first two children, who happened to be boys, were at their grandmother's house doing what boys do—running and wrestling. Activities like coloring get their attention for around a ten-nanosecond time frame, and then they are trying to write on each other with the crayons or use them as miniswords. As my mother-in-law had only had girls and she had been an only child, she assumed that the children were abnormally hyperactive and were probably great candidates for being medicated with something akin to elephant tranquilizers. I had to break the news to her that not only was this what boys were like, but this was actually considered good behavior and it could get far worse. Not that she mentioned it, but her next assumption may have been that her new son-in-law's parenting skills were on par with used dishwater. However, she did babysit my sister-in-law's son and realized very soon that the saying "boys will be boys" is not only true, but a curse.

7 Elmer J. Fudd, millionaire, owns a mansion and a yacht. If you need to ask, don't bother.

deficit disorder,[8] the girls can actually sit still for more than 18 or 19 seconds and absorb what the teacher is saying. Some boys don't recognize that the teacher is in the room until the teacher is standing on the desk screaming at the top of his or her lungs to shut up and sit down. It is hard at this age for the boys to learn anything because they use their heads more for battering rams than for learning.

In later years, boys turn the physical roughhousing into a competition about everything from grades to games. A boy can't walk up a flight of stairs without challenging someone to beat him to the top. You'd think that with all the challenges, boys would love competition. They do—when they win, that is. If a boy loses at something as simple as the board game Candy Land, then you'd think he was just told that the monsters under his bed were planning their big attack for tonight. Girls at this age don't know how to handle this level of outrageous competition. It is like walking into a lions' den wearing zebra-striped pajamas. Luckily, the girls' ability to concentrate balances against the boys' competitive nature.

As a general rule, boys are harder to rear earlier on. They think nothing of going on the playground swings as high as they can and jumping off even if it will launch them into thorn bushes, or climbing the kitchen hutch that is displaying the good china just because they have nothing better to do. Meanwhile, the girls are (usually) sweet little things…or at least know how to act that way when an adult is in the room. The older they get, however, the more the roles reverse, and the boys become easier.[9] After all, do boys spend hour upon hour on the phone? Do they form little cliques and hate another girl one day and like her the next? Do they hog the bathroom experimenting with makeup even if you have the stomach flu? Suffice it to say that girls continue to get harder to understand and get along with as they grow up because, well, because they are turning into women.

---

8 With a bit of Tourette's syndrome thrown in.

9 "Easier" and "easy" should not be confused with each other. After all, it is "easier" to kill a great white shark with a rusty spoon than to pick up and move Mount Everest spoonful by spoonful, but you still aren't going to call it easy!

Mind over Matter

or

Mind over What the Heck Is the Matter Now?

A man's brain and woman's brain are hardwired about as differently as an IBM supercomputer and the game Operation. I'm not going to say who's who, especially because when men get upset, they tend to make that annoying buzzing sound. Biologically speaking, the brain is divided into two halves. The left half is considered the analytical side, and the right side is considered the artistic side. They are attached and can "talk to each other" by a mass of tissue in the middle called the corpus callosum.

Scientists have shown that the corpus callosum is very thick in women, a veritable superhighway of data transport. In men, the corpus callosum is more of a backyard alley full of trash cans and sleeping hobos that gets plugged up when more than a few people are meandering there at the same time. That would seem to favor the female brain in the ability of both sides interacting, but, getting back to the superhighway analogy, it is more like an eight-lane road that allows traffic to go either way—any way—it wants, regardless of what is barreling down from the other direction. In contrast, if you sidestep the urinating hobo in the alley, you can usually get by.

For most men, you'd think the artistic right side would have atrophied away with disuse, so the left side would be sending thoughts over through the corpus callosum to the right side like lemmings heading toward a cliff. After all, many men can't match clothes,[10] and they all secretly like the velvet paintings in the Dogs Playing Poker series.[11] However, men do actually use that artistic side. They have adapted the entire half to creating bad pickup lines and humor along the lines of belching the national anthem. If it hadn't been for that development, a guy's left brain would only fill half the skull so it would rattle around like the last peanut in a can, causing permanent brain damage.

A man actually uses the left side of his brain for constructive things. This part of a man's brain is exceptionally powerful. He can use it for higher math, problem solving, and inventing. However, the right brain gets lonely every few seconds and needs to be heard, even if it has no bearing on the immediate issues.[12] Therefore, it tries to imagine how every woman who walks by would look naked[13] and then shunts that image over to the left side. The left side takes a moment to admire the handiwork of the right side and then tries to get back to the business at hand. The right brain will go on tossing random things over, trying its best to keep the left brain from doing its job. Usually, it is quite successful. The left side of the brain is not stupid, after all, and so is quite pleased to be distracted and not have to work.

Now some women may roll their eyes at this section, thinking that we couldn't possibly be so shallow, but there will be no eye rolling from the men, because they agree. All men live through it every waking and sleeping moment of their lives. The hormone level is forever

---

10 I've got a doctorate and give lectures around the world. My wife *still* has to match my clothes, complete with putting a tie around the outfit, before I pack. If I were allowed to actually pick my own outfits, people would think I pick my clothes by blindfolding myself, spinning around, and launching myself in the direction of the closet, and then putting on whatever my hands touch first.

11 Vincent van Gogh would have had one on his wall if they were around during his time.

12 Sort of like listening to a congressman.

13 Which is not so good if you are visiting your grandmother in the old folks' home.

set on "11."[14] At least, they all *would* agree, but most male readers are no longer paying attention to the words on this page because ever since I mentioned naked women in the last paragraph, they may have continued reading the words, but their comprehension level is now hovering at about the level of overcooked broccoli.[15]

Women's brains, on the other hand, are a flood of activity. Neurons to the left are firing. Neurons to the right are firing. Hell, if you could open up the skull, it would look like the Chinese New Year. Unlike in men, both sides of the brain are robust and energetic. The left and right sides are blazing away with ideas, anxieties, worries, plans, etc. So what would happen if you were in a crowded room and everyone was talking at the same time? To a man, it is chaos. It would be like trying to do long division in your head while reciting the state capitals alphabetically while playing dodge ball. To a woman, it is business as usual. That's why they can talk about seventeen or eighteen subjects in a two-minute interval, whereas a man's brain will simply explode and dribble out his ears if more than two unrelated things are happening.

There are two types of memory: short term and long term. In short-term memory, things get placed on a temporary shelf before being discarded. Long-term memory is when an event gets recorded in the brain for posterity. As you'd expect, men and women differ on their abilities with short- and long-term memory. As a general rule, the short-term memory of a man stinks like a long-lost diaper in the cushions of a couch.

If a guy goes to the local store to buy three things, he may come back with three things, but only one of them will be what he was supposed to get in the first place. It is not that he doesn't want to get what he is supposed to; he truly can't remember. That could be an exceptionally infuriating thing to a woman if one of the things on the

---

14 "It's not ten. You see, most blokes, you know, will be playing at ten. You're on ten here, all the way up, all the way up, all the way up, you're on ten on your guitar. Where can you go from there? Where? Eleven!" Nigel Tufnel.

15 To get men's attention back, you have to mention female nudity a second time. The right side of the brain sees this word and sends a message to the left to stop skimming and look for any exciting context so the guy has to back up and actually read the paragraph for comprehension.

list was something she had an urgent need for, like feminine protection. Not only is the short-term memory shelf on the small side, it is built on an angle so the few things put there still tend to roll out. He can't remember to call when he's supposed to call, even if his wife has threatened his very existence if he doesn't. If he is being introduced to someone, he can't remember their name by the end of the sentence.

Once a man is used to being around a woman, he gets used to hanging up his brain on the coat rack when he walks through the door of his house. When a male is younger, he's got his mother. A boy will sit there screaming for his mom to help him find his sneakers even if he is wearing them. Later in life, many males take on a wife. After several years of marriage, a man could starve to death if his wife is late from work because he's forgotten how to operate a can opener.

Naturally, this lack of focus infuriates women, who have to compensate for men's forgetfulness by reminding them repeatedly of things (also known as nagging). If a woman asks a guy to take out the garbage, chances are that he is going to forget the first six or seven times. It is only when she is standing right in front of him ranting and pointing furiously at a huge pile of garbage, under which presumably exists a trash can, that he gets up and does the job.

In contrast, a woman's short-term memory is laser sharp. She not only remembers exactly what was said, but can quote it back verbatim. This ability upsets men. If a man says he'll be home right after work at 5:30 p.m., and he gets home a tad late (happy hour ends at 10:30 p.m.), the wife will be mad at the man. The man may try to weasel himself out of the doghouse, but she's got the hard evidence on her side. Trying to win an argument with a woman over something involving short-term memory is like pleading innocent to a bank robbery even though you stopped to pick your nose in front of a dozen security cameras. The jury isn't going to be out for too long before the verdict is returned. And with a woman, justice certainly isn't blind, but it is swift, decisive, and eviscerating.

What people don't realize, however, is that the opposite is also true. The long-term memory of men is actually quite good. Just look at how well a man retains information like business discussions, college classes he actually bothered attending, sports trivia, and the bra sizes of former girlfriends. The long-term memory of most men is a paradigm of stability, even though a man might accidentally leave his child at day care because he forgot it was his turn for pickup.

The only problem with a man's long-term memory is that it has a sort of tribunal panel that passes judgment on whether the memory is good enough to put into the long-term vault. What color dresses were the bridesmaids wearing at his wedding? What was the entrée at the reception? What color hair ribbon was his wife wearing when he proposed? Unimportant. It gets filed in the recycle bin. Who was the MVP of Super Bowl XLIX? Critical data.

His wife, however, thinks these details are of the utmost significance and a man's brain must have little competence not to remember events that have such phenomenal bearing on day-to-day life. Unfortunately, sometimes the wife's birthday/anniversary accidentally gets thrown in the delete pile. Therefore, a woman can help a man's memory prioritization in this area by unleashing such wrath that it would make any survivors of Sodom and Gomorrah wince, and with that, the memory should be better engraved in a man's brain.

Because a woman has such good short-term memory, she naturally assumes that her long-term memory is without question. After all, she can recount previous events in great detail. The problem here is that a woman's long-term memory is highly selective.[16] She may remember that she and her husband were late for her sister's wedding because her husband took the wrong route. However, her memory will fail to recall that her husband had been pleading with her to take less than two hours in the bathroom so they could get on the road at a reasonable time. A woman may recall how her husband foolishly locked the keys in the hotel room. She'll forget that she made him change his clothes several times to match her outfit so that he had no idea what was where by the time he made it out.

There appears to be a transfer problem between the short-term to long-term memory. A woman has a built-in editing function that

---

16 Also known by a man's definition as wildly inaccurate.

can delete the bad portions of a memory while anything silly her husband ever does will remain right at the top of her recollection, available for recounting at any social gatherings or company meetings. It is kind of like how the old USSR Communist Party would have events reported in the paper. If the headline read, "Jubilant Crowds Fill Streets to Greet Premier," they could accidentally fail to mention that he was escorting the first shipments of toilet paper to arrive in the region in months. If the headline was "Soviet Scientists Develop Plant That Produces Larger Tomatoes," they could fail to mention the six-legged frogs, man-eating worms, and other oddities found near the Chernobyl power plant, along with the fact that the new tomatoes ripped through your colon like a bowling ball dropped through one-ply toilet paper if you dared eat them.

Fights arise between couples because of these memory differences. A woman can recount a past event, completely deleting all essential details. A man, not thinking the event was that important at the time, did not bother to file the details away and so can't rebut her story. Unless there is a witness in the wings or recorded evidence, the guy won't be able to defend himself, and he will lose yet again. One other thing to keep in mind if the witness is female is that it is possible for women to have synergistic selective memories. They can both recall what the guy did wrong, leaving out any facts that would incriminate someone with the double-X chromosomes.

If, on the odd occasion, that a guy has placed this memory in his long-term vault and can fully validate himself, the woman then goes to Plan B and keeps switching the discussion until she finds a memory that the guy hasn't stored away or one where he was at fault, not that those are hard to find. She can then pick up the argument at this totally random point and bring it on to victory.

Let's say that the couple is fighting, and she is mad because she feels the husband doesn't like her parents, and that is why they are always late when they are supposed to go over there for dinner. Now, this fight may have started because the guy didn't remember when his mother-in-law's birthday was, but the fact that they guy can't remember his *own* mother's birthday can't be submitted as evidence. She'll recount things like last year's Christmas and Thanksgiving.

Now, what if the guy remembers that she forgot to pick up her mother's gift, so that they had rush to a very crowded mall to stand in line. He remembers this because this event was burned into his soul as he was left in line to pay for the double-support bra while his wife was gathering "a few" other things in seventeen other stores. Meanwhile, he was desperately trying to think of anything but what this gift was going to be used for.

On Thanksgiving, maybe she burned the mashed potatoes and had to redo them. Maybe she can blame him because he was supposed to buy more potatoes the last time he was shopping. If he still has the grocery list and potatoes wasn't on it, that *should* exonerate him. Right? Wrong! She could make the argument that she didn't write it on the list because she was upset that he said her mother's stuffing tastes like papier-mâché since it has as much moisture as sandpaper. Can the man refute this? No, and it wouldn't matter if he could since she could go to the next argument.

Was either of the events the man's fault? No. Does it matter if a guy has perfect memory? Hardly. If he did or can't remember if he didn't, she has proved her point about him not getting something somewhere, and not only is the case open and shut, but the jury has issued its verdict, and the judge is tying a noose.

The Bathroom

or

Marking Your Territory Is *Not* a Laugh-Riot Excuse for the Woman if Your Urine Aim Is Subpar

L et me say a few words about restroom etiquette. Most people have a hang-up about public restrooms. Women are, by far, the worst in this fashion when it comes to actually using the restroom for its designed purpose, mainly being the excretion of body wastes, rather than for some secondary reason, usually a social gathering place. For some women, it would come as a shock to learn that behind the stall doors are actual working toilets. I assume they think the stalls are minifortresses of solitude for some women to spend some alone time. To many women, actually using a toilet in such a public place would be along the same lines as whipping out a bedpan while at a Tupperware party. You just don't go to the bathroom when another living being could hear. Most women are happy giving the perception that they never have to move their bowels—ever.

Why are these restrooms so popular for women to visit en masse? Because they exist everywhere, and men are forbidden entry. Not only do women not want men there, but men certainly don't want to be there. Men are more likely to accidentally open a door with a sign warning of a nuclear spill rather than open a door with a skirted stick figure on it. Put one of those signs on the exit to Sing Sing, and you wouldn't even need any guards. I'm not sure what the exact repulsion is, but men avoid women's restrooms like they avoid dating Lorena Bobbitt.[17]

When women are in restrooms together, men get this paranoid feeling that all women talk about is men, and usually not in the most flattering terms. That is completely untrue—the part about men being paranoid, I mean. Since the women are truly laughing behind men's backs as soon as that restroom door swings shut, men are perfectly justified in being unnerved. Simply put, you aren't paranoid if people are actually plotting against you. Inside that bathroom, women can come together like wolf packs, comparing notes on the weaknesses they've seen in the prey outside, whether it is a mother complex or some insecurity, and so can emerge organized and dangerous.

In some rare situations, women will find it absolutely unavoidable that they must use the bathroom to (gasp) go the bathroom. There is a certain amount of emotional trauma when this happens. It is uncomfortable for women to do this in front of other living things.[18] In a peeing situation, many women need a buffer zone of around ten feet to actually accomplish the mission. In a, let's say, more extreme expelling situation, the buffer zone increases to encompass the entire restroom facility.

Therefore, women will have to do a fair amount of reconnaissance before actually heading into the stall. If there is another person in the bathroom, then they pretend that their visit has to do with

---

17 For those who do not know who Lorena Bobbitt is, she was the wife of a man whom she found out was cheating on her. Rather than divorce him, she decided to take matters into her own hands—literally—and cut the man's Mr. Friendly off. She then went joy riding in the car and she tossed Mr. Friendly, yes—she was still holding it—from the window. Police, having been called, not only took John Bobbitt, the unfaithful husband, to the hospital, but found his missing pal (how is that for a game of hide-and-seek that you really don't want to win?). Surgeons were able to successfully reattach it to Mr. Bobbitt, who then went on—I am not making this up—to star in pornographic films.

18 Living things would include pets and plants.

primping their makeup. Only when that person is gone does the woman make her approach to the toilet bowl. What happens if both women are primping waiting for the other to leave? Then it becomes a question of how bad the woman has to go. It is a test of wills (and bladders) where one woman will eventually give up and go start the entire process over again at another bathroom.

Most women pretty much refuse to sit down on a public toilet. Either they use up nearly a whole industrial-size roll of toilet paper making a disposable barrier to sit down upon, or they go for the "hovering" approach. I'll grant you that most women complain about men when it comes to properly aiming into toilets at home, but these same women who try to combine straddling and hovering above the public toilet bowl have about as much marksmanship as a blitzed Stevie Wonder at a grenade-launching range.[19]

So what happens when another woman walks into the bathroom during the act? Then the first woman plays possum. She'll sit there with as much stealth as a commando waiting for the enemy to depart so that she may finish her mission. Not only do women not like to actually "go" in a restroom—they don't like other women to do it either. I've actually heard women complaining about a woman who had the gall to enter the restroom and relieve herself while they were chatting about their boyfriends.

And that brings up a striking difference in how men and women act in a restroom. Women like to talk in the restroom. To a man, this is about as taboo as complimenting another man's butt. As a general rule, dead silence is observed in a men's room, with the possible exception of a "How about them [insert name of local sports team]?"

---

19 OK, so now I've made a joke that mentions Stevie Wonder after I previously talked about Michael Jackson. I'd hope the reader doesn't read any racist tones into it. But when you need an example of a famous blind person, who do you use? Invariably it comes down to Stevie Wonder and Ray Charles. Ask people to name a famous blind person, and they often draw a blank after those two names. For a musician, there is Jeff Healey. Considering there are only seventy-five people left in the world who know the hit "Angel Eyes," the comment would fall flat. His band did win Canadian Entertainer of the Year back in 1990, but I believe the competition was Eskimos juggling herring. Other famous white blind people? How about Homer? Unfortunately, the average person buying this book immediately thinks not of the famous Greek poet who wrote The Iliad and The Odyssey but of Homer Simpson, who is not blind. What can I say but, "Doh!"

The proper and only response to this question is "Yep." No elaboration is needed or wanted. For men in the bathroom, this is considered "chatty." Men aren't even supposed to look around. They are to stare straight ahead and down at their feet even when—make that especially when—they are at the urinal.

When men enter a restroom, it is strictly about business at hand, or in this case, in the hand. Get in and get out as fast as possible. Think of it like invading the beaches of Normandy—it needs to be done, but you don't really want to be there, and you *really* don't want to hang around admiring the scenery. There is even a protocol for what urinal can be used. If you are the first one there, usually you take an end one. That way if a second guy comes in, he can take the other and be separated as much as humanly possible. With more people, the rule is to maximize distance so only when nearly everything is full is one allowed to use urinals side by side. It would freak the heck out of a guy if he was in a bathroom with a bunch of urinals and the next guy decided to use the one right next to him.

At home, the guy does allow himself far more time. To a woman, a bathroom is a changing room, a makeup center, a salon, and quite often a Fortress of Solitude if there are kids are around. To a man, a bathroom is, well, a bathroom…and maybe a library. Guys do like to keep busy, so if you saw him with a newspaper or magazine tucked under his arm, you knew where he was headed and you could avoid that part of the house for the twenty minutes it took him to complete his assignment and another twenty minutes to allow the air to become breathable. Now, it is a smartphone. So considering what happens with phones and bathrooms these days, we should all think of another person's phone as a biohazard on par with eating food accidentally (or purposely) left on the floor of the New York subway system.

Romance

or

Dull Pencils, Long Stories, and Other Things Men Don't Think Have a Point

R omance is important to women. To a guy, it ranks somewhere between curly fries and curly fries with cheese…and that is only if he isn't hungry. If a man is on a date and it goes well, then he assumes it was romantic. If it doesn't, then it wasn't. A guy could be cleaning out a backed-up septic system and have a prostitute come down in there, have sex with him, steal all his money and clothes, give him VD, and he would still describe it as romantic.

To a woman, romance is more of a feeling than a sensation. And therein lies the problem. Men measure emotional moments about as accurately as they could measure the depth of the Grand Canyon with a ruler. Women crave romance. They need it like men need food, water, and *Sports Illustrated* swimsuit issues. And yet men simply don't know how to give it to them. It's like giving a six-year-old a Swiss Army knife and expecting him to know how to perform open-heart surgery. He may try, but it will inevitably end badly.

For a man to be able to find and maintain a woman, he is going to have to learn the basics on how to romance a woman. Unfortunately, it is easier to recite *War and Peace* verbatim, backward even. Romance can be many different things to many different women. After all, you didn't expect them to agree on something that would have made all men's lives easier, would you? Romance can be horseback riding, walks along the beach, a trip to a special concert, or something else that *some other* boyfriend is doing for one of *her friends*.

I should note that there does exist the mutant guy who does know how to romance a woman. He will create endless grief for all those other men around him. A man attempting to duplicate his success is not considered romantic by a woman because he is copying another man's moves. Moves are specific to the man, like fingerprints and ball-scratching technique. Romance is supposed to be spur of the moment and original, even if it requires several weeks of planning and you need a second mortgage to fund it.

Maybe it is best if we give a definition of what romance is. Romance must be at once spontaneous and well thought out. It must be both straight from the heart and deep from the wallet. It must be simultaneously breathtaking and soothing. A man's got a better chance of reanimating dead flesh than pulling off something that meets these conflicting requirements. And yet that is the task that stands before men, an ever-present impediment thwarting their attempts to get what they most desire: a woman who is so awash in the sea of sensory stimulation and passion that she barely notices the guy fumbling for twenty minutes trying to get her bra unclasped.

Women will argue this point and say that romance is as simple as bringing a single rose home unexpectedly. However, if a guy brings flowers home, the first impression the woman has is that he is guilty about something, and she is going to find out what. After she's subjected the man to an interrogation that violates the Geneva Conventions, she may then relent and thank the man for the gesture. The man, having been about to confess to kidnapping the Lindbergh baby to make the torture end, is now not so much feeling romantic as suffering from post-traumatic stress disorder.

How important is being on the receiving end of romance to a man? About as important as macrame is to cows. To a man, romance is an endless source of frustration. A guy finds sucking on a concrete milk shake easier and more pleasurable than trying to think up what would tickle a woman's interest. To a woman, a sunset is an endless source of beauty to be drunk in by the soul. To a man, seeing a sunset means he's way late for happy hour. To a woman, a horse-drawn carriage is a tie to the chivalry of the past. To a man, a moving horse has no interest unless he's got money riding on its nose.

When a man finally gets the woman he wants, then he feels he can stop working so hard on this whole courting thing. And herein lies another problem besetting couples. Once a guy works so damn hard romancing a woman to get her, he feels that he can finally relax, sit back, open up a cold one, and enjoy it. The weekend's arrived. Mission accomplished. The *Eagle* has landed. The woman, on the other hand, becomes accustomed to the level of romance in the dating relationship and comes to expect that it will continue throughout life. When it doesn't, there is hell to pay, and hell is having a bad hair day.

Once married, a guy thinks he can get sex by just showing up au naturel at the bedside.[20] Meanwhile, the woman looks over to a guy that used to be Fabio[21] and is now Flabio. She's going to expect him to work for it like before they were married. A guy just can't keep up that level of romantic intensity. He feels like he's paid his dues. Usually the guy gets married when he can't think of anything else romantic to do. That's his last gasp. The romance tank is empty. As he's walking down the aisle, he thinks he's approaching the finish line for all that romantic mumbo jumbo, and he's about to find out he hasn't even left the starting gate.

---

20 Or anywhere else in the house. Therefore, it is a good idea that any new house or apartment have drapes.

21 Fabio is a model who used to have long hair and model for the covers of romance novels. They'd put a shirt on him unbuttoned down to his waist, turn on the wind machine to get his long hair flowing, toss a woman in his arms, take a picture, and that was his entire day's work. You could say that he mastered the "lost in her wonder" look in his eyes, but anyone hearing an interview with him would realize the lost look wasn't so much a skill but a lifestyle. One day when he was riding a roller coaster, a bird flew by and hit him in the nose, blooding him up. A collective cheer resounded around the globe from the men.

Feelings

or

Emotional Responses, Not Grabbing Your Wife When She Walks By

---

Ask a man how he is feeling, and you may get all the way up to a one-word answer, such as "hungry" or "tired." You'll only get that if a man is chatty. Otherwise expect a shrug of the shoulders. Why is he not going to express his innermost thoughts? To a man, he just has. That is it. The well is dry. Pencils down. Women just can't understand that men don't have this internal boiling cauldron of "stuff" that they do. If a woman is asked how she is feeling, you'd better clear the afternoon. If she says she has nothing to say, then she really has a lot to say even though you don't want to hear it, and you had better beg to hear it now, or you'll be hearing about it later. Get it?

Do you want another example of feelings? Too bad. Remember, I'm a guy writing this, so it was painful enough getting the first paragraph done. Thinking I can actually get a second paragraph on feelings accomplished is like expecting…

The Differences in Sports

or

How Can You Call It a Sport for Men if It Doesn't Have Balls?

A n absolutely huge difference between men and women is their perception of organized sports. In general, women don't see sports as one of the focal points of their lives. Women are even shocked that this would qualify as a topic in this book, never mind that it gets a longer listing than the section on feelings. Men would schedule major surgery around games. If it were the playoffs, we'd be willing to zap ourselves with defibrillators rather than go to the hospital if we were having a heart attack. A woman cannot understand what the big deal is in missing "just one game" when other plans come up, like the birth of their child.[22] However,

---

22 Luckily, there are now televisions in the birthing rooms. If she is in full labor and the sound is turned down low, she may actually forget that it is on. Do not remind her by cheering for or against a team. She is none too pleased that there is no sharing of the "physical joy" of childbirth. If she doesn't think that every ounce of your being is focused in this birthing process, and you are within arm's reach, chances are that you will be reeducated. One warning—if the doctor is a sports fan, best to turn the television off. We don't want him turning at the wrong second to see "the catch" and missing his own catch.

most men cannot be fully convinced that the Earth will not fall off its axis if they are late for *the* game.

The game can be defined as any game being played by a local sports franchise (anything from the nearest pro sports team to a Cub Scouts tug-of-war) or a team from a school the man went to (or that is somehow connected with someone he knows), or that the man has a bet on. Will the outcome of a game be changed by a guy a couple hundred miles away screaming at a television? To men—yes, it will. It is perfectly acceptable to scream suggestions to the coach or threaten the obviously paid-off referees via the television…and think that it matters. And you crazy women thought televisions could only *receive* signals.

With men, sports are truly an all-consuming passion. Let's face it—men will think nothing of watching a pregame show that is longer than the actual game. After watching the game, a guy will then sit through a postgame wrap-up to tell him what he just watched. Watching the Super Bowl can be a twelve-hour event! He used to take breaks during commercials, but the poor guy can't even do that now, as that's when the best commercials of the year are rolled out.

To a man, sports time is all relative. If a woman asks a man to take out the garbage, he may say, "In two minutes, hon!" However, this is sports time. Two minutes can last for forty-five regular minutes. If he is supposed to take his wife to her mother's house for her birthday, this misperception can have dire consequences. It is now *her* version of altered time that comes into play as the next time the guy wants action, it actually won't be when hell freezes over, but it will still be a pretty damn long time.

When the man is focused on the television, his mind is racing uncontrollably, dreaming up defensive and offensive strategies, even though his wife's perception is of a couch sloth glued to a single spot and devoting his minuscule energy reserves to flatulence and reaching for the next chip. However, because his mind is racing so fast, the theory of relativity dictates that time for him is slowed down. Therefore, the man perceives that it is only a few minutes even though hours may pass. Now doesn't that sound better than that old perception of guys who have their IQ drop and butt size rise every time the TV is turned on?

Men even buy things solely because they are labeled "sports." As a general rule, men hate dressing up. A tie to some guys is as comfortable and natural as a noose. How to get him to dress up? Put him in a "sports" coat. What do these things have to do with sports? You don't see businessmen in a negotiation spontaneously break into a huddle to discuss strategy. A man will also buy sports drinks and eat sports bars even if he is the type that watches a show he hates because the one he liked is finished, and he's too lazy to get up and look for the remote when it is not within easy reach.

Women will claim that they like sports as well, albeit to a lesser (sane) degree. However, if I may generalize, the sports that women like are some that men don't even acknowledge as true sports. Yes, all this is changing (God willing) with the surge in popularity of sports like women's basketball, softball, and soccer. However, the predominant "sports" women still like these days are things like figure skating, gymnastics, and synchronized swimming. How the hell ballroom dancing became an Olympic sport is beyond the comprehension of all men—even the ones doing the dancing. Men just can't deal with sports that have a subjective ending determined by judges. In men's sports, you know who wins because he crosses the line first, throws farthest, or jumps longest. In a boxing match, you have a fair idea who won because the loser is the one sprawled on the canvas.

Meanwhile, in women's sports, you've got an international panel of judges who are about as impartial as the English soccer fans.[23] In many of these sports predominantly watched by women, you may as well get it over with and give out all the medals before the events

---

23 English soccer fans are one of the most unusual groups of individuals on the planet. Usually, the British have a reserved demeanor. They pride themselves in the whole "stiff upper lip" thing. You couldn't get emotion out of them if you tripped at dinner and impaled their spleen with your butter knife. They may even apologize to you for getting your knife all bloody. However, these very same people lose their minds when a soccer ball is involved. They have stampeded and killed each other over games. Countries have banned their fans for fear of them. So apparently, this is what you get from repressing your feelings for the last several centuries.

begin since the judging can be so bad. Also, women like knowing the personal history of every person competing.

To appeal to women viewers, the Olympic Games have been altered in the last decade or so. Ninety percent of the time they are showing the obstacles the athlete had to overcome to get to this event, such as the bad acne that held them back from going to dances in the seventh grade, or parents who were only willing to give up bringing them to the rented-out skating rink every other morning at 3:00 a.m. since they actually had jobs and thought spending money on other things like food and rent weren't such bad ideas. The other 10 percent of the time, the network squeezes in a few moments of the actual competition. Sorry, but men don't care how the guy donated blood to save his half brother's dog Roofus. If he can bench-press a Buick, then we care.

The Differences in Shopping

or

No, This Is Not Considered a Sport

I t is not true that women are the only ones who like to shop, although men would have women believe that. The difference is that when men buy something, they call it an "investment." That way, it doesn't sound like they are frittering away their money on adult toys. How else can they justify two-seater sports cars with a family of four? Or how about computers with enough power to operate the space station even though the only thing they ever do with their computer is play Tetris and download videos of skateboard accidents? Sure, they may mutter phrases like "minimization of depreciation" and "value-added loss," but it all comes down to the simple fact that, mentally, boys never truly grow up and so will always like toys. Don't believe me? Put a Rock'em Sock'em Robots game on the counter and count the nanoseconds it takes for the guy to break down and start trying to knock the head off one of the robots.

Besides buying *investments*, men despise shopping. The second-to-absolute-worst type of shopping is buying clothes, even if it is for himself. Why? My theory is that every man bears the scars of childhood when his mother brought him to Sears and made him try on back-to-school clothes. Boys never trusted the privacy of those stall doors that didn't have locks and were open on the top and bottom, especially when you were short enough that you felt you were allowing the entire department store to see your tighty-whities.

You'd get an outfit on, come out, and then your mother would twirl you around a few times, make you walk up and down the aisle like a G-rated catwalk, and then send you in to try yet another outfit on. She'd also grab the front of your pants and tug them around to see how snug they fit, giving you a reverse wedgy in the process. Mothers would strongly deny that it is possible to damage their little boys' self-worth, considering these are the same creatures who think it is socially acceptable behavior to run up to their sibling, grab on, and pass gas—then try to hold on as the sibling tries to escape the impending stench. And yet, this exposure in a public place is probably the source of our nightmares of being naked in front of the class/boardroom.[24]

So what is the singular worst type of shopping for men? Hands down, it is buying presents for your girlfriend or wife. If you buy her jewelry, it won't match any outfits she currently has, so she'll have to go spend several hundred dollars to get the necessary clothes to go with the jewelry. What about buying clothes? A man is as lost in the women's department as in the maze of the Minotaur, only being with the Minotaur is much less dangerous.[25] A man will stand there with a look on his face like he is an Alzheimer's person in a mirror maze.

When a saleswoman tries to help, she only makes the situation worse. She'll ask questions like "Is she a summer person or a winter person?" This question makes about as much sense to a guy

---

24 Let it be known that I had a wonderful mother. However, my brother and I have taken it as our duty to tease her about the imaginary emotional scars we incurred in our youth. The worst for me was if you ever had something on your face and she'd lick her thumb and rub it off. Now you had mom spit over your entire cheek. She'd do things like that, and then we'd post the child abuse hotline number near the phone.

25 In Greek mythology, the Minotaur was a creature with the head of a bull and body of a man. According to legend, he was born by the king's wife. Previously, the king had ticked off the god Poseidon, so Poseidon had his wife fall in love with a bull. She let the bull have its way with her, and there came the Minotaur. A beautiful love story, if you ever heard one. Anyway, the Minotaur became violent as he grew, probably due to the junior high years when all the boys kept asking him if he was horny. They built a maze to keep him away from the rest of the population. He wasn't bright enough to get out, but those who came in were beaten to death. Not quite Romeo and Juliet, but close enough.

as when some women pluck out their eyebrows and then arbitrarily draw another one in somewhere on their forehead.[26] He ends up buying something less suited for her having coffee with friends and more suited for working at a transvestite bar.

How about buying her chocolates? She'll complain about her diet, but then still eat them, and then complain about the exercise she's going to have to do to lose those calories. Perfume? Only if you know what she normally wears. Otherwise, you risk getting her something that gives her hives.[27] Scented candle? Sure, she can throw them in the closet with the dozens of other gifts of last resort.

Women, on the other hand, view shopping with the same anticipation as men feel heading for a strip bar. Their pulse quickens, their face becomes flush, and their breathing is erratic. Shopping is a nearly transcendental event for them, even if they were just going to get a new pair of socks.

When men shop, they know exactly what they want. They head to the closest store with the cheapest version of the desired item (unless it is electronic in nature). They walk directly to the aisle, find said item, and get out. Mission accomplished. Turn the lights out. Women must go to every store they know in town that could even remotely carry the item. They'll spend twenty dollars in gas to find a bargain saving twenty cents on paper plates. The fleeing Hebrews took a shorter, more direct route out of Egypt than women take hunting so-called bargains. The meandering doesn't stop when women get to the store, either. Most women have to circle each and every clothes rack and go down every aisle, even if they just went in to use the ATM. Why they haven't petitioned to have shopping as an Olympic sport yet, I don't know.

---

26 Usually when this happens, they draw it in a bit high so they end up having a surprised look twenty-four hours a day.

27 If shopping for perfume, you may think they mixed up the prices as the smallest bottle costs so much you'd think it was filled with unicorn tears, and the giant vats of the stuff cost only a few bucks but would probably sting like hell if actually applied on the skin.

The Essence of a Couple

or

Two's Company, Three Is a Crowd...

Unless They Are Twins

A lot of people make a living from the fact that men don't understand women and women don't even want to imagine how low they'd have to sink to begin to understand men. Think how many marriage counselors would be out of business if men came to realize the intricacies of a female mind that seems at the outset like a bunch of haphazard connections and if women were to fully comprehend how pathetically simple a man's mind is. There are even books written on the subject of how men and women act like they are from different planets. The problem with these books is that it makes some couples think that they actually *want* to understand each other. Big mistake.

The best to be hoped for is just to accept each other. Do men truly want to understand how a woman can think she has absolutely nothing to wear when she's got enough closets and bureaus full of clothing to get the country through a nuclear winter? Do women truly want to understand that it is absolutely (and pathetically) true that all men think about is sex and sports with the occasional sandwich thrown in? Both groups point at the other in bewilderment and exasperation. Even couples that have been married for twenty or thirty years don't claim to understand each other; they just accept their partners. Hell, there are some couples that don't say a dozen words to each other a day. To the outside world, they look like a loving couple staring into each other's eyes, but it is really just a case of there being nothing left to say after all those years.

So let's talk about being a couple. Now, this doesn't seem to be the most rational of things when you step back and think of it. If you are living alone, you can watch whatever you want, eat whatever you want, and even go to bed at any time without worrying about keeping the light on when you read or getting yelled at for passing enough gas to make your sheet look like a hot-air balloon. Your house can be clean or dirty. The toilet seat can be up, and that is not considered a crime on par with trying to assassinate the president. When you decide to be a couple, nothing is ever the same. Everything is a compromise...well, if you consider doing what your wife wants as the definition of compromise.

Yet, biology pushes most of us to want to be mated up. It seems odd to go out to dinner by yourself. If you do, people at the restaurant assume you know you are doing something out of the norm and seat you in the back corner where the lighting is bad so you can hide in the shadows. You are near leper status in the outside world. Even going to the movies is met with suspicion if you are alone—and that is a place where you are supposed to just sit and be quiet.[28]

There is this thing out there called "love" that makes people do the craziest things so they can be with one person.[29] Most people bandy the word around pretty readily—they may love a football team or a car or waffles, but you don't want to drive your car off a cliff if you have a disagreement with your waffles. Love is the crack cocaine of

---

28 There are select theaters where people sit alone. Unfortunately for Pee-wee Herman, the former award-winning star of a hit children's show, he was alone but still caught in a vigorous "debate" with a "special friend," and that got him arrested.

29 In some places in Utah, love can be between a man and multiple wives. Of course it doesn't work the other way around where the woman can have multiple husbands. I guess that means men just have more love to share.

emotions. People want it, it is addictive, and you do some stupid-ass stuff once you are on it.

As a general rule, women fall into and out of love quicker than men do. If a woman says "I love you" too early in the relationship, the man starts hyperventilating and looking for the emergency exit even if they are on a flight at thirty thousand feet. To say men don't do well with commitment is like saying elephants don't do well learning ballet. That brings up a host of problems for women. If they are in love, when do they ever say it? There are some guys who are happy to date the same woman for decades, so if she doesn't eventually push, she has as much chance of walking down the aisle as she does walking on water.

So when does a woman say, "I love you?" To be absolutely safe, she can wait until after the first child is born, but most women want to be a bit riskier than that and push the timing up a bit. If the guy says it first, then it is certainly a green light for the woman to return the comment. And that leads to yet another problem—men may want to say it, but they are afraid the woman won't say it back. If a guy says "I love you" and the woman returns a "that's nice," she may as well perform open-heart surgery on him without an anesthetic.

Therefore, some guys hint around a lot. He may start with "I really enjoy being with you." Of course that is followed up by the ever-popular "You know, I really, *really* enjoy being with you." If a guy says that to a woman, he is basically saying, "I love you, but if you don't say it first, I'm jumping off a pier," which is especially dangerous for those men not living near a body of water.

So what if a man says "I love you" early in a relationship and the woman is head over heels for him? *She* should run like the wind. Do not pass go, do not collect $200. Unfortunately, many men use this phrase to mean "I'm horny, and I can't think of anything else to say to get you into bed." I am not breaking any "bro code" rules here. Guys are welcome to give any lame line they want to. If a guy asks a woman if she got hurt when she fell down from heaven, and that works, bless him. Emotional bribery is a wee bit different.

Once they are past the whole "in love" thing, the woman may eventually have to ask the dreaded "Is this relationship going anywhere?" Now, if a woman says this, she isn't talking about hitting the late show. She is talking marriage. There are some guys who finally pop the question to get engaged, hoping they can then put off the marriage another decade or so.

So how do men fall in love? Usually, they fall into and out of love much slower than women do. Glaciers can come and go before a man admits it to himself and the world. Now, this comes with its own set of problems. If the woman wants to break it off, then many men lose their minds. If there is a murder/suicide on the news, you never have to ask if it was the guy who did it. If you polled people (who are men), they would say that the crazy meter pegs a bit higher with women than guys. However, if you really want that meter broken, you need a spurned guy.

So here you are trying to mix two things that seem from the outside not to go together well. I like brownies and I like ice cream. Whoever first had the idea of combining a hot brownie with a cold scoop of ice cream should be up with the other great inventors of history. When the right man and the right woman eventually do get together, it is absolutely worth the years of dating faux pas, miscues, and train wrecks.

What Men Look For

or

Beauty Is Only Skin Deep, but That Is How Far Men's Eyes Can See

M en are often accused of being superficial when it comes to their likes and dislikes of women. It is absolutely unfair to accuse men of this. Men appreciate scintillating conversations, sparkling senses of humor, and individuals who possess a depth of empathy for their neighbors. For some men, however, when a beautiful woman walks by, the blood supply that is meant for his brain leaves and goes to other places, leaving him incapable of any articulate comments. Sure, he'd like to engage a woman in a discussion of Chaucer or the latest revelations of the superstring theory, but he just can't seem to make his tongue move in such a way that he can make noises that don't sound like the Animal Planet channel.

A guy has barely enough blood in his brain to keep it from drying out.[30] Women just don't comprehend the basic biology associated with men. It's quite a handicap to be working at a job and all of a sudden become mentally incapacitated. Architects would have trouble with Legos, firemen would have difficulties putting out matches, and

---

30 By the time a teenage boy is done high school, his brain looks like an old raisin bathing in about a teaspoon of brain juice.

I don't even want to think of what happens to surgeons on the job. We men are deserving of sympathy and understanding for our affliction rather than the scorn heaped upon us. I'll stop short of making any temporary claims to the Americans with Disabilities Act.

Many women will read this and declare that all men are pigs. What can men say in their defense? Oink. Tell us something we don't know. I am not saying that all men are chauvinists (although more than a few are) who don't respect women or think they are equals. I am saying that each and every man is a pig in that he is totally hung up with women and sex. Some men hide it better than others, but they are pigs nonetheless. A couple men will deny their true nature, but just throw two bowls of quivering Jell-O side by side in front of a man and see if he can take his eyes off of them.

It doesn't matter how they are dressed or how they were brought up, men fall a few branches down on the evolutionary tree when an attractive woman walks by. Men know in their hearts they are obsessed with sex and they have come to accept (and relish) it. Women, on the other hand, are shocked each and every time they get to know a guy and find out that in his heart he too is piggish. It's like opening up a carton of milk and being surprised that it is actually filled with (gasp!) milk. What women need to do is lower their expectations a bit—give up and realize there will be milk and just hope that it isn't past the expiry. For those women who don't believe me,[31] just ask every one of your married friends whether their husbands are pigs. If you don't believe them, ask a minister's wife, right before you remind her that lying is against one of the Ten Commandments. They will all give you a look like you asked them if they were fond of breathing.

I'm not saying that being a pig is a bad thing. It is biology. When men are in their teens, sex is what they breathe and eat. Now, that doesn't mean that teenage boys have to act on their impulses, but it doesn't help anything to deny that those impulses are there. Some women may still not be convinced of the pig thing, and there are a hell of a lot of men who would deny this. I offer this as final proof. How often does a nineteen-year-old boy actually think about sex?

---

31 Probably there are some nuns still locked away in convents somewhere who have little contact with the opposite sex.

Every ten or fifteen minutes? More than that, maybe? The actual es-timate—and keep in mind that I am not making this up or exaggerat-ing—is every nineteen seconds. A teen can't go through an average minute without thinking of sex multiple times. So if your daughter is out on a date, you may still think of her as a little girl who likes to climb up in your lap, but three times a minute, the guy is also think-ing of her being in his lap, but in a far different manner.

So what are men looking for overall? A man wants a woman who doesn't need him to spend the equivalent of the GNP of Peru every time her birthday swings around. He wants a woman with a great sense of humor, meaning that when she is laughing in his presence, it is more often with him than at him. A man wants a woman who ac-tually says exactly what is on her mind rather than hinting for days.[32] However, all that is optional if her sex drive is stuck in high gear.

---

32 If we are wishing here, I may as well throw in a hope for world peace and that there is never a reunion tour for 'N Sync.

What Women Look For

or

If You Ain't a Bad Boy, You Best

Hope to Be a Good Banker

Women declare themselves to be not nearly as shallow as men. They set their sights for looks *and* money. Isn't that so much better? It used to be assumed that women were more ethereal when it came to picking men. Women's lib has ended this illusion, as now women can be seen gathering together to discuss the pros and cons of particular men's butts.[33] Ever see women at a strip club? They go absolutely insane. You'd think the men were packing gold bars in their Speedos. Women are now more than glad to discuss men like they are pieces of meat. So what do men think of this change of events? Men only *pray* to be treated like objects. If you ever hear about a male teacher propositioning a young girl, you want him strung up by two particularly sensitive orbs. If you hear about a female teacher propositioning a young boy, many men think, *Damn…Where the heck was that when I was young?*

Some women who are actively looking for men think nearly all of them are jerks. I would disagree with this—immature, yes; jerks,

---

33 Personally, I am sick to death of women ogling me. I can't walk down the hall of my office building without women commenting, "What an ass."

no. So why should a woman complicate her life by bringing in a man when she thinks it will have the same effect as bringing a hornet's nest to a day care? These women blame the sorry state of their male companions on society, nature, nagging mothers, hormones, etc.

Many women will gladly state to every living being that will listen in person or read hourly/daily on Facebook that every guy they go out with is a jerk in the end. It is a never-ending cycle. First, they are miserable and not dating anyone. One day, they somehow find a guy willing to go on a date, and instantly, that guy is the love of her life. All other men pale in comparison. Finally, life has bestowed the richest of gifts—true love—on them, and things will never be the same. Usually, that is about day three in the relationship. As inevitable as the rising sun and old meat taking on an unappealing smell, all of a sudden she will report that the guy is a no-good bastard who somehow escaped the bowels of hell to torment her life for no apparent reason. All men are jerks…until she somehow has another date.

OK. So what exactly is the common denominator in all these individual relationships? Certainly not the man, if she is the one sifting through guys like a panhandler looking for gold. The woman in these cases is either doing something to terrify men into fleeing…or she is subconsciously actively going out of her way to pick jerks. Let's handle the first case of women who don't realize they scare the hell out of men.

Remember that whole thing about women falling in love too quickly? Yes, I know that cell phones have whittled the average attention span down to the point where people check their Facebook status in the middle of sex, but it wasn't *that* many pages ago. Well, let's say the guy is nice to her—and by "nice" I mean that he actually stops the car at the end of the date for her to get out. If he comes home from work the next day and finds his apartment has been jimmied open so she can leave her toothbrush in his bathroom, he may realize there is an issue. If she hacks into his Twitter account and threatens any woman on his list with bodily harm if they ever contact him again, there may an issue. If she has told her parents to fly in from Iowa to meet him and help check out church availability, there may be an issue.

And that brings us to the amazing number of women who will go miles out of their way to find jerks, much to the exasperation of nice guys. All men may be pigs, but that does not mean that they're not nice pigs. Many women subconsciously step on nice guys to get to the jerks. Ever hear the story about how the nice guy laid his coat down in the puddle so the woman could cross the street without getting muddy? Well, she was crossing the street to get to a jerk who wouldn't offer his coat to her if she had icicles hanging off her breasts.

Nice guys are considered as exciting as a *Brady Bunch* marathon. After all, a nice guy will get the woman home on time, respect her wishes, and (horror of all horrors) please her parents. If the parents like the boyfriend, a woman will usually drop him quicker than, well, than a greased pig. A nice guy assumes a woman wants to be treated with the utmost respect. He will care about her opinions. He'll try to do things she wants to do. In turn, the only attention she'll pay him is extinguishing her cigarette in the nice guy's navel, which is especially cruel in this day and age when most women don't smoke and so have to make the special effort to take the habit up just to have one to stub out on the poor guy.

So What Is a Nice Guy to Do?

or

It Is Hard to Win a Race When You Don't Even Know Where the Starting Line Is

For the most part, men don't have absolute control over how they look and how much money they make. Those men who think that toothbrushes are a luxury item or dream of the day they can move up the corporate ladder to work the milk-shake machine may not have tons of choices on whom to date. After years of hearing the word "no" from women, even if they haven't even asked the women out or looked in their direction, some men give up the pursuit. Quite often, you'll find their computers littered with enough viruses to bring down the space station since all their time is spent with cybersex. They spend their time "chatting" with hot young co-eds who are actually other geeky men whom I can't even begin to explain. That still leaves quite a pool of nice guys who have trouble finding dates.

The question then becomes, what can the average man do to make himself more attractive to women? Don't expect me to have the answer. It would be easier for me to find Jimmy Hoffa's body with a quadriplegic bloodhound—with a cold, no less—than know what the hell women look for in a guy. Hell, at the time of this writing, many women are absolutely drooling over the sexiness of vampires. Yes, the things that come out at night and kill them by biting them and draining their blood. It is a cottage industry of books and movies. Meanwhile, if a real guy so much as gave the average woman a hickey, she'd knock his teeth so far in that he could floss with his tonsils.

Most men assume that if they use the white knight approach, the women will eventually be won over. Therefore, you find many men "being there" for women as their friends and confidants. They open doors for women, pay for meals, and treat them like royalty. They are there to pick up the shattered pieces of the woman every time her relationship crashes and burns, whenever she is dumped by a moron whose greatest goal in life is to make the show *World's Greatest Police Chases*. Schmucks. Nice schmucks, but schmucks nevertheless. Let me be clear here—the shmuck ain't the "bad guy" since he's got the girl—it is the nice guy who bears the title.

You can tell who the nice guys are by lifting up their shirts. If you see hundreds of indentations on a guy's back, that is from years of women with stilettos walking all over him after he rebuilt their egos enough so that they would crawl back to the loser boyfriend who tried to pick up their best friend/roommate/mother. When it comes to dating women, nice men finish last—assuming they finish at all.

Many men work hard to garner a woman's trust. What happens to this relationship? She uses him as a sounding board as to why the cretin she is dating treats her so poorly, standing her up, ignoring her, even repeatedly dumping her. I have talked to a woman who literally had a cup of beer dumped on her head, and when I said the guy wasn't worth it, she went out again that night looking to make up with him. Again—the cretin guy is out having a great time, and the knight, rather than riding a great white steed, is riding a couch watching a *Star Trek* marathon. She then goes out after all the abuse she's endured and sleeps with the bad guy yet again. Why won't she sleep with the nice guy? Because she "doesn't want to ruin their friendship." As soon as a woman uses the word "friend" to describe the guy, his chances with her are over. That particular guy has as good a shot being with that woman as he does shoeing that great white steed while in full gallop.

Once attached with the label of "nice guy," a man can only hope that a woman is burned more times than a pyromaniac with half-inch matches before she eventually gives up and looks at him. After years of partying and wild sex with multiple jerks, she'll settle down, give up on those crazy, kinky all-nighters, and look for a guy who is willing to take the garbage out every night. What if the nice guy wants a bit of that naughty girl she doled out to the guys who treated her like crap? No problem. He's entitled to want anything he'd like. Getting it, however, is another story entirely.

Some nice guys try the "cool" approach to get women. They act like they are completely indifferent around the woman whom they cannot stop fantasizing about being trapped in an elevator with, with nothing more than a loofah sponge and whipped cream. The woman will respond by showing true indifference. She'll pay him about as much attention as she would a fly on a cow patty. What about the nice guy who attempts the "cool" approach like wearing leather jackets and driving motorcycles? When he ends up getting the jacket caught on the handlebars, knocking the bike down, and pinning himself under it and having the date have to go for help, his chances with her are about as good as Pamela Anderson's[34] on *Jeopardy!*

Am I saying that there is absolutely no hope for the nice guy? Of course not. I am saying that there is extraordinarily little hope for the nice guy. What may this little hope be? Alcohol. When some women imbibe enough alcohol, their standards may nose-dive like a kamikaze pilot to the point where they include men who would not take full advantage of trying to get women into this stage in the first

---

34 Pamela Anderson is an actress who somehow was never able to win the Academy Award. She was best known for being on the television show *Baywatch*, in which her total contribution consisted off running on a beach in slow motion with a bathing suit on that let the world know that she was part of the mammalian class. Sure, you can laugh at her, but she made millions and it was the top syndicated show in the entire world. Well, she also may be known for a sex tape with her husband Tommy Lee from the rock band Mötley Crüe. To say that Tommy Lee is a big star is something that can be taken more ways than one. Yes, he is one of the premier drummers in the history of rock, but it wasn't his drumstick that he may best be known for.

place. If kissing ensues when she is in the company of a nice guy, she may sober up the next day and realize the nice guy is not so bad after all since he didn't try to take advantage of her. Besides, women keep count of the number of different men, not the number of encounters. Once the make-out barrier has been breached with a nice guy, she may figure that the damage has already been done, so she might as well do it again.

I should also here describe the "Pedestal Phenomenon." Many men are taught to treat women with what borders on reverence. It is a man's duty to make life easier for the woman. General chivalry like opening doors for women, taking your hat off in their presence, and not gawking when they bend down to pick something up is considered a positive characteristic by most people. It is also a man's job to make a woman feel good about herself. She should be showered with compliments, gifts, and attention...appropriately. Unwanted compliments, gifts, and attention are reasons for police involvement.

So what happens when a man is chivalrous and complimentary? The woman feels like she is placed on a pedestal. That's a good thing, right? Wrong. If she is up there, the only way she can see you is by looking down at you. She'll listen to all those compliments, and as she starts believing them, she then questions why a woman as hot as she is is hanging out with an unworthy man like you. That's when you get dumped for a guy who puts her down because she has to look up to him. Get it? If so, please send a letter to me via my publisher so I can get it as well.

Where to Find a Date

or

Where to Mingle if You're Single

Women make up a little over half of the world's population, and yet men still have a tough time meeting them. You'd think that with over three billion women running around the planet, any man putting up a half-hearted attempt would stumble over one. The problem is not so much tripping over them, but them walking all over you. Since there are so many women and it is still so difficult to find one to date, the only logical conclusion is that women are purposely trying not to be found.

Why would they do this? Because many want men to have to work for every last scrap of attention they begrudgingly mete out. Some women want men to beg, grovel, and otherwise humiliate themselves in their efforts to garner a woman's attention. It's basically the first step toward the domestication of the male species. What can men do about this? Nothing, due to the fact that a man's backbone is made of instant cottage cheese when it comes to trying to get women to think they are datable material.

What about women who have a tough time meeting men? Usually the problem here is that they are not putting out the necessary vibes. On the off, off, way-off chance that she is looking for a nice guy who won't use her toothbrush to clean the gum off of his shoes when he's leaving her apartment, she's got to let the nice guy know she's accessible to date. The nice guy's usually been burned so many times that he's permanently lost his eyebrows and nostril hair, so he quite often does not notice subtle hints or thinks the woman is looking for another *friend* to unload some mental baggage on. Therefore, any hints the woman puts out cannot be anywhere near subtle. That eye contact from across the crowded room for 0.4 seconds isn't going to instill enough confidence for the guy to risk getting torched again. He needs a few more well-placed clues. A hand on his knee or tongue in his ear should get the point across.

So where do people go to meet each other? In the olden days, there weren't a whole lot of options. The village only had so many men and so many women, so there wasn't much to choose from. If the woman had less hair than a Sasquatch,[35] and a man had more ambition than a potato, then it was considered a good match by all. These days, it is different. Not only has the population increased, but modern transportation has dramatically enhanced the range over which men and women can find each other. With health clubs, churches, the Internet, and meddling relatives, the avenues to meet prospective mates have exploded.

So exactly how has this changed the dating possibilities? Back in the village, the choices were limited, so people settled. These days, people have the ability to travel the entire world searching for their soul mate. Therefore, they search and search and search. They end up in their midthirties alone, realizing their biological clock is ticking louder than Big Ben.[36]

A lot of people suggest going to health clubs to meet people. Personally, I don't get it. For men, statistically, there's always going

---

35 "Sasquatch" is the Native American word for a Bigfoot. While a big foot has some good connotations, it is usually in reference to a predictor of another feature on a man where bigger is usually better. To a woman, it is not the most endearing of terms. Is it fair that if a woman has extra hair, she is treated like an infectious leper, while a guy can look like he is wearing a carpet on his back and shoplifting cotton balls by shoving them in his ears and nostrils? No, but if I were to make a list of negatives women have to face in life compared to men, then this would like less like a guide book and more like the *Encyclopedia Britannica*.

36 The clock, not the porn star.

to be guys there who are better built than you are, so she's not even looking at you as her first choice. Therefore, by waltzing up and talking to her, all you're really doing is blocking her view of the beefcake behind you. Besides, if you've truly been working out, then you've got sweat stains starting at your armpits and draping down to your waist, and you smell like a dog that was accidentally left outside during a rainstorm.

Watching a woman build up a sweat can be quite erotic, whereas a man building up a sweat is about as repulsive as the jockstrap he is wearing. And to top it off, a guy feels tremendous pressure at a club to pretend that he is in shape. If a woman is at an adjoining machine, the guy always feels compelled to ratchet up the weight he is pumping, especially if the woman is doing the same exercise. A man would rather have his intestine exploding out of his diaphragm than admit that a woman is stronger than he is—even if it is his first time in a health club and she has been working out regularly for years. If he's not lifting or pushing something, then he is running or climbing. Try to talk to a woman when you're doing this, and you sound like an obscene phone call, except that you are less coherent and charming.

For a woman, a health club sounds like a great deal—she can get fit while eyeing some stud muffins. However, women obsess more about shapes than *Sesame Street*. Unless a woman can't count all her ribs, she thinks she may as well have "Goodyear" tattooed down her side. Therefore, if a woman goes to the gym, she will hide her figure in sweats that are baggy enough to be used to smuggle bowling balls. Any guy now looking over at this woman doesn't know if she's an actual female under all those clothes or a cousin of Jabba the Hut.

And then if the woman does work out, she—at least theoretically—may sweat. Once a woman breaks the mildest of sweats, she then feels as attractive as foot fungus. The guy truly doesn't care, but that doesn't matter. So she may have started out at the gym to meet guys, but she ends up dressed in Hefty bags glaring at the women in spandex while avoiding men like they are trolls covered in infectious herpes lesions. Not the best recipe for snatching up those single guys.

Other people suggest that you can meet singles at church. That one's a bit odd for me as well. Personally, I think asking a woman's sign during a gospel reading is in somewhat poor taste. Besides, what you'd really want to do with the woman qualifies as a sin in most religions.[37] Therefore, it seems a bit hypocritical to be doing this on sacred grounds. Even if you don't believe in God, it still doesn't mean a guy would go out of his way to tick him off in case he actually does exist. As I've said before, it is difficult for a woman to get asked out unless she drops significant hints. Kneeling and bowing may be a normal part of the ceremony, but not when he's wearing a sleeveless shirt, and she has on a tube top and miniskirt to show that they are open for a night out.

The place you spend the most time and probably have the best chance to meet someone is on the job. However, workplace dating is usually a no—no. The only time that rule usually gets bent is at the office Christmas party, where for some reason the mix of booze and photocopier-toner fumes turns the copying room into a red-light district rivaling Sodom and Gomorrah. Once the alcohol wears off and you're both back to work on Monday, it is difficult to get budgets worked out when you don't know if the other kept any of those Xerox imprints.[38]

Dating a person you work with is bad for a multitude of reasons. First off, if there is a breakup, the two of you are forced to still see each other day after day. That is like getting wounded and then each day having to pull the scab off so that it never heals. While the relationship is on, all your coworkers somehow feel they have permission to ask all sorts of personal details on how the two of you are doing. Is it just casual groping, or is the relationship leading somewhere? Other coworkers can feel a bit awkward since they may have complained about your date's work before you were going out. Your girlfriend may have been known as the dragon lady beforehand, and

---

37 Technically, even *thinking* what you'd want to do is enough to get you a few extra days in hell.

38 Of course now it could be worse as copiers can make PDFs so one click of the button and the entire country can see the "full moon."

now your coworkers are afraid that you'll reveal all the jokes they've been saying behind her back all these years.

Knowing these pitfalls, the partners in many office romances decide to keep things secret so they can avoid those fates. To make it look like they are not dating, they go out of their way to avoid each other while at work. Unfortunately, this act is usually about as convincing as WWE wrestling and Fox News.[39] Somehow, everyone at work figures it out, and then it is worse than not telling them because the coworkers can't help but discuss among themselves how the relationship is possibly proceeding. Rumors are worse than truth each and every time. Every time you two come out of the same room, people will be wiping down the furniture.

One tried and true method of finding a date is admitting that you are failing on your own and asking your friends for help. They will then try to match you up with a friend who is also desperate. There are so many things that can go wrong here that it is difficult to recount them all, so let me touch upon just a few scenarios. When a friend says he's got someone for you, first think of all the nonwinners he has dated and then dumped. So chances are if he is still single, the person you are being paired up with is someone who is below his standards. Sometimes, it is *way* below his standards.

Either he's a true noble friend looking out for your benefit or, more likely, he's pawning off his cousin who recently lost her job as a carnival oddity. Sometimes your friend is going steady, so you get fixed up with a friend of his girlfriend. Many women friends have an unusual mutualistic relationship. An attractive girl subconsciously or not so subconsciously seeks a friend who is not-so-attractive so that she is always the prettiest girl in a group, whereas a not-so-attractive girl seeks an attractive girl as a friend so that when they are paired, she can get the scraps. This relationship has more than a passing

---

39   OK, so I may tick off a few readers with the Fox News comment. However, the only reason they haven't linked the Democrats to Nazi time travelers who went back to kill Jesus Christ in the hopes of thwarting the writing of the Bill of Rights is because they haven't thought of it yet. I could make the same complaint about MSNBC making fun of the Republicans, but that would involve someone actually watching MSNBC.

resemblance to remoras and sharks.[40] Therefore, if your friend's girl-friend is good looking, you may end up dating someone with a "really incredible personality" who just happens to have a teeny problem with an overproduction of saliva to the point where she drowns small animals if she tries to pet them.

After all the trials and tribulations of finding a date, one has to think that the old custom of arranged marriages wasn't so bad after all. You'd certainly expend a lot less energy since you have as much control over your dating as the weatherman has over the weather. The only problem with bringing back arranged marriages in today's age is that there would be no incentive to keep oneself in physical shape so as to appear attractive to the opposite sex. By the time the two people were old enough to marry, after years of eating all the lard-laden, sugar-encrusted items that pass for food in this society, their combined weight would be enough to make the *Queen Mary* list to one side (the boat, that is). So maybe it's best if we keep dating the way it is. Otherwise, our country could easily be taken over by nearly any other country since we'd all be essentially turned into Weebles, and our national flag would have a picture of a Krispy Kreme doughnut on it.

---

40   The shark knows it is one of the coolest things in the ocean. A remora is...not. Another name for a remora is sucker fish, as it is built to stick to the shark. Why does the shark put up with this? Because for the luxury of hanging around a top predator, the remora eats the parasites and dead skin off the shark.

Asking Someone on a Date

or

Putting Your Self-Esteem

through a Cheese Grater

Having a woman say "no" when a man asks her out is a devastating thing for a man's ego. The ego is basically the man's third testicle; it likes to be stroked—and hurts like hell when it is smacked. The big difference is that a man eventually recovers from a scrotum shot but will forever feel the emotional sting not only every time he sees the woman who rejected him, but when she parades around the meatheads she'd rather date.

Therefore, a man plays the game of asking a woman out without actually asking her out to see how she'll react. If he asks her without asking her, and she agrees, then the man may really ask her. Sound confusing? Not as much as some of the lame pickup lines some guys use.[41] A man thinks he's got this stealth approach going

---

41 According to askmen.com, these are the top ten bad pickup lines: (10) Great legs, what time do they open? (9) You must be tired because you've been running through my head all night. (8) Guess what? It is your lucky day since I picked you to talk to. (7) That shirt's very becoming on you. Of course, if I was on you, I'd be coming to. (6) Can I buy you a drink or do you just want the money? (5) Can I have your phone number? I seem to have lost mine. (4) Do you believe in love at first sight, or should I walk past you again? (3) Excuse me, but I think you owe me a drink. [Why?] Because when I saw you across the room, I dropped mine. (2) Is your last name Gillette? Because you are the best a man could get. (1) Do you come here often?

when making these pathetic advances, but it appears on a woman's radar like the Spanish Armada. It is like sending the UCLA marching band on a reconnaissance mission.

Nevertheless, a guy has got to play the game to protect that ego. There are several standard modi operandi. He may try the "anyway" approach. In this tactic, the guy was going to the movie/restaurant/hot tub *anyway*, so she could tag along if she wanted, but it certainly wouldn't be any big deal to him either way. Under this approach, a guy has to act as nonchalant as if he were asking her for the time even though he's been building up to ask her out for several weeks, thrown up twice in nervous anticipation, and had to schedule an unnecessary root canal just to "accidentally" bump into her.

Then there is the "friends" approach, in which a bunch of people just happen to be going to a place, and the guy would be willing to give the woman a lift to be with the rest of the gang. If the woman ditches him once they arrive, then the guy knows the relationship is a dead end before he travels that road and so can take the necessary U-turn. Best to do that before he finds her with another guy in the backseat of his car and has to chauffer them back to her apartment—and then bleach down his car's upholstery.

A variation on this is the "disappearing friends" technique in which several people are going somewhere, but they mysteriously drop out at the last minute.[42] Since the guy already asked her, he can play it like he is "obligated" and so will still take her. Sure, these techniques are pretty hokey, but they're better than getting that third testis drop-kicked. It may be shaped like a football, but it should be treated with a bit more TLC.

In this age when society is striving for equality among all groups, women want the freedom to ask men out about as much as they want the freedom to unclog septic systems after an outbreak of food poisoning at a maximum-security penitentiary site. It's like a can of mace; they want it but don't want to ever need to use it. And why would they? Women have got an ego to protect as well. They may throw up words like "chivalry" and "unladylike" to explain away why they don't ask men out, but the idea of a walking hormone factory

---

42 The option here is if the guy wants to pay the friends off so that they disappear.

turning them down sounds about as appealing as French kissing a waffle iron.

Therefore, women have to play a game too, so that a guy can know she is receptive to a date. If a woman can lower a man's fear of rejection, the man will be more amenable to asking her out. How to do this? She can smile at him, talk to him, laugh at jokes that would normally be considered pathetic, or go to more drastic measures like pretending to actually be interested in guy things. Unfortunately, men pick up on subtle hints with the same acuity that a dog understands algebra. The women are then not only stuck without the romantic, enjoyable date, but are now involved in activities that they despise.

Case in point. There are many women out there who will act dumb just so they will not frighten away the intellectually challenged men. Remember that "third testicle"? Many men like their ego stroked about as much as...well, they like it stroked a whole lot. Women, knowing this, will sometimes play down their natural abilities as a backhand way not to accidentally make a man feel intimidated. Some women may try to do poorly on tests, in athletics, and socially so that the man looks better in comparison.

Nothing else floors the "nice guy" as much as this. Here he is being rejected by a woman who doesn't even consider him remotely interesting enough to date, and yet she turns around and believes she is not good enough for the guy who thinks Chutes and Ladders is a mentally taxing game or escargot has something to do with NASCAR. I'm not saying the guy must be smart for a woman to want him, but a little common sense would be nice. Any common sense would tell a guy that a smarter woman means she'll probably have a better career, bring home more money, and that means an easier life for him. After all, pride doesn't sound nearly as good when you think a fancy night out is when you are allowed to supersize your meal. If she is bringing home the big bacon, that is going to mean one freakin' huge high-definition television with more stations than you could count.

Quite often, women get pretty bored waiting for men to pick up on the hints. Back in junior high, it used to be easier. She'd tell one of her friends, who would tell one of your friends, who would tell you. You'd then give her an answer through the same chain. Either that or she'd send a note asking whether you liked her or not, and all you had to do was circle "yes." Whole relationships could be carried on without the two people speaking to each other or even acknowledging each other's existence even when they are walking by in the hallways. Sound a bit immature by today's standards? Well, ladies, don't forget that you're dealing with men. Men may be taller and have more body hair than when they were in junior high, but that brain is still as juvenile as ever.

Let's face it, junior high boys titter over everything that rhymes with a dirty word or any object that in the slightest way could resemble a body part. Are grown men that different? If you are a woman, walk by any guy and say you are anal retentive about x. No matter what guy it is, if you look hard enough, there will be the briefest smirk on his lips. So as to passing notes, etc., men would *love* for the junior high approach to continue throughout adulthood. That takes all the pressure off of worrying about being rejected. Maybe that explains their fascination with Internet chat rooms; it is just like passing notes.

So what's a woman to do if she doesn't want to embarrass herself trying to get the guy to notice her? She either goes home and watches bad movies on Lifetime[43] or goes to a place like a bar where the men ask out any female organism that is higher on the evolutionary ladder than a sponge. Of course the caliber of guy there is on par with starved hyenas. Will these guys be jerks? You may as well ask if your dog will try to kiss you after licking himself in a manner that is anatomically impossible for humans to do. Therefore, it behooves a woman to do whatever she can to get a guy to notice her short of lighting herself on fire rather than head to a human meat market.

After all these millennia, humans have found a new way to meet each other, and that is online. It can be done in two ways, either through a dating website or through chat rooms. With the dating sites, you pay money for a computer program to ask you thousands of questions

---

43 I believe the original name of the network was "Movies So Bad, Men Would Rather Spend a Lifetime Getting Beaten with Sticks Than Watch Another Minute," and it was shorted down to just Lifetime.

so that it can match your personality correctly with the ideal mate. Unfortunately, ideal means matching you with someone seven states or an ocean away. However, if you were able to drive to an airport, take a flight, rent a car, canoe down some rapids, and endure a yak ride, you could get to your soul mate. Quite often, that is not particularly practical, especially if you want to swing over after work.

Therefore, you've got to settle with someone a bit more local from the dating company. The biggest issue with this is when you first meet your date; you get to see who an objective independent program tells you is your match. If the person looks like he or she lives behind the dumpster at McDonald's and has the tendency to swat away flies that aren't actually there, then you have got to wonder what the computer thinks are your significant flaws.

Therefore, people are tempted to not be 100 percent truthful on the applications so that they get someone better. If they say that they weigh 160 pounds, that may have been true way back in high school...—for one leg—but now that is the average weekly bacon delivery. If they say they have six-pack abs, they could mean what multiple six-packs do to abs. If the person says he or she likes hiking, it will probably go no farther than hiking up his pants after his second box of Pop Tarts.

When the two people meet, they should probably choose a neutral site rather than one person driving over and picking up the other. There are multiple reasons for this, but we probably only need to discuss one—the blind date may be a raving lunatic. If the man picks the woman up at the house and there are seventy-five cats living with her, the evening won't be good.[44] If he doesn't own any shirts with sleeves, it is best that she doesn't get in the car.

---

44 One major difference between men and women is that there are very few men who end up in life being a crazy cat person. Meanwhile, it is a clear warning sign if a woman has three cats when she is young that her house may be overrun when she is older. There will be dirty litter everywhere that cats walk through and then walk on plates, pillows, etc. When the woman starts talking to them and then answering back in a high-pitched voice, then the break from reality has really set in. The next thing you know, she is dressing them up in little costumes and taking pictures to make calendars out of. Little does the woman know that those cats are plotting their revenge after each embarrassing moment. Every time the woman is walking downstairs in her house, it seems the cats are "accidentally" getting under her feet. Sure, these women can keep telling themselves it is accidental, but "Mr. Fluffy" is lethal.

Unfortunately, not only will he/she have to deal with the potentially crazy date, but also the trip home. There are some clingy women who simply refuse to leave a car since they can't take a hint that the date is over. She'll be talking about what she and her second cousin twice removed did during the summer when she was eight while the guy has resorted to using the tire jack as a crowbar to pry her out of the car.

If men have it bad, women have it worse when it comes to blind dates. A man can be crazy both emotionally *and* physically. Whereas men should prepare themselves for a date by taking some extra cash out at the ATM, a woman needs mace, a Taser, and nunchucks in case he is one of those men who thinks "no means yes, but the woman needs more assurance by being groped." If a crazy guy knows where the woman lives, he may pitch a tent on her front lawn to make sure no other guys come along because she is obviously meant to be with him forever just because she complimented him on parting his hair neatly.

The person can also try finding a date on his own by going into chat rooms. Chat rooms are where random people can send random messages. If a guy is talking with a woman, he may think he is acting smooth, but it isn't necessarily the case. If the man starts making sexual suggestions and the woman responds favorably, chances are very good that it is actually a person with the stem still on the apple, if you know what I mean.

Whether in an online dating pool or a chat room, one of the things a person usually does is post a picture. Around 99.9 percent of Photoshop sales are due solely to people buying it so they can spruce up their online photo. Whether it is a woman putting her face on Angelina Jolie's body or a guy morphing his features with Brad Pitt's, the pictures are usually not the most honest things on the Internet, and that is saying something for a thing that tries to make you believe that a deposed Nigerian prince on the run wants to deposit millions of dollars into your bank account to split with him if only you'll give him your account number. It does make meeting at the restaurant a bit difficult when you are both looking for people who look like they walked out of a J.Crew catalogue when you should be looking for people who look like they were part of the slave crew of a Viking ship.

The Date

or

Time to Await Your Fate

What does a guy have to do to get ready for a first date? Basically nothing. If a guy is really hopeful about the night, he may apply deodorant. That is in stark contrast to a woman, who must change her clothes, apply makeup, change her clothes, fix her hair, change her clothes, gather opinions about her appearance, change her clothes, and then repeat the entire process—and this for someone she plans on dumping at the end of the evening.

This does not mean that a guy does not care about his appearance; it's just that he has no idea what in hell to do with it. Telling a guy to look good on a date is like asking him to hold his breath for twenty minutes; best case, he gives you an odd look and refuses to try, and worst case, he tries, passes out, and smashes his head on the bureau on the way to the ground. Sure, there are a lot of guys who think they know what women think as sexy, but they end up looking like a discotheque refuge or an escapee from a Village People tribute band. Therefore, a man often decides to either give up trying to look good and save his brain cells to memorize "spontaneous," witty small talk or always wear the outfit he got a compliment on one time years ago from a cousin who was trying to make small talk because she forgot his name.

In the teenage years, when a guy arrives at the woman's house, he should go to the door and knock. Under no circumstances should he stay in the car and honk the horn. Parents of the woman will consider the horn honking as rude as pulling the finger of the dead guy at a wake and then passing gas, claiming it was the deceased. But isn't the favor of the parents considered the kiss of death for a relationship? Yes. Women like to rebel, and that can be translated into doing whatever the parents don't want her to do, even if she doesn't want to do it either. However, for the man, the father's wrath may be death itself. By sheer mental effort alone, the father will try to make the man's head implode if he seems to be even the remotest threat to his little girl's innocence, even if she is as innocent as Madonna[45] during a casting call.

When the guy is invited in, invariably the woman will not yet be ready. Therefore, the father will offer to "entertain" him. "Entertain" is an unusual word. I don't think General Custer would have said he was entertained by Sitting Bull and his Native American friends. Time alone is exactly what the father is salivating for.

The father will offer the date a seat and then turn on a blinding light usually reserved for interrogating suspected terrorists. The light should have a heating element on it that should increase the temperature around the guy to the point where his skin starts to blister. He should start perspiring enough to make his armpits smell like warm mayonnaise and cause the stain to extend all the way to his waist.

The questions then begin. It's a combination *Jeopardy!* and Hanoi Hilton.[46] The father wants to know exactly what his itinerary is. Are they going to a movie? If so, what movie? How long does the movie run? Who produced the movie? How long does it take to get to the theater? Has the oil been properly changed in the car that will have his daughter in it? What is the capital of Honduras? If a train were leaving Boston at forty-five miles per hour and one left Chicago going sixty-five miles per hour, in what city would they pass

---

45 The singer, *not* the mother of Jesus Christ. I'll probably get myself in enough trouble with people in this book without ticking off The Big Guy.

46 Hanoi Hilton is *not* Paris's younger sister. It was a torture site in Vietnam. What's the difference? Paris gets to torture the entire country rather than select individuals.

each other? The questions are intricately designed to trick the boy into admitting that there exists a small block of time that the boy can try to take advantage of his daughter.

Why does a father roast the guy like a pig at a backyard barbecue? Does he think that every guy his daughter wants to date is a sex fiend? Yes, he certainly does. Why does he think this? Two reasons: (1) because it is true, and (2) because he remembers what he was thinking when he used to go pick up a date. He remembers back to his younger years when he was hornier than the New York Philharmonic. He looks into the eyes of the young man in front of him and knows that the pimples on that kid's face are bursting with hormones. The father has to sit there pretending he doesn't know what libidinous fantasies the male in front of him is contemplating, and the guy has to sit there pretending that his most lecherous thought is lip-synching in the church choir. Ground rules will be laid down, the primary one being what time the woman is to be back home. If the curfew is 11:00 p.m., then it is 11:00 p.m. It is not 11:15 p.m. It is not even 11:01 p.m.

Breaking this rule is met with the same leniency as trying to wing the Pope with an AK-47. Young women quite often like to rebel against their parents, and so flaunt the rules. However, it is not she who pays the price for these violations. If you think some societies are a bit strict for chopping off a person's hand for stealing, then you really don't want to know what the father is pondering when the dating rules are bent. Therefore, a guy must do whatever it takes to get the girl back on time—and while he's at it, he should make sure his shirt is tucked in and not inside out, or his internal organs will soon be in the same shape.

Once the girl is ready, she'll finally make her appearance, much to the relief of her date. At this point, he's paid his dues and is ready to gnaw through the door to get out of the presence of the Grand Inquisitor. Until the couple is completely out of sight, there should be no physical contact.[47] Giving her a quick kiss while in the presence of

---

47 A guy not even making eye contact with his date is a plus in the father's eyes.

her father is like flaunting drugs in front of the Dallas Cowboys.[48] Any action more bold can result in the complete uncoiling of the man's small intestine. Getting a quick kiss in the car before driving off is also a no-no. There is every guarantee that the father will be looking out some window of the house with his teeth clenched tighter than a vise and his hands groping for a substitute for his "little girl's" date's neck. Hell, some fathers still hate to see their little girl kissed, even if she's married to the guy and has three kids.

So where does a guy bring a woman on a first date if he success-fully escapes her house? If the guy is petrified that he's going to say the wrong thing to his date or, worse yet, be too shy to say anything at all, then he should bring her to a movie. That way, the deepest he has to get into a conversation is "So, you want more popcorn?" What movie to take her to? Most men will make the assumption that he should take her to a touchy-feely movie where people are talking about and sharing (gasp!) emotions. Big mistake.

Going to a chick flick sets a bad precedent. Start now and he'll end up being one of those pathetic male souls who tape *General Hospital* every day so they can keep up with the problems of even more pathetic losers who still end up getting more sex than he does. Besides that, after seeing a romantic movie, the guy will have to live up to some romantic ideal he can't possibly attain.

So what is a guy to do if the woman insists on seeing a love story? First off is to do everything he can to get out of it. If it helps, he can imagine that he is in a Vietnamese prison camp (Hanoi, not Paris, if you didn't read the earlier footnote) and his captors are stopping by any second with bamboo for that special manicure. The man can say that he'd *like* to go, but that the reviews were dreadful[49] or that he

---

48   OK, so this one is a bit outdated. For a while, the Dallas Cowboys were featured less in the sports section of the newspaper and more in the police blotter. Yes, athletes can be caught with things like pot. Only a cowboy would have been arrested for 213 pounds of pot. The second time—yes, there was another time—it was only 175 pounds. For a while, there was a long line of limos that followed the team bus. The limos contained "personal entertainers" for the team. What did the coach think of all the shenanigans? Apparently he was the biggest partier of them all.

49   Technically true if you only read movie reviews in things like *Guns and Ammo* and *Mercenary Soldier* magazine.

wants to read the book first[50] or that it's that time of month and he'd be too emotional.[51]

Will any of these excuses work? Absolutely not. However, it is at least established that the guy is going to hate the experience. Won't that be a hindrance if this is a first date? Of course it may. It could not only snap the bud from the beginning of a flowering relationship, but dig up the roots and urinate in the empty hole. Better though to never have this relationship take off than for the man to end up as the eventual husband who is forced to accompany his wife to craft shows and to agree that watching ultimate fighting is barbaric and beneath people of dignity.[52]

If the man has no choice but to go to a romantic movie, he'll have to go.[53] However, throughout the movie, he should do a fair amount of muttering during any especially romantic scenes. If the lead actor is revealing any feelings, the man can toss in the occasional "God, spare me!" in a voice loud enough to be heard by his date and potentially the row ahead of him so that he may get a few dirty looks. As for actually watching the film, the man instead should either stare up at the ceiling or assume the standard position for an emergency landing in an airplane. With luck, the woman will hate the experience enough to never want to go to a romantic movie with the guy ever

---

50 Technically, this one is true as well as you *never* want to read this book and you *never ever* want to see this movie.

51 All right, so that one is a lie, but desperate times call for desperate measures.

52 Ultimate fighting is a combination of kickboxing, freestyle wrestling, and back-alley brawling. It takes place in an octagonal rather than traditional square ring. Why an octagon when that is far less practical? Because it summons up the memories of old Bruce Lee movies where all the greatest fighters in the world would be flown in to some remote island by some maniacal villain to battle to the death. It may sound farcical to women that people would be willing to risk their lives being beaten to a pulp just for "glory." However, these are *men* we are talking about. You know, the species willing to skateboard down a flight of stairs or drink a gallon of milk to see if they can't puke. Just me saying that it is impossible to drink a gallon of milk without puking will make a good percentage of men reading this book take on that challenge as being the exception to the rule. Besides, I'd *still* say that is more realistic than people breaking into song in everyday life.

53 If the movie stars Meryl Streep, Meg Ryan, or Renée Zellweger, the man should ask to put his head underneath the wheel of the car so that his date can drive over it rather than go. A man found leaving one of these films may just as well make an appointment with his local veterinarian and get himself fixed. He doesn't even deserve a human doctor.

again, but not so much that her fists curl up into balls of rage and little drops of spittle start to accumulate at the corners or her mouth whenever thoughts of the man and romance are uttered in proximity to each other.[54]

For an established couple, going to the movies is no big deal. However, there is a certain amount of anguish in the early movie dates. Paying for two tickets to the movies without the guy getting his arm around her is as good a financial investment as buying previously scratched lottery tickets. The guy knows he wants to make a move. The trick is when.

Before the movie starts, he's allowed to make casual conversation. Putting an arm around her now makes the scene as casual as the election of a new president. Conversation becomes as strained as baby food as you're sitting there with your arm awkwardly draped over her shoulder not knowing what to do or say next. Therefore, the guy's got to wait until there can be no significant conversation. If he does it during the movie, he has no particular excuse to be moving his arm. He's just got to fling it over and hope she snuggles into it rather than not acknowledging it or—worse yet—leaning forward. Oh, that one sucks.

The previews are the time to do it. He can do the concerned approach, like "Can you see OK?" or "Are you warm enough?" meanwhile putting an arm around her to emphasize the care in his voice, not that he pays any attention to the actual answer. Pathetic? Absolutely. But it is better than nothing. The big issue with the arm-around-the-shoulder thing is that it is great for the first fifteen minutes. Then the blood starts draining from the arm, and the shoulder starts locking up. It can then feel like needles are being stabbed randomly around your arm. If you move it, you could be sending the wrong message to your date, that you don't value touching her.

Therefore, you've got to try to get blood flowing again. You can do so by rubbing her shoulder, but be careful you aren't giving her a friction burn. There is little romance if she has to excuse herself to

---

54 As a general note, it is usually considered in bad taste to ruin a woman's evening and then expect her to make your night. Putting any moves on now will be met with the same open-arms greeting as the Poles expressed to the Germans during the blitzkrieg.

apply aloe lotion. The other thing you can do is clasp and unclasp your hand rapidly and repeatedly. This has to be done nonchalantly, lest she think you are about to make a grab for an area of the road you haven't paid the toll to travel on yet.

The movie make-out, however, should never be attempted except by established couples and, even then, most women aren't too keen on it as it can be considered trashy. After all the horror stories her father told her, making an unsolicited move on her in the theater while she is busy watching the movie would be like shooting a cap gun in the VFW during happy hour. She's just as likely to turn around and snap his neck before she realizes it is just a kiss. In general, women are not into public displays of affection except to hold hands, and even that isn't so much to show affection, but to mark her territory against other women.[55]

For the man with enough confidence in his social skills to be able to say something remotely unpathetic, he can offer to take her to dinner for the first date. He should never take her to an establishment that has a menu comprising the various ways a beef patty can be placed between two pieces of bread. There should not exist the ability to "supersize" the meal. Instead, the menu should have the meat from at least twelve different animals other than cow and chicken and have a wine menu thicker than a phone book if he really wants to impress her.

Above all else, the man should have a plan in mind before he picks her up. Under no circumstances should he ask where she wants to go. If so, he starts off sounding wishy-washy, and women don't like that. They want a warrior, not a worrier. Women desire men with

---

55 When you walk a dog, it seems that they want to urinate on every tree, fire hydrant, car tire, or elderly person with a walker that they pass by. The reason for this is that they are marking their territory—by peeing on it, they are imparting their particular urine's smell so that other dogs know that piece of land is their property. Dogs, however, are not much on squatter's rights and so pee on top of the first dog's spot so as to supersede the first deed to the land. So why do it at all? Pretty much to annoy the owner of the dog who has to stand there acting like he doesn't see his animal pissing all over his neighbors' shrubs so often they the leaves have started to turn brown and drop off. Let's just be grateful women are content with the holding-hands method instead to mark to other women that the property is taken.

distinct opinions and objectives. That way, they can have something to beat out of men over the ensuing decades of a relationship.

Dinner has more opportunities to be suave, or at least to think one is doing so. By going to a restaurant that actually gives you a menu rather than having one printed above the counter, the man shows that he is not cheap (even though he probably is) and is sophisticated (even though he probably isn't). A man, since he is usually paying the bill, cannot help but look at the prices. A good rule of thumb is the fancier a restaurant gets, the higher the price of the meal and the smaller the portions they'll serve.

Fancy restaurants don't even try to hide the fact that they are trying to shake you down for every cent you have while concurrently trying to starve you to death. They even go to the point of taunting men by placing a few morsels of food on a humungous plate just to make it look even more minuscule. That is like giving a woman a magnifying glass and telling her to hold it up because she is going to be excited when he goes au naturel. Chances are, she's not going to be expecting a "big" event. In some French restaurants, you can find yourself maxing out your credit card and still being so hungry that you'll be trying to suck the nutritive value out of the linen to get some sustenance. The guy finds himself making excuses to drop off his date early so he can gorge himself at the Golden Arches.

Another oddity of taking dates to fancy restaurants is that the amount a woman eats is indirectly proportional to how much her meal costs. If she orders a prime rib, most women will take two or three bites and claim to be full. Many women are concerned about their weight, and so they try to give men the false impression that they barely eat enough to keep an anorexic gnat alive. Men, however, are not thrilled to see forty-five dollars' worth of the forty-six-dollar steak pitched. These women may as well not order their own meal and just eat the garnish off the guy's plate.

Why do women do this? My theory is that they order expensive items to see how much the guy sweats. If he acts completely calm, chances are that he has got enough money to pay rent. If he looks like he has had a sudden and severe onset of grand mal seizure, chances are that he doesn't have loads of money and so may not be as good a catch.

So what can a guy do to impress a date at the restaurant? One thing is for the man to order for the woman. Why this is impressive is something men really don't know. It's not as if women don't like to talk. Talking is part of the essence of being a woman. A good two thirds of the X chromosome is devoted to developing language skills. It's like a woman seizing the television remote and thinking that she is doing a man the favor of not having to sprain his thumb as he clicks through the channels at light speed. Men wouldn't allow the remote to be pried out of their hands if the other end was held by an amorous orangutan with morning breath. My guess is that women like men ordering because they want men to get it out of their systems now so the women won't have so much work later in marriage.

What should a guy talk about while waiting for the food to arrive? It is easier to mention what not to discuss. First off, do not mention former girlfriends. A woman will figure that the two of you are no longer going out either because she dumped you due to some significant defects or you dumped her because you can't handle a relationship. Either way, you're damaged goods. Another no-no is talking about the family. You've either had a happy childhood, in which case you're a goody-goody mama's boy, or you've had a bad childhood, and now you're carrying enough mental baggage that you'll need a spare bedroom to keep it all in. How about how excited you are to be on a date with her? That will buy you a one-way ticket to Patheticville. Showing too much enthusiasm turns a woman off like asking her to wash the skid marks out of your underwear. What about your hobbies or interests? Sure, if you want to watch her eyes glass over and her head hit the salad plate.

So what's left? Keep the conversation revolving around her. That, after all, will be her favorite topic. She'll take over the talking without even realizing it. By doing this, the guy limits what he has to say, and she still thinks he's a scintillating conversationalist when he barely has to open his mouth.

Above all at dinner, the guy has to pick up the tab. Even if she's the heiress to the Rockefeller fortune and is insisting, he's got to get his hands on that bill, or his hands won't be getting on much else. If the bill is larger than expected, he should not show any panic on his face. They say some animals can smell fear. Well, women can smell cheap. If the woman insists on paying, and the guy finally agrees to that after a significant discussion, will the woman still think of him as stingy? Actually, she won't think of him at all. His name will be permanently scratched off her mental list. He could dress up as Thor in drag, light himself on fire, and run past her, and she'd never even notice him.

What if she insists on paying at least half? Then the guy will have half a chance in hell of going out with her again. A guy has got to make picking up the check sound like it is absolutely no big deal. Even if he has to delve into his college fund, shake down his grandmother, and sell one of his kidneys, he's got to pick up the tab to have any chance of a close encounter later in the evening.

Any romantic dates that won't break the bank? There's always a picnic. Forget the PB&J, though. What is saved in money is going to have to be paid back in emotionally wrenching time and creativity. Nothing is allowed to be ordinary. Forget the Wonder Bread. You'll have to pick up a baguette or some other piece of bread that is hard to spell and deteriorates into a heap of crumbs when you try to break it. Throw a piece of cheese in it? Again, you'll have to get something with an unusual spelling like feta or brie. You want a drink? If you're over twenty-one, then the *only* beverage that can be served is a bottle of wine. If it has a screw cap, then that will be the only screwing that will happen.

So how does one pick wine, whether it is red or white, blush or chardonnay? I've never had a clue. If I'm at a business dinner, I clutter up the space in front of me and refuse to make eye contact with the waiter so there is no way I'll get the wine list. I know picking wine has got something to do with matching the wine with the entrée. Red wine is supposed to go with beef, and white goes with chicken, fish, and light pastas. Why? Who the hell really knows? Do you pick the type of soda with the chicken nuggets or cheeseburger?

Sure, a lot of people claim they know about wine, but these are the same people who think that truffles, which are mushrooms that grow out of animal dung, are a delicacy. Hell, while we're speaking of it, you might as well throw some truffles in the picnic basket as well. You do have a basket, don't you? Think you're going to look sophisticated brown-bagging it? Why don't you just pick her up on a moped? Throw in a few exotic fruits and an entrée picked up at any run-of-the mill French café, and you're in business. Oh yeah, this was supposed to be cheap. Sorry, but it's about time you learned: love may be blind, but it can smell money a mile away.

If the date is going well (you haven't accidentally poked your [or her] eye with the fork, and you're not wearing more spaghetti than you've eaten), you may be thinking of going for a second date. At this point, it becomes important to know if she is actually enjoying herself or if she'd rather give herself a frontal lobotomy with an ice pick than spend any additional time with you. Therefore, you've got to start hinting as to whether she'd like to go out again.

Unfortunately, men don't hint well. "So are you having a good time?" is about the best line men have come up with after thousands of years of dating. If she shrugs her shoulders and says it's OK, then it is an epic disaster. Let's face it, if she's allowed to eat anything she wants to for free and all she has to do is put up with your company, and she still thinks she got a bum deal, then you've got to work on your communication and/or bathing skills. Assuming she does actually make some suggestion that it isn't the worst day of her life, then you have the green light for asking her out again. Warning: don't do this now. Asking for a date while on a date sounds about as desperate as asking for a rope when at the bottom of a rapidly filling septic tank.

The most stress comes at the end of the date. The whole date can be considered a success or failure depending upon whether the guy gets a kiss at the end of the night. A woman will have decided whether a guy is going to get the kiss probably before the date starts. However, the guy has got to read every move throughout the night as to whether he's going to get the green light or get checked into the boards.[56]

---

56 Being checked into the boards is a hockey term. In this particular sport, you can be skating down the ice minding your own business when a member of the opposing team can barrel down as fast as he can to slam you into the wall. That is perfectly fine, even if it results in your ribs now sticking out through your skin. In most sports, if you are involved in a fight, you are thrown out of the game. In hockey, you get two minutes in the penalty box. Even with all this action, it is now being beaten in the ratings by people playing poker. Go figure.

So what can a guy use as a key to whether to try for the kiss? The best one is when you're dropping her off at the end of the night, you ask her whether she wants you to walk her to the door. Now, the woman lives here. She's made this walk by herself tens of thousands of times. If at this stage of her life, she asks for help walking to the door, chances are high that she'll be willing to give a kiss. If instead she jumps out of the car before it comes to a complete stop and tucks into a ball as she dives through the front window of her house rather than taking the time to open the door, chances are fairly low that a kiss will be in the offing.

When the two of you get to the front door, there is usually a bit of small talk. So how does one go from mild pleasantries to a lip lock? First off, give a quick glance down at her lips. Does she return the look? If so, good. If instead her lips turn into a snarl to bear her canine teeth, then bad. So what's the next step? The guy should move forward about one one-thousandth of an inch. If she in kind moves forward, he can then move forward, and the two will eventually meet in a kiss. If the woman rocks back, then the guy can call off the ill-fated attempt and pretend the whole thing never happened, thus saving face rather than sucking it.

The thing to watch out for here is the parents if she still lives at home. The house may be dark, but there is no doubt the father is up, along with his blood pressure. Why is he in the dark? Because it is easier to see you from behind the curtain. The father has somehow turned from his nine-to-five job of senior payroll accountant to army commando ready to cut the Achilles tendon of the enemy to immobilize him if need be.[57] Sometimes, the mother will call him off, but you can only count on this as much as a couple dozen sandbags holding back a flooding Mississippi River. If you plan on making a move on his baby girl, I'd put on the inflatable ducky and get ready for the typhoon.

---

57 The Achilles tendon is the thing that connects the calf muscle to the heel. I don't mean to imply that the father would cut this vital thing for absolutely no reason. There would have to be something serious for this to happen, like the man complimenting his daughter, thus trying to get her in a compromising position, or not complimenting his daughter, thus hurting his little princess's feelings.

Not to put any additional pressure on you, but the first kiss will dictate her thoughts as to what kind of lover you are. Tense up and give her a quick kiss, and you'll be considered to have the sexual dynamism of Sheetrock. A little too much on the wet side, and she'll be telling her friends all about the slobbering basset hound she had a date with. Too long and you're a pervert. Too short and she'll assume other things are as well. So just relax and have fun.

After all the pressure is poured on, what's a guy to do? One of the tried and true techniques for the initial move is the cheek caress. By gently placing his hand under her chin and guiding her face to his, a guy demonstrates both physical tenderness and emotional strength. This technique does take practice, though. Move in too quickly, and you'll end up giving her a double face slap reminiscent of a Three Stooges skit. Too hard and she'll think you've escaped from the World Wrestling Federation and are trying to place a full nelson on her. The next thing he's got to watch out for is how wet his lips are. If they are too dry, it will be like sucking on sandpaper. Therefore, he should slightly wet his lips with his tongue as he makes the approach. Remember—slightly—too much licking and he'll look like Jeffrey Dahmer.[58]

Once the man makes lip contact, he should keep it for no less than two and no more than five seconds. The trick here is to leave her wanting more. As she rocks back for breath, bail out and fade off into the night. That's easy to say, for very few men have the willpower to break off a successful smooch. For inspiration, think of her father behind the curtain with a two-by-four. If she leans back in for an open-mouthed kiss, well, even if the father is approaching with a tire iron to pry the two of you apart or to wrap it around your skull, you still wouldn't have the willpower to back off.

After the date is over and it is deemed successful, a guy's got to act casual, like it couldn't have been anything but. If he sees the woman the next day, he should not attempt a high-five or perform any sort of victory dance. Doing something like that is a clear signal that he expected that a night with him was supposed to be an

---

58 Jeffrey Dahmer was not just a run-of-the-mill serial killer, but one who liked to eat his victims, bringing a whole new meaning to "finger-licking good."

unqualified disaster and anything else is a lucky aberration. He'll get her wondering why she should tempt fate yet again. However, if *she* acts cool, then the guy figures he's displayed the sexual charisma of aging Brussels sprouts and would land about as gracefully as the *Hindenburg* if he asked her out again.

So when does he ask her out again? Monday? Again, it sounds too desperate. She'll think that she's the only one he's able to get a date with. If she thinks that, then she'll wonder whether she is hurting her social standing by lowering herself to the level of going out with the likes of him.

Here's the conundrum: unless other women are clamoring to get him, she doesn't want him. Yet if he actually does go out with a different girl, then she especially won't go out with him again since she'll feel jilted. So what the hell does a woman actually want? She wants to go out with a guy who could have any woman (within five hundred miles, give or take five thousand) and whom every woman wants, but who has picked her—but could pick another—but can't because he feels entrapped by her unique feminine wiles. Now isn't that simple?

Around Wednesday is the right time to ask the woman out. If he asks Thursday or Friday, she's tempted to say no. Why? Because she doesn't want him to think that she can't get any other plans for the weekend besides his last-minute offer. She'll have this attitude even if she has spent the last several days cursing at the telephone like a drunken sailor at a Justin Bieber concert waiting for him to call. This lesson holds true throughout courtship. Even if the couple has gone out every weekend for the last two years, she'll be pissed that he is taking her for granted by waiting until "the last minute" before making plans with her.

Couldn't she just make the assumption that they'll be going out this weekend if they have for the past seventy-two weekends straight? Sure, but this way women ensure that they remain the focal point of men's lives. A man should get to the point that he doesn't blow his nose without thinking how that will impact her schedule. Couldn't she make the plans instead? Yes, but it is eminently more fun for women to make men sweat it out trying to figure out what women actually want to do. Most men would rather face death figuring out the riddle of the Sphinx[59] than continually attempt to guess what women want of them. Many men finally break down and decide to get married because they just can't take the pressure of coming up with something to do on dates.

When a guy really wants to ratchet up the relationship, a good plan for a date is for him to make her dinner. Why is this so good? Not only can the guy try to impress the woman with domestic talents he doesn't really have, but he gets her *into his apartment*! I'm not saying here that the only thing men care about on dates is whether anything physical will happen. I may be implying it like hell, but I'm not outright saying it.

In preparing, keep in mind that the dinner *must be elegant*. Therefore, every dating bachelor eventually learns that he must know and be able to perform one or two fancy recipes. For me, it was chicken cordon bleu. It sounded fancy, looked fancy, and tasted like I actually knew something about cooking. I'd throw in a salad with several types of lettuce I'd never heard of, bread that was not (believe it or not) presliced, and a dessert that took hours to create. I then had to pretend I cooked like that on a routine basis. Keep in mind that this is quite a stretch for a bachelor who routinely under-cooks macaroni and cheese because he does not have the patience to wait the full ten minutes to boil the noodles until they are soft.

Not only should the food be good, but also the atmosphere be should be right. I'm not talking here of having enough oxygen in the room to breathe.[60] I'm talking about having the place looking nice enough that one could assume that individuals with opposable thumbs inhabited it. It doesn't matter how delectable the food is if she has to arm-wrestle a member of the rodent family for first dibs or has to eat off a board stretched across two milk crates in place of a table. That may have qualified for furniture in college, but in the real

---

59 Most people know the sphinx from the statue next to the great Pyramids of Giza. It has the face of a man and body of a lion, which turned out to be far more intimidating than their original ostrich body. The sphinx was said to give riddles to passersby who, if they weren't able to answer them, were devoured. I don't know about you, but I'd be even more intimidated if it was the other way around with the head of a lion and body of a person. I mean, really, I can imagine the terror of seeing the jaws of a lion closing in on me, but what is a man's mouth going to do? Give a vicious hickey?

60 Although it would be a plus if the place doesn't smell like a condemned YMCA.

world, it is about as clean and elegant as Ray Charles's spittoon. So what to do to spruce the place up for a date? Candles are an absolute must. For most bachelors, their life experience with candles is blowing them out on birthday cakes once a year as a child. We are not talking about those candles. For many men, what I am about to say may sound incredible, almost as unbelievable as the Loch Ness Monster, Bigfoot, and Donald Trump's hair. There are—I kid you not—stores that specialize in selling just candles.

Candles! That's it! Look around and all you see are more candles! You can have scented candles, colored candles, ornamental candles, etc. If these stores have diversified at all, then they sell scented soap as well. So what the heck is it that makes soap and candles have enough in common to devote an entire store to them? The only thing I can think of is that they are two objects that men can't imagine buying, never mind comparing the difference between. Come to think of it, men don't care much in the buying department unless it has a motor attached or has the words "high def" associated with it.

Where do they so cleverly hide these stores from men so that we don't even know they exist? Believe it or not, they are in nearly every mall. Because men care so little about those shops, even if the man is staring directly at the store, his brain is able to take the entire image and shove it into his blind spot. It is only when a woman drags a guy in there and shows it to him that it becomes part of a man's reality, sort of like herpes.

Not only should a bachelor have the appropriate candles, but he should have the appropriate candle holders. Leaning lit candles up against the salt shaker just doesn't cut it from a safety viewpoint. It also helps if there are napkins on the table (that haven't been swiped from the local fast-food restaurant and aren't just paper towels folded in half) and the silverware is not plastic and does not have food particles from previous meals clinging to it. No sporks.[61]

---

61 The spork is the must underappreciated of all utensils. For those uninitiated, it is the spoon with serrations so it can also operate as a fork. The manufacturers of silverware are aware that it would dramatically cut down on the number of products they could sell. Therefore, the spork has been relegated to the plastic variety only. If you put a sharper edge on one side so it could also act as a knife, men would never use anything else.

At the risk of making another statement that sounds too far-fetched to be true, it is possible that there is more silverware at each place setting than just a knife, fork, and spoon. If there is a soup being served, then there is a thing called a "soup spoon." If there is a salad, then there is a "salad fork." Does the salad fork work any differently than a regular fork? If you try to pick up steak with it, does it bounce off or something? No. Apparently the same fork can work for both, but that isn't allowed for a fancy dinner.

So why can't each person have one fork apiece and just do a good job licking it off between courses? It's got something to do with manners. If time permits (and I get some cash, maybe in the manner of a significant government grant), maybe I can study up on this "manners" thing, along with the theoretics involved with matching appropriate clothes, and I can put out an advanced book of survival tips for men.[62]

And you've got to have music playing. Rather than play anything you actually like, you should play something more toward the classical end. Yes, I know AC/DC and Led Zeppelin qualify as classic rock, but I'm talking about classic as in Bach, Beethoven, Brahms, and other dead people who used to wear funny wigs for some inexplicable reason. An acceptable alternative to this is a piano soloist, light jazz, or something else that is one step up from elevator music.

Most guys usually have to stoop to buy the one token CD for mood setting. If he doesn't have one, he's got to go and get one. Once home, he should listen to it several times before she comes over so that he learns to stop cringing when it is playing. For many men, this is like having the choice of which golf club he would like to be beaten with.

Not only must the table look good, but the apartment should be cleaned—of course only the parts that she is going to see. No

---

62 Naturally, I'll need some hazard pay for a mission this dangerous and unpredictable. Maybe some rations like beef jerky and Mountain Dew to make sure if I can't figure things out, I've got something to fall back on. If I look "changed" when I come back—for example, if I do things like wear a sweater tied around my neck for no apparent reason with a pastel shirt underneath—I hereby authorize my friends to tie me into a chair and force me to watch a marathon of Arnold Schwarzenegger movies while I am only allowed to eat beef nachos to get me back.

sense going overboard. Pushing things under the bed or building a six-foot wall of crap behind the closet door that could seriously injure the next person who opens it are perfectly fine ways of eradicating clutter. Many restaurants do basically the same thing: they look nice from the front, but the back has a dumpster full of rotting food with enough flies to carry off an entire cow and rats that can bench-press a Buick.

One problem area is the bathroom. There's not a whole lot the guy can do about the bathroom besides actually cleaning it. Many bachelors clean their bathrooms about as often as we elect a president. Unfortunately, women just can't get in a romantic mood if there are multiple layers of sticky urine sediment that prevent her from sitting down when she has to pee, or if she does sit down, she gets the sensation of sitting on a giant Post-it pad. Not only does the toilet have to be cleaned, but the floor around the toilet, the sink, and even the shower. The simple fact is that if the woman is thinking about getting close to a guy, and she knows he attempts to get clean in a shower stall lined with green and brown algae, sliding between the sheets will need to involve a body-sized condom.[63]

The guy also has to clean the dining room. That should include the dining room table that has been holding the last six months of junk mail, his sweaty gym shirts, and the old pizzas in varies stages from moldy all the way to fossilized. The kitchen has got to be clean in case she comes in to help get the food. There is usually a leaning tower of dishes in the sink that would be the envy of Pisa. Those have got to be cleaned. There are brown boxes with handles around the kitchen. These are known as cupboards and are where the man is supposed to store clean dishes when not in use. So what does a guy clean first? The bedroom, of course, as he hopes that is where the most time will be spent.

---

63 Here are a few hints to see if the bathroom is actually clean. Is the entire toilet white or more of a splotchy yellow-brown? If it isn't white, go back and do it again. What about the floor near the toilet? The tile is supposed to be the same pattern as the rest of the room. If the two feet around the toilet are a different pattern, best to go back and do it again.

The first thing in the bedroom is that the bed should be made. Most men are confused by this statement. "Made" does not mean having to buy wood and nails to construct a frame and throw a mattress on top. Made means that the sheets must be tucked in with the top curled down over the blanket that is also tucked in. The comforter then has to be neatly over everything with the pillows tucked under it. Most men don't even know what a comforter is, never mind have one.

There are some women who go so far as to have decorative pillows on top of the bed whose sole purpose in being made is to be tossed on the ground when the person goes to bed, only to be put back on top when a person leaves. The foreskin after a bris is about as useful as these decorative pillows, but for some reason, women love them. It is also important, apparently, that the sheets be washed so that there is no odor or staining. If the man has been having a successful dating life, again, it is even more important that the sheets are washed.

The floor of a bachelor's bedroom usually has several different piles of clothes going from "somewhat washed" to "bearable" to "usable in an emergency" to "this should really be incinerated." *All* piles need to go. Now, there is no need to go crazy and actually wash, dry, and put them away. Out of sight, out of mind is the standard rule of thumb. The closet does wonders for hiding things, as does the space under the bed. One word of caution—if you've stuffed so much under the bed that the four legs are not actually touching the floor so that it rocks like a ship at sea when you get on it, or you suffer nosebleeds being that high off the ground, you've exceeded the acceptable limit.

When the man's date arrives, he should invite her in (obviously). If she's brought a change of clothes with her, then that is certainly a good sign for the (late) evening, and the man can consider himself golden unless there is a tragic accident with the flaming shish kebabs he's preparing. However, that much good luck is extremely doubtful unless you are Brad Pitt or an elderly millionaire with a hacking cough.

When she's at the apartment, he's got to act cool. He does not want her to know that before her arrival, he put out a grease fire in his attempt to make deep-fried calamari that sent his roommate to the hospital.[64] Instead, he wants to give the impression that the place is always clean and he always cooks extravagant meals and he always changes his underwear on a daily basis.

It is important to note that if anything permanent does happen in the future, his then wife will be a bit miffed when she finds out that he is, in fact, a slob whose adeptness in the kitchen is on par with that of a blindfolded rhino. Therefore, it is important to have affidavits from people like roommates and family members stating that he didn't become a slob after marriage, but that he has been one throughout his life. That way, the guy can throw the "for better or worse" thing at her. If she didn't check under the hood before buying the car, that is her problem. Too bad for her if she has buyer's remorse.[65]

When the couple is ready to eat, he should start by opening the bottle of wine. When men shop, they usually tend to purchase the lowest-priced brand of the item they want. Do this with wine, and you'll end up with something that is more appropriate for removing paint (and stomach lining) than drinking. It is also important to know *how* to open the bottle. First off, the guy *must have* a bottle opener—not a bottle-cap opener, but something designed to remove a cork. Accept no substitutes; a pocketknife or pair of scissors will take twenty minutes to get the bottle open, and then there will be more debris floating in the liquid than when the Japanese bombed Pearl Harbor.

I probably should go through the proper way to open a bottle of wine. First off, the top comes wrapped in some metallic material. I believe they glue the stuff on just to make men like me look as debonair as a street clown with his fly at half mast when trying to get the bloomin' thing off. The guy should take a knife and go around the outside of the lip of the bottle in a fluid motion. Sawing at it with a butcher's knife would give the woman the impression that she's dating someone less like James Bond and more like Leatherface from *The Texas Chainsaw Massacre*.

---

64 Thank God both for the drop-and-roll technique as well as that wonderful invention of 911.

65 Some states have a lemon law for bad cars, but not for guys.

After the metallic paper is gone, remove the top to expose the cork. Twist the corkscrew about three-quarters of the way in. Too little and you'll have trouble pulling it out (known as corkus interruptus), too much and you'll drill through the cork, spewing chunks in the wine (it may not lose its flavor, but it certainly loses its class when you have to put it through a strainer). Rock the cork back and forth gently, working it out slowly. Trying to physically yank it straight out will usually end with the bottle shooting out of your hand one way and the decorking hand ending up in the forehead of the aforementioned date. Physical abuse, even if accidental, is not the best way to begin a relationship.

Wineglasses are the next necessity. It is hard to pull off a sophisticated attitude when you are pouring into a glass that was formerly a jelly jar. No regular glasses, plastic cups, soup bowls, McDonald's cups (even if they were rinsed), or any other container, no matter how well it can hold liquid. The glass must have a stem to it. There is no substitute for a wine glass. Will the wine taste different if sipped from a beer mug? Absolutely not. It doesn't matter to the woman. If she sees the guy drinking wine from a mug, she is going to assume him to be the type who in later years will, rather than paint the exterior of the house, decorate it by hanging a collection of mismatched hubcaps. She simply doesn't want to end up sitting on a couch in her front lawn staring at a Trans Am that has been up on blocks for the last seven years.

The man should only fill the glass half full. Yes, the guy wants her to drink a lot, but he doesn't want her to think she's drinking a lot, or she'll start counting and cut herself off. Instead, he should just keep her glass "fresh" by bringing it back up to half full when the level gets low. As the night progresses, he can inch up to filling it three-quarters full. Oh, and about pouring: it helps to give a little twist when finishing up on the pour so that the wine doesn't dribble down the side of the bottle. It looks nice and gives her the impression that the guy knows more about alcohol than funnels, shotguns, and tap sucks.

So you've got her in your apartment with a little bit of alcohol in her. Exactly how much is key to the situation. Too little and the "wit" you are trying to so cleverly show off is in the "nit" variety. Too much alcohol combined with something happening that shouldn't have, and the guy will be spending the next several years in an orange jumpsuit with a twenty-four-hour-a-day roommate who is incarcerated for something to do with puppies and a blender. If she's smiling and looking like she is actually enjoying herself, then that is the time for the guy to show his moves.

Each guy has got to come up with his own set of moves that suits his personality. How to do this? Through a painful, tortuous process of trial and error. There's no way of telling whether a woman is laughing because she finds your wit so dazzling or because you've done something foolish. I'm going to refrain from discussing the moves I personally crafted during the dating phase of my life. After all, a man's dating technique should be as individual as his fingerprint. What works for one man may be disastrous for the next. That sounds so much better than having my wife say that all my previous moves were dorky. Would she actually say this? Absolutely not. She would never put my dorkiness in the past tense.

Going Steady

or

There May Be No Ring on Her Finger, but There May Be One in Your Nose

A fter a while, you may find that the two of you are going out on a routine basis and not seeing others. Some type of actual commitment is usually hoped for here. Many men panic at this stage. Even if he hasn't gone out with a different woman in two years because (a) he really likes his time spent with this one and/or (b) he couldn't get a date with another woman if fifty-dollar bills were velcroed to his body, he may still not know whether there is a true commitment.

Earlier last century, a guy would pin a girl. No, not like in a wrestling match, although that does usually indicate some type of serious relationship. The pin I'm talking about here is one to wear on her shirt. By accepting it, the woman gave a nonverbal commitment to see him exclusively, and when the relationship ended, she'd give the pin back. It acted like a scarlet letter *A*[66] as something to ward other

---

66 Actually, that may be a bad example. This reference refers to the book *The Scarlet Letter* by Nathaniel Hawthorne, in which a woman in Puritan times ends up having a child out of wedlock. As such, society shuns her by making her wear a scarlet letter A on her clothes for the rest of her life to stand for "adulterer." These days, that could be considered an advertisement to men.

men off. It meant that she was taken and all other guys were to keep hands off. This commitment wasn't as serious as a ring. The pin was kind of like leasing a car; everyone called it yours, so you got to drive it around for a while before needing to make the actual decision to buy it.

These days, giving the woman a pin has gone the way of the dodo, phone booths, and kids who can spell.[67] A guy may as well offer her father two goats and a sack of change as a dowry to take her away. Even saying the word "steady" will get a chuckle out of a woman because it is so antiquated. Besides, the only thing steady in a relationship is the girl's father's conviction that the guy is trying to corrupt his defenseless daughter.[68] So what can a guy do to find out if the two of them are actually seeing each other exclusively? Believe it or not, there's painfully little he can do. The only thing that will let him know for sure is when she introduces him to someone, she'll refer to him as her boyfriend. At this point, he knows he's in.

A warning to women: there are some men thick enough to think that dating and sex for months (or years) on end does not involve any actual commitment. He hears the word "boyfriend" and the next thing you know, he's wearing a fake moustache, checked out of his apartment, legally changed his name, and moved to another state in efforts to avoid the woman. Tell this man that you "love him," and he'll be found swimming the wrong way across the Rio Grande.

I don't recommend it, but if a guy wants to press the issue of whether he has reached boyfriend status, he could introduce her to someone as his girlfriend. However, he runs the risk of having her wince, break out in cold chills, or "correct him," which is quite embarrassing, especially if he is introducing her to close friends, family members, or his clergyman.

---

67 LOL on c-ing u kds txt.

68 He'll think this even if the guy has been living in a monastery while his daughter has dated the entire football team, three at a time.

Breaking Up

or

Now I Understand Why

Animals Can Gnaw Their Own

Leg Off to Escape a Trap

Obviously, most relationships don't work out. If they did, we'd all have ended up with our childhood sweethearts. Considering that you may have picked each other for the sheer fact that you both had a retainer and could understand each other's lisping, that is not a good thing. Most of us were fairly naïve the first time we picked the person we thought was going to be the love of our life. Instead the relationship turned into a never-ending episode of *The Twilight Zone* where things were great one day, and the next, the person had changed so much you were hunting around for giant seed pods under the bed.

The big question is who decides to break up with whom. If she decides to break up with him, then it is important for the guy to handle it gracefully. Even if he has an engagement ring in his back pocket, it is best to handle it like he wholeheartedly agrees and was about to break up with her if she didn't with him. After all, the last thing he wants is for her to walk by him with a look of pity in her eyes, and then her friends to also look at him like he is somewhat pathetic. The next thing you know, everyone is treating him like a monkey in a zoo, keeping their distance so he doesn't throw poop at them.

The most that he can hope for is for her to agree that it is a mutual breakup. Under no circumstances should he ask her not to dump him. After all, what happens if a guy begs for her to give him another chance? Well, whether she says yes or no, his dignity takes such a kick in the head that it will look like something out of a Picasso painting. If she says no, then he's basically gotten dumped twice with an exclamation point, and he's only one strike away from her taking a restraining order on him.

The only thing worse than her saying no is her saying yes. Getting back together means that she dumped you but took you back because she felt pity for you but could dump you again at any time when the pity thing dries up. Gee, doesn't that sound comforting? That's like trying to push water back into a raisin so it will magically be a grape again.

If he wants to break up with her, the best approach is to blame himself for the relationship not working. Whether he's "just not ready for this type of commitment" or he "just doesn't know what he wants in life right now" and "doesn't want to drag her through the emotional turmoil he himself is embroiled in," it is easier giving a ridiculous line like those than the real reason. After all, would he rather explain to her that she's boring him to the point where he'd rather take up recreational do-it-yourself acupuncture than keep spending time with her, or that she requires more maintenance than a nuclear power plant?

The big problem with this approach is that she may actually not only buy it, but bank on it. If she does, she may be willing to stick by him while he "figures things out." After going back and forth for about two or three weeks[69] discussing why he doesn't want to break up with her but really wants to, many men confuse themselves to the point where they talk themselves back into the relationship. It is sort of like how Moonies get new recruits; he gets no sleep, and there is

---

69 Or months or years.

a lot of happy repetition from the woman who says how much better things will be once they work through this together. Men then have to wait a few more weeks before they can start the whole process over again.

Without a clean snap, the breakup can last forever. So men should remember, if a woman breaks up with him because she's trying to "find herself," he should let her go because she really is trying to dump him nicely. Pass into the night gracefully. Besides, anybody using a phrase as pathetic as that should be replaced. In the entire history of the human race, that phrase has only been used as a dump line. Take it for what it is, or the next line will describe why she actually is breaking up with you, and that experience is about as pleasant as chewing on a light bulb sandwich.

Serious Dating

or

Don't Be So Sure It Is Love Rather Than Lust, If You Two Installed a Stripper Pole

At some point, you go past the boyfriend/girlfriend stage and into the couple stage. When you're in this stage, your personal identity disappears like office supplies when the work cabinet is left open. If someone says "you," they mean that in the plural. People view you the couple as something that always goes together like salt and pepper, a pail and shovel, and pimples and teenagers. Now people don't ask if "you" are busy, they ask if the two of you are. It becomes expected that the two of you will socially act as one unit; Siamese twins without having to share internal organs. A man knows he has entered this stage when there is a guys' night out, and he finds himself having to ask for his girlfriend's permission to go. He hasn't taken any vows yet, there are no children to go home to, and yet here he is with his hat in hand (while she's got some other part of his in hers) asking for permission to see his own friends.

Some women will lay the old guilt trip on guys who want to have a boys' night out with a question like "So being with your friends is more important than me?" That is a no-win question, much along the line of "What do I do with the pin I just pulled out of this grenade?"

Sure, she is important, but the question really is whether the one night every other month with the guys matters in the grand scheme of the cosmos compared to the day in, day out he's been spending with the girlfriend.

If he is with her every single day, does it matter taking a night off? To some women, yes! It is, after all, theoretically possible that the one night he goes out with the guys, there could be an earthquake at the establishment he attends. During said earthquake, he falls through a fissure that traps him underground with a vivacious woman who also gets pinned underneath the rubble. Even though he begins by resisting her stunning charms, the temperature drops for the evening, and the two people need to huddle close together for enough warmth to make it through the night. One thing leads to another, and then his girlfriend is the one out in the cold. Well, either that or a stripper gives him a lap dance. Either way, it isn't good.

Most women are OK with the guys' night out as long as the women can have their night too. However, there are some women who cannot bear the thought of the guy having any fun without her. Therefore, if the guys ask the boyfriend somewhere, she's going to want to go as well. She'll end up going to concerts, movies, and parties that she has no intention of enjoying, and she'll make sure he doesn't either, so that eventually he will just want to stop going out at all.

If she's never been over fifty yards from an electric outlet, she'll still be there camping. If she thinks Barry Manilow[70] is OK but a little on the loud side, she'll still be there sitting next to her boyfriend during a Metallica concert with hands over her ears asking how anybody can actually enjoy this garbage. There will be enough "Can we go yet?," "Is it almost over?," and my personal favorite, "Do you really think this is fun?," to suck the life out of a rain forest. You can either

---

70 Many people may not remember Barry Manilow these days. He was a multiplatinum singer who had his greatest success in the 1970s. He started his musical career writing jingles like McDonald's "You Deserve a Break Today" and Band Aid's "I am stuck on Band-Aid's brand because Band-Aids stuck on me." He then went on to perform a string of hits. However, since the songs tended to be a little on the slow side, he was blacklisted by the male community. When men are in a group, they extol how much they can't stand the singer, but if they are alone in the car and one of his songs comes on...

argue with her all night, which would kill the evening, or give in, which would kill the evening. Either way, it is about as pleasant as cleaning New York City subway urinals with your personal toothbrush.

Even if he doesn't realize it, a guy starts to dread the men even mentioning going out because he knows that when it happens and the girlfriend insists on going, the evening is going to suck like an aardvark on steroids. The Pavlovian response[71] has been built in; he shudders at any mention of a guys' night out. By the way, the guys are usually just tickled pink to have her tag along as she successfully steers them away from anything that could be considered fun. At this point, she's won and he is considered domesticated. He may as well hook up a harness to his neck and go plow the front yard.

The opposite is also true. There are some men who feel rejected when they get left at home while the women all go out together. Don't be. Do not go. Do not ask to go. Do not even ask them where they are going. They do not want you there. A man would be as welcome as a chain smoker at a Lamaze class. Is he afraid the women will talk bad about the men in their lives? A man should put any uncertainties behind him. Sure, they are going to talk about all the guys. They are out for a good time, and a good time includes telling each other all the ridiculous things that men do. Problems with your hygiene, conversation skills, or bedroom repertoire will be laid out in graphic detail for all the women to dissect, analyze, and poke fun at.

Many insecure men will ball up in a fetal position hearing this. However, it is not entirely a bad thing. By having all the women together discussing all the guys, a man's girlfriend can be relieved that all the things he does to drive her insane are common things to all

---

71 Ivan Pavlov was a Russian psychologist who became known for discovering classical conditioning. In his famous experiment, he would ring a bell and then feed a dog. The dog became so conditioned to the bell meaning food was coming that the ring alone would get the dog to salivate. No food was needed. This phenomenon basically works for all animals. If I get a glare from my wife, I immediately start to sweat. Now, I don't know what I did wrong, but there has got to be something, and she'll soon tell me what. I have been trying to use this phenomenon on my wife. Rather than ask for a new beer when the older one is finished and I can't get up because there is something good on television, I've been trying to just shake the bottle rather than shake and then ask. Unfortunately, my wife must be a bit slow in the learning department, because all she does is shake one of her fingers back at me.

men. Men are all insensitive, horny slobs, and by being with other women complaining about their guys, a woman will understand that. It is then a question of getting over it or moving into a convent.

How does a man know he's reached the couple stage? The big sign is when he feels free to leave things at her apartment, especially an extra toothbrush. Leaving a toothbrush at a woman's apartment is a big deal. It does not mean that he has an irrational fear of gingivitis. Instead it means that he will be expecting to spend nights there often. It is a cleaner way for a guy to mark his "territory" without having to pay rent. So what does a guy do to get to that stage? Nothing. He should make no attempt to bring the subject up. Let her do it. If he shows up for a date and brings the toothbrush with him, she will think he is quite presumptive and will shoot him down like a duck in duck season.[72] She may also think the relationship is moving much too quickly, panic, and hit the eject button.

This is in stark contrast to a guy. If a woman brings a toothbrush to keep at a man's apartment, he is overjoyed because that heavily implies multiple overnight stays, and that can only be good, right? Absolutely. It is as great an idea as trying to figure out what a lion ate by going up and smelling his breath. What the guy doesn't realize is that there is a huge slippery slope here. Once she gets the toothbrush in, she'll then opt for a few changes of clothes, and then it is an extra makeup kit. In no short order, the guy's bathroom has been turned into a Mary Kay warehouse, his dresser is full of her clothes while his get relegated to the pile in the corner, and she has become as permanent a fixture in the dwelling as the plumbing.

At this point, the guy may freak. He'll look around his bachelor pad and realize it is more of a maxi pad. What he wanted was sex, and what he got was a very significant other who is beginning to plan his life with her in it for the long haul. I'm not saying that men have a fear of commitment, but watching someone's goldfish for a day would be a major step for a guy. If he does not think of the relationship with the same intensity as the woman, he's then got to remove her stuff out of his apartment. Can he do this without completely

---

72 With this hunter having a howitzer.

breaking up with her? About as easily as escaping from Alcatraz with only a used toothpick.

Another sign of the serious couple is that the opposite families accept that they'll be together. A man's parents expect that when he comes over, he'll obviously be bringing her. The only problem with this is that parents naturally assume marriage is in the offing and keep hinting at when the two of you will be getting engaged and bearing them grandchildren. Mentioning the ticking of her biological clock or his expanding waistline is not beneath them. His parents will be giving her big hugs and kisses, to the point of ignoring their biological son. It may even get to the point that when there is a fight, they will instinctively assume that he performed the bonehead move, because she is an angel. Unfortunately, if a relationship reaches this stage and then falls apart, the parents look at their own son like he just played kick the can with a Ming vase. They then compare all future girlfriends to the one that got away, which makes the current girlfriend feel about as welcome as ants at a picnic.

Of course, he and she can be considered a couple and *not* have the family accept one of them. There are times when he invites her to go along with him to his parents', and when they walk in, the parents get a look on their faces like he's got a dozen sticks of dynamite strapped to his chest. Why might the parents not like her? One easy reason may be her appearance. If she's got her hair poofed out so that she is a foot taller, is wearing fishnet stockings, and has enough makeup on to be considered a Superfund site, thenthey may be thinking you are renting your girlfriend by the hour.

And then there is the time when the guy has to meet her parents. Does he face the same dilemma that the woman faces? Not quite. The mother may warm up to him a bit, but with the father, it is a matter of degrees how much he does not like the guy. No one is good enough for daddy's little girl. Not now. Not ever. So what is a guy to do? Be polite, hide any visible tattoos, and never show any sign that he is physically attracted to his daughter. If she comes out wearing something low cut, he'd better conjure up a vision of the New York Giants offensive line in the locker room after a game in the mud. Under no circumstances, no matter how many years they've been together, should a man's soldier ever stand at attention in the presence of her father. There shall be no guttural sounds if she bends over to pick something up off the ground, or even a glance downward to acknowledge that she exists below her shoulders.

Will the girlfriend's father ever warm up to a guy? About as quickly as the Ice Age ended. Therefore, it is best for the man to compliment the mother and get on her good side. She can then potentially act as a buffer in case he brings the daughter home late and the father has decided to teach the lesson of punctuality by puncturing holes in his spleen with a screwdriver. A good preparation for a man meeting his girlfriend's parents is to streak in front of a firing squad.

Living Together

or

Oh, the Parents Are Going

to *Love* This Decision!

The option of living together before marriage is a relatively new chapter in human relationships. Many people frown heavily on it. As those who support the option like to claim, you want to take the car out for a test drive before you buy it, or if you are in a nice restaurant, you have a taste of the wine before the waiter leaves the bottle.

However, those who don't like it can point out that once that car is driven off the lot, it begins to depreciate rapidly in value, and if you are in a restaurant and a waiter tries to pawn off a bottle of opened wine that another table rejected, then he/she has lost their tip. In the instance of cars, the dealers try to spruce up the idea of a car being used by calling it preowned instead. If I can extend this analogy one step further by relating the car dealers to parents of the girl..., they'll certainly let you take the car out for a spin to see if you like it, as in a date, but they don't want you opening up the throttle and speeding down the highway to see what it can do. And if there ever is an accident, you are most certainly buying the damn thing.

It may sound in the above paragraph that men own women like property, something they'd pick up at the mall, and once the men are done with them, the women find themselves on a rack in the Goodwill store. However, the reverse is also true, and men bear the stigma as well. Once people who have cohabitated move out, quite a few people in society view them as damaged goods.

If you go to the grocery store and see a can of soup that has a dent in it, you *know* the soup still tastes the same on the inside. However, you still go out of your way to reach around it and find the undented can. Now, the vast majority if people have been, let's say, "handled" prior to marriage. However, that doesn't necessarily show. If the person has been living with another person, then the chances go from an almost certainty to kind of creepy if something didn't happen—and there is the dent.

When a couple lives together and then breaks up, things change a bit—besides the fact that people know they are no longer getting benefits. The problem is that every other new boyfriend/girlfriend will always have it in the back of their mind how they stacked up against the former live-in. OK, so maybe it is about sex, but it goes beyond that.

The new person will wonder what their new love ever saw in the old partner that they may/may not have. Why didn't it work out previously? Something must have been not quite right to start, and then it went horribly wrong. After all, if a train crashes, you don't see people hopping the next one until there is some sort of investigation as to why the first wreck happened. The new partner will wonder if the person they are dating was the dumper who may have set impossible standards or the dumpee who is hiding some phenomenal flaw that will come out in time.

Why is this trial period of living together so new to human history? Simply because it couldn't have happened without modern birth control. The idea of temporarily living with each other when the only methods of birth control were abstinence (then what's the point of living together?) or coitus interruptus[73] (a man in this state

---

73 To put this into a sports analogy, that is in football where you are allowed to do all the running and catching, getting pounded on by the other team. But when it comes time to take the ball over the goal line, you have to put the ball on the one and walk away.

is as trustworthy as a starving wolverine at a baby bunny birthday party) is akin to playing hopscotch in a mine field. Sooner or later, there's going to be a puck that slips past the goalie. In this case, though, the referee can put a guy in the penalty both till death do they part.

The idea of living together is usually a gradual one. Managing two apartments is difficult work. The two of you are sleeping together every night already. You never know exactly whose apartment you're going to end up at. Headaches start to pile up. You've each got to plan to have changes of clothes at the other's place (unless you start wearing her clothes, which is a different book entirely). You've got to let others know where the hell you are going to be that night in case someone needs to reach you.

Most importantly, the two of you are paying two separate sets of bills (rent, cable, electricity, etc.), and you think that by living together, you can cut expenses. Although this is theoretically true, it doesn't pan out that way for the guy. Now meals have to be planned a bit rather than alternating between frozen pizza and macaroni and cheese. If the apartment needs something like towels, they won't just magically appear one day with the name of a hotel on them. Furniture must actually be purchased at a store, unlike the usual way of waiting for bargains at garage sales where you can buy a mattress that has been passed down through three generations and has helped conceive a dozen kids.

Having a very practical reason for living together like only paying one rent (coupled with the thought of rampant sex), many couples decide to live together. Why not get married? People give a variety of reasons: they want to know where their careers are going before they permanently settle down, they think marriage is a mere formality and nothing more than words on a paper, or the man breaks out in hives every time the subject is mentioned. Whatever the reason may be, the parents will think it sucks like a black hole with an attitude.

Because parents are known to hate the idea of living together, many couples decide to conceal the fact, which is about as easy to hide as chicken pox in a nudist colony. This deception can only work if the couple lives far enough away that the spontaneous visit is a rare event. Having her mom pop over to give her daughter a casserole only to find her dressed up as a prison warden and the boyfriend as an escaped convict isn't good. The mother may be able to conclude that he didn't happen over with that outfit while her daughter was coincidentally wearing hers.

So how does a couple attempt to pull off this deception? First off, they have to decide whose parents would be wigged out more, and this person will become the default resident. If the idea of living together is brought up, and his mother tears her shirt and claims she has no children, then the apartment should be his. If her father collects guns and/or works at the post office, then the apartment should be called hers.

One problem becomes how to decorate the place or, more appropriately, how not to decorate the place. If the guy's parents come over and notice a teddy bear calendar hanging up on the wall or prints of famous paintings of kids dancing in meadows, they're going to get a hint that things aren't all that they seem. Although if they come over and there is simple order to the place rather than the usual standing chaos the guy lived in all his life, that will give them a hint too.

All hanging decorations should be gender neutral. It is just too difficult to start yanking things out of the wall every time a parent comes over and then nailing them back up when they're gone. Not only is it difficult hiding the stuff, but the landlord is going to have a tizzy fit when his apartment walls have so many holes that it looks like the lunar landscape. So what kinds of decorations qualify as gender neutral? Just about as close to zero as Mike Tyson[74] winning *American Idol*.

---

74 For those unaware of Mr. Tyson, he was the youngest heavyweight boxing champion ever. In his early days, he caused abject fear in his opponents. Everything seemed intimidating about him, with the exception of his voice. You would think by the look of him that he must have a hell of a sense of humor and just sucked on a helium balloon to get the actual pitch that came out of his mouth. The irony would then be that he was in press conferences saying—I kid you not—that he wanted to eat the children of his opponents. Doing that in a voice that sounded like it should be coming from a Muppet on *Sesame Street* made it that more amusing. One would have thought these were idle "boasts," yet he later did tread on the cannibalistic line and bit part of the ear off his boxing opponent Evander Holyfield. Technically, however, he did not eat it and spit it out. And you thought a ball grabbed at a baseball game was a surprising souvenir to bring back from a sporting event!

For a guy, living in an undecorated room is no big deal. He'd just as soon live in a cave as long as it didn't mess up his TV reception. Women, however, handle looking at blank walls about as well as being locked in a white room in a straightjacket. After a while in that environment, a woman will go crazy and start nailing pages from catalogues and staple-gunning dead flowers to the walls just to have something on them.

The furniture has also got to be somewhat gender neutral. Flowery bedspreads and drapes are going to be a problem to explain for a guy unless he pulls off the excuse that he got them cheaply at a yard sale. Heck, if I had had any drapes at all hanging up, my mother would have thought I eloped. Most guys just can't bring themselves to the point to enter a store to pick up things to garnish the window.[75] Blinds or a pull-down shade? Sure. After all, you don't want the world peering in when you're walking around wearing nothing more than a five o'clock shadow, especially if you've just stepped out of a cold shower. However, putting up something to "accent the colors of the room" is about as big a giveaway as Monica Lewinsky's dress.[76]

The next thing the apartment must have is ample closet space. The guy will need this to start shoveling his stuff into when her mother pulls the car up out front, or vice versa. Depending on how strict her mother is, the guy may want to have room for him to hide in there as well. Be sure to keep some snacks in there in case it is an extended visit. Oh yeah, some ventilation would also help. If her mother does find him in there and is wielding a sharp implement in the general direction of his nether region, then his only hope is to

---

[75] In graduate school, I became roommates with my brother. Somehow, we got our hands on two small drapes. Since they were too small to actually cover the living room window and there was no way in hell we were going to take the time to buy a curtain rod, we nailed them right into the wall. Nobody even noticed until they tried to close them.

[76] There may come a time that people don't quite remember the story behind this. Miss Lewinsky was an intern at the White House when Bill Clinton was president. Their relationship went a wee bit beyond the professional realm, and he was accused of having sex with her. While it was technically true strictly in terms of intercourse, it was less so in terms of certain body parts being in places where they normally shouldn't be. There was quite a bit of denial until it was found out that a dress did exist that had, let's say, a bit of his overexuberance on it.

convince her he hasn't come out of the closet in more ways than one. Otherwise, the only way he'll have children is bribing foreign officials at border crossings.

When the two of you are living together, life can seem quite rosy for a while. It seems to be the best of all worlds. Each person can have the freedom to come and go as they please while still having the commitment of living together. However, for many couples, this world is unstable, sort of like daydreaming while barreling down the highway. You can pass through the physical roads of life while your mind takes an emotional journey full of enchanted places. In the end, your mind gets wrapped around the guardrail.

Don't believe me? Well, the instability works its way in through the cracks and loosens the stones of any foundation. Your relationship may start off strong. As an analogy, we could use the Washington Monument. Things start to go bad, and then you end up more with a Leaning Tower of Pisa. Eventually, the building, rather than being erect, is lying on the ground. There is no such thing as Viagra for buildings, so most architects decide to demolish it and start again rather than save it. The same can possibly happen in open relationships.

Let us say the woman was going to surprise her boyfriend with his favorite meal, so she goes shopping and slaves over the stove for an hour or two. Meanwhile, he decided he felt like a burger and stopped off at Mickey D's. When he gets back to the apartment with special sauce hanging off of his chin, she is going to be as pissed as Peter Best when "Love Me Do" comes on the radio.[77]

Technically, did the boyfriend do anything wrong? No. He didn't tell her he'd be home at a certain time. However, she'll tell him in a voice usually reserved for interrogating suspected serial killers that he *should have* checked in with her. What is that tinkling sound you

---

[77] Don't know him? Peter Best was the original drummer for the Beatles. In the early days of the band, he was considered the biggest heartthrob of the bunch. John, Paul, and George, however, dumped him. They picked up a studio drummer named Richard Starkey who went by the name of Ringo. In short, Ringo ends up with countless millions and married to Barbara Bach while Peter is someone you are reading about in a footnote.

hear? That is a rock thrown through just one of the windows of your glass house of freedom.

Another time, the guy will have rented a few videos, and she'll have decided to go out for a few drinks with friends. Not knowing this, he won't start watching the movies because she could be home any minute. Any minute turns into any hour, and his once-pleasant mood deteriorates like wet tissue paper. Not that she was interested in seeing *Biker Babes from Mars*, but it is the thought that counts.[78] Yes, things do indeed work both ways, and the two of you will start to find ways to curtail the other person's freedom while maintaining your own.

Then there are the chores. At the beginning of the move-in, each person is responsible for cleaning his or her own messes. Usually, that starts off without a problem. An hour or two into living together, that changes. It may start off innocently enough when one day one of you (he) is in a rush and leaves dirty dishes in the sink. When that person (he) gets back home, he or she (but really he) may have honestly forgotten they were there and went off to do something else. Meanwhile, the other person (she) views the dishes as a sign the other person is taking him/her (you get the point) for granted and is secretly wondering if this is the first step toward indentured servitude.[79]

Meanwhile, the offender, not actually hearing a verbal complaint, figures that leaving chores until later is not a problem as long as they get done. Eventually. Unfortunately, eventually means different things for different people. Some clock it with a stopwatch, while others use a calendar.

As the sink fills with dirty dishes that then begin to take over the counter, one partner may finally start hinting that all is not well in paradise. As the odor from the kitchen starts wafting through the

---

78 Besides, it was *Biker Babes from Mars II: Electric Boogaloo* that really broke cinematic ground.

79 An indentured servant is not a slave. Instead, this is someone who enters a contract with a person for a set number of years to do basically anything the person wants them to do in exchange for food, lodging, etc. Once the terms of the contract are up, the servant is free to go. The contract terms for marriage, if I can remember the vow, are "until death do us part," but that's not the same as a slave. The difference? After ordering the servant around, the master can't turn around and think the spouse is in the mood for sex.

entire apartment, more hints may be given. If the hints are not picked up, the neat roommate eventually snaps and would try to stab the offending roommate if he or she could actually find a knife in the clutter.

Couldn't this also happen in a marriage? Possibly, but in a marriage, the individuals know that the other person can't just walk out over silly arguments, and so feel more empowered to tell their partner what is bothering them (sometimes over and over) before it gets to the point where she is now thinking of showing him where the Brillo Pad is located by dragging him over to the sink by the hair and showing him like you would show cheese to a grater.

If the chore thing doesn't start arguments, then the money thing will. People who are not married usually keep their own checking accounts. It is mostly expected that the bills will be split in half. To say that this may be a headache is like saying Atlas may get a backache.[80] The couple may decide to write two checks for every bill that comes in, but that becomes tedious, and you have to get both people together to get anything done. The next option is for one person to pay the rent and the other to pay the bills, with the inequality being made up with buying groceries, making out a separate check, and/or charging for doing laundry. Again, it starts out nice, but it is a disaster in the making.

First off, there's usually one person who doesn't think paying bills promptly is a significant priority. Meanwhile, the other person gets a wee miffed at having his or her credit rating slashed like teenagers in a *Friday the 13th* movie. The once-pristine credit rating cultivated over years of proper fiscal management now has more black marks on it than the movie *101 Dalmatians*.

Therefore, one person takes on the (gasp) responsibility of paying bills, and the other person is subject to this person financially. If a month goes by without one roommate paying the other, that is the price of love, and it is no big deal. If three months go by, then that

---

80 Atlas was a Titan from Greek mythology. He and the other Titans waged war against Zeus and the rest of the gods. When they lost, Atlas's punishment was to hold up the world on his back for eternity. It could have been worse—one of his Titan friends was forced to go bra shopping with his girlfriend for the rest of eternity.

person is still great, but may have a bit of growing up to do. At six months, all hell breaks loose, so either the first person is physically threatening violence, or the second takes the day off and moves out, leaving the first person with the bag.

Proposing

or

That Little Rock Costs What?

There comes a time in a man's life when he thinks that he's found the woman he wants to spend the rest of his life with. He'd be willing to climb the highest mountain, swim the deepest sea, walk the last mile, dig the deepest grave, yadda, yadda. However, a few men would do all these things anyway not out of love, but because they think their partner's backside is hotter than a Miami sidewalk in summer. These men get that confused look when they are trying to distinguish between lust and love, sort of like that look dogs get when they hear a high-pitched noise.

Here are a few clues to help tell the difference. If a man still thinks she's the most beautiful woman in the world even though she's got a sniveling cold and hasn't bathed in several days, then it is love. If he thinks she's beautiful only when she is partially nude swinging around a pole, then chances are it is lust. If he wants to tell her how much he loves her after he's been dragged shopping, it is love. If he tells her he loves her because he wants her to make him a sandwich, it is, well, lazy. If a man takes a woman home to meet his parents, it is love. If he takes the woman home to meet his fraternity brothers who are all standing around with fistfuls of dollar bills, then it is lust.

Marriage cannot live on sex alone, although it is nice to give it that old college try. Lust is just peachy as long as there is love there as well. Otherwise, time will play its little tricks and give him an ever-lengthening forehead, add several chins to her, turn his rippling abs to rolling flabs, and make her tanned skin take on the appearance of an old baseball glove. If the relationship is based only on sex, then the couple will one day look at one other and be calling their divorce lawyers faster than Speedy Gonzales with the runs. If friendship isn't the foundation, it is like building the rest of the house on quicksand at the base of a volcano...next to the Native American graveyard.

When a woman tells her friends that she is engaged, they inevitably ask her how the guy proposed. They are all looking for something romantic and will actually be *grading* the man on his performance. Propose in a nonromantic fashion, and forever will you be known as the Dud to all your wife's friends. Your future wife knows this and wants to be swept off her feet during the proposal. She'll be somewhat miffed if she gets the ring during the halftime break of a televised football game.

If the proposal, for lack of a better word, sucks, then she may still say yes. However, the woman will retain the right to bring the episode up throughout her life in any argument the two of you may have, whether it be germane to the disagreement at hand or not. Don't take this ace and stuff it up her sleeve, or you'll find yourself losing arguments in later years about monetary retirement vehicles and vacation destinations as she starts crying about how she's trying to compensate for that crappy proposal at the McDonald's drive-through that left her an emotionally scarred hull of the person she wanted to be.

The big difficulty with planning a proposal is that the woman without question wants and needs to be surprised when you ask, while at the same time, she is being romanced like never before. Usually, these two things are mutually exclusive. If you are taking her on a weekend to the country and the two of you have been hinting about marriage, she'll naturally be expecting the ring. A standard proposal there may score high on the romance scale, but low on the surprise scale. On the opposite end of the spectrum, presenting the ring after knocking down the lavatory door while she is using it would certainly rate high on the surprise scale, while the romantic scale would hit negative numbers. Therefore, it is better to err on the side of romance rather than surprise.

So what are some options as to how to propose? As mentioned, a weekend in the country is quite nice, unless the two of you already live in the country, which means she won't think it is romantic at all to have the question popped behind Billy Joe's milking barn. If you already live in the city, then don't bother proposing on a subway that can be considered secluded if it has less than three people per square foot.

I guess the rule of thumb here is a change of venue. However, many men lack the finances to bring the woman away at this time. After all, he's just spent his retirement funds, hocked his television set, and rolled his grandmother just to get the money necessary to buy the diamond ring. Spending more money right now, considering the rent payment is now late, is about as good an idea as a hemophiliac ordering a drink with an umbrella in it at a biker bar.

If a guy does have the money and takes the woman on vacation, there are a few things to keep in mind. First off, she knows he's going to propose, so he's got to surprise her with how he does it. One way some men have surprised women is by putting the ring in her champagne glass. That works great unless, of course, she swallows the ring, which later perforates her colon on its way out (high on surprise, low on romance).

Then there is the option of sneaking the ring to the waiter earlier in the day and having him present it to her with dessert. Again, this can work quite well, but the guy then has to trust that the waiter doesn't hate his job and isn't just looking for any excuse to quit and hightail it out of there carrying away three months of an almost-but-not-yet-engaged man's salary (again, high on surprise, low on romance).

As stated before, if she figures out that she is going to have the question popped, then she'll be disappointed. If he realizes he's not going to get the surprise she craves and so delays popping the question when she is expecting it, that will put her into a really unfavorable mood, as she was probably mentioning to her friends that it was going to happen and now has to go back empty handed.[81] Trust me— she has told everyone she has ever known who has ovaries that she's going to get engaged and will not like every woman giving her that expecting look when she gets back. Catch-22, you say? Naturally, I say. And the fun is only starting in the marriage game.

For those on a budget plan, another place to propose that many feel is romantic is the place where the two of you met. By bringing her back to that special spot, a man can forever have that place immortalized in their hearts. Exceptions to this plan include the basement of a fraternity, the bathroom of a singles club, a *Star Trek* convention, and the drunk tank at the local police station.

When proposing, the man should get down on one knee. That is good for at least two points all by itself on the romantic scale. The difficulty here is that everyone around him will know what he is doing. What had been a private moment now becomes the evening's entertainment for the rest of the room. A Cyclops riding in on a unicorn while carrying Jimmy Hoffa will not unglue women's eyes when there is a proposal in progress.

Whoops, that brings me to a point that I should have mentioned at the beginning of this section. When a man proposes to a woman, you must know that she is going to say yes before you ask. Having a good hunch is simply not good enough. Being rejected when the two of you are alone together is like having her rip your still-beating heart out of your chest. Being rejected when the two of you are surrounded by others is like having her not only rip your heart out, but feed it to her dog amid the cheering of the crowd. At least if the guy is on one knee, he doesn't have far to fall to the ground as his body involuntarily curls up into the fetal position.

So how does a man make absolutely certain that she is going to say yes? Most men take the wait-and-see approach. They wait in a relationship for month after month and year after year until the woman breaks down and starts screaming as to when the hell you're ever going to propose. Ergo, problem solved.

---

81 Technically, it is empty fingered.

Some women are a bit subtler about it. She may leave a copy of *Modern Bride* magazine in her apartment for you to see when you come over. If that doesn't work, she may start leaving them in your apartment, your car, your place of employment, etc. And if that doesn't work, she may take the next step and rip the pictures out of the magazine and staple-gun them to your chest.

Once the woman has dropped the hint, the guy can be sure that his proposal will not be rejected. However, he can't just blurt out a proposal over pizza at the bowling alley because he'd be back to failing on both the romance and surprise scale. He must wait a little bit so that he can take her off guard with his proposal. What he has to watch out for here is, if he waits too long, one day he'll get a post-card from her and his best friend in Las Vegas.

Sometimes, a guy does not want to have to wait for the woman to bring up the subject of marriage. He's found the love of his life and wants her married to him before she realizes what she's done. He must then try to find a way to be tipped off as to what way she would lean when taken off guard. If it is near her birthday or a holiday, he can ask her if she wants something special for a present. If she sug-gests the new Pearl Jam CD, then he's got to explain to her that she can get something truly extraspecial. If she then suggests the Pearl Jam double-album live CD/DVD combo, then he should abandon the whole effort because she not only isn't on the same page as he is in life, she's in a different section of the bookstore.

If the closest holiday is over three months away, then the present idea will fly like spit off the Empire State Building. Therefore, he'll have to get a bit more creative. He can ask about her future plans and see if she mentions him. If she cites things like joining a convent, becoming a groupie for a death-metal band, drug smuggling for the Colombians, or trying to find the true meaning to sexual fulfillment after she's done dating him, then not only is she not ready for him, but she never will be. If that doesn't work, he could mention that he was recently in a jewelry store. If she panics, he can back off and claim he was thinking about buying his mother that nose ring she has had her eye on lately. If she gets excited, he can keep talking and see if she starts pressing for a diamond. If she thinks that he is talking about a jewelry store because he may want accessories to start cross-dressing, then again the relationship is in significant trouble.

So what does he do if she continues to remain aloof? He keeps getting more and more desperate with questions, but he should still never propose without knowing the final answer. Think of the consequences! What happens if he asks, and then she wants time to think about it before she gives him an answer? What does the poor slob do? She's obviously wondering whether he's the best she's going to be able to land in life or if she'll be able to roll the dice again and come up with something (anything) better. That is certainly not the pat on the back that the old male ego was looking for. He can't take the proposal back—that would be like pulling a life preserver back into the lifeboat because he's just seen someone else he'd rather save. However, she's not allowed to take the proposal as a rain check to be cashed in at her leisure.

If she doesn't give an answer within a few days, he can demand an answer or the proposal becomes null and void. So if she finally does say yes, then that *still* bites like Lassie with rabies. For the rest of his life, when he walks down the street with her, he'll be wondering if she's kicking herself every time she passes a guy who looks like he can bend steel bars with his butt muscles.

So if he (a) has taken the above quiz and gotten an acceptable score, (b) knows the answer is going to be yes with the same certainty that you know the sun will rise tomorrow, (c) is doing something she thinks is romantic and he probably thinks is dreadfully dull and/or expensive, and (d) knows that bringing out a ring will make her squeal like a stuck pig, then he should go ahead and pop the question. When she then agrees, the couple can spend a romantic moment together. He's probably more inclined to try to get her into bed at that moment, whereas that is the last thing she wants. Instead, she wants to tell the world the good news. His only hope is a mobile phone with a low battery.

Now the guy may think the hard part is over. After all, she has agreed to the marriage, and so it is only a matter of logistics before it is over. That's like Admiral Byrd thinking he just had to bring an extra pair of thermal underwear and a couple pizzas for his trip to the

North Pole. The Manhattan Project[82] wasn't as tense as what they are going to go through now. Pressure? Neither member of the couple has seen pressure like this before unless they met in a Siberian salts mine. What is so daunting a task as to make mere mortal men curse the gods that have set such a Herculean task before their very feet? It is time to plan the wedding. Heaven help them both.

---

82 The Manhattan Project was the US top-secret mission to build an atomic bomb to help end World War II. The fate of the world was hanging in the balance because if the Germans did it first, we'd all be eating sauerkraut for breakfast. It involved 130,000 people, thirty different sites—and it was still kept a secret! If a single woman on the project had been proposed to, the veil of secrecy would have collapsed in nanoseconds because there is no force on the planet that can stop her telling people.

Section 2

Planning the Wedding

or

If You Are Tying the Knot, Make Sure It Is Not a Noose

The Golden Rule of Planning a Wedding:
It is the Bride's Day.
Whatever She Says, Goes.
Period.

So you've proposed. Now it is time to plan the wedding. At this point, more work will have to be done than went into building the Pyramids at Giza, only more people are needed to get the wedding off the ground, and the labor rate is higher. When will the wedding be held? How many people will come? Will it be in a church, garden, home, mountaintop, etc.? Will you be forced to perform the chicken dance or the hokey pokey at the reception? All aspects must be planned and scrutinized. Backup plans must be made. If animal sacrifices were allowed in this country, the goat would go the way of the dodo after the first June to ensure the proper karma for the wedding.

There will be more issues demanding attention than you would think two people can handle. Those two people are going to be busier than sumo wrestlers at an all-you-can-eat buffet. For these two, it will be like they are an octopus at a Whack-A-Mole competition. Wait a minute! I bet you men out there are just assuming that you are one of the two decision-makers I was referring to? Ha! Ha! Ha! Sorry. You've got as much say as Helen Keller with her hands tied behind her back. The two decision-makers are your soon-to-be wife and soon-to-be mother-in-law. You as a prospective groom are about to feel like a ship lost at sea in the middle of a typhoon. The only thing you can do is batten down the hatches and ride the sucker out, praying you don't drown before the storm breaks.[83]

The first lesson for a man to learn about planning his upcoming wedding is that it has nearly *nothing* to do with him. Now many men will protest this fact—single men! All married men, however, will attest to this truism, as long as you don't take the poll within earshot of their wives. Yes, it is true that the man is needed to start the whole wedding shebang going, but his role is akin to the guy who flips the coin at the beginning of the football game. Once he tosses that coin and the game begins, he sits down and watches the action happen around him. For all practical purposes, he has become a vestigial organ, as useless as an appendix or a US vice president.

Simply put, the wedding is not "their" day but *her* day! Did you see the Golden Rule back on the first page of this section? That ain't filler—it is something you are going to have to live with day in and day out (sometimes hour in and hour out) until the wedding is done.[84] All planning is centered on the *bride* in *her* flowing white gown as *she* walks into the church to the tune of "Here Comes the *Bride*." Anyone know of any groom songs? That's because there aren't any. Zip. Nada. All eyes in the house are focused on the bride making her entrance while the groom gets about as much attention as Tito at a televised Jackson family reunion.[85] At this time, the groom really doesn't mind anyway since he and his usher buddies are too busy praying that that last round of tequila shots from the night before doesn't make them lose the cleaning deposits on the rented tuxes.

---

83 OK, so I don't exactly know what "batten" means either, but it certainly doesn't sound like a particularly fun thing to do when you are scrambling around on the slippery deck of a ship surging up and down with rain pelting you, knowing that if you go overboard, you've got about two minutes before hypothermia sets in.

84 Naturally, after the wedding, you are so used to doing what your wife says when she says it that it sets you up perfectly for married life.

85 This joke made a bit more sense prior to Michael Jackson's untimely passing. However, one would have to admit that a Jackson 4 reunion tour would have trouble drawing a full crowd at a slumber party.

Many women start thinking about their wedding day when they are little girls. They picture what type of flowers they'd like, what their maids of honor will wear, whether it will be an outdoor or indoor ceremony, etc. Meanwhile, the boys are running around playing wholesome games like cops and robbers, cowboys and Indians, or some other game where the two groups are allowed to pretend to maim each other with weapons.[86] These boys are completely unaware of the schemes the girls are conjuring up to lure them into the bondage, I mean bonds, of holy matrimony.

The first decision to be made is the date. The woman is going to have a definite idea about whether she wants an indoor or outdoor wedding (which will have direct bearing on which season you may have the ceremony if you live in a northern state). Many men may protest the idea of an outdoor wedding since you cannot predict the wedding pattern several days in advance, never mind several months. **Lesson 2: Practicality is not part of planning a wedding**. Many men will approach their wives with graphs, flow charts, and other assorted data on the possible problems associated with weddings in outdoor locations. After explaining the cons effectively to his future wife, he will then need to find a competent doctor able to extract the various sheets of paper lodged in the various orifices of his body.

Going back to the basics—the Golden Rule is as unmovable as Mount Everest or your bowels after attending a three-day cheese festival. She has been thinking about this event nearly all her life, while men just think of the wedding as the pregame to an exciting night of partying followed by wild sex. A word of caution—if you men relay this thought to your fiancées, the women will ever so politely correct the offending male individuals with a verbal berating so

---

86 In the olden days, kids used to actually go outside to see friends. Now, they can stay inside, go online, and play with tons more friends than they ever had before. Of course they have never actually met these friends face-to-face and often don't even know their real names. Cap guns have been replaced by games where you can machete off alien heads in wonderfully intricate graphic detail. These kids will grow up to be amazing strategists if a zombie apocalypse ever broke out. However, they'd get winded climbing a staircase.

severe that any exposed skin will blister and the hair will look like he's been skydiving.

Now many men should be confused by now. It seems that the future wife and mother-in-law are making all the decisions, so all he should have to do is kick back and be sure he arrives at the appropriate church on the appropriate day wearing the appropriate tux. WRONG! **Lesson 3: A man must act interested in every detail of the wedding and act like he is choosing along with the women when he really has no say**. Now lesson 3 is a difficult one to master, but it is the only way a man can skirt cartloads of trouble. The woman wants the man there at nearly every step of the planning, will ask opinions of the man at each juncture, and will expect an answer to every question she poses. Fine. The only problem is that she does not listen or care one whit what the man actually says. I have come to believe that at this stage, the soon-to-be bride and mother-in-law hear the soon-to-be groom's voice like the teacher on a *Peanuts* cartoon.

For instance, the bride and her mother could turn to the groom and ask if the wedding should be held at the church closest to the reception hall or the one that she grew up going to. If he says he doesn't care, they'll look at him with utter disgust. He couldn't get more of a negative reaction if he suggested they get married in a cave with the ghost of Osama bin Laden performing the rite. If he does answer, they usually give a dumbfounded look like he just wet himself since the answer is so ridiculous. They then ignore the ridiculous remark and pick what they were going to before they ever asked.

Lesson 4: The wife considers everything even remotely associated with the wedding a Big Deal. Every detail will be agonized over with her mother, while the man, for the most part, simply does not care. What color dress do the bridesmaids wear, what flowers are needed, what will be the entrée at the reception, ad nauseam, all must be coordinated as a conductor conducts all the members of a symphony orchestra.

It will be difficult for men, but they must be able to operate lessons 3 and 4 at the same time. If she is considering what length shoelaces the ushers should wear, the man has got to try his damnedest to feign interest. One trick is to have a pocket full of Warheads sour candy. At every opportunity, the man can toss one in his mouth and bite down so he can get a very concerned look on his face. If he doesn't, she'll report the infraction to all women she has ever known so that he is universally shunned like Michael Vick at a PETA meeting.[87] Most people would rather go flick a bear cub's nose while the mother bear is watching than cross a bride.

87 Mr. Vick was a talented football quarterback who terrorized defenses with his ability to pull the ball down and scamper for thirty yards just when it looked like his offense was pinned down. Like many pro athletes, he was competitive on and off the field. When it was found that he was deep into pit-bull fighting, the public turned on him fairly quickly and he spent some time in jail, forfeiting the top salary contract in the league at the time. It goes to show that you can't go out of your way to harm things with a heart and mind. Had he been throwing lawyers and politicians into an arena to battle to the death, I'm not even sure that qualifies as a misdemeanor.

Announcing the Engagement

or

Telling the World, Whether

It Cares to Hear or Not

I t used to be customary that a man asked permission from the future father-in-law for his daughter's hand in marriage. Women, believe it or not, didn't particularly care to be left out of this—or any—decision-making process. Therefore, asking the woman's father first is now only done by pure traditionalists and men desperately trying to suck up to their future in-laws. It's not the smartest move anyway—you've got to get two yeses rather than one. That's like your boss giving you a raise and then you going to the board of directors to ask if they thought that was a prudent decision on your boss's part. After all, what are you going to do if he says no? If you stop seeing her, you lose out on the love of your life, and if you ask her anyway, you know that every Thanksgiving dinner, your father-in-law is thinking of carving up more than the turkey.

Once you and your now fiancée decide to get married, you should tell both sets of parents. Considering that the bride's father is now going to have to take a second job to go along with a second mortgage to pay for the damn wedding, it is customary to go to the woman's house first. Unless the parents live far away, they should be told in person. Hopefully, they will accept the engagement as good news. If she is knocked up, quitting school, or dropping her career to follow your rock band around the tri-city area, do not expect her parents to greet you with open arms. If the arms are open, quickly look to see if their hands are clutching any objects that would be considered effective for bludgeoning purposes. With proper advanced planning on your part, they would have gotten to know you and begun to accept the idea that you might be taking their daughter away from them and defiling her on a routine basis.

If the parents seem amicable after hearing the news, now is still not the time to press your luck. Let them get used to you. And while I'm at it, here are a few don'ts. Now is not the time to presume and call them "mom" and "dad." They did not raise you before your engagement, nor do they want to start doing so now. Do not ever cry in front of them whether you are happy or sad. In the parents' generation, a man who cried would be labeled an absolute loser unless he had just lost a limb. In our modern enlightened era, however, a man who is in touch with his feelings enough to express them in so open and honest a fashion is now referred to as an absolute nonwinner. You don't want your father-in-law referring to the upcoming event as a same-sex marriage.

Do not borrow money from them even if you are broke enough that your idea of dining out is eating whatever food you find between the couch cushions while you're visiting friends. Parents of your wife-to-be would rather live with the thought of losing a daughter than know they're gaining a bloodsucking leech who is going to move in with them and drain the life out of their golden years. If you are staying at their house overnight, do not feel it acceptable to walk around in your underwear or in the buff. Do not drink milk straight from the carton. Do not freely express gas. And above all, do not discuss how great your sex life has become now that you are seeing their little girl. They don't want to think of the two of you together, and they especially don't want to think what it took her to get so good.

Once her parents are told, it is time for your parents. Again, the personal touch is most appreciated, as in if you live within a five-hundred-mile radius, your mother will never forgive you if you don't drive over and tell her in person. With a guy's parents, you don't need surprise and probably can't get it anyway. If you call over to your parents and ask if both of them are going to be home, chances are good that telling them anything else besides the two of you being engaged will be massively disappointing. Telling them that you just received an ambassadorship will get a "that's nice," as it is good, but it isn't getting them any closer to grandchildren.[88]

After the parents, now you should tell your friends. When a woman tells her friends, there is usually a lot of shrieking and jumping up and down. She shows the ring off, which is then followed by more shrieking and jumping up and down. Men don't do this. Men react more as if you had just told them you enlisted in the army. After a few minutes of stunned silence, you usually get a response like, "Uh, congratulations?"

Why the lukewarm response? Because some men view the bachelorhood days as carefree times of little responsibility and the ability to date as few or as many women as you'd like. Theoretically, this is true, but it isn't really practical. In the real world, finding any date—never mind one who is mildly interesting—is a laborious, time-consuming process that rarely comes to fruition. Finding multiple wild dates with nubile nymphomaniac twins is possible but is as likely as raising the *Titanic* by blowing into it with a long straw from an overhead boat.

Then comes the time to put the wedding announcement in the society page of the local paper.[89] You may not recognize this section. Most men don't even know it exists. It's usually the part of the paper men throw out along with the coupons (and every other section not relating to sports or comics). Anyway, one day, your fiancée's picture will be there announcing her engagement. An engagement usually involves two people, yet it will only be her picture in the paper (that

---

88 As a note of caution, once grandchildren do come, you nearly become invisible to your parents. You are more a transportation vehicle taking the grandchildren to and from them. If you walk into the house and your wife is holding the baby, they'll knock you down to get past you and to that child.

89 Depending on when this book gets published, local newspapers may have gone the way of the dodo bird, eight-track tapes, and children playing outside.

would be under the Golden Rule of Planning a Wedding). When you read the print next to the picture, it says, "Mr. and Mrs. [in-laws' last name] announce the engagement of their daughter [fiancée's name] to [finally your name]." You do not come into the sentence until the end, kind of like an afterthought. She is the main act. You are just the backup band. She is Led Zeppelin ready to pound out the rock. You are the Men at Work cover band when people are mostly at the concession stand and finding their seats. Most warm-up bands have to nearly light themselves on fire to get any attention from the crowd, and only then if they hand out marshmallows for them to toast.

Setting the Date

or

The Happiest Day of Your Life...or Else

There are two possibilities here. You can plan a wedding that is less than six months away (also known as the quickie) or take the more standard approach of planning far ahead. Very few things that take six months are regarded as "quick." Governments can rise and fall in this time. Wars can be won or lost. However, planning a wedding can take each and every drawn-out, grueling day. If you reach behind you and can feel something cold and hard prodding you between your shoulder blades, and the two of you have let it slip that grandchildren are coming far sooner than expected, assume this is a shotgun held by her father and go for the quickie. Otherwise, you (not really) and your fiancée (she and only she) will have to decide between the two approaches.

First off, she will decide at what time of year to have the wedding. Believe it or not, something like this really matters to the woman! Now, I can follow that if the woman wants an outdoor wedding, it would make sense to have it in the summer, but after that, we men don't care what time of year. Some women dream of a fall wedding because of all the colored leaves. The only time you'd see the leaves is on the quick limo trip from the church to the reception, but that doesn't matter. Maybe she wants a spring wedding, when the flowers start blooming. Forget those silly April showers and all the mud they bring. It's her dream to marry a certain way, and you are there to do little else but follow orders.

The first thing she will do is come up with a list of possible dates at the time of year she wants to get married. At this point, you still have a modicum of veto power. Think hard about these dates. Is one of them Super Bowl Sunday? Are there any playoffs you would be concerned to miss? If you don't cross the big sports-conflict dates off the list of possibilities now, then it becomes destiny that that day is picked and enough nonrefundable deposits will be put down so that you cannot change it to watch the big game. Naturally, you can't say why you are vetoing this day. You can always offer up that it is the anniversary of an earlier girlfriend, and your fiancée will drop that date like a greased pig with oozing boils. Of course this may backfire years later when your wife realizes you can't remember your own wedding anniversary after theoretically being able to remember a former girlfriend's.

After she's picked several dates, you must then find the *right one*. By the time you are done, you'd think sucking a bowling ball up a straw would be easier. First off, you've got to go to the church to see if it is free that day. Chances are that it is free that day, but the wrong part of that day. You see, there are morning marriages and afternoon marriages. Your fiancée will have a definite preference on when she wants to be married, and it will be opposite the time the church has open. Then you have to look around that date to find when the church is available at the right time. Maybe you need to change churches and, if so, the facilities have to be vetted along with the priest/minister/rabbi/voodoo cult leader. A church can have a wonderful location, but you don't want someone performing the rites if he has got the appeal of Edgar Allan Poe on downers[90] or the long-windedness

---

90 Edgar Allan Poe was uniquely adapted to writing horror, such as "The Tell-Tale Heart" and "The Pit and the Pendulum." He didn't have the carefree life in which he wrote chilling stories for the fun of it. His father left when he was young, and his mother died of consumption. When he went to school, his fiancée married someone else. He was fired from one of his first magazine jobs for being drunk all the time. Later in life, he married his thirteen-year-old cousin. When he finally achieved the initial success as a writer with "The Raven," his wife got tuberculosis and died two years later. He later died of alcoholism. In short, not party central.

of a revivalist minister who is going to be condemning everyone to hell for sinning right before the reception party.

Unfortunately, you can't just book the church. You've got to go find out if the place where she wants the reception also has an opening that day. It won't. You then have to go back and forth between the church and reception hall until you get an acceptable time and date. At this point, run—do not walk—to the church and reception hall to book them both before some other slob walks off the street and books one of them, which would throw you right back to square one. While at the church, feel free to pray like hell that the limo driver and photographer will also be available that day. Getting your second cousin Jimmy to get you guys in his pickup truck that he considers clean because he emptied the ashtray and take pictures on his cell phone when his photography skills had before been limited to selfies in the bathroom mirror just doesn't cut it as an acceptable option.

Choosing a Church

or

God Help You Get through This

Y ou (I really mean your fiancée) can decide to get married anywhere, but the most popular place is still a church, even if she hasn't gone to a service in twenty years and can't remember what the religion was about. Often, the woman wants the wedding in the church she went to as a child for sentimental reasons. However, practicality dictates that the best church would be one with a more central location to where the guests are going to be coming from. Practicality, much like common sense and frugality, has as much to do with a wedding as a shark feeding frenzy and good oral hygiene. Therefore, you are off to the church of her childhood even if you have to book flights with three connections, rent a car to drive the next few hundred miles, and then borrow mules to get you over the mountain pass to get there.

Even if she hasn't been to the church in forever and does not have a clue who the current minister is, that will not stop her from boldly marching up the stairs to the rectory, brashly knocking on the door, and then making *you* do the talking. You may be nervous, not even knowing if that particular religion practices sacrificing virgins, but by and large ministers/priests/rabbis are nice people who will try to set you at ease. However, unlike the caterer, limo driver, photographer, etc., this person actually cares what happens to the two of you after he or she has been paid and the ceremony is over. Therefore, the minister is going to interview the two of you.

Now here is a person sitting in front of you who is representing God. However, you cannot help but lie to this person. "Do you go to church often?" the minister may ask.

"Oh yes," you lie. Feeling guilty, you try to rationalize this statement in your own mind by arguing that you at least go *toward* a church. It's just that you don't actually stop at the church, but instead pass by it on the way to the local Hooters restaurant.

Or he may ask, "Are you two living together?"

"No," you reply. "We're waiting until we're married."

Now even though you two spend every night together, you've decided to go the financially draining route of still paying rent at two separate apartments. Lies. Lies. Lies. Hopefully the church also comes equipped with a confessional that you can stop in on your way to the reception.

You will also have to do some questioning of the person of the cloth in order to make sure you are planning a wedding that he or she will actually consider having in this church. Do they allow the special music you wanted? Usually, ministers are lenient toward flutes, pianos, and even rhythm guitars. However, they tend to frown upon punk bands that will be smashing their instruments on the local furniture after their song is over. Go figure. Will you be doing the standard vows or making up your own?[91] Does the minister have a dress code? Even if the reception is a beach party, he may not feel comfortable leading a service in front of a group of people wearing thong bikinis and Speedos, especially if you are asking him to wear one as well.

You should also ask whether the minister will require you two to take wedding classes. Some religions push people to explore issues on money, children, responsibility, and the like before allowing them to get married in their church. Actually, that isn't such a bad

---

91   If the minister is doing the standard vows, you can see if he'll slip that "obey" back into them after "love and honor." Your wife should be too nervous to notice at the time, so make sure it is caught on video.

idea. Just because both people agree that Frosted Flakes is a great cereal or think she looks "smoking" in a tube top doesn't mean they have thought through the whole marriage deal beyond the first few weeks.

If the couple appears before the minister wanting to get married for a tax credit or because it was the greatest way left to tick off the parents, he isn't going to be happy to have you two stand in front of him so he can pronounce you husband and wife until death do you part when you have as much chance of sticking together as greased Teflon. In other words, if they have a class, suck it up and go. However, in the case of the Catholic Church, in which priests are supposed to be abstinent, it is like Willie Nelson teaching money management classes[92] or Pat Robertson teaching religious tolerance.[93]

Once all that is done, you should wrap up the loose details by finding out exactly which hours you have the church. If you have a morning wedding, the people helping out[94] (florists, cameramen, etc.) can go in at their convenience and set up. However, another wedding is coming in right after you, so there ain't no dillydallying after the ceremony is done. If the wedding is running late, the receiving line has to be abbreviated to have the guests run by the wedding party and high-five them. If you have the late wedding, you can take your time leaving. However, setting up is done in a mad rush. As soon as the previous wedding leaves, the setter-uppers must storm the church like Navy SEALS taking over Grenada. Hint: if other people don't move fast enough, a significant level of civilian casualties is acceptable. You should also figure out how much the church will

---

92   As successful as Willie Nelson was for singing country, he had the slight problem that the IRS swung by one day and picked him on a minor discrepancy—owing $16.7 million. One could look at that as bad, but it doesn't compare to Mike Tyson, who made over $1 billion and at the time of this writing is now broke, owing Uncle Sam $38 million. Go figure that Mike Tyson is not a math whiz!

93   Pat Robertson is a minister who actually ran for president. His views were a tad extreme for one who professed divine knowledge, including the idea of nuking the State Department, assassinating world leaders opposed to us, and thinking Haiti had a devastating earthquake because they literally had a pact with the devil. Apparently when Jesus said to turn the other cheek, Mr. Robertson was thinking of the lower one.

94   "Helping" is an unusual term as you are paying them enough money for a Tahiti vacation for their effort this single day.

cost you. Don't haggle. This time is the only time where someone is not purposely trying to rake you over the financial coals for the sheer enjoyment of it...usually. Besides, the minister will be saying a personal message about the two of you, so you probably don't want to be referred to as "the chiseler" during the blessing.

Choosing a Reception Hall

or

It Will Cost Me How Many

Limbs for an Open Bar?

The choice of the reception hall sets the flavor of the entire wedding. This decision is where the big bucks can come into play. It can be as cheap as Cheez Whiz on Ritz crackers at your grandmother's assisted living home or a fully catered gala event with heads of state in attendance. For the sake of simplicity, I will explain the middle-of-the-road route: having dinner in a banquet hall.

The first question you must ask at a banquet hall is whether it can accommodate the number of people who will be attending the wedding. If the room is too big for you to fill with friends, it looks like you are as popular as Woody Allen at a family reunion.[95] If it is too small, people will feel like they are in a mosh pit. If the restaurant manager agrees that the room does suit your needs, ask to see the room anyway. Why? Because managers will lie to get your business. Before you feel aghast at the impropriety of that, remember how much lying you did to the minister.

---

95 Not that she was invited, but I don't think Mia Farrow would have been trying to catch the bouquet at Woody's last wedding since he divorced her and married their adopted daughter.

One of the major problems with many restaurants is that they want to maximize their seating capacity. If your wedding contains about 150 people and they only have rooms that comfortably fit 100 and 200 people, they will try to shoehorn you into the 100-person-capacity room. That way, they can make more money on the big room. How can a restaurant do this? There are several tricks they use. First, they put so many chairs around each table that they are actually touching, and then they bunch in so many tables that only dwarf anorexics are able to move from one table to the next without knocking over several pieces of furniture. So how does a person sit down at their seat in all this chaos? He or she must either crawl over the top of the chair or lift the chair out of the way, get into position next to the table, drop the chair back into place, pull it in, and then offer a napkin to the person at the next table to help stem the flow of blood emanating from the fresh head wound inflicted by the chair.

Another trick restaurants can use to maximize seating is the "shrinking dance floor." Under this scheme, the restaurant nonchalantly either sets up tables on or partially on the dance floor. Of course this becomes a bad idea when you've got a table of people who may potentially be drinking heavily with another group of people inches away flailing around on the dance floor doing the Macarena. After a couple of accidental elbows to the head, you've got the makings of a good bar fight. As much as it would spice up the wedding video to see Cousin Ted using Great-Aunt Ethel's walker to give Cousin Jimmy's knee the ability to bend in both directions, it is best to avoid it.

The next big decision to decide on is the menu. Here is where a man should butt in if his fiancée makes a bad decision, even if it results in a stiletto to the forehead. A bad decision here is anything but chicken. Chicken is basic. Most people like it or can at least tolerate it. If you get fish, then half the crowd won't eat it. If you get some type of beef, nearly no one is happy because some like it raw while others prefer it burnt to a crisp. Throw in a few salads for the vegetarians, and most guests should be OK. If the bride's father has the big bucks, maybe he'll spring for a buffet. Otherwise, chicken. If you order salmon stuffed with brie cheese, Aunt Marge will complain about the gas it is causing her due to lactose intolerance, and Cousin Phil will be ordering pizzas sent to the restaurant.

Besides the main menu, you probably should spring for some hors d'oeuvres.[96] You figure, after the wedding, all the guests go down to the reception while the bridal party stays at the church taking pictures of every combination of people there is. So back at the reception hall, you've got a bunch of people standing around in uncomfortable clothing for what seems like (actually is) hours. The only thing these people have in common with each other is that they somehow know either the bride or groom. So how many times can they say "that was a nice ceremony" to random people until they are bored out of their minds? Roughly two minutes. Having a table with hors d'oeuvres allows people an excuse to break from boring conversations. Getting some cheese and crackers out is the least you can do for your guests to cover up the many, many awkward moments before the party gets into full swing. If you don't give someone an out, you'll end up with some guys talking about trying to nail one of the particular bridesmaids, not knowing that her father, overhearing the conversation, wants to nail them with real nails.

Then there is the bar. You can have a cash bar or an open bar. A cash bar means that people have to pay for their drinks when they get them. An open bar means that they try to drink as much as humanly possible while hopefully not lapsing into a coma because they don't have to pay. It's a safe bet that the guests will ask for the top-of-the-line booze at an open bar, whereas at a cash bar, they are used to drinking paint thinner. What these guests don't realize (or just don't care about) is that the restaurant keeps tabs on all these open-bar drinks and then presents the bill at the end of the night. For an average-sized wedding, a restaurant may need a couple people just to carry an itemized bill out. Unless you are fairly sure your father-in-law is adequately embezzling from his place of employment, you should opt for the cash bar. The only good part to an open bar is that the father-in-law will be so mad at the bill that he will forget how many positions you are going to attempt with his daughter that night.

---

96 "You" technically means your father-in-law. Every financial decision in the wedding planning adds another year of working before he's allowed to retire.

The big thing you'll have to check when finding a restaurant is the total price of the evening. Now, the average person would assume that if you ask the restaurant manager how much it will cost per person, you need only multiply said cost by number of people, and you'd be done. That is exactly what the restaurant wants you to think. Did you actually want to have time to dance after the meal is served? Better check how many hours they are giving the room to you before you get smacked with extra rental hours! Did you want the restaurant to actually serve the cake rather than have the guests line up to scoop parts of it off? Better check that that the cake-cutting service is included! Are you going to have a champagne toast? Some restaurants even have an uncorking charge for the bottles! If restaurants could, they'd be renting the silverware. Make sure these details are done. Otherwise, at the end of the night when most everyone is toasted, the manager will be more than happy to present to either you or your father-in-law a bill that looks more like you are buying the restaurant rather than using its services for the night.

Choosing a Baker

or

You May Want to Be Baked for This One

You will need a cake whether you like cake or not. "Wedding doughnuts" just doesn't have that traditional sound. Therefore, you will need someone to bake this cake. If you go to a professional baker, the first thing he'll ask you is how many people it is supposed to feed. He will then give you a list of types of cakes with prices related to the number of people it is supposed to serve. Now, I can't imagine that he is going to make cakes different sizes if you say 140 people as opposed to 150. Yet if you say 150, you will be paying more. However, people are afraid to cut corners here just in case the baker does possess this mystical power to bake a cake for the exact number of people. As a general rule, I tend not to try to shortchange people who can spit in my food.

You may have a relative who is quite a "renowned" baker[97] and will offer to make the cake in lieu of a gift. REJECT THIS OFFER. A wedding cake is a special cake, and there are more things that can and do go wrong with this confectionary delight than giving a six-year-old with a vial of superglue. In my earlier years, I worked at a restaurant that specialized in weddings, and I saw lots of accidents

---

97 These days, you qualify as a baker if you are able to add the right amount of eggs and oil to a prepackaged cake mix.

with amateur cakes. The biggest mistake the nonprofessionals make is underestimating how much a wedding cake actually weighs. They just plop layer on top of layer until the cake is deemed large enough to feed the Seventh Fleet. They don't take into account that unless the cake is phenomenally stale, its weight will cause it to collapse in on itself.

Therefore, unless the cake has proper hidden supports (as the pros do it), it takes on a shape that would be deemed unnatural any place on earth except the town of Pisa. If left unattended, most of the cake usually ends up toppling onto the floor. We're only talking dessert here, but since so much tradition is built around the damn thing, the bride will cry as though the maid of honor has been swarmed and terminated by killer bees. It just doesn't cut it to do the "bride feeding groom, groom feeding bride" by getting on your hands and knees to lick cake off the carpet. The problem is that the cake is a *symbol* of the marriage. If it crashes right out of the gate, the bride may think the marriage is also doomed to an early failure. Flour and sugar are simply not a good prognosticator of whether the marriage will last. The herpes flare-up from the stag-party stripper, on the other hand…

Decorating cakes by nonprofessionals can also be quite bad. Nonprofessionals concentrate on taste. Wrong. The cake must look good. Taste runs a very distant second as to what matters on a wedding cake. If it tastes like wet cardboard but looks glamorous in the wedding pictures, it will be considered a success. Besides, most people are full by that time and don't eat the cake that the father of the bride paid all that money for anyway.

But back to the decorations. Besides having a plastic bride and groom on top, the cake has elaborate frosting decorations and may even be garnished by real flowers and ribbons. I have—I kid you not—seen a cake at a reception that was intricately decorated with ribbons, etc. The problem arose in that the person who decorated the cake did not know how to fasten the ornaments properly and so stuck in *pins*. The poor waitresses were then forced to go through the cake piece by piece trying to ensure they weren't serving the cake-of-death, hoping the dinner wasn't going to turn into more of a Last Supper as it led to perforated intestinal tracts.

If you don't believe that looks are more important than taste, you'd be surprised to know that some bakers decorate an imposter cake made of Styrofoam. Only the top part is real. After the bride and groom cut the cake, the waitresses then take it out of sight and put it on a shelf. The cake that is served to you is actually just a standard sheet cake in the kitchen. Tricky, but effective.

You can get many types of cake, from the standard yellow and chocolate all the way up to an elaborate carrot cake. Stay simple. The outside is shellacked with frosting, so no one can tell without X-ray vision that you opted for the cheaper one. Besides that, the more complex a cake you have, the more people will be guaranteed not to like it and have yet one more thing to complain about.

Choosing a Photographer

or

Posting Thousands of Selfies Doesn't Make You a Photographer

M any photographers become photographers because they were considered too pushy to become used-car salesmen. When considering good photographers, you'll find that most of the older ones are usually escaped Nazi war criminals, while the younger ones may lack the same level of experience but have the advantage of youthful vitality as they are smacking people around with their equipment to get the picture they desire.[98]

Unfortunately, photographers can be broken down into two groups: timid and aggressive. The timid photographer, even though he may know everything about lighting, shutter speeds, and all that other camera jargon, ends up taking pictures of the back of Aunt Selma's head because he was too intimidated to knock her down to get the good shot. At a wedding, everyone is trying to get a good look at the couple getting married (since there is *nothing* else to do), so a photographer who isn't willing to swing a few elbows to get ahead of people to get a clear shot gets lots of pictures mostly

---

98 British soccer fans make excellent photographers.

of the backs of blue-haired ladies. In the corner of these pictures are two people who—besides one being dressed in white and the other in black—could be anybody doing anything anywhere. Therefore, you've got to get a photographer who is at least a wee bit aggressive. After all, a wedding album is to be cherished forever.[99] Meanwhile, Aunt Selma's hip that she broke getting knocked down by the photographer will eventually heal (albeit slowly because of her advanced age) and will probably only require a minimum of physical therapy.

As trivial as it sounds, selecting a photographer should begin the day of or after you book the church. A good photographer is in high demand—and he knows it. In a capitalistic society, demand is going to push the photographer's price so high that they get about twenty dollars every time they push the button on their camera. And push he will! There's more clicking than at a dolphin family reunion.

Because they are so expensive and because a bad photographer can be really bad ("How was I supposed to know you wanted a picture of that ring thing?"), it becomes quite an ordeal to find the right one. The best way to start is to get recommendations from friends on how bad their photographer was and then cross that person off the list. Eventually, you will get a few people that you (not really you but your future wife and mother-in-law) will want to personally interview.

First off, ask to see some wedding albums the photographer has done. You'll notice in these albums that the groom is conspicuously absent for the first third of the album. This is normal. Remember the Golden Rule of Planning a Wedding. This is the bride's day, not yours. The photographer is *supposed* to start at the bride's house so that he can take pictures of her "getting ready." If the groom is featured in too many pictures, then your future wife and mother-in-law will consider the photographer a hack with no clue of what weddings are about and will immediately scratch that person from the list.

Note: Lest I forget to mention, the photographer hardly ever takes true candid shots. Nearly every picture the photographer takes and puts into the wedding album is a fake. He starts off at the bride's house. Even though the bride has spent a minor fortune getting her

---

99   After the first six months of marriage have gone by, the wedding album gets opened as much as an occupied coffin.

hair professionally done (even though it then gets covered up by the veil), the photographer will make the bride and mother pose as if the mother is helping get the bride's hair *just right*—even though the frantically nervous bride would gouge the eyes out of anyone (including her own mother) who messes with her hair. Even the bride's father does not escape this charade. This man is perfectly capable of dressing himself (I'm not saying he could actually pick out a matching outfit—just that he knows he puts on underwear *before* his pants), but another popular "candid" pose is that of the bride fixing her father's tie. Fake. Fake. Fake.

More absurdly, the actual wedding shots are usually fakes! One of the biggest moments in your life is never truly captured on film! You see, it would be slightly disruptive for the photographer to be standing front and center with light bulb flashing every few seconds while you're supposed to be concentrating on your vows. Besides that, the minister/priest/rabbi tends to get a wee pissed off when he/she can't read the holy text because of all the little stars he/she is seeing from the 250-megawatt bulb the photographer uses. Therefore, most of the big shots (exchange rings, kiss the bride, etc.) are missed! These shots are posed and shot *after* the real ceremony when all the guests are getting trashed at the reception because there is nothing to do but drink while waiting for the bride and groom to finally arrive.

If the photographer is deemed acceptable, then a price must be negotiated. Let him set the first price, and then try to ensure there will be no hidden costs that will jack up an already overinflated bill. Your job at this point is to pin this guy down, or he'll bankrupt you easier than Imelda Marcos set loose in Foot Locker.[100] You've got to ask questions like, "Do I have to pay you for your travel?" Otherwise,

---

100   Imelda Marcos was the former wife of the president of the Philippines. Once the country elected her husband, he declared martial law so that he could save the country all the money and anguish of elections. With all the savings, Imelda spent money like never seen before. The Philippine people were thrilled to live in poverty so Imelda could satisfy her fetishes, like three thousand pairs of shoes. Now, most men are aghast when they hear a number like that. However, I'm betting more than a few women are drooling over this idea. Men do not *remotely* get the fascination and love some women have for shoes. As excited as a guy would be judging a pillow/Jell-O fight at the Miss Universe pageant, some women are that excited to see things they shove their feet into. Go figure.

he's going to take "the scenic route" from his home to the church and then to the reception.

Next off, you have to ask him how much of his time is covered under the price. Don't forget, you've got to pay this guy to be at the bride's house an hour before the wedding up until the dancing at the reception. If you don't specify timing, you'll find the photographer leaving soon after he eats (yes, you're supposed to pay for his meal at the reception even though you're already paying him to be there). Naturally, if he is "leaving" because his time is up, you would then find yourself begging him to stay. He'll agree, but it will cost you a *tiny* bit extra. This is the guy who gets paid so much an hour that surgeons salivate. Therefore, the photographer just played you like the banjo in the movie *Deliverance* (out of proper taste, I'll stop the allusion to *Deliverance* here even though there is a much more accurate one involving Ned Beatty—you[101] playing Ned's part).

On a final note about the photographer, you'd think that after all the money you'll be shoveling his way, you would own what he did. Sorry. He owns and keeps all the negatives or data files. If you want to give people in your wedding party some pictures, he'd be glad to print some copies. KA-CHING! How about pictures to some of your elderly relatives? KA-CHING! Friends who couldn't make it? KA-CHING! KA-CHING! You have no choice but to be nice to this legal blackmailer, otherwise he won't "touch up" the photos to remove the extra zits you broke out with from the tension leading up the ceremony. You can't even bring the prints to the store to copy as they are copy protected. Try it at your local Walmart, and the machine starts blinking/buzzing to alert the world to your criminal activity, so you then have to slink away feeling like quite the deviant.

---

101 Meaning your father-in-law and his ever-thinning wallet.

Choosing a Person to Do the Video Recording

or

Who Can We Trust to Push a Button *and* Be Sober?

M odern technology has brought another wrinkle to weddings—and along with it, one hell of a headache. Video cameras are now plentiful enough that major events like weddings are now considered a must to be recorded. Paying a professional to do this is absurdly expensive and should *never* be suggested on your part. If you do, I'm sure you'll easily be able to hear the grinding of teeth every time you see the now-pauper that is your father-in-law; that is if he has the strength to grind his teeth after selling so much of his blood. We are also not talking about someone taking video on their phone. Just because a person can point, click, and paste to Facebook before people even leave the church doesn't make him the prodigal son of Stephen Spielberg.

A better option is to ask a mutual friend. The problem here is that just because a person owns a video camera doesn't mean he knows how to use one.[102] Sure, the guy may get the lens cap off, but usually he thinks he's pressed "pause" when he hasn't, so he ends up taking twenty minutes of footage of his feet before he realizes the camera is going. Amateurs have no clue what they are doing at a wedding, so it is up to you to give them strict instructions. Unfortunately, since the person is usually doing the taping as a favor to you, you have to phrase your demands as suggestions. Some he'll take, some he won't.

First off, remind the man to charge the batteries (multiple) *right before the wedding*. Otherwise, just as the bride walks down the aisle, the batteries will quit because he forgot all the extensive footage he took of Junior eating sand at the beach.[103] Your wife will then be mad at *you* for trusting such a dimwit of a friend when you[104] could have just spent the money on a real videographer. Even your future father-in-law will be pissed at you. Why will he be mad at *you* when you were saving him money? You don't expect him to be mad at his little girl on her big day, do you?

Also, make sure that your video guy knows to be *early* for the wedding. He should not arrive just ten minutes beforehand and think he can easily make his way through the gathering throngs of people carrying an armful of bulky equipment without accidentally laying out one of the grandmothers. He should also scope out the place he is going to camp out one day before the actual wedding. Otherwise, he'll have no clue where to stand during the ceremony. If he stands to the side of the altar, the only part of the ceremony he'll capture on film will either be the back of the bride's dress or the beginnings of the groom's bald spot. If he stands in the back of the church, he'll get pictures of the relatives who didn't care to show up in enough time to get good seats. Besides that, in a Catholic wedding, people

---

102 In this day and age of cameras doing videos, you basically have to ask *why* someone now owns a video camera. If this is a person who spends an inordinate amount of time near women's bathrooms and is not of that gender, you may want to check that he won't break any parole violations by being near any recording equipment.

103 Important safety note: Don't ask to see their previous footage. The excitement in a person's life is inversely proportional to how many pictures and videos he takes of it.

104 Actually that poor bastard known as the future father-in-law.

will be popping up and down in the pews often enough that the film becomes a jumbled mix of backs of heads followed by derrières followed by backs of heads. He could stand behind the minister, and that would be the best of all views since he would be getting the faces of the bride and groom as well as the congregation. However, he'd be a bit conspicuous, and anything that could remotely take eyeballs away from the bride is as forbidden as asking your mother-in-law for a lap dance.

The best place for the cameraman to be is in the balcony—assuming the church has one. It is out of the way, so he won't be banging into or being jostled by others. He'll also have a good view of the bride, assuming he knows how to zoom in. One of the problems here that you may want to remind the video guy of is that the camera may be taping the picture of the bride and groom in the front of the church, but it will be recording *his* voice. This isn't a Hollywood set with a sound crew—the only sound that camera is going to pick up is what is next to it. It gets a little disturbing when you get your wedding video back and see a picture of the two of you exchanging vows but hear this guy talking about how his hemorrhoids are flaring up because he's been sitting too long or, worse, making comments about which members of the bridal party he'd "like to do."

With any luck, the guy captures the basic "I do" and "kiss" highlights. Now the guy's job becomes really difficult. Up to this time, all he had to do was point the camera in the direction of the woman with the big poofy white dress. Now he has to handle the reception with many things going on. Because the reception starts before the bride and groom get to the banquet hall, the video guy has a wee too much free rein on what to videotape and lots of time to exploit it. Don't ask me why they feel this compulsion, but video guys think they must shoot continual footage while the bride and groom aren't there. So what does he take pictures of? Friends and relatives who are a bit miffed that this guy is walking around shoving a camera in their face every time they put some hors d'oeuvres in their mouth. Let's just say that it is hard to have a mouthful of food and still look glamorous for the camera. Eventually people are scared of even approaching the food because they are too self-conscious that they'll look like a pig as people can later count all the trips on the video they made to the snack table.

You may be able to forgive all the excesses the cameraman is going to immortalize, but then there's the stuff he doesn't tape that really gets you. Sure, he got the wedding (assuming he was taping when he thought he was taping and paused when he thought he was paused). But now he is at a party and would like to have a little fun and imbibe from the selection of alcoholic beverages. Since he is a guest doing a favor rather than a paid professional, he is allowed to do so. Unfortunately, this means that he may be paying a wee bit less and less attention to what is going on around him. Cutting the cake? He may be in the bar line for another shooter. Bride dancing with father? He may be trying to pick up one of the members of the wedding party. Last dance between the bride and groom? By now he's trying to pick himself up off the floor.

In the final analysis, you get what you paid for. The cameraman has done you a favor from the kindness of his own heart and the cheapness of your own wallet.[105] Therefore, you can't complain. Well, you can, but not so that it would get back to him. So now you are left with footage of you and your bride at the church. It may not be possible to hear or recognize either of you up at that altar, but you do know it is you. You also will have a lot of candid moments at the reception, some of which can be used to blackmail guests at a later date. What the heck. You'll play it the day you get back from the honeymoon, and by the time you get the urge to play it again, whatever you recorded it on will be obsolete, so you won't be able to anyway.

---

105 Yes, it is your father-in-law's money you "saved," but don't expect him to be thanking you. It is like he is drowning in a pool of debt, and you are trying to help him by not urinating in the pool to add more water.

Getting the Wedding Invitations

or

You'll Be Stationary Picking

Out This Stationery

At first, most men will not think getting invitations should be a big deal.[106] Unfortunately, they are forgetting Lesson 4 in that *everything* to do with the wedding is a big deal. The future couple with the mother of the bride in tow will arrive at the stationery store and explain that they are in the market for wedding invitations. The owner of the store, realizing he or she is going to be able to take that trip to Cancun after this single sale, will gleefully push other customers down, using a cattle prod if need be, to bring you to the Books of Invitations. Let me warn you—these books are terrifying things. It reminds me of what I imagine the Necronomicon (Book of the Dead) you see in mummy movies. The first thing that will strike you is that they are enormous. These books—yes, I do mean to

---

106 Most men have spent their lives card shopping by going into a store and grabbing the first card that mentions the right occasion (birthday, anniversary, etc.) and the right person (grandmother, sister, whoever else your mother yells at you to go get a #*&# card for). Apparently—and I know this seems crazy—you are supposed to read these cards and match your feeling to the right card. There are a ton of reasons men are cringing right now—admitting you have feelings is bad enough, but reading about feelings is enough to have most men dry heave.

be using the plural—are *huge*! You will be expected to go to the first one, clean and jerk it up to your chest, and get it to a table before the weight causes your intestine to explode into your scrotum.

You will then open the first book. Your fiancée will be perched on one shoulder, and her mother will be hanging over the other. You will turn the page where the first invitation is pasted in, and the debate between the two women will begin. Your opinion will be asked, but only for their amusement. No thought you express will be given any real credence. Your job devolves down to nothing more than a page-turner. As the debates continue page after page, you will find your eyes start to lose focus in the monotony of staring at paper saying in various ways that a person will be invited to witness a love only rivaled by Romeo and Juliet's. At this point, the two women will stop and ask what you think of a particular card. Now, they have already made up their mind about the card. It is, in their opinion, either a completely tasteful or tasteless card, and if you do not verify their previous decision, they'll stare at you like you left your fly open at a day-care center. At this point, you may try to pay attention lest you will be caught again, but I can guarantee that no man's mind can bear the painful monotony of the Books of Invitations.

Therefore, men will have to take a different approach in order to survive this ordeal. First off, accept the knowledge that you will be slipping off into a near-catatonic state. Once you hear your name, however, you must arouse yourself to action. Instead of giving a true opinion, say something like "Yes, I see what you mean" or "Hmm, I guess I'd have to agree with you." While muttering these lines, it is a good touch to rub your chin in thoughtful contemplation. The women, thinking that you have made a decision, will then do what comes naturally and ignore it.

After what seems like a near eternity, the women will have the choices narrowed down to about half a dozen invitations. This time they will insist that you pick your favorite. Once you do, they will both quickly decide that that card is utterly ridiculous and wonder how it got chosen for the final round in the first place. Finally they will pick the appropriate card. Now you are done. Right? Ha! Ha! Ha! Sorry, buddy, but you've got a *long* way to go. Not only do you have to choose the card, but you will have to decide on a host of other things to go with it.

First off is picking the font (i.e., what the writing on the invitation looks like). Who actually cares, you ask? Dear Lord, how many times do I have to keep referring you back to Lesson 4? In the grand scheme of things, your wife will forget about this, but at this moment it is *important*. Any man who considers this issue as anything less than the signing of the Declaration of Independence will be deemed an insensitive clod who (as tears well up in the eyes) must be having second thoughts about the whole marriage thing. Now, there will be several standard fonts for which there is no extra charge. There are also special fonts that will cost a "little" extra (you can almost feel the stationery-store owner salivating as little extras keep jumping into the bill). Why would a special font cost more? Does it use more ink? No. Does it need special paper? No. Does the owner of the stationery store want to extend his weekend trip to Cancun into a three-day affair? Yep. Naturally, your fiancée will tend to gravitate toward that special font.

Now there are yet other decisions to be made, such as the color of the paper and (I don't expect you to believe this, but it is true) the color of the envelope on the *inside*—you know, the part people see for approximately 6.3 nanoseconds as they are opening the envelope, taking out the contents, and throwing it away! Believe it or not, you actually have to pick this color—and the women with you actually care and will sit there debating the pros and cons of each and every shade! Should it match the bridesmaids' gowns or the maid of honor's gown or the season the wedding takes place in or...You'd think people routinely saved the torn-open envelope to bring to the wedding to ensure it blends properly.

After the excruciating pain of selecting everything to do with the invites, the man is about to dive headlong through the front store window because that would be less painful than spending a few more seconds in that store. But wait! You are *not done*! You now have to pick printed accessories to the wedding.

Do you want napkins printed with your names on them? God forbid the guests would have to wipe their cake-encrusted faces on a plain napkin! How about matchboxes with your names? Who cares if no one smokes anymore? Balloons? What says "love" better than helium-inflated latex?[107] By this time, the stationery-store owner has become a shark in the water, and you are bleeding profusely. He or she will try to sell you anything in which your names can be engraved. I have no doubt that you could get wedding toilet paper under the guise of promoting a closer intimacy between the couple and their guests. Meanwhile, the stationery-store owner has canceled his trip to Cancun altogether and is now heading for an extended Hawaiian vacation.

My best advice to a man going into the hell pit known as the stationery store is to not bring any sharp implements with him lest he decide to take the easy way out. I would then give the bride's father a financial cooling-off period before entering the household again—say a minimum of two weeks. Maybe you can speed the healing process by giving him a commemorative candle engraved with your and your wife's names that will be present on every table at the wedding.

I will say one more word before leaving this section. Part of the invitations is the cards for the seating arrangements. When people go to a wedding, it is not first come, first serve. People cannot amble in and sit wherever they want. If they could, by the time the last people arrived from the church, the parents would be sitting at the table next to the kitchen door. Planning who sits where is an elaborate chess game. The table front and center in front of the head table belongs to the immediate family. After that, it gets dicey. You see, the closer someone is to the table, the more important that person is deemed.

Suffice it to say that if you go to a wedding and you find yourself at the back table between two kids who are using their knives trying to stab each other rather than eat their food, there was some debate between the couple if they were willing to put up with your company

---

107 There are other latex items that have more of an association with "love."

to get the gift you brought. The other problem with arranging seating is that you have to consider who will get along with whom. You've got to consider divorces and family rivalries on one side and people who don't know each other but would come to blows if they did on the other. As a general rule, men are not considered smart enough to accomplish this puzzle...end of discussion.

Choosing Flowers

or

Flower Power...a Thorny Situation

S imple. Threaten to douse yourself in gasoline and then play with welding equipment if you are asked to pick anything to do with flowers. If your fiancée will not take no for an answer, take the easy way out and start swallowing glass. Trust me. It'll be easier, quicker, and more fun having the hospital repair the internal damage you have inflicted on yourself rather than picking out floral patterns.

Don't believe me? Well, there are the flowers for the altar at the church. Then there are the flowers for the pews that hold the family members. Don't forget the wedding party! All the bridesmaids will be carrying bouquets. And wouldn't those ushers be upset if they didn't get their spiffy boutonnieres? Of course they wouldn't, but that is beside the point.

Then you've got to deal with the reception hall. Some couples go for flowers on the head table and then some type of flower arrangement on each of the guest tables. The bride is obviously going to have to have her special bouquet. Since she'll want to keep that, she then has to buy another bouquet to throw at the reception. Each of these decisions is agonized over with more scrutiny than goes on in the jury room for murder trials. The flowers have to be picked according to the color theme of the wedding. Flowers also have "special meanings." Gardenias mean joy, while apple blossoms connote good fortune. Why? Who knows, and what man actually cares? See what I mean about picking flowers? Flowers may be pretty, but the situation they present is anything but.

Selecting the Bridal Gown

or

White? Really?

This decision is another that would be painful for the man to help with. Luckily, he is forbidden to assist on this one. Women and their mothers read tons of bridal magazines before venturing forth to bridal salons to look at dresses. These two women may cover salons within a hundred-mile radius to find this mystical "right dress." Most men don't take this search seriously. However, most men think they are fashion jet-setters if their socks are the same color.

A bride must decide what material she wants the dress made of. The fabric could be chiffon (nothing to do with lemon pie), taffeta (which wrinkles when looked at), or a host of other materials that one would think are entirely impractical to be used in the manufacture of clothing. The neckline could be off the shoulder (which means she'll need to buy a special bra so the straps don't show), Queen Elizabeth (a high collar that flares out behind the head and looks about as comfortable to wear as underwear made of sandpaper), or many other styles. Sleeve choices include things like a Gibson sleeve (puffy at the shoulder and tight around the wrist, which makes their arms look like a sheep's legs), a bishop sleeve (regular sleeve with a large cuff, which will make it so much fun trying to find her hand to put the ring on when the pressure is already on you), or many other choices.

The waistline could be antebellum (dips to a point in front of the dress),[108] basque (dips below the waist, making her legs look munchkin size compared to the rest of her body), or some other type. For a headpiece, she could choose a tiara (a crown that looks foolish on anyone other than royalty who are looking foolish already with their stupid wave), Juliet cap (hat covered with lace that does a good job hiding that expensive hairdo the bride just had), or multiple other things. The skirt choices include, among other things, mermaid (tight-fitting dress that doesn't flare out until past the knees, which allows the bride only the ability to take baby steps all day) and bouffant (skirt that spreads so far out from the body that you nearly topple over trying to reach her when it comes time to kiss the bride). Other choices include veil, train length and style, shoes, and the color. Shoot me now.

Unless this is a second marriage or she looks like she is shoplifting a beach ball, the color of the gown is usually white. White is the symbol of virginity. However, in today's society, most men and women have, shall we say, already tested the merchandise they are about to buy. Some women decide to buy bridal gowns that are off-white if their virginity is vastly improbable, as in cases where she was previously married, she has a bulging stomach, there are "performance" videos available of her on the Internet, the wedding party consists of mostly her own children, or the minister is asking the couple to say "I do" and most of the congregation is thinking "I did." An off-white color for bridal gowns is often called "candlestick white." That is because "ugly yellow" doesn't really attract buyers.

---

108 The word "antebellum" also means "before the war," and that doesn't have good connotations whatsoever.

'

Picking the Tux

or

Paying Bucks for the Tux Sucks

B ring your best man to the closest tux place. Pick tails or no tails, cummerbund or vest.[109] Get a few measurements. You can be in and out in under fifteen minutes. You then have the rest of the afternoon to scout out places to have the bachelor party.

---

109 Sure. As if you are picking anything. Your wife has given you the basics, and you are there to make it happen.

Transportation

or

The Only Driving a Bride

Does Is You Nuts

E ven if you have a new Cadillac or Ferrari, you can be guaranteed that the woman will insist on renting some other vehicle to take her from her house to the wedding and from the
wedding to the reception. Total traveling mileage may be less than
two miles, but you will still have to rent something expensive for the
entire day. Whether it is a horse-drawn carriage, an antique car, or
a limousine, the woman will need some type of transportation. This
decision is one of those that the man really has nothing to do with.
The picture in the woman's head of "the perfect wedding" includes
her vision of what she wants to arrive in, and that may have been
cemented in around the age of five, so talking her out of anything
is often like talking a fish out of swimming. There are drawbacks to
each choice.

The horse-drawn carriage is a romanticized method for the bride
and groom to travel. Quite often, a synonym for "romantic" is "freakin' impractical." Obviously, a horse-drawn carriage can only be
used with moderate weather. If the weather is cold, those few miles
of traveling are going to be agonizing. The bride could show up

with enough goose pimples to look like, well, a plucked goose. If it is raining, the gobs of makeup she applied to herself are now going to come coursing down to make her look like a rabid raccoon. Therefore, if you are going to opt for the carriage, ante up a few more bucks for some type of canopy.

Also of note is that most people fail to realize that a horse is a biological animal and as such will have biological responses. In other words, it may leave a pile of poop bigger than some dogs in inopportune places.[110] There does exist the chance that someone from the wedding party may step in said pile and have no choice but to carry this reminder with him or her for the rest of the day. If the pile is upwind of the reception, you may find that the guests don't quite have the appetite you'd planned on.

An antique car, on the other hand, is a synonym for an old car. Old cars break down. Old cars don't have spare parts that can be bought straight off the shelf. Usually a part has to be ordered from some other part of the country, if it is actually in this country. No matter where you actually live, you can be guaranteed that no one within a surrounding state will have that "special part." Therefore, if the car breaks down a week before the wedding, it will take them several days just to locate a replacement part, another day or two to ship the part, and then another day or two before they realize the problem is actually another part. In other words, you agonize every day for the last week before you realize you truly are screwed. If the car breaks down *during* the wedding day, you are beyond SOL. Having her arrive in a tow truck driven by a guy named Mel with more grease on him than an oil derrick will put her in a sour mood, especially if her beautiful white dress now looks like a Dalmatian.

A limousine is the "safest" mode of transportation in that there are fewer things that usually go wrong. As you're checking out limousines, the salespeople will be telling you of all the great features. These features can include wet bar, phone, and television with Blu-ray. If you were going on a long trip, these things would be nice, but

---

110 If the horse drops his load when the bride arrives to the service, it doesn't matter the volume or the smell. People have to pretend it is not there. Nothing is allowed to detract from the vision of the bride.

the limo only gets used for less than an hour for the day. Do you think the bride and her wedding party are going to plunk in a DVD of *Steel Magnolias* on the way to the wedding? Are you going to try to drink your money's worth of booze from the church to the reception? No— not that you can't try though. Borrowing someone's minivan would be more practical and cheaper, but no self-respecting bride would be caught dead in it. Now, she doesn't mind you having to drive one for years on end once the kids come, even if your only previous car has been a pickup. However, that day, her transportation is going to be special. Luckily, they don't allow Roman litters carried by slaves anymore.

Registering for Gifts

or

How Many Toasters Can You Get
and Still Pretend to Be Thankful?

T he couple getting married will be getting lots of gifts. Amazingly, the man will not particularly care for any of them even if he normally *loves* presents. These gifts are like the evil alternate-universe Christmas. To further rub salt in the wound, the cash envelopes will be taken by the bride to buy more things that the husband doesn't like. This is not by coincidence, but by design. Remember the Golden Rule.

Since it is quite often difficult to shop for couples getting married, stores have graciously come up with the idea of having the couple "register."[111] The couple (she and she alone) first picks a store or two from which they (she and only she) would deem it acceptable that their guests shop from. A list is then generated of what the couple (just her) picks out and is put into the company computer. That way, if someone wants to buy a gift, they need only go to the store in question and find out the gifts, match that up with the price range, and then realize that they need to bump their range up because either

---

111 Just like your credit cards graciously charge you interest to help remind you to pay your bills in time.

the couple was greedy or everyone else rushed down and got the cheap stuff. Simple.

Now, a new couple needs many things to start their life together. If they have just bought a house, they will need tools to do necessary repairs. Therefore, tools of all types would come in handy. A hardworking couple may also want some electronics for entertainment that they couldn't previously afford. Sound good? Too bad. These gifts belong to the realm of what a man really likes and, therefore, they do not make the cut.

Instead, the gift list centers on what the woman wants. So what does a woman who is starting a marriage deem she needs more than anything else? China. You know, the stuff that—just maybe—you may eat off of once every three or four years. Other than that, it just sits in the cupboard. Why does she feel this is necessary? Because it is not out of the realm of possibility that an important guest may come over and—heaven forbid—you don't want them eating off of the ordinary plate you are able to eat off of every other day.

Picking the right china is quite difficult for a man, especially if he despises the entire concept of china. The first thing that needs to be picked out is the pattern. A man will tend to pick out the simpler patterns because he naturally assumes they are cheaper. That would be a bad assumption along the lines of walking into a recluse's apartment, seeing chainsaws everywhere, and assuming he is a lumberjack on the weekends. Simple can be considered elegant. Therefore, by doing less, they can charge more. If you are a man, you will not be able to make out any rhyme or reason to how they could possibly begin to (over)price this stuff. Therefore, always look at the price tag without your fiancée seeing you look at the price tag and then pretend to make up your mind, picking out the cheaper stuff—cheaper does *not* mean cheap. You will also have to decide on accessory dishes. Will your wife want cups to match the plates? Absolutely! Saucers for the cups? Most definitely! Smaller appetizer dishes? A necessity! Soup bowls? Without a doubt! It would be simply barbaric not to have them.

You then have to pick out the silverware to go with the dishes. Here, you find your future wife debating the merits of four- versus five-tined forks, while you are eyeing the cutlery section to see if the clerk would take pity and euthanize you. Don't forget that after all this is done, you are going to need a very large, very expensive cabinet that does little else but display the china. You may never use your china, but that big ol' cabinet taking up every last ounce of free space in the dining room will be a constant reminder each time you stub your toe on it of how much inner satisfaction you have knowing that if important guests arrive, you'll be ready to serve them food on nice-looking dishes.

As unbelievable as it may seem, there are gifts even more useless than china. The good news is that they are not as expensive as china. The bad news is that these gifts are so ridiculous that men still cannot abide putting them on the list of things the "couple wants," which makes the wife mad because she deems them a necessity. What I am referring to here are the dust ruffle and pillow shams. In case you don't know what the dust ruffle is, it is the material that goes over the box-spring mattress and hangs down to the floor. Properly fitted, it hides the space between the bottom of the bed and the floor. It goes without saying that the dust ruffle must be picked to match the bed comforter. You don't have a comforter? Add that to the list.

What is the purpose of the dust ruffle, you may ask? Well, in the years before indoor plumbing, it was never a pleasant moment when in the middle of the night, you realized you had to get out of bed and make a trip outside to relieve yourself. In the wintertime especially, I could imagine I'd rather run the risk of my bladder achieving the size of a grapefruit than make my way to the outhouse by trudging through several feet of snow at 2:00 a.m. with a wind chill of −70°C that is making my testicles want to disappear back into my body cavity to get warm. Therefore, people used to keep bedpans under their beds for the emergency that couldn't wait. The dust ruffle was invented to hide the bedpan.

Newsflash: unless a modern-day person is exceedingly lazy, he or she would rather walk down to the bathroom. That is why the bedpan industry is not the booming market it once was. I'm sure if you took a poll, you'd find that most households do not have or at least do not admit to owning a bedpan. Now it is true that I could be wrong, and the bedpan industry may be limited due to a case of poor marketing. Maybe they could see increased sales with a better ad campaign, like with a celebrity endorsement from Tiger Woods.[112] It could be that technology has not kept up with today's needs. Heck, we've invented the smokeless ashtray. With a bit of reverse engineering, I'm sure we could come up with the odorless bedpan. Throw on some designer colors, and we may really have something. If we do, maybe it'll be vogue to get a bedpan. You probably should get a male and female. What the hay, you may as well throw a few more in for the kids and a couple guest bedpans for those overnighters you may have. Then again...

What makes dust ruffles even worse than their utter lack of usefulness is that it makes your day even harder. If you decide you want to make the bed,[113] the dust ruffle gets easily discombobulated. It shifts up and down as well as side to side as you are trying to arrange the sheets. Fixing it with a heavy mattress lying on top of it is no easy chore, so sometimes you have to flip the mattress off the bed to put the dust ruffle down carefully. You then have to gently place the mattress back down and then—even more carefully—tuck the covers in. Any slight movement will send the dust ruffle askew, and you'll have to start making the bed from scratch.

Then there are the pillow shams. A pillow sham is a decorative cover that goes over your pillow and pillow casing. In the morning after you make your bed, rather than hide the pillows under the covers, you can stuff them into pillow shams and then lay them on top of the covers since they look so pretty. At night, simply remove the pillow, fold the pillow sham, and place it where it will not be wrinkled. The entire idea of a pillow sham is yet another inconvenience in your day that you really don't need or want, but your loving wife will, and she won't be too happy if you mistreat either the dust ruffle or pillow shams.[114]

---

112 At this point, his golf game has gone to crap, so it is fitting.

113 That is, your wife tells you to.

114 Many women start off the marriage with things like dust ruffles and pillow shams, but it is difficult to keep up. Once kids come and mothers are losing sleep, they magically disappear. Do not ask where they have gone to. Making fun of an exhausted wife for years of having them may make them magically reappear at night—and she may promptly choke you with them while you sleep.

Knowing how many fights can occur when registering for gifts, most men tend to opt out of the whole process. This is not a good idea. More than china will be picked. If a man does not go, he will be forever destined to sleep on floral sheets, wake to the sun beating in through floral curtains, shower behind a floral curtain, and dry his body with a floral towel. The man *must* go to retain the veto vote. You will get yelled at for it, and your manhood may be called into question more than a few times, but you must hold firm to the way you want your bedroom and bathroom to look—or more correctly—not to look.

Many men may go the extra step and demand that they register at a place like Sears that has tools and electronics. He will then make a list of the things he wants and demand that they be put on the list. The woman will put up a mild argument and then "give in." Here is where the Great Women's Conspiracy kicks into action. Shopping for wedding presents is nearly always done by women. Therefore, they can see what the man wants and promptly ignore it for what the woman wants. Not only does the man think he has won a battle he has actually lost, but now the woman can bring this situation up at a later time as an example of "letting him get his own way."

Music

or

Singing through the Pain

There are two times you have to be concerned with music. The first is at the church, and the second is at the reception. Church music can be quite basic (if the man plans it) or quite elaborate (if the woman plans it). Most guys really don't care too much. Throw a few bucks to an old lady who can squeeze out "Here Comes the Bride" on an organ, and he is content. However, there should be a few warm-up tunes before the wedding starts so that the people in the church don't realize waiting is about as boring as watching bass fishing on TV. Many women would rather have a string symphony during this time to entertain the guests. It only costs about as much as having Bruce Springsteen give a private concert.

Your fiancée may want to have one of her friends sing a few songs during the ceremony. Either that or she may have a friend or relative play something on an appropriate instrument, like a piano, flute, or guitar (nonelectric). What you have to watch out for here is having one of her friends or relatives who has "been singing or playing all of her life." Just because a person enjoys something and has been doing it for a long time doesn't necessarily mean that the person is actually good at it. Mike Tyson could practice singing "You Light Up My Life" for years, and I can guarantee you that it is not going to be a pretty sight when he performs. Therefore, you have got to convince your wife that any potential performer should be auditioned or have a reliable[115] reference.

The problem here is that if you are auditioning a friend or relative and he or she is simply not good, it is difficult to tell that person that he or she didn't make the cut and won't be performing at the wedding. The next thing you know, that person is whining, and then his/her parents (who are also your relatives) start complaining about their poor spurned child, and then other relatives come in to tell them to stop griping because their child was no good to begin with and it is about time that someone finally said so after years of everyone suffering through his/her performances at every reunion. By the time the wedding day rolls around, the family is getting along about as amicably as roosters at a cockfight.

What it comes down to when deciding if a relative is going to do something musical at a wedding is that you must get a reliable (nonrelated) witness who has seen this person perform (better than a drunken barroom karaoke) in the last several years. Being the best snowflake in the fifth-grade winter pageant does not cut it; neither does six straight years in saxophone summer camp. Remember: the bride may deny it vehemently, but she wants to be the center of attention. If all the guests are chuckling through the ceremony about how many notes the "musician" dropped rather than paying attention to her, that won't set a good precedent for her mood for the latter part of the evening.

The second musical thing you will have to consider is what type of music will be played at the reception. Here, you have two choices. You can either have a band or a disc jockey. Since you are paying either of them significant cash,[116] you can be and should be much more critical of them. Not to put pressure on you, but a bad decision here can screw up the entire day: guests don't dance, the party

---

115 Meaning *not* the person's mother. If they share any genes or want to get into the other person's jeans, you can't trust the person's opinion.

116 The money can be found in the husk of the once-vibrant being that is your wife's father. He may not look like his former self as the financial burden has crushed the spirit, zombifying him.

never really picks up any momentum, and everybody sits at their tables drinking and flees from the scene when the requisite amount of time has passed before good manners allow guests to leave. Your wife has been physically planning this day for months to years. She has become obsessive about every detail. Emotionally, she may have been planning her wedding day most of her life. To see the party implode after all her work will send her into a tailspin that will make the towering inferno look like a campfire.

Who do you think she'll blame? Hmmm...Herself after all the countless hours she put in? No. One of the mothers for butting in too much/not enough at the right/wrong time? Pretty doubtful. Well then, how about, oh let's say, YOU! She'll think back on all those times she was freaking out about some absurd detail while you carelessly frittered away your time on things like trying to keep your job or—heaven forbid—not acting like you were going to lose bladder control when the minister didn't act like this was going to be the greatest day of his or her life as well as yours.

So let's take this seriously. This choice of music is one in which you actually care what decision is made, unlike nearly everything else in the day. We'll start with the band. Bands that play weddings basically come in two types. The first type is one that is playing small gigs just killing time before their big break. Let's call them the "attitude band" since they have one and are not afraid to show it early and often. This type of band is dangerous to have at a wedding. They really don't want to be there, and your guests quite often don't really want to have them there. You see, they think playing at this wedding is somewhat beneath them. Picture William Shatner[117] being asked to play a supporting role in a high school play. Yes, he truly does need the practice that badly, but he's not about to admit it.

Since the band does not want the evening to be a total waste of their time, they are going to play a lot of original songs, trying

---

117 Mr. Shatner was the actor made famous for playing Captain Kirk in the original *Star Trek*. Basically, his character would beam down to a planet and nearly every crewman would be killed while he'd be locking lips with some alien vixen. The acting was...poor, unless you compare it to him playing a cop on *TJ Hooker*, where it was atrocious, unless you then compare it to him singing "Rocket Man," in which case you are looking to stuff raw meat into your ears in the hope a passing pit bull will gnaw them off.

some of their new experimental work on your guests. In case you're wondering, they take musical requests from your guests about as well as a state trooper being asked to hold a drunk driver's beer while he performs his sobriety test since his fourteen-year-old date can't because she is already passed out. This is not good. Guests at weddings don't like any sort of novelty in their music whatsoever. Musical novelty is greeted with as much acceptance as lepers at an open audition for *Playboy*. People only want to dance to what they know. Anything slightly out of the ordinary and they'll immediately rush back to their seats to sit on their hands.

Other serious problems exist with bands that think they are rising stars. As with happens with stars that are fast and hot, they tend to burn out. You make sure you book the band you want well ahead of time, you lay down a deposit, and the next thing you know, the band has broken up over "artistic differences." Artistic differences? What's the big deal on doing yet another cover of "Old Time Rock and Roll" that someone's artistic integrity is going to come into question? Usually "artistic differences" boil down to things like the band not being able to practice anymore because the drummer's mom has kicked them out of her garage or the lead singer not being able to come up with enough lyrics to describe all the angst he feels when he can't afford his second Starbucks latte of the day.

The second type of band is what you may refer to as a "professional cheesy band." These band members aren't reaching for the stars, just their next paycheck. They are not in music for the artistry or the fame, just the extra spending money. As such, they aim to please so that they may get another gig. Contrary to the first type of band, the PCB does nothing novel or innovative besides add a few unnecessary notes to old standby songs. All the band members are always cheery—too cheery. You'd think they were Valium smugglers. Whether they are singing, announcing the cutting of the cake, or trying to find out which one of the guests left their lights on in the parking lot, you'd think they were naming the next winner from the Publishers Clearing House Sweepstakes. Unlike the attitude band, they are happy to take requests. Unfortunately, all the songs pretty much sound the same. If you don't pay attention too closely, whether they're playing a tune by Frank Sinatra or Frank Zappa, you'd think they were playing one long version of "Tie a Yellow Ribbon" by Tony Orlando and Dawn.

Therefore, if you are going to opt for a band, you may want to go with the second type as the lesser of two evils. At least they try to mold themselves to the particular crowd they are entertaining. The second type knows that after nearly a lifetime of devotion to music, working to get money to pay for lessons, countless hours of devoting themselves to their private muse of music, and even potentially majoring in it in college, their lifetime peak will be playing dinky little weddings. Once these bands get over any suicidal tendencies, they usually work out fairly well.

One of the problems with any band is that they are going to take breaks. You can't really expect them to sit there cranking out the music for hours on end. Therefore, they stop every so often to take a ten-minute break. Band members tend to rely on their innate natural clocks to mark this passage of time. Unfortunately, their circadian rhythm is whacked to hell and back since band members are usually up all hours of the night and gauge each minute by how long it takes to smoke a cigarette or how long it takes for the Prozac they just popped to get them unnaturally cheery again considering that some members have to get up early to work the grill for the morning Denny's Grand Slam breakfast.

Therefore, ten minutes to them may mean half an hour in the real world. Meanwhile, the party usually stops dead in its tracks when there is no music. If nothing is done in the meantime, these minutes can become quite awkward as the guests try to entertain themselves. The people who are drunk will usually be the first to fill the void with humor that the rest of the crowd doesn't deem funny (or coherent). They'll assume that they just can't be heard and so will tell their jokes louder and louder, which drives people away from the tables, with the only place left to go being the bar. Unfortunately, the line at the bar is long since the band is trying to convince the bartender that they should be considered part of the wedding party and so are entitled to free drinks.

Some bands recognize this awful pause in the party and bring along an MP3 player. It is relatively easy these days to hook an MP3 player up to some speakers, and you can literally walk away for hours. However, since the band doesn't want to be shown up and have more people dancing to canned music than while they were playing, they tend to play Muzak[118] so that nobody can have too good of a time.

The alternative to getting a band is hiring a disc jockey. You should personally interview the DJ. If he has these rather large, thin, round black things on which the music is recorded, run away. These antiques were known in their day as "records." Now, they are usually referred to as "vinyl." People who actually use the word "vinyl" when referring to a record do so because that way they can sound like a *collector* rather than *a loser caught in the past.*

Records have serious problems. First off, since they aren't made in any serious amount anymore, a DJ who still uses them can be guaranteed not to play any music even remotely new. This DJ would be the one to play a lot of the "Beer Barrel Polka" mixed in with Bee Gees hits. Besides that, records don't age well, so they'll be skipping beats more often than Karen Carpenter skipped meals.[119]

Most modern DJs have now skipped over CDs and have gone right to MP3s. The only problem with this is that you are paying a guy a lot of money, and you used to at least see him lugging in boxes of CDs, CD players, etc. He broke a sweat. If the guy works from MP3s,

---

118 Music has been described as the universal language, able to soothe the savage breast. No, it is not "beast"—that is a misquote perpetuated by Bugs Bunny. Muzak is a version of music that has had its soul ripped out. It is often found in elevators and uptight department stores. They take popular songs and remove anything that could offend someone, namely the lyrics, and any instruments that don't rhyme with "gorgan." When you hear it, your brain recognizes it as something it knows, and so you can't help but try to guess which popular song they are mutilating now. You'll hear this sappy thing, and know you know it but can't pull it up. However, when you finally realize that they made "Stairway to Heaven" into a peppy jingle, you'll cringe, but not as much later on when you find yourself humming this travesty.

119 Karen Carpenter was the singer of the highly successful group the Carpenters. Unfortunately, she passed away due to anorexia nervosa. Some men may scoff at a disease that can be solved by going to McDonald's, but it is a serious issue. So why does it appear at first glance that I was insensitive to this topic? It could be so that I could draw attention to the plight of these mostly women. Of course if you are cynical, you could think I just did the footnote to cover for the inappropriate joke. If that were the case, though, you'd expect me to have been insensitive in other parts, and that's just, well, silly as I'm sure this book will put me in contention for the Pulitzer.

he brings in a laptop, some speakers, and he's good to go. If the guy has set up playlists prior, he can go into a coma and still get paid for the day.

Either a CD or MP3 allows you to start exactly at the right song. What you have to make sure of here is that the prospective DJ has songs you want to hear. The best suggestion is that you bring *two* lists with you to the DJ interview. The first is the list of songs you want to hear. You'll have to pick out the special songs—first dance, last dance, father-daughter dance, mother-son dance, ad nauseam, as well as the stuff you just like to listen to.

The next list of songs is by far more important. These are the songs you DO NOT want to hear at your wedding. If you do not put in this list, your party will be at the whim of your guests who will be requesting everything from bad rap ("Ice Ice Baby") to bad country ("Achy Breaky Heart"). Because you are doing the hiring, you can ban whole categories of music with a simple edict! If you hate rap and have one teen who likes it and keeps requesting it, and the DJ obliges, Aunt Selma isn't going to be getting up to shake a leg to "Big Booty Hoes." You will also want to ban particular songs. One of the big ones that comes to mind is "The Chicken Dance." "The Chicken Dance"[120] is a song only played at weddings. Why? Because this is the only time old people get to act ridiculous in public just like their kids do on a daily basis.

Another song men will want to ultimately avoid is anything that could break into a conga line. A conga line is bad for several reasons. First off, men are continually harassed to do the damn thing. When they finally get pushed up to doing it, they realize the last person in line is another male. They are then left with the uncomfortable decision of whether to grab the waist of the man in front of them and

---

120   For those of you not familiar with "The Chicken Dance," you haven't been to too many weddings. I kid you not, it is a Swiss accordion song from the 1950s. You'd think a song like this couldn't possibly be popular, but it has been recorded over 140 times and sold more than forty thousand records. The older crowd usually loves it, as you get into a circle, make duck-bill motions with your hands, flap your "wings," shake your "tail feathers," clap, and then swing around the circle. Why do they love it? Maybe you can blend in if you have Parkinson's. OK, I apologize for that one as well. The Pulitzer may be slipping away.

have that man not like this scenario, or not grab the man's waist and just tail along. If he just tails along, the man will be uncomfortable because he'll think other people are labeling him a homophobe who is not secure in his own masculinity. A no-win situation if I ever saw one.

Since you are the guest of honor, a conga line that forms may have you as the leader. Then you're really in for it. You'll then have to weave around the reception hall, trying vainly not to get in the way of the waitresses or knock over tables. You've also got to make sure you don't conga yourself into a corner and have the mob crush you against a wall right before your wedding night.

I'll bet you're assuming I'll put the nix on those line dances like the electric slide and the macarena. Actually, I encourage them. Men—real men that is—hate these dances, and women love them. Since women do not need men to get up there and dance and know that trying to get the men on the dance floor will be about as successful as getting men to go to a Barbara Streisand concert, they will actually *leave the men alone*! This will be your only chance of the night to get an alcoholic drink with your buddies in the wedding party. If the song goes too quickly and you want another drink, see if the bartender will hide you behind the bar for a few minutes.[121]

Whether you have a live band or a DJ, one of them is going to have to act as a master of ceremonies. He or she will have to announce the wedding party when they finally arrive from the church, tell everyone when to sit down when the cake is to be cut, direct the special dances, etc. If your MC is too timid, your reception will never come under any type of order. You should view the crowd of people at your wedding as having the collective intelligence of grazing sheep. Without some type of herder, they'll basically sit there chewing their cuds.[122] If you have one of those exuberant MCs and the power rushes to his head, he ends up sounding like he's announcing events at the Ringling Brothers and Barnum & Bailey Circus

---

121 If you don't tip the bartender the first time, expect him to sell you out the second, maybe even by clanking a glass so people start physically looking for the groom.

122 Yes, I know that it is cows who chew their cuds rather than sheep, but I'm allowing myself a bit of poetic license if you don't mind.

or a monster truck rally. By the sound of his voice, you'd think you were about to stick your head in the lion's mouth rather than feed your wife a piece of cake.

Above all, make sure that the MC has a lot of wedding experience so that he knows how to run the damn thing. Give him the list of names of the wedding party and tell him how to pronounce them. Make him repeat the list back to you if necessary so he doesn't screw up. The biggest names not to screw up are yours. If you two are going to be known as Mr. and Mrs. Koch (pronounced with a long o like the drink Coke) and he says it with a short o, then it is going to illicit a lot of semisuppressed tittering.

The last thing you want to make sure of with the DJ is that he knows what to play when. The basic job here is to have him act as a kindly drill sergeant. When the wedding party arrives, he has got to get the crowd settled, the people announced, and everyone seated. He has to keep the smile on while doing everything short of threatening the lives of people if you are ever going to get to the partying part of the day.

Picking Wedding Bands

or

Is It Better When Prisoners Get to Choose Their Own Handcuffs?

Picking the wedding rings is a painful process, to put it mildly. In Greek mythology, Prometheus was punished by being tied to a rock in Hades and have vultures come and eat his liver every day only to have it grow back again. The gods punished him in this way only because jewelry stores hadn't been invented yet. Otherwise, Hades would have one hell of a jewelry selection that poor Prometheus would have to go through day after endless day. I'm not saying that buying the wedding band is actually as painful as the liver thing. It isn't good, but there is no permanent physical scarring.[123] The good news is that you'll have your fiancée there to help you out. The bad news is that you'll have your fiancée there to help you out.

Going back to the jewelry store after buying the diamond is like going over to the bully's house after he just beat the snot out of you to complain that you still have the full range of movement of your left arm. He'll happily make sure that that arm would become as useful

---

123 Financial scarring definitely and emotional scarring maybe, but not physical.

as a street hooker's chastity belt. Here the jewelry store has simultaneously sucked any idea of financial savings you ever had away from you and still made you feel guilty for not selling one of your kidneys to pay for the better-grade diamond. You now have to go back to them and admit that they didn't suck you completely dry, so that they can have another crack at it.

You and your fiancée will have two different opinions on what types of wedding bands to get. She'll want matching ones so they'll look good in the wedding photos (which is the only time for the rest of your life when it could possibly matter if the rings look even remotely alike). She'll also want either white gold or yellow gold. She'll then need something that goes well with her diamond ring. Meanwhile, you are thinking "cheap and simple, simple and cheap." All you really want is a circular piece of metal (major burrs sanded down) that is a fraction of a grade higher than what would turn your fiancée's or your own finger green.

You'll have a few things working against you here. The first is that you hate to see your fiancée get her mind set on something and then tell her it is out of your price range. After the first visit, you can barely afford a plastic decoder ring, never mind something else made of gold. The second thing against you is that ever since buying the diamond ring, you're still having nightmare flashbacks that make you wake up screaming in a pool of sweat. Therefore, you may be willing to agree to almost anything.

Your first instinct is to let your mind wander away from this mental madness and torture. You'll imagine yourself in a place much more fun, like a gator-infested swamp. At this point, you'd gleefully sport an alligator-skin purse just to taunt the local animals rather than be at the jewelry store. After all, this is the place that recently convinced you that three months of hustling your tail off at work making deadlines, missing deadlines, mandatory overtime with no pay, etc., is only worth this tiny, itty-bitty rock. And they'll tell you up front that the clarity or cut of that rock is probably not so good (even though you can't see any problems yourself because the damn thing is about as big as the tip of a blunt pencil) because you couldn't afford a good rock with the piddly job you've got. It may be difficult, but you must concentrate on the matter at hand. Otherwise, you'll end up having to wear a frilly diamond-chip-encrusted flower-engraved girly ring for the rest of your life. By the way, that's how long you'll be paying for it too!

Express to your fiancée that you want to keep things simple. You want a plain wedding band. A simple circular piece of metal is enough to show to the world that you are, indeed, married. Women may not understand this because they react much differently than men do when getting jewelry. Unlike women, men don't go running off to other men showing the ring off. Men don't gather with their male coworkers at the water cooler to titter about the ring. To men, jewelry is nothing more than expensive trinkets that you now have to worry about losing.[124] To women, they are incarnations of your love for them. Ergo, the size of the jewelry, how often you get jewelry, how deeply in debt you have to go to acquire jewelry, all translates into how much you love them. In every sense, when a woman utters the words "size doesn't matter," she is lying through her teeth.

---

124 There are exceptions to the men-loving-jewelry rule. There are some rappers who don't feel that they are dressed unless they are about to toss their back out by wearing so many necklaces. Being half Italian myself, I can say that some members of this community have enough gold around their necks to rival an Egyptian pharaoh's burial. The men who do this then have to unbutton their shirts down to their navels so the rest of the world can "admire" their medallions—that is if you can see them through the forest of chest hair.

The Bridal Shower

or

The Only Time "Women" and "Shower" Are Used In the Same Sentence and Not Considered Exciting

I f you want to see fine acting, forget Broadway and go to a bridal shower. Everyone there is pretending to have a good time when boredom is oozing out of every pore of their bodies. A bridal shower is duller than earthworms mating. It is duller than watching the Stamp Collecting Channel. The shower is usually held about a month before the actual wedding. The purpose of having a party that no one actually enjoys is that the guests get suckered in to buying yet another gift for the bride.

Traditionally, the maid of honor hosts the shower. All the female relatives, close friends, and sometimes coworkers meet at a rented hall room or at a house large enough for the expected crowd. Usually only light hors d'oeuvres are served. Not feeding this crowd that really doesn't want to be there is as close to criminal as you're going to get. Low blood sugar and blue hair are a lethal mix. Yet if you feed them a big meal, then you really won't be able to keep anyone awake. Besides that, the women will need that little plastic fork to nonchalantly jab into their leg every so often to help maintain consciousness during this party. If the silverware were metal, you'd have women dropping left and right from blood loss.

Everybody sits in a circle in good view of the bride. The bride then opens presents. Most men love opening presents. They abhor it here. Usually opening gifts is a fun thing; however, women have found a way to suck every last bit of enjoyment out of it, leaving it an emotional black hole. First off, the card is read aloud. For each one, the bride secretly prays that it is just a "To/From" card rather than some long-winded Hallmark that rambles on endlessly about the virtues and bliss of marriage. Each present is unwrapped slowly and methodically.[125]

The present is then named and held aloft. The bride first gives a speech on how indispensable that particular item is to everyday living, even if it happens to be her third shower caddy of the evening. Every woman who has ever owned that particular product then stands up and gives a complete testimonial to its merits. These speeches are followed by a general discussion and question-and-answer period. Once all that could possibly be said about an item had been thoroughly reviewed, then and only then may the bride start on the next gift.

Meanwhile, the maid of honor has the duty of taking notes on the proceedings. No, I am not kidding. The maid of honor needs to write down who gave what and maybe a quick comment about what was said so that after the party is over, the bride can then more easily write the thank-you cards. Men don't like thank-you cards. They don't like writing them, sending them, or receiving them. To men, thank-you cards are about as useful as the British royal family at a crop harvest.[126] If men were running these parties, the groom would

---

125 Usually, there is one elderly aunt who has flashbacks from the Great Depression and keeps proclaiming, "Save the paper!" This rather than the proper way of opening a present, where the wrapping paper ends up looking like it was in a chainsaw duel. To accomplish this ridiculous endeavor, each piece of tape is supposed to be peeled off with as little tearing of the paper as possible. Once done, it is folded up neatly. Yes, it is environmentally friendly, but when it takes ten minutes to open each present, the boredom hits a level that makes Alcatraz solitary confinement feel like Disney World.

126 Or any other manual-labor event.

say "Thanks, guys," chug a beer in their honor, maybe butt a head or two, and that would be that. Nothing more needed. Nothing more expected.

With women, it would be considered a major faux pas not to send out the thank-you cards. For the next several days after the party, all of the bride's spare time will be consumed with writing these cards, which puts her into an ever-so-pleasant mood. Naturally she'll find it easier dealing with this frustration by venting it at the groom. Even though you did not ask for these gifts—nor particularly want most of them—it will be your fault that she is tied to the chair writing cards. You can offer to help, but licking stamps just doesn't cut it. It's best just to stay far, far away. If that isn't cutting it, offer to do the thank-you cards for the wedding. That may appease her a bit, and it really isn't any extra work for you. When you start to do the cards after the wedding, there is a phenomenally high probability that you will do something she doesn't like—poor handwriting, writing the wrong thing, putting the stamps on slightly crooked, etc.—which will get you fired from the job (which is what you want anyway).

The Bachelor Party

or

Stud or Dud

The bachelor party is the antithesis of the bridal shower in that it scores a zero on practicality and a ten (hopefully) on fun. Planning of the bachelor party is a duty usually bestowed upon the best man. Since this can be a night in which things can easily get out of hand as rules of proper decorum and behavior are too casually tossed aside, you should pick your best man carefully. Only the very best of best men will take the time for adequate planning of the bachelor party to ensure that things do indeed get significantly insane.

You see, the bachelor party is the only time when men are actually given somewhat of a green light to go out for some significant fun. A subset of these parties may be at a strip club, so it is important to note that at no other time—again, forever—is a man allowed to see a woman naked unless it is in a *National Geographic* magazine at a doctor's office. If you include when the lights are on, then your wife may also be on the no-see-naked list. Now, I'm absolutely *not* saying that a strip bar is the place to be. Any regular bar, racetrack, or one of the guys' houses for poker is fine and much less likely to involve someone needing to post bail at the end of the night.

What first needs discussing is when to have the bachelor party. Usually, the bachelor party is a surprise party. Therefore, you will have nothing to do with the planning. Be that as it may, you *must* get to best man and beg him if need be *not* to have the party the day before the wedding. I know that the day before the wedding is the last day of "freedom," and so men band together and think that these precious remaining hours should be celebrated to their fullest. Good intention. Bad idea. Hitler invading Russia was a better idea. Digging burning bread out of a plugged-in toaster with a wet knife is a better idea. Skinny-dipping in piranha-infested waters with a filet mignon loincloth is a better idea. At your bachelor party, chances are that you'll have a fair amount to drink and stay out pretty late. If you were to have a hangover or feel physically ill on your wedding day, your wife will forever hold this against you.

I've actually been to weddings where the groom and/or ushers have had a hard time standing during the ceremony because they felt so hung over. When they got to the reception, they just sat in the corner until they were absolutely needed for a dance and then promptly dragged themselves back to the corner once their task was complete. It wasn't pretty watching the bride smile on the outside but knowing that inside she was a seething volcano who would make sure the marriage wasn't going to be consummated for at least a week, and even then not without a tremendous amount of begging.

If you have a negative effect on the wedding because of being sick/tired, whenever you have an argument for the rest of your life—not that it has one iota to do with the wedding—she will bring up how callous it was of you to ruin *her* wedding day. You will pay dearly and often for this mistake. I don't care if you give her a back rub every night, clean every dish throughout the marriage, and have each anniversary present encrusted with diamonds, it is never enough to make up for putting a damper on her big day. Therefore, make your objections known to your best man. Go out the week earlier, and that way, you don't have to worry about staying late/getting drunk, etc. You'll just have to worry that you've followed the unwritten rules of the bachelor party.

One important note is that cell phones should be banned. Women should not be allowed to call to check up on the guys. More importantly, there are some idiots who like to take pictures or videos of whatever they deem interesting. Your fiancée knows you'll be going out for a wild night. She does not want—nor do you want—pictures taken that could eventually make their way back to her, your mother, her mother, your boss, etc. If any clown in the party whips out the phone, politely point this out to any married men who are there, and they will bring him out to the alley to educate him on the matter.

At the end of the night, the men should gather to get their stories straight. All men should go home and tell their wives/girlfriends that they had a "nice time." That's it. Final and only comment. That way, the guy who spent twenty dollars to get a fifty-cent garter from a stripper, the guy who did multiple power pukes in a minivan belonging to one of the wives, the guy who tipped the gorgeous waitress enough to carry her through a semester of college, etc., will not get into trouble. Do not allow for elaborations. Otherwise, the women will share stories, document the inconsistencies, and then try to break the weakest man.

Legal Matters

or

The Least Expensive Time a

Couple Has a Legal Issue

Make sure all legal matters are cleared up well ahead of the actual wedding day. The first thing is the wedding license. What the license requires varies from state to state. Therefore, you should actually get this done well ahead of time. First off, they'll make sure you are able to get married. Call them picky, but all fifty states frown upon things like marrying your fourteen-year-old sister while you're still hitched to your first cousin.[127] They also may require things like blood tests to make sure that venereal diseases are known about. Any surprises here, and the next license applied for will be by the "clean" partner for the kind that James Bond carries with him.

The bride and groom should also decide what should be done about the last-name thing. The bride can keep her last name, change it to the groom's, hyphenate the two names, or mix the letters together, toss them into a hat, and pull them out one by one to see what she comes out with. A rarely used option is that the man changes

---

127   OK, so I'm not sure of West Virginia on that one, but I'll get back to you on that.

his last name to the bride's. Regardless of gender equality, he may as well change his first name to "Whipped" because that's how he'll be referred to from here forward.[128] Many men in today's society are quite liberal when it comes to women's rights, but they still hold that they want the wife to take the husband's name.

Let's face it, it isn't easy for the woman to change her name. To do that, she has to change her driver's license, auto insurance, credit cards, bank accounts, mail, passport, employment records, fingerprints, retinal scan, etc. It is like entering the witness protection program. The major stumbling block (besides sheer hassle) that can make the wife want to keep her last name or hyphenate it is for her professional career. If clients have been dealing with Dr. Johnson for the last several years and are now told they are dealing with Dr. Smith, they may not make the leap that they are talking to the same person. Husbands can understand this trepidation, but that still doesn't mean they have to like it. Their only option is to act concerned about difficulties of a name change but also kind of mention the problems of not changing the name several hundred times a day.[129]

The best argument a man can give to convince his bride to change her name is to mention the consequences if they plan on having children. A woman will find it difficult to have a different last name than the children she bears. Mention this—over and over again if need be, even when she is sleeping—especially if you detect a sign of weakness. Throw in a few lines like "It may be difficult to get a house loan/car loan/bank account if they assume we're not married because of different names" and "The greatest present I could give you is sharing our name," and you may be on your way to convincing her to change. All bets are off if her first name and your last name or horrendous together—for example, your last name is Wang and her first name is Anita.

The other big legal decision is whether to sign a prenuptial agreement. Since most people get married early in their career, there is no need to sign a prenuptial agreement to see who gets the milk crates

---

128 If there was a guy who had the job of recycling used septic tanks from the inside out, *he* would still point and laugh at the guy who took his wife's name.

129 As it gets closer to the wedding, it may go up to hundreds per hour.

you are currently using as furniture or the dishes that could easily be replaced at the local Goodwill store. If, however, the marriage occurs later in life or one of the people entering the marriage has some family money, then a prenuptial agreement may be wanted—by one member of the two. Love may be blind, but it can still smell cash a mile away.

The idea of a prenup is a bit funny. Here you are promising before God, family, and friends a lifetime of being with your spouse for richer or poorer, in sickness in health, for better or worse—and you're already planning on what to do when you bail. It's like jumping off lover's leap but not telling your partner you're wearing a bungee cord.

Bringing up the idea that you want a prenuptial agreement is about as successful as asking if you're still allowed to date other women after you get hitched. The woman is immediately suspicious that you are ready to eject at a moment's notice. If you feel it is an absolute necessity, have your lawyer draw up as many documents as need be for her to sign, like adding her name on your credit card, setting up a will, putting her name on the house lease, signing her up for a CD music club, etc., and throw in the prenup near the end when her eyes are partially glazed over.

If she notices, blame the lawyer. Having tipped him beforehand, he can then explain that it is standard practice for his profession to include the prenup in these legal matters and that you knew nothing about it. You can then argue that the two of you don't need one. He will then argue that if your fiancée is so sure of the marriage, then she won't mind signing one. If she then chirps in with questions like "Is there any minimum time I have to stay with him before I qualify for the cash?" or "But do I still get all the money in the case of accidental death?" then maybe it is time to take a closer look at your relationship. If you are thirty-plus years older than her, I can guarantee that it wasn't your bod so much as your wad that she is interested in.

Rehearsal

or

Practice? Are We Talking about Practice?

T he marriage ceremony requires people to be in the right place at the right time with the right amount of sobriety. Usually the night before the ceremony, a rehearsal is given at the church. The ushers, bridesmaids, immediate family, special readers, ring bearer, flower girl, and whoever the heck else won't just be sitting there watching the ceremony is supposed to attend. They'll all meet at the church where the minister will guide them through the steps. Most likely, the minister has performed this same ceremony count-less times, and he certainly has better things to do at night than act as a choreographer. He'll try to keep the pace brisk so he can get back to ministering to the poor, aiding the sick, or YouTubing skate-board accidents.

This is usually the first time everyone is together, so it is a bit fun. You are surrounded by your best friends, and your fiancée is sur-rounded by her best friends. You'll be chitchatting along while the minister is explaining things when all of a sudden you realize that the rehearsal is over and you don't have a clue what to do the next day. It's a bit embarrassing to say to the minister, "Sorry, but I haven't been paying attention to a thing you said. After the years of tuning you out during your sermons, I guess I just fell into my old habit, but

I probably should have been listening this time. Could we start this whole thing over?"

Too scared to say anything, you'll say nothing and hope that your best man was paying attention. After all, it is his job to make things go smoothly. During the ceremony, he should be able to whisper to you where you are to go and what you are to do. That is why you picked him to be your best man. That is why he is here. Isn't it? Of course not!

You picked him because he is your best friend. This is the guy who stuck pens up his nose and made you laugh in history class when your teacher was discussing the Holocaust, costing you two weeks of detention. He taught you how to make Jell-O shots, which caused you to go to the hospital to get your stomach pumped. This wasn't your study partner making sure you got your rest before the SATs, but the one that thought a double date till the wee hours of the morning was a better idea. And now what have you done? You've laid your fate into the hands of a guy who holds the fraternity record for longest belch.

The only thing people remember from the wedding rehearsal is that they are told they walk too damn fast. The ushers get paired up with the bridesmaids, and then they have to practice walking down the aisle slowly enough that if the photographer ran out of batteries, he'd be able to go back to his car to get some, maybe have a quick cigarette, get back into the church, put the batteries in the camera, and still not miss the shot. When the bride enters with her father, they must walk even slower.

They have even made up a special walk for these two. Both people put the left foot forward and then bring the right foot parallel. They then bring the right foot forward and then the left parallel. Sure, everyone likes to see the bride, but with this walk, they have time to break out the canvas and draw a picture. Why do they do this so slowly? The only reason I can come up with is that if you spend a thousand bucks for a dress that is only going to be used for a few hours, you're going to make sure everyone looks at it until their eyeballs have the image burned forever into their retinas.

Traditionally, the bride's parents pay for the wedding. The groom's parents are supposed to pay for the rehearsal dinner. As with many time-honored traditions that link us to our past and bind us to our ancestral heritage, this is stupid. Sure, you may get an inward chuckle now that your parents are "only" taking a nose dive on their savings account while her parents are taking out a second mortgage and giving up on the idea of retirement just to give you two this day. However, time may change your perspective of the situation. If you and your wife end up having two, three, or more girls, you'll find that you like this tradition about as much as getting a second circumcision.

The purpose of the rehearsal dinner is to thank all the people who will be helping in your wedding. Not only do they and their dates get free food and drinks, but you should get the ushers a little gift, and the bride should get the bridesmaids a little gift. The bride usually gets something artsy-craftsy to remind them of the wedding. In other words, she gets them useless knickknacks that they'll feel guilty to throw out for the rest of their lives. Do not let your bride pick out gifts for the ushers, or they will get useless knickknacks, too.[130] If you are made to get them something that reminds them of the wedding, get them a beer mug with the wedding date or something else written on it so that you can pretend it has sentimental value. If your fiancée doesn't impose put any constraints, get fun gifts like video games. The men may not remember where they got them, but at least they'll enjoy keeping them.

The night should be kept somewhat tame if it is the day before the wedding. It is best that everyone tries to get a good night's sleep. Even if you are too nervous to actually nod off, you should at least try to save your energy. Therefore, don't think about how this is the biggest decision of your life and all the things that can possibly go wrong and how you really don't know where you are supposed to stand/walk/sit during the wedding because you were yucking it up with the guys. Just put all those little thoughts out of your head, because if you are tired, you are even more likely to make a mistake in front of every close friend and family member you've ever had.

---

130 The difference here is that the men won't have any remorse tossing these things out. You can only hope they do it at home rather than flip it in the garbage on the way out of the restaurant in full view of your fiancée.

The Wedding Morning

or

Better Wed Than Dead

I t is considered bad luck for the groom to see the bride before the wedding. Even if the two of you have been sleeping together every night for the last several years, the bride will usually not stay the night this time. Consider this the second-greatest blessing you will receive today. On the morning of her wedding day, the woman loses any remnant of sanity she once possessed. As a matter of fact, "possessed" is a good word to describe her. If you would like to witness how your bride acts during that morning without putting yourself in harm's way, just go rent *The Exorcist*. Usually, the bride stays with her family, and she can torture them. Maybe this is why the tradition started for women to be away from the men; if she torments her parents all day long, then maybe it is not so difficult for her father to give her away later in the day.

If it is a morning wedding, then you should be ready to go immediately. If you are staying at home, you should set several alarms. If you are at a hotel, set the alarm *and* ask for a wake-up call. I don't care if you *never* sleep in. Because of all the tension, you may not get to sleep until the wee hours of the morning, and then that li'l ol' biological alarm clock you have will keep hitting the snooze button instead of getting your butt out of bed.

Your tuxedo should have been picked up the day before, along with anything else you need. When you wake up, you should immediately get ready. Whatever can go wrong will go wrong. Plan on this. Both Murphy's Law and O'Reilly's Corollary are in effect.[131] This will be the day you've run out of toothpaste or you've cut yourself shaving and blood is spurting out so fast, you'd think you were in a *Rambo* movie. Be smart and eat before you put the tux on, or you'll have your big pictures taken with jelly-doughnut stains on you. If there are any animals, keep them away from you. This could be the day they have a little accident that you'll go skidding through. After trying to launder the stains out of it, you'll shrink the tux and end up looking like Pee-wee Herman.[132]

If it is an afternoon wedding, the temptation is to just relax and enjoy the day. Instead, you should be panicking like a Twinkie at a fat farm. The problem with the afternoon wedding is that it lulls you into a false sense of security. There you are, thinking you can leisurely get everything done, when Father Time comes along and smacks you upside the head with every delay he can think of: landslides, typhoons—whatever can happen between you and that church.

Case in point. Usually, men are so cheap that they'll rent the tux for an absolute minimum amount of time. Therefore, you may find yourself with this little errand to do the day of the wedding. Since the chance is that you'll be getting married on a Saturday or Sunday, check the hours of the store. If they close at noon and you get there after an extended lunch with the best man, you are screwed (not in the good way). Even if you do get in the store, you have to be careful. You must get your tux and make sure it is the right one. Check everything. Do not trust the rental place. I made the mistake of not checking when I rented my tux for the junior prom. When I went to put it on later that day, I realized that they forgot to include buttons for the shirt. By the time I was able to pick up my now highly irritated date from her highly irritated parents' house, I was two hours late and

131 As most people know, Murphy's Law is "Whatever can go wrong, will go wrong." For those of you who don't know, O'Reilly's Corollary is "Murphy was an optimist."
132 That would be Pee-wee Herman when he was doing the kids' show, not when he was arrested in the adult movie theater having a "conversation" with "Mr. Johnson."

came with an assortment of poorly sewn buttons to keep my shirt closed. Talk about making a lasting impression—I think her father wanted to impress his fist into my skull! Therefore, bring a checklist, or you could find yourself using a stapler to keep your shirt closed.

Meanwhile, your bride will start the day by having her hair professionally done. There will be what seems to be endless primping and fussing (and some money thrown in) until both she and the hair stylist are satisfied. When they finally have reached that point at which the hair is deemed a work of art able to rival the *Mona Lisa*, they will throw on a headpiece and veil so that no one can see it. The bride will also have to have her makeup professionally done. Usually there is enough makeup applied so that it can be seen by people in the back row of the church (even if you are getting married in Notre Dame). From the back of the church, your bride will look glamorous. Up close, she'll look like she's trick-or-treating as Tammy Faye Bakker.[133]

Your fiancée will then head home to get final preparations in order. She'll make sure the flowers (corsages, etc.) are all right when delivered. If they're not, heads will roll. The bridesmaids will arrive, along with the photographer and limo driver. She may not have to say anything, but the entire crew is ready to do her bidding without hesitation or question. Think Genghis Khan in white. The photographer will take, "ahem," candid shots of the bride getting ready that will take hours for him to meticulously pose so that they look "natural."

Wherever the bride is has become the command center of the entire operation. Updates and any big decisions are passed through her. You are a different story. Your lone responsibility is to show up at the church on time, preferably with your fly up. They don't even trust

---

133   Tammy Faye Bakker was a televangelist's wife. She was known not only for massive amounts of makeup, but long false eyelashes and—I kid you not—eyebrows that were tattooed on. She and her husband would stare into the camera "praying" for your financial well-being so hard that she'd start crying. Since she had inches of makeup on, it would go streaming down her face creating a toxic pool that would frighten away the EPA. People sent them so much money that they had no idea what to do with it all—even their dog house was air conditioned. A sex scandal eventually brought down the show, and they divorced while he was in jail. Apparently, it wasn't a match made in heaven.

you with this single chore. That is why you have a best man—to help you from screwing up the one thing you are supposed to do.[134] The bride is General MacArthur, while you wouldn't be allowed to lead a Cub Scout troop on a trip to the mall. For most men, this is a good thing. Asking for more responsibility is like asking the IRS to go over your taxes.

---

134 OK, so you may need a backup to your backup.

The Wedding

or

One Ring to Rule Them All, One Ring to Find Them; One Ring to Bring Them All and in the Darkness Bind Them

Y ou should plan on arriving at the wedding about forty-five minutes to one hour before the wedding starts. That way, you'll be maybe ten minutes early. Expect a car accident to slow traffic down even if the church is only a few blocks away. Either that, or you arrive with plenty of time to spare but then realize you forgot to bring the ring and now must make it back to the apartment and return in the time it took you to leisurely first get to the church. At this point, speed limits won't mean much to you, especially since you are driving so fast most signs are nothing but a blur anyway. Keep the windows up, or you'll wind up looking like Don King's[135] half brother.

---

135 Mr. King made his reputation as a boxing promoter with hair that must have been over a foot long and looked like he had plugged a hair dryer directly into a nuclear power plant. He managed most of the best boxers of his time, and they inevitably sued him. How he continually signed up new boxers with his reputation of picking their pockets is amazing, unless one figures his clientele is used to having their heads used as door stops.

It may not surprise readers at this point that I was almost late to the wedding where I was a groom and another where I was best man. At my own, my brother and I decided to take the scenic route across the state rather than the highway since we had so much time to spare. Looked shorter on the map, until we realized every village has seventy-five stop signs. By the time we got to the correct city, we were scrambling to get our tuxes, go to the hotel, change clothes, and speed off to the church. In all the hurry, my poor brother forgot to bring the priest's check, and we didn't have time to go back for it. Luckily, he was a trusting soul. When I was best man for my brother (notice a pattern here?), we both assumed that the pressure was off because he only lived a mile from the church. What could possibly go wrong? By the time we got there, the bride was arriving and we had to sneak my brother in the back way so that he would not see her before the ceremony.

Your ushers, on the other hand, should really be at the church half an hour to forty-five minutes early because they have an actual job to perform. They have to escort all the guests to their seats. Actually, they only take in half of the people. You see, when a couple arrives, an usher escorts the woman arm in arm to a seat while her date sheepishly follows behind. I'm not sure why and how this tradition got started. Maybe it is since the ushers were close to, but did not get the honor of being best man, the next-best thing was to allow them to walk off (at least temporarily) with everyone else's date. For that brief time, they are "studs on the run" as every man has to give up his date to the usher, who can then strut in with tons of women. OK, so most of the women they are escorting have more wrinkles than the laundry in a bachelor pad and are starting to get facial hair, but there are times quality can be sacrificed for quantity.[136]

The thing the ushers have to remember here is that friends of the bride usually sit on the right-hand side of the church while friends of the groom sit on the left-hand side. Here is another tradition that has no real significant bearing on today's world. Maybe in previous times when marriages could be used to unite warring families, it was

---

136 Not really.

nice to all start on the same side so you knew whom you were allied with in case a fight broke out. But unless a significant amount of the crowd is composed of vying Mafia families, then the odds of a ruckus are pretty remote. If ushers get this rule confused (as mine did in the first five minutes), no real harm is done. However, the ushers also have to remember that only immediate family members are to sit in the first few rows. Forgetting this rule *will* get the ushers into significant trouble. All that strutting the usher did earlier to give the hot-looking cousin a seat up front will come crashing down on him when he has to ask her to move in full view of a packed church. From stud to dud in no time flat.

Meanwhile, you and the best man are in a waiting room behind the altar. The minister will usually come in to give you a quick pep talk along the lines of "Have you really thought through the serious commitment you are about to make here?" You'd think he was the guy who was hired to give the pep talks to the Buffalo Bills before the Super Bowls.[137] What he is actually doing is making sure you really are willing to go through with the ceremony. He'll make sure the back door is unlocked, and if you don't bolt for it, he'll leave you two alone and get ready to begin. Pretty soon you'll hear the organ crank up, and then the wedding has begun.

When the ceremony begins, you'll be at the front of the church with the best man. You'll be staring out over the crowd when it hits you that no one is paying attention to you. Everyone—including your parents—is waiting for the entrance of the bride. The only way you'd garner any serious attention is if you spontaneously combusted. Maybe.

The processional music will start, and in walk the ushers arm in arm with the bridesmaids. For esthetic reasons, the ushers and bridesmaids are usually paired according to height. Heaven forbid you pair

---

137 If you are second best at anything, that is usually quite an accomplishment. In the Olympics, second place gets you a silver medal. For the Buffalo Bills, losing four Super Bowls in a row got them a litany of jokes. What do the Bills stand for? Boy I Love Losing Super Bowls. What do Billy Graham and the Buffalo football team have in common? They can both make a stadium of fifty thousand people say, "Oh, Jesus." How do you keep a Buffalo Bill out of your yard? Put up a goalpost. What do you call a Buffalo Bill with a Super Bowl ring? A thief.

them according to interests so that they can have a better time at the wedding and reception. Even though everyone is gathered for "your day," you can consider it an easy bet that the single ushers will want to be paired with the single bridesmaids. Single ushers are always hoping that the aura of love at a wedding, combined with their dapper threads (and more than a few drinks), might lead to a night of unwedded bliss.

When all the couples have entered, the maid of honor will walk in alone. After that, the organ will crank up "Here Comes the Bride," and everyone will stand to see the bride walk in with her father. If they are walking properly, it should take about twenty minutes for them to get to you. You should have plenty of time to go feed the parking meter or get a quick bite to eat.

When they do finally get to you, the father will offer her hand to you and then go take his seat. This act is known as "giving the bride away." The tradition dates back centuries to when women were considered one step above clean laundry. Your bride will quietly allow her father to give her to you so that you are now in charge of her. You will remember this moment well. Sure, there is a tremendous amount of happiness as you see the beautiful vision who is about to become your wedded wife. However, the moment is probably more memorable as the last time it looked like you were in charge. After this point, big decisions (as well as most little ones) usually need her stamp of approval. With luck, she'll allow you to pick the pizza toppings on your birthday.

The two of you will then approach the minister. First off, he'll say a few words about the sanctity of marriage. One minute, he'll be praising the power and beauty of love, and the next he'll be expounding on the pressures that can tear a couple apart. This schizophrenic roller coaster of a diatribe may not be the sugarcoated pom-pom speech you wanted, but it is closer to what marriage is really like. You'll then have a few people of your choosing get up to read a passage from the Bible. The people you pick are usually a couple of the runners-up for ushers or bridesmaids. For them, it is kind of like working like hell during off season and tryouts to finally make the big sports team in high school and having nothing to really show for it save a few splinters in the butt from keeping the bench warm. They don't get to wear the spiffy clothes, and they don't get to sit at the head table, but at least you threw them some bone of recognition. It goes without saying that the passages picked to read should have something to do with love rather than being lost in a desert or fire and brimstone raining down to level cities of sinners.

After that comes time for the vows. Here you can read your own vows or repeat what the minister says. These days, making up your own vows is trendy. "Trendy," however, does not translate into "good idea." You run many risks when you write your own vows. First and foremost, since this is one of the biggest moments of your life, you can bet your mind will be about as sharp as overcooked spaghetti. You'll barely remember how to tie your own shoes, so don't bet that you can remember those vows you wrote.

Another problem is that what sounded so deep and meaningful to you before (when you stayed up till 4:00 a.m. with a six-pack of Milwaukee's Best, beating your head against the coffee table trying to come up with something) may now sound either corny or pathetic. The third problem is that men tend to promise the moon, and women remember the vows verbatim and so can and will hold it against you at a later time. Meanwhile, your bride will craft vows that sound nice but don't commit her to anything more significant than not purposely trying to push you down the staircase. Even if she does make any big promises, men don't remember the vows, so it doesn't matter anyway.

Repeating what the minister says clearly has its advantages. If nothing else, it allows you to look up exactly what you've promised at a later date when your wife tries to convince you that it is your job as the husband to (a) check out any noise (real or fictitious) your wife hears in the middle of the night, (b) kill anything she wants killed (from a spider to a mouse to a bat to a coworker who wears the same clothes as she does, etc.), and (c) buy her feminine hygiene products. You'll still have to do what she says, but you at least won the argument for a Pyrrhic victory.[138] You can dance around the room doing your best Rocky Balboa impersonation savoring the moment, but

---

138 King Pyrrhus fought the Romans. In two of the battles he had with them, he won, but his losses were so devastating that he would have been better losing. It is kind of like kissing the most beautiful girl in the bar and then realizing her boyfriend and his friends would like to talk to you outside about redecorating your spleen.

then you'll have to put your head down and sheepishly perform the duty she has ordered you to do anyway.

The next stage of the wedding is the exchanging of the rings. First off, you've got to get the ring from your best man. Hopefully, he'll have remembered to put the ring in an easily accessible pocket that is not occupied by his keys, spare change, a prophylactic, or some other things that in his panic will not allow him to get the damn thing out. He'll hand you the ring, and you'll place it on your now-wife's finger as you repeat what the minister is saying. She'll then put a ring on your finger. Some recommend a touch of Vaseline on the ring so those of you with fat knuckles (you know who you are) can have it put on without dislocating the finger. No time for a two-minute timeout while you fight to get your ring on.

Then it is time to kiss the bride. Kissing the bride at the end of the ceremony sounds pretty easy. After all, you've done it countless times already. However, you haven't done it when being stared at by every important person in your life. You are about to kiss your wife, and that kiss is going to be judged by everyone in the room. If you kiss too short, people will deem you unaffectionate. If you kiss too long, you are deemed crass for displaying too much public affection. And then there's the approach. You've got to be smooth, self-assured, without rushing in so fast you head-butt her to the floor. You've also got to display sensitivity, so that means eyes closed. However, you should line up the target before the approach so you don't muckle on to her nose. There are no do-overs, so you'd better get it right.

Once the kiss is done, the organ will crank up, and that is your cue to leave the altar. Don't think your job is actually done at the church. You've got another hour of work to do before you get paroled and can go to the party. Take your bride arm in arm and walk at a normal pace toward the exit. Everybody will be standing and cheering like you just negotiated peace in the Middle East when all you did was repeat what someone else said and put a ring on someone else's finger. Rubbing your stomach and patting your head requires more coordination. The best man and maid of honor will be next, followed by the ushers and bridesmaids. At the entrance of the church, all of you are supposed to stop and set up the receiving line.

The receiving line is where everyone in the wedding party stands in a single row, and then each and every guest who attended the wedding gets to personally talk to every person in the wedding party. Conversation here is about as lively as chocolate-pudding night at the geriatric center, as groups have as much in common as members of the Teamsters and the Bolshoi Ballet. Yet each group will engage in a bit of forced small talk as they wait to shuttle to the next person. When the guests reach your wife, they all comment on how beautiful she is. Most male guests take this opportunity to kiss the bride. You are expected to sit back, smile, and let a string of men plant their lips on your new wife. There will be more germs passed here than in a New York City subway public restroom.

When the people finally get to you, you'd expect them to say something nice about, well, you—or even anything about you. After all, you got all spiffed up. You theoretically were part of the main attraction—at least it said so on the invites. Nope. After people gush to the bride about the bride, they step over to you and continue to compliment the bride. "Isn't she beautiful?" "What a lovely dress!" Yadda, yadda, yadda. The best you can hope for is a quick "Congratulations." The worst you can hope for is elderly relatives who pick this time to have an in-depth conversation with you about nothing in particular, or even worse, their health and bowel movements. One guy will start up a conversation with you about how the arthritis has really taken a toll on his shuffleboard game, while a woman may talk about how her garbage disposal is not acting properly ever since she put the remains of a KFC family feast down it. Your job is to politely shove them out the door so you can greet the next guest. If you don't expedite the line, it will move as slowly as a line at the DMV during lunch hour.[139]

---

139 The Department of Motor Vehicles may be the most despised government organization. Well, if it is fear then the nod probably goes to the IRS. And then if it is sheer disgust, that probably goes to Congress. Contempt? That depends on whether your party is in the presidency or not. OK, so beyond all that, the DMV is not loved. It is the organization that stands between you and the ultimate freedom in life—your driver's license. Whether you are registering your car or renewing your license, it will cost you bucks each and every time you walk in the door. That wouldn't be so bad, but the lines are something you'd more likely see in Disney World. Of course the only time you are able to get there, unless you take the day off, is lunchtime, and that is when they send everyone on break except one elderly lady who hasn't been able to hear properly since the Reagan administration.

After the guests have gone through the reception line, they head for the banquet hall. You have no such luck. You are being sent to purgatory. It is now time for pictures. Most men assume that taking the wedding pictures should last about fifteen minutes—tops. The Donner Party[140] had more giggles than you are going to have. Hopefully, you ate well earlier because you ain't going anywhere for a while.

The photographer first sets up the absolute-must shots. As discussed earlier, most of the wedding pictures you see in the wedding albums are shams. You basically have to relive every moment of the wedding you just went through, pausing at every junction so the photographer can take pictures. Once you've relived the entire wedding, stopping to pose ten minutes for every five minutes of wedding, you're still not off the hook. The photographer then takes pictures of every combination of people possible. He goes for the entire wedding party; just the groom and ushers; just the bride and bridesmaids; the groom and groom's family; the bride and bride's family; the bride, groom, and bride's family; the bride, groom, and groom's family. A wedding has more combinations than a pizza parlor.

All this is bad enough, but he can't just tell which people to stand together so he can take the picture. He's got to pose each and every person in each and every shot. No matter which position a person has his head in, the photographer thinks it is wrong and feels obligated to run up to that person and tilt it at the angle he finds appropriate. Personally, I learned to hold my head in an upright position in the first few months of my life and now consider myself fairly adept at this procedure. I thought I was well beyond needing lessons to learn to look at a camera. So why all of a sudden does some guy think I look so much better cocking my head at a forty-five-degree angle while jutting my chin out? Probably because he has to make it look like photography is an extremely difficult job. Otherwise, people will

---

140 No, the Donner Party was not a wild bash you'd see on MTV. It was a party of people in 1846–1847 who were crossing the Sierra Nevada on their way to California when they became snowbound. With no food, they resorted to cannibalism. Unfortunately, showing people eating each other would be more highbrow that what they normally feature on MTV.

wise up, and instead of paying him hundreds upon hundreds of dollars to keep pressing a button, they'll just get someone with a high-resolution camera to take pictures, and with the right software, they can e-mail everyone in the wedding party their own personal album.

Starting the Reception

Or

If You Aren't Having Fun, You

Better Pretend You Are

When you finally arrive at the reception, you are not allowed to walk in. You first have to be announced. Unless people really weren't paying attention, they should know your names by now. After all, your names *were* written on the invitations, the two of you *did* somewhat stand out in the church, and the guests weren't even allowed to leave unless they ran the gauntlet known as the reception line. Be that as it may, you and the bride, the wedding party, and both sets of parents will have to line up outside and wait to be called in by the DJ, assuming he hasn't lost the piece of paper with your names on it.

When the wedding party is all lined up outside, the DJ will put on some appropriate instrumental music and start calling people in. As mentioned previously, he *should* be well versed with the names. No matter how badly he screws up, there is nothing that can be done about it at this point. Usually the parents are first in, followed by the ushers escorting in the bridesmaids, and then the bride and groom. No need to do any slow walks—it is time to get the party going. The bride has sort of a rock-star aura to her, so everyone wants to talk to her and touch her. If the groom lets everyone who wants to greet the bride actually do so between the entrance and the head table, by the time the food is served, it is going to be colder than a polar bear's day-old turd. It is the groom's job to drag the woman through the crowd, potentially against her will as she doesn't want to deny her adoring admirers.[141] Everyone is waiting for dinner. There is the whole rest of the night for mingling.

While people are getting settled, the wait staff will be pouring the champagne toast. The irony here is that most people don't really like champagne. People say they do because they don't want to admit that they don't like something that is considered classy. But let's face it, what is really considered classy for food? Caviar is nothing more than fish eggs, escargot is snails, sweetbread is pancreas from cows that are under one year old, and truffles are an edible fungus. So when the toast actually happens, people will take the obligatory sip and then conveniently forget about the rest.[142]

The best man is supposed to get up and give a toast to the bride and groom. Keep in mind that while you were busy taking the last of the pictures, he hightailed it to the reception hall and tried not only to make up lost time in the alcohol department, but tried to get his blood-alcohol level to the point where he will feel "relaxed" giving the toast. Let's just hope relaxed isn't incoherent or inappropriate.

He's got two basic options. First off, he can go the serious route and end up giving a speech that is so generic and bland it could have been said at anyone's wedding. Pray that this happens. His other choice is to go for humor. He may describe some of the events and girls in your previous life that are hysterical when told in a fraternity basement, but lose a little charm when your entire family, elementary school teachers, and in-laws are now staring at you. What is worse

---

141 Did I mention that there is a Golden Rule of Planning a Wedding?

142 It seems to be a good idea for the champagne to just sit there on the table until the end in case people change their mind about drinking it; i.e. they've used up every bit of cash on booze and so have no choice, or they have effectively inebriated their taste buds to the point where it doesn't matter. The wait staff will more than likely remove the glasses after a while. It isn't a bad idea to remove unwelcome alcohol as there is often a teenage element that would drink paint thinner if they could get a buzz.

than talking about old wild girlfriends? Talking about wild times with the bride. While she is up there in a white dress, she is not going to think it is hilarious hearing about any potential earlier indiscretions, like if he caught the two of you getting friendly in the linen closet.

You then take your place at the head table. All the restaurant workers will start serving you immediately because you are hopelessly behind schedule. Here it is, 7:30 p.m., and that juicy chicken cordon bleu that the chef was told to have ready at 6:00 is now drier than the surface of the sun. Usually they will start with a salad. A big urge here is to mingle with the crowd and thank them for coming. Do this and the wait staff will whisk your food so fast you'll hear a sonic boom—and you'll need that food to slow down the alcohol to your brain. Restaurant workers get paid a few bucks an hour. They make most of their money on tips and per event. Therefore, there is very little incentive for them to give you time to eat your meal in a relaxed and dignified manner. As soon as you're finishing off one course, that plate will be whipped away and replaced by another. Take a bathroom break now and you'll have to order Domino's to get anything to eat.

At any time of the night, people may start hitting their glasses with the silverware. Once a few people start doing it, the lemming effect takes over and the entire crowd is clinking their glasses. When people do this, the bride and groom are supposed to kiss. Even if you are several tables over talking to some friends, you are supposed to find your bride and go kiss her. I recommend doing it. Not only does it make everyone happy to see the bride and groom kissing, but you may as well enjoy the last sign of public affection your wife is going to show in this lifetime. Leading up to this moment, spontaneous acts of passion could strike anywhere. You two could be at a movie, and the next thing you know, you could be in a passionate embrace. Now that you are married, when you go to the theater, you will watch the movie. As it stands from now on, any spontaneous outbursts of desire must be submitted in writing at least forty-eight hours before the event is to occur, and authorization for this is granted sparingly. It goes without saying that this spontaneous outburst will not occur around people she knows, if there are people allowed at all within eyeshot, and there can be no possibility of it being photographed or videoed.[143]

The wedding cake is usually a near work of art. How else can you explain why dessert cost hundreds of dollars? A set of paints is only a few dollars, but *Whistler's Mother* is worth millions. Apparently that is the same type of thing with eggs and flour. The cutting of the cake is yet another tradition for which people have to stop what they are doing and watch the bride and groom. Unlike many other wedding traditions, the cutting of the cake does not have a traditional song that goes with it. Therefore the DJ quite often plays a song like "The Farmer in the Dell" and changes the words to say, "The groom cuts the cake, the groom cuts the cake, heigh-ho, the derry-o, the groom cuts the cake." If that isn't ridiculous enough for you, the DJ then announces each and every movement by changing the words to this verse. It isn't like people need a soundtrack to every moment of a wedding so that people will understand what is going on.

The groom now has to make a momentous decision. When he feeds the bride, he has to decide whether to go against his natural instinct and politely feed his wife or do what he really wants to do and smear the cake all over her face. The bride knows there is a mental conflict brewing within her husband akin to that of an eight-year-old with a slingshot in a china shop. Therefore, she is usually giving the groom the evil eye so as to warn him not to do anything he will regret deeply and often. After the bride has spent months planning her perfect day, as well as hours getting her hair and makeup done and then donning an expensive snow-white dress, she does not have the sense of humor that the groom thinks she has.[144]

The best choice here is usually a compromise. You can feed her and then nip the tip of her nose when she's had a mouthful. Then it is her turn. When she picks up the piece of cake and shoves it so far

---

143 Including satellite photos.

144 Quite often, women are considered by the men in their lives as not having as robust a sense of humor as they themselves possess. Women would counter this with the suggestion that men think they are a whole lot funnier than they actually are. With the "pull my finger," nose flicking when we get someone to look down at their shirt, wet willies, etc., they may just have a point.

into your face that you'll be squeezing frosting out of your sinuses for the next several weeks, you then look like a wuss for being so nice to her. Better that, though, than getting her with the cake and having every guest be a witness to you upsetting your bride on her wedding day. If she gets upset, the whole crowd will turn on you like you're a wounded gazelle at a cheetah convention.

Once the cake is cut, the wait staff whisks it away, cuts it up, and serves it to the guests. The top tier is saved for the bride and groom. It is a tradition that part of the wedding cake be frozen and eaten on the first and tenth anniversary. I don't think I'm breaking any secrets when I tell you that that cake is going to taste heinous after sitting in the freezer for a year. It tastes somewhat like the inner sole of a sneaker, only a bit more difficult to chew. Who would start such a stupid tradition? I've got my bet on the antacid makers, although I guess it could be the refrigerator manufacturers. After all, that cake is going to take up nearly all the room in your freezer for nearly a year before you finally take it out and discover it is putrid. In the meantime, you're probably forced to buy a freezer chest to keep the real food in.

The myth used to be that the bride would throw her bouquet to the eligible women, and the one who caught it would be the next one to get married. The wife considers the bouquet she carried in the ceremony to have some sentimental value. She would no more let someone else have it than she would let another woman wear a long white dress to her wedding. You couldn't pry those flowers out of her hands with a crowbar and dynamite. Therefore, she'll have to buy a special alternative bouquet for throwing.[145]

When the time is announced for the throwing of the bouquet, several women will bustle through the crowd because they are desperate to get married and aren't going to take any chances on

---

145 Along with everything else at the wedding, nothing can be better than what the bride has. Therefore, the secondary bouquet she throws will be nice, but not that nice. For some women, they take this principle of not showing up the bride to an extreme. If you go to some weddings, the bridesmaid dresses are absolutely hideous. They could look like pink Hefty garbage bags. Of course these ridiculously self-conscious brides take the chance that they are so heinous that people can't take their eyes off of them, like not being able to stop watching a train wreck.

missing out on something that could cause them good luck in this department. They may be approaching the dance floor with a smile, but they are ready to instill an "accidental" world of hurt on other women who come between them and that bouquet. The second set of women is usually goaded to being up there by the married women who for some reason cannot abide having any friends who are single and happy.

All the women get into a line. The women who are desperate to catch the bouquet "somehow" end up smack in the middle.[146] The bride then turns her back to the crowd of women and tosses the bouquet. As the bouquet is flying in the air, you can look into the eyes of the extreme set and see each one of them calculating how bad it would look to knock down the seven people in her path, especially if one is the flower girl. Usually three is the maximum before they realize their antics would draw too much negative attention and likely show up on YouTube.

Once the bouquet has been tossed and caught, the bride then sits down on a chair in the middle of the dance floor. The groom is then supposed to remove her garter belt. With that flowing gown, it is not the easiest thing to find her leg, never mind something on it. You may think it funny to try to reach a little higher than you need to when searching for the garter, but your wife will not think this is amusing. There will be whooping and hollering from the guys in the room to do just that. They may even start chanting for you to go farther. It is best to remember that the night is young and you, at some point, will be alone with your new bride, and you may want

---

146 Hopefully, there aren't any younger women who want to play and amble in front of the more aggressive set of females dead set on catching that bouquet at all costs on the mystical assumption that it will somehow help them land a husband after decades of hopeless failures resulting from either telling the guy on the first date that she may already be in love with him and wants to be impregnated since her eggs are starting to shrivel, or how she hopes he won't disappoint her like the other men who mysteriously disappear after the first date as she is used to a lifetime of men inexplicably leaving. These women have to keep smiling so as not to show their desperation, but they want these kids moved. Sometimes, they'll do the "smile and hug" to the younger girl, like she is so happy to see her, but that hug moves the girl off to the side. If the girl then gets moved to another semidesperate woman, there is another smile and hug so that she eventually gets passed off to the side like a human hot potato.

her in a good mood. In other words, remove the garter quickly and efficiently.

The single men are then supposed to gather. They too can be broken into two groups. Unlike the first group of women who are desperate to get hitched, the most anxious group of guys are the ones who are looking over at the woman who caught the bouquet and want to put the garter on her leg. The second group of guys are the ones who just can't keep their competitive nature in check. If the woman is attractive, the edge goes to the first group. If not, then that second group just can't help going for it. She could be a shaved-down yeti, and these guys will go for the win while the first group dives out of the way.

So anyway, the woman who caught the bouquet sits down in a chair. The guy who caught the garter then approaches. The woman extends her leg, and the guy starts putting the garter on. Usually, the crowd is goading the guy on to put it as high as possible. That is, everyone but his date, who is going to make sure that he will pay for any enjoyment he gets out of this act. Oh, I should mention that the woman's date may also be less than pleased that people are chanting for another guy to feel her up. Therefore, the guy with the garter is in trouble one way or another.

After the hours your guests have spent waiting in the church and waiting in the reception hall, they are getting about as agitated as a hyperactive five-year-old chewing on coffee grinds. The crowd wants the party to begin. Too bad. Before everyone is allowed to finally start having a good time,[147] all the obligatory dances have to be danced. First off, the bride and groom have to dance to "their song." By the way, the art of dancing has been lost on this generation. Gone are the days when the couple could gracefully waltz across the dance floor swooshing and dipping. Nowadays, it is too much of a bother

---

147 For all the brides out there, I am *not* saying that people didn't enjoy the wedding after all the planning you did. I'm just saying that they can have a little personal fun right now. Yes, the people who came to your personal wedding are forever blessed to have had their eyes gaze on the radiance that was your presence. The vows they heard you utter will forever ring in their ears to give them solace in their darkest times. The love they experienced will forever warm their souls. Your personal wedding will be the highlight of their lives, even above their own. Feel better now?

to even keep one arm out to the side. Couples usually just hold on to each other's waists and spin in a slow circle that may or may not move to the beat of that song (or any song, for that matter). Not quite the *Ziegfeld Follies*.

When the song is finally over, it is time for the bride to dance with her father. Again the crowd is touched with a bit of sentimentality. Temporarily. The room quiets as the song starts and father takes daughter into his arms. "Daddy's Little Girl" or some other schmaltzy song plays, and the audience looks upon the sight of father and daughter. However, this mood dissipates faster than gin at a Shriners convention. After that song, it is time for the groom to dance with his mother. The music hasn't gone through more than five bars before the crowd again becomes bored. To you, it may be a touching experience, but to the crowd, it will seem like this song is longer than the time it took for the *Titanic* to sink. Once those songs are all done, the wedding party usually takes to the dance floor.

By this time, the older folks have given up on the idea of actually enjoying themselves at the wedding and have gone home because it is way past their bedtime. Meanwhile, the children who have come have now collectively lost their little minds. The kids are sleep deprived since they not only lost their nap, but are now losing their standard night's sleep. Since they skipped dinner and ate every piece of cake and ice cream they could get their hands on (and possibly drank the fancy ginger ale that all the adults left), their blood sugar is as high as a kite in a hurricane. By this time, all children will be doing their best impersonations of Woody Woodpecker, leaping all over the place banging into everything with their heads. The parents of these little cherubs have tossed in the white towel and given up on the idea of a quick dance together before leaving because the kids have sucked the life out of them.

So what do you do at this point? If you're really sadistic, you could have more specialty dances. One of the specialty dances you can have is what is known as the Dollar Dance. In this one, any of the men present can line up and pay to dance with the bride. These are the same guests who just chipped in for engagement gifts, wedding gifts, and are shelling money out to come down to see the ceremony, and you are shaking them down for their last couple bucks. The way it works is that the guy pays the best man a buck and then gets to dance with the bride for a good eight or nine seconds before he is bumped by the next guy. Meanwhile, the groom feels like he should be wearing gold chains, a loud, colorful suit, and maybe a hat with a feather in it if he is collecting money from men to be with his wife.

From here on in, the reception is supposed to be a party. However, both you and your wife are in about as high demand as doughnuts at a police station. Not only are you trying to enjoy some time with your new wife, but you should make an attempt to say hello and thank the guests who traveled to see you. After all, as a new couple who probably doesn't have much to start with, you are hoping they got you a cool wedding gift. The least you can do is remember the names of the people who showed up. You will also want to spend time with the ushers. By this time in your life, it is usually pretty rare that all your favorite buddies are gathered in the same place.[148] You are going to want to dance a few dances with your wife, and then as you are running over to do a shot with your buddies, you've got to stop at least at one table to ask how your guests are doing. It is here that the elderly relative tries to continue the arthritis/shuffleboard story he started back at the receiving line. At this point, you need a diversion. Look around the table to find some hapless person and ask if he has heard this fascinating story. When the relative turns to the victim to start the story over for his benefit, you leap away from the table like somebody just threw a grenade on top of it.

Before you know it, the reception draws to a close. Before your last dance comes up, you and the bride are supposed to go change into something less formal. Why, you may ask, since you expect the bride to keep these new clothes on until just nanoseconds after you can get her back to your room? Because you two will be heading off on your honeymoon, so you want to ditch the gown and suit.

Since the gown costs as much as putting an addition on your house, you really shouldn't be scrunching it up in your suitcase while you go on vacation. Instead, the gown gets packed way in the back of

---

148   If it isn't rare, it will be soon.

the closet where it can be properly ignored as it yellows. "Yellows?" you may ask. Yep. For a piece of clothing that women spend hundreds to thousands of dollars on, you'd think that the damn thing would age a bit better than deli meat. If a man spent that much money on a piece of clothing, it had better be wrinkle proof, stain proof, and bulletproof. The only clothing a guy owns that yellows is T-shirts that get heavy-duty armpit stains and underwear that…well, never mind that and let's get back to the bridal gown.

For those women who hate to see the yellowing, they can bring the gown to a dry cleaner who will treat it in some special way and then package it in a box to prevent this phenomenon. Then it can be put into the closet and properly ignored. Once again, I smell conspiracy. I wouldn't doubt that the bridal stores are paid a fair penny to spray on yellowing dust as the gown leaves the showroom. If this dust isn't removed, it slowly works its magic over the years. It's kind of a planned obsolescence: either the bridal shop gets a kickback from the local dry cleaner, or the gown yellows to the point it can't be worn by some future generation.

As for your suit, it is being rented by the day, so you are going to want to give it to someone who can be trusted to bring it back on time. Usually this honor falls to the best man. Is it because he is the most fiscally responsible? Is it because he is the most reliable? No. It's because he's usually broke, so he'd best get his tux in on time so he doesn't have to fork over any extra cash. If he remembers his, he'll remember yours. Usually.

Once the two of you are changed, then it is time for the last dance. Everyone usually makes a circle around the two of you as you dance to the final song of the evening. At first you think everyone is quiet because it is such a touching moment, but if you actually look up, you'll see that half the guests are out-and-out exhausted because it is frankly way past their bedtime, and the other guests are now realizing they are plastered to the point where they will have difficulty finding their room, never mind the person they came with. Therefore, it is best if you keep your eyes closed and pretend it is magical.

Section 3
Married Life

or

Married Life, Peacekeeper Missiles, Civil Disobedience, and Other Oxymorons[149]

---

149 Sure, we men may talk a tough game like life used to be so wild before marriage, and somehow we decided to give it up and walk down the aisle. Truth is, men are pretty useless without women and love being in love even if their ability to express it is closer to that of a member of the vegetable rather than animal kingdom.

Understanding Sex

or

The Birds & the Bees & Begging to Please

I f you were to ask men and women to list the most important aspects they are looking forward to in marriage, you'd get slightly different responses. Women would talk about the eternal companionship as they grow old together, the ability to share feelings on multiple levels, and the depth of empathy. Men think the other stuff is "nice," but sex is still the first thing they'd mention,[150] along with someone to make meals so they don't exist on grilled cheese and takeout.

All men will freely admit to the world that they personally are ultimate sex experts,[151] virtual sex machines they may claim, but they'd still rough up a Cub Scout if they thought the kid had some clue that they didn't about what really turns women on. Secretly, men are ridiculously insecure in that they fear they might be missing some magical technique to make women have mind-shattering multiple orgasms. I'm not talking here about the standard methods, but something hidden in an ancient scroll buried in a cave located in the

---

150 At least that is the way they would answer it if they were out of earshot of their wives. Otherwise, the men's answers eerily match their wives'.

151 Naturally, all men can't be the best. If you ask women, it clearly isn't the case that the average guy isn't so hot. How all these other men are so deluded, I'll never know.

Himalayan mountains; the man nibbles here while his left hand rubs there and his right foot massages this and his right elbow caresses that and—bingo—the woman is his lifetime sex slave.

Why are men so insecure? Because all men sucked like fish out of water when they first started to have sex. When it comes to a teenage boy, females were a greater mystery than the Bermuda Triangle. You see, all that men are taught in sex-education class is the very basics. They are shown how to wear a condom, told where the baby comes out, given a few words about VD, and then class dismissed. Is there any mention of what actually can make a woman climax? No. We are left to go through a painful process of trial and error that can leave both parties emotionally scarred for life. Some men get their hands onto porno tapes, and then they are really screwed up by the time they get a chance to be with a woman, doing things like dressing up like a pizza-delivery kid.

Usually the sex-education class was taught by a gym teacher who was about as qualified to teach sex as the pope. The guy wore sweats for a living, so he looked extremely uncomfortable as he stood at the front of the class with jeans and a collared shirt that had pit stains all the way down to his waist. His teaching technique quite often consisted of stammering and/or rambling for a while until he was finally able to get the film projector started. Since a budget for anything to do with sex ed got past the school board just about as easily as an introductory course in ritual animal sacrifices, the teacher had to rely on black-and-white movies made in the 1950s. These movies more often talked about how your body was changing and told you you'd better shower or you'd get zits. Somehow, you were supposed to intuit sex from that. That's like learning Egyptian hieroglyphics by watching music videos on MTV.[152]

In earlier times, if a student asked the gym teacher a personal question about his current sex life, the teacher usually would distract the class by screaming and pointing to the back of the room, and then, while everyone else looked back, he'd dive out the nearest window. That's why sex ed used to be taught only on the first floor.

---

152 In ancient-history class, it is taught that MTV actually used to play music videos. Go figure.

Nowadays, a school realizes they've got a tad more responsibility, so they put sex ed on a higher floor or at least nail the windows shut. So now the sex ed teacher has to take a different approach.

> Student: "My boyfriend doesn't like condoms, so I am using a sponge with spermicide. Do I have to worry about getting herpes?"
>
> Teacher: "Hmm, good question," he says as he contemplates whether he can survive a three-story drop if he tucks and rolls. "Why don't you take a few extra laps around the gym and that should help."

> Student: "I've been getting some severe cramping during my periods. Is there anything I can do about it?"
>
> Teacher: "Well," he says with his hand cradling his chin, "a few laps wouldn't hurt."

The History of Marriage

or

They Don't Call It the Bonds

of Marriage for Nothing

A t one point in our early evolutionary history, when all people looked like rejects from the World Wrestling Federation, men and women wanted about as much to do with each other as salt and a gaping abdominal wound. They each went their separate ways and only came together when it was time to breed. When that time hit, females released something into the air called a pheromone, which is Greek for "stupid time." A few molecules launched into the air, and you've got guys willing to kill, maim, threaten, annihilate, torture, etc., every other male within ten square miles of that female, all in the name of "love."

Meanwhile, the female goes into what is known as the estrous cycle. Unlike other cycles like motor-, bi-, and uni-, she stays put while the action comes to her. To say that a female animal is very receptive to sex during the estrous cycle is like saying that birds are receptive to flying when a cat is bounding toward them looking for an afternoon snack. During this time, a female would do nearly anything for sex. No holds are barred, no act is too dangerous, no attempts too ridiculous. You know, it's like an average day in the life of a modern guy.

Then an amazing thing happened in our evolutionary development. No, I am not referring to the invention of fishnet stockings. I am referring to the development of opposable thumbs. Opposable thumbs allowed us to hold on to things. To be better climbers, we could hold on to tree branches. To make tasks easier, we could manipulate simple tools. To give men something to do when the women weren't in their estrous cycle…well, let's never mind that.

Now that people had the ability to use tools, it became evolutionarily advantageous to become more intelligent so that they could use more sophisticated tools. Therefore, the brain size kept getting bigger. The problem here is that bigger brains meant bigger heads. That is why we ran into that little problem of childbirth becoming akin to trying to shove a basketball through a golf hole.[153]

The problem with getting bigger and bigger heads to accommodate these brains is that the birthing process looks less like the "Miracle of Life" and more like a scene from the movie *Alien*. Therefore, human babies have to be born prematurely. What do I mean by this? When a human baby is born, the only things it can do for itself are breathe, poop, and suckle. It is true that some women will claim that that is all men can do on Sundays, just substituting a beer for a boob, but that is beside the point.

Compare that to a baby kitten that is just itching for a fight moments after birth. For a human baby to be born at the proper time so that he or she isn't a twenty-four-hour-a-day blob of mental, physical, and emotional exertion, a woman would have to carry the child for approximately twenty months rather than the current nine. The only women willing to do this are probably into S&M activities like bondage, whips, and dating accountants.

So what is a female going to do with a completely dependent and helpless human being? Most women would say "divorce him," but I'm still talking about a baby here. Let's get back to our prehistoric roots. A woman of those times couldn't very well spend her time gathering food, finding shelter, protecting territory, etc., along with

---

153 I say "we," but women will ever so politely remind me that men have as much to do with the pain of childbirth as the guy who christens the ship has to do with building the damn thing.

the continual responsibility of child rearing. She needed to find a way to keep the male around to help her care for their offspring. So what could make a male give up freedom and accept significantly more responsibility? Why would a male choose to phenomenally increase his workload by now having to bring home food for a horde of people rather than pick something up on the fly, or build large shelters rather than kick back in the open air?

Enter a new phase in evolution: continual estrous. Human females may not be in heat continually, but they theoretically are able to have sex at any time rather than just once a month. The possibility—no matter how remote—that something could happen will keep the man around. There may be some debate among married men today about whether a guaranteed once-a-month sexual marathon is better or worse than the possibility of sex at any time of the month, but the choice is hers rather than his. It is kind of like giving up a guaranteed thousand bucks a month for some lottery tickets. Sure, you might end up becoming a millionaire, but there's a better chance of being struck by lightning—twice—while standing next to a leprechaun riding a unicorn.

At this point in evolution, the male was supposed to go off hunting and bring food home to the family. So how was a protohuman to do this when he was walking on all fours? Putting the kill in his mouth and dragging it back a mile or two may tenderize it a tad, but it also makes it a wee bit dirty, never mind putting a bit of strain on the teeth. Dragging things home became counterproductive, so another solution had to be found.

The male had to free his hands up so that he could carry food home. Therefore, we reached a point in our evolutionary history where people learned to walk upright. The male could then make a kill and carry food home to the family. The woman could hopefully show her appreciation by allowing conjugal visits that would mean more kids that would mean more food he has to bring home. It was a vicious cycle that would only end when he was so tired after bringing home enough food to feed the brood that the only thing hard were the calluses on his hands, which took away one of the advantages to those opposable thumbs.

Groups of people began living together so that men could share the hunt and women could share the responsibilities of child rearing and food gathering. Why did it get divided up this way? Because they flipped for it, and women lost the toss and had to stay home with the screaming kids rather than get the far more relaxing opportunity of battling saber-toothed tigers.

At some point, the idea of marriage came about. In gorilla colonies, the alpha male, who is usually also the largest, basically can have any female he wants. He even mounts the other males in a show of dominance.[154] Anyway, human beings have evolved past that. At some point, the other men in the tribe realized that it may be true that the strongest man could beat them up on an individual basis, but if they ganged up on him, they could knock the ever-living tar out of him. Even the weakest man could drop a pretty good-sized rock on the sleeping alpha male. That may not sound like a fair fight, but the male sitting there watching one guy having multiple females while all he had was his opposable thumbs didn't think life was particularly fair to begin with.

So back to the marriage thing. The alpha-male scenario was over. The idea of random sex had its problems. First off, the males could not tell which children were their own. More importantly, each male bothered the heck out of each woman by asking if he was "the best." After multiple crushing defeats of the male ego, everyone decided that monogamy was the best way to go. That way, it was only one woman lying to one guy.

The Bible has the first marriage as being between Adam and Eve. Adam was molded out of clay and brought to life by God. Most women will admit that this is an appropriate material for a guy to be made of, especially his will. Before Eve came along, Adam kicked around the garden doing not much of anything but naming animals. After a week or two of this, Adam started going a bit stir crazy. Considering that there are over five billion species of insects alone, you can imagine that this job lost its pizzazz fairly quickly. God then decided to give him a partner in life.

---

154 And you thought kicking sand in another guy's face at the beach was bad! Now, there isn't sexual contact, but it still isn't something to write home about.

Enter Eve. God knocks Adam out and does a bit of surgery by removing one of his ribs. You'd think that getting a woman would instead involve removing his backbone. So what happens to Adam and Eve? Rather than live a life in paradise, Adam becomes the first man to have his little head do the thinking rather than the big head.

The serpent appears to Eve and convinces her that she should eat the forbidden fruit. Why? She falls prey to being the first woman who was never satisfied no matter how good she had it. She takes a bite and then tells Adam to take a bite. The whipped individual that he is, he does bite, and then the party is over. After they get evicted from the garden, they go on to have a dysfunctional family in which one son kills another and then leaves them forever.[155]

Eventually, the church decided to get in on this marriage thing. Before that time, there were no game rules, and so nobody knew what exactly was expected of them when entering into a committed relationship. Because of this, there was total chaos. As an example, let's say that you are playing baseball, and you are abiding by all the rules of the game. Now let's say that your opponent is playing by a different set of rules. If she chooses to take twenty strikes while you take only three, then it will be difficult for you to compete evenly. Now let's say that she also decides that she can bring the baseball bat with her to first base and club the baseman into a coma so he drops the ball and she is safe. Again, this makes the playing field uneven. What the church did was come along and set up rules to play by—though whether they were the best rules is clearly up for debate. Since religion was ruled by men, you can be guaranteed that the rules heavily favored their side. Getting back to the baseball example, women may have a few extra strikes, but they had to now play blindfolded so could barely find the plate, never mind know when to swing.

In other words, the women, more often than not, got the raw end of that deal. Since the rules were set up so that the men got educated, had the jobs, and owned the land, a woman on her own had the

---

155 It is kind of depressing when you think about it. You'd think God's publicist would have told him that a happy ending tends to sell more books. And then you've got the movie rights. You've got to leave them wanting more in case they go for a sequel.

financial stability of a New York City bag lady. To top it off, the priest would patiently explain to women that the only way not to spend eternity in a magma lake being poked by an imp was to do what her husband said. If they didn't believe him, they could always read it in the Bible themselves…well, if they were allowed to read. Therefore, women were trained to be desperate for a husband, which was great for men since "desperate" and "standards" didn't need to go together. As long as a guy wasn't missing limbs, he was a catch.

So once a couple got married, sex was now considered acceptable. At this time, there were few ways to reap the joys of sex without reaping the, *ahem*, joys of parenthood. Sure, there were some tribes that had been able to curb the birth rate by taking advantage of the fact that sperm cannot live through high temperatures, and so men boiled their testicles to keep their sperm count down.[156] Most relied on what is known as the rhythm method, where the guy does not fully complete the act. People practicing this for long periods of time are commonly referred to as "parents."

---

156 I wish I was kidding.

The Art of Conversation

or

Talking for the Sake of Talking

M en and women have dramatically different views on what is meant by conversation. This point alone may be the greatest single reason for the difficulties between the sexes. To put it bluntly, men think conversation should have a point, whereas women think conversation itself is the point. When a guy comes home from work, the last thing he wants to do is relive every moment of his day verbatim. Yet this is exactly what women want to do, and so they expect that is what men should want if they weren't callous, insensitive slobs. Hence, you throw these two sexes together at the end of the day, and you generate enough electrical friction to rival the Grand Coulee Dam.

A guy comes home from work and wants to unwind. "Unwind" for him is another word for dropping about seventy-five IQ points and going into a near-catatonic state in his favorite comfy chair. If his brain were a computer, he'd be hitting the reboot button. If he can hurry this process up with a cold beer, then so much the better. That means watching TV, surfing the Net, or some other activity that does not require any outgoing communication skills. A woman, on the other hand, wants to discuss not only everything that happened to her, but everything that happened to all her coworkers. If her brain is a computer, she is backing up important files, doing a disc defragmentation, and upgrading for the tasks ahead. A guy just doesn't stand a chance against that. He can't even remember the names of the people he works with, and the woman expects him to keep all her friends' life stories straight from day to day.

There will be no getting around the work debriefing. His debriefing usually goes something like this: "Work suck. Boss suck." That is about it. Men haven't gotten past the troglodyte stage[157] in communication skills (and sometimes hygiene). When it is his wife's turn to launch into *As the Job Turns*, a man may need to refer to cheat sheets to remember who is mad at whom over what. Smart men will understand that this is the way she decompresses. Not giving her this time will not allow her to relax, meaning you may pay in another way, such as your dinner being more fit for use as a prison shank than for eating. She may also stop talking altogether. Some men may think they got their way when this happens. These men are about to get a lesson in geology. You see, a woman is like a volcano. If she continues to let off steam, then she is all right. If it builds up, she looks calm on the outside, but when she blows, she will be taking the countryside with her.

At some point, his wife is going to want some more significant verbal input on a man's part to ensure that he is actually part of this conversation. That is why he can't lose total concentration. He's got to train his subconscious to notice gaps in the conversation. If his wife has stopped talking, he had better start, or she'll read him the riot act (which can seem to last as long as a reading of *Moby-Dick*) and then repeat everything that was missed on the first go-around.

So what is he supposed to say at the point when she stops talking? Here he has to learn an advanced memory skill. He's got to quickly search that short-term subconscious memory and find out if she was talking about a male or female coworker. If the coworker

---

157 So, technically, a troglodyte isn't a real thing. In the movies, they had troglodytes as these hairy, brutish cavemen that usually had a single horn coming out of their forehead. I can guarantee you two things on this issue: (1) they have never found a skeleton matching this description, and (2) women don't need men to be any hornier than they already are.

was male, he should make the mental assumption that if she wants his opinion about another man, that man must have done something wrong. Therefore, the husband says something like "What was he thinking about?" That should cover most situations the guy could have gotten himself into. If she was discussing a woman, he should say something like "And she put up with that?"

That will not only cover situations where that particular woman was correct, but will also work in situations where there is a disagreement between two females. The rule of thumb is that when there is a disagreement between a male and a female, the male is always wrong. If the two individuals are female, then one of them may possibly be wrong—however, there usually is a male lurking in the background of the scenario who is ultimately at fault.

Many men may not like the idea of continually "admitting" that being male is the equivalent of being at fault. These men will offer reasons why the man supposedly at fault in the latest office drama held his point of view. He can back up this argument with facts, figures, online searches, bar charts, horoscope readings, etc. What does a man accomplish by sticking up for other men? Does he stand the remotest chance in hell of convincing the woman that a guy can be correct? About as much chance as convincing a cow that eating grass is boring.

I should pause to note here that I am *not* comparing women to cows. I hate to admit it, but if anyone resembles cows in the home, it is men. We need to be herded to and from the kitchen at dinner. If there is a kid's sporting event or concert, it is usually the wife who reminds the guy for the seventy-fifth time and makes sure he is ready to leave at the right time. Four stomachs and a low-watt brain? Yeah, we are guilty as charged.

The only thing that arguing will accomplish is interminably dragging out a conversation the guy didn't want to be having in the first place. In the blue-moon chance that a man wins the argument due to some indisputable evidence, he is faced with a hollow victory. For the rest of the day, the man will end up getting the cold shoulder. He should know that this is the only piece of a woman's anatomy—and the only temperature—he'll be getting. He can stick to his beliefs and position as long as he likes, but that's not going to end the nuclear winter that has settled over his household.[158]

An incredibly difficult problem to get over is the difference between what a woman says and what she means. Ever hear of the phrase "no means no"? Well, it is phenomenally important to obey while dating, but you can throw that one out the ever-lovin' window once you're married. When a man asks questions like "Do you want to talk about it? Did I do something wrong? Are you upset?" a woman may answer, "No." The man may take her word for it and merrily skip off to go watch reruns of *Baywatch*. Meanwhile, the woman is so mad she has become capable of spitting acid so caustic that silverware would melt in her mouth. If a guy even thinks he may need to ask if there is an issue, then the answer is a colossal "YES!"

So what is a man to do when a woman says that there is no problem and that she doesn't want to talk? He should do what she wants him to do, and that is to *beg* her to talk. The vast majority of men don't realize this, and their marriages suffer. They know that when *they* say they don't want to talk, that means that they (gasp!) don't want to talk. When a woman asks a man if he wants to talk about a problem, and he says no, she naturally assumes that he actually does because she would certainly say no but mean yes. She'll then keep pushing the guy to talk as she would like to be pushed to talk, and the guy will eventually get frustrated. She will then get mad at him because he did not make it clear that he really didn't want to talk.

When a woman says she doesn't want to talk, and the man figures out that she does want to talk and does the requisite pleading talk to get her to talk even though he really doesn't want her to talk, she will then talk. A woman, now feeling that her husband really does want to listen, will then start discussing the problems of the day. Here is where men make another critical mistake. When a woman talks about her problems, a man usually jumps into the middle of her

---

158   To be fair to women, it should be noted that men are often sore winners and poor losers when it comes to everything else. A guy loses so much as a game of cribbage to his wife, and he may be smiling on the outside, but his insides feel like he has been fed a diet of lemon juice and razor blades. Heaven forbid he wins anything, and he is strutting around the house like he just won an Olympic gold medal in studliness.

conversation and offers what he thinks is the appropriate solution to her dilemma. Thinking that he is then done with his job of listening, he skips over to the fridge, cracks open a beer, and tries to catch the tail end of the slo-mo chest-heaving beach rescue on said *Baywatch* show.

If two men are discussing a problem, the point of this discussion is to solve said problem. Once said problem is solved, men stop talking. A woman does not want to hear answers to her problems. In fact, she doesn't want to hear anything at all from him. She wants him to sit there and listen. That is how a woman sorts through her emotions of the day. After a stressful day, a man shuts down, and a woman opens up. Throw a few kids running in and out between your legs chatting incomprehensibly, and you really get lost trying to stay quiet while getting the kids to be quiet so you can understand what the heck your wife is saying.

Are there other words or phrases a female says besides "no" that a man has to watch out for? Does a shark have any teeth? Does Boston have any drivers willing to give you the finger?[159] Women have so many words or phrases that mean things so completely different than you'd ever find in *Webster's Dictionary* that they should qualify as having their own language.

An example may be in order. Let's say the husband and wife are going to go out to dinner. If he doesn't particularly care where he wants to go, he may ask her if she has a preference. She may respond, "I don't care." She'll say this even if she knows the exact dish at the exact table served by the exact waiter at the exact restaurant she wants to eat. A man will then blindly make a suggestion, at which point the woman will say she is "not in the mood" for that restaurant.

---

159 Depending on how you look at it, Boston has the best or worst drivers in the country. The signs with numbers on them in other places around the country are known as "speed limits"—in Boston, it is the number that if your car hits this minimal limit, they are allowed to plow you off the road. All people there can drive with one hand wildly gesturing out the window in what is *not* the universal sign of peace and the other leaning on the horn—I don't know if they have mastered the ability to drive with their knees or how they stay on the road. In Boston, if your car has not issued a sonic boom when entering from a ramp or if you aren't within a slice of cardboard away from the next guy's bumper, they consider you a speed bump. Most people can't even pat their head and rub their stomach. Boston drivers can do all the above while texting and changing the radio station.

He'll then have to keep going down the list of restaurants until he happens upon the one she was thinking of in the first place.

Time is not an object to the woman. He may have to pore through the Yellow Pages[160] to get to the correct restaurant, but she will patiently keep rejecting each and every restaurant until he gets to the correct one. Why would a woman perform this macabre charade? Because she wants a guy to be "decisive." She also wants to get her way. Unfortunately in the long run, this guessing game has the reverse effect. Any decisiveness is beaten out of a guy. After several years of marriage, it is a wonder a guy can even figure out what condiments to put on his own hot dog without asking.

In woman-speak, a woman will often ask questions when she wants to tell a man to do something or (more likely) correct his errant behavior. If a guy comes out of the bedroom dressed for the day, and his wife says, "Are you wearing that?" Well, of course the man is wearing the clothes! Does she think that he fell into his closet and there was enough static electricity to have clothing adhere to his body so it actually looks like he is wearing them? Does she think a man likes to take random clothes for a bit of a stroll around the house before he puts on his real outfit?

She is not wondering anything. She is telling him that the attire he is now wearing clashes like Black Panthers and Ku Klux Klan members at a pajama party. She is also telling him that *he will* march back into the bedroom and put on a different outfit. When a man realizes that he has lost veto power in dressing himself even though he has been doing so most of his life, it is a somewhat humbling experience. She may as well help blow his nose. Heaven forbid if the guy then returns with another outfit that is rejected. He then feels like a two-year-old who can't figure out what side of his underwear belongs in the front.

A woman can also say something like "Are you going to serve that to the baby?" Let's say that you have food in a bowl with a bunny at the bottom of it, and you are heading toward the child you just strapped in the high chair. Chances are fairly high that you were

---

160 That is dating me. The only thing yellow pages are good now for is leveling the legs of furniture.

probably going to give the contents of that bowl to said child. A man's job is then to figure out exactly what he was doing incorrectly.

Looking down into the bowl, he may realize that the food chunks are about the size of the baby's fist and would get lodged immediately in said baby's esophagus if he could possibly fit it into his mouth, or it is so hot from the twenty minutes in the microwave that it is still bubbling. If he does not know what the problem is, then he should pretend he does. For the man who does not want to allow his wife the condescending attitude she will naturally assume, he can pretend that the food was actually for him.[161]

Whenever the question a woman asks appears obvious, the answer never is. What she expects as the correct response will either incriminate the man or make him feel like a moron. Why do women do this? Because the answer will either incriminate the man or make him feel like a moron. 'Nuff said.

---

161 Note: strained apples and chicken is not all it's cracked up to be.

Differences in Entertainment

or

If the Wallet Doesn't Open,

It Doesn't Count

When the couple decides to have a night of fun together, they usually have very different ideas of what they mean. For a man, that means dragging the woman into the bedroom. For the woman, it means to stay as far away from the bedroom as possible. She even (gasp) wants to be out of the house entirely and (ungh) spend money. To her, sex can theoretically happen any day, so "special" means to go out and do something different. To him, "special" means they order pizza from the fancy pizza place.

So what do women want to do when they go out? Dinner and dancing is quite a popular thing for women to want to do when they think of a special evening. To a guy, the dinner part is no big deal. After all, dinner magically appears for him every day at dinnertime. Sure, he may have to "help" a bit by reminding his wife how hungry he is, but it is always there. Heck, if things are hectic, takeout is only an app away. No, to a woman, getting dinner means going out to a restaurant and sitting down at a table with people waiting on *her* for a change. The idea of nothing to clean up after eating is a minor version of heaven to many women.

As to loving to dance, this idea puzzles many men. You'd think women would have enough of the rhythmic swaying thing when they vacuum and dust.[162] The problem here is that most guys just can't get into dancing. Men may complain about the style of music or having to get dressed up or that he's paying a significant amount of money for the ability to move back and forth in a two-foot-by-two-foot area, but the fact is that they are afraid of looking stupid. They look around the dance floor at the guys who keep a beat about as well as a man being electrocuted. Then they worry that they'll be yet another man flailing around on the dance floor doing the married man's shuffle, where every sense of rhythm has left their bodies, and they just step back and forth looking like they are in desperate need of relieving their bladder.

If men are asked to go country line dancing, then it is a different story. They do not think they'll look stupid. They know they'll look stupid. Any man doing the "tush push" or "slappin' leather" by definition is open to ridicule. Even uttering these dance moves out loud is enough to qualify for a purple nurple from the closest male person.[163]

Because of this, most men flat out refuse to do any line dancing. These men are continually harassed by their wives to get up with them to dance. They are the intelligent ones. Some men break down under the pressure and finally head onto the dance floor, especially at a wedding. Within the first two minutes, the guy has hip-checked his aunt into the hors d'oeuvres table, opened a major head wound to his niece with his elbow, and stepped on his wife's foot enough

---

162 I would consider it a life saved if any man reading this does not point out dirty swaths of carpet behind the couches in lieu of taking his wife out when she asks to do something.

163 A purple nurple is an act done only by men on other men and is hopefully confined to junior high and, even there, only to a select few individuals. It is when one guy goes up to one of his friends, grabs his nipple, and twists as hard as he can. The idea is that unexpected pain is somehow linked to being construed as a humorous event. Throughout the history of men, this is the best idea they have come up with for the usefulness of male nipples.

times to pulverize most of the tarpals, never mind having all his buddies bestowing humorous nicknames on him.[164]

So what can couples do together that they both like? Guys like going to sporting events. Many women would rather receive reverse liposuction than go to see a live sporting event. Football is no fun to some women because they don't understand the rules.[165] To them, it looks like one guy mounts another, gets a warped ball passed to him, he hands it to another guy, and then a bunch of guys climb all over each other, a whistle blows, and they pat each other on the butt. To these women, they may as well watch a movie about Caligula.[166]

Baseball? Rather than pat each other, the athletes are always adjusting themselves. Who knew that something men are born with and have lived with all their lives needs to be repositioned after every pitch or swing of the bat? Throw in the hot dog and beer that costs as much as filet mignon at most fancy restaurants, along with the realization that the game moves as fast as frozen molasses, and women really have a spiffy time. Hockey is even worse because women like to be comfortable when they go out. The idea of sitting in a cold arena on a cold seat drinking cold beer does not leave them hot. Then you've got pro wrestling and monster truck shows, which, believe it or not, women don't even consider *real* sports. Go figure.

So watching sports is out. What about playing sports? If a woman has spent several hours in the bathroom working on her appearance and another hour picking out her wardrobe, chances are about as high as a dachshund's testicles that she is going to want to run around

---

164 Perhaps, "the Wayne Gretzky of the dance floor" or "Dread Astair."

165 Let it be known that I am not saying women can't understand football. It is just that many don't want to. The idea of getting to know something so that you can fritter away an entire Sunday as well as Monday (and sometimes Thursday nights) obsessing about something out of your control—or worse—joining fantasy leagues where you pretend to have a team by drafting them with a group of your friends so that you can have an imaginary league to obsess about the rest of the week—is a phenomenal waste of time on par with trying to count the grains of sand in the Sahara Desert or, worse, beer cans at a NASCAR tailgate.

166 Caligula was the third emperor of Rome and known to be a bit more on the eccentric side. Some examples would include making his horse a senator, claiming to have fought a battle (and winning it) with the god Poseidon so that his war chest was all seashells, having himself declared a god, and, from some accounts, having affairs with his grandmother and sister. And you thought current politics was a little on the seedy side...

getting sweaty. Naturally, there are many women out there who love to play sports and are phenomenally good at it. When these women play, they are not usually there in a dating capacity. These women are smart enough to know, as discussed previously, that most men are neither good winners nor good losers. Therefore, an evening of fun with a guy has to involve something where whining and gloating cannot be factored into the discussion.

Museums? Men are generally not the most culturally sophisticated beings on the planet, so their idea of art is usually pictures of women lying on cars. Going for a walk? That would involve, well, walking. So that usually leaves going to the movies. Now all you have to do is pick which one both of you would actually enjoy. Piece of cake.

Differences in Fixing Things

or

Repair Despair

A s mentioned earlier in this section, the ability of the human species to learn how to make and use tools was a pivotal event in our evolutionary process. Men of course believe that if some tools are good, then a whole freakin' lot must be better. Men love tools like dogs love sticking their noses in other dogs' business. Most men believe that there is no such thing as enough tools, even if they have no idea how to properly use the ones they have.

You can basically break men up into three groups: (1) men who walk around hoping that something breaks so they can get their tools out and fix it; (2) men who have plenty of time to go out and buy tools, but not quite enough time to actually fix anything; and (3) men who hope nothing breaks, ever, lest they become exposed as incompetent in the whole "fixing things" department. As time passes, the latter group is becoming more and more prevalent. I, personally, am their president. If there is a leak that needs to be fixed, I can get my tools and, in no time flat, make it far worse than it ever was before. Give me enough time, and the leak can become an indoor Jacuzzi.

An incompetent male with tools has several problems. The first is that no matter how bad he is, he usually refuses to let his wife do the job, lest he be exposed as less than what society deems a real man. He would rather electrocute himself than have his wife install a new dimmer switch. The second option is to call a professional. That is also bad as it usually ends up that the longest part of the guy's visit is tallying the bill. As if that isn't bad enough, the professional usually has a smug look on his face when he presents the bill at a labor rate of $120 per hour that he had to round up to after just five minutes of work.

Unfortunately, the third problem is usually the worst—invariably if a guy is unhandy, his father-in-law is a phenom with tools. It doesn't matter if a man is a powerful attorney who makes a six-digit salary. If his father-in-law comes over and sees a hole in the wall from a child who did not successfully round a corner when running at top speed with socks on[167] or a door that doesn't close properly, he'll give the guy a look of disgust that will easily convey that he is at an utter loss as to why his daughter would want to mix her gene pool with his.

Women are phenomenally different when it comes to tools. In fact, you don't even need to use the plural form of the word when it comes to most women. If there were such a thing as a tool chest just for women, you could open it up and find only a butter knife. For a woman, that is the only tool she needs. It can be a screwdriver, pliers, wire cutter, etc. To a woman, it is the ultimate wonder tool. To a man, it is a butter knife. He'd no sooner use a butter knife as a tool than he would use a blowtorch to weld a hole in a full gasoline tank. If there is a second tool to be found in the average woman's toolbox, it is usually a shoe that can act as a hammer. Given enough time and women, with butter knives and shoes, they could make an exact replica of the Eiffel Tower.

When it comes to kitchen tools, also known as utensils, the exact opposite is true when it comes to food. If something needs to be cut,

---

167 My house had a hole in the wall from the kids, and it was there for months. Every now and then, I'd walk by it and nod thoughtfully, but I had absolutely no idea to fix it. Nailing a piece of plywood over it didn't seem to be the best choice, and hanging a picture at knee level would have drawn a fair amount of suspicion. My wife eventually took care of it one time when I was on a business trip. I had to admit that she did a wonderful job. Naturally, my eldest slipped just days later and put a hole back in nearly the same spot. Yep, there is only one area where my wife considers me "handy," and that is usually not related in any way to the word "helpful."

a man will grab the closest knife and start hacking away. Men know of a total of two knives: butter and sharp. If they are carving into a steak, then they use something sharp. Otherwise, they go for the basic butter knife. Women? They've got bread knives, pastry knives, paring knives, carving knives, and a host of others. If they sold one knife for cutting chicken and one for cutting steak, a woman would decide that she would absolutely need both to function properly in society.

Each knife has its own purpose and place in the kitchen. A guy can certainly learn what the different types are, but making him care is another story. Do you think a guy would actually take up an extra five seconds searching through one of the kitchen drawers to find a special knife to cut his pastry? I think not. Most women are simply grateful that men use utensils at all while eating.

When it comes to instructions, women tend to read them sixteen or seventeen times before beginning the project. They should be able to quote them verbatim before starting. Usually men pay as much attention to the directions as they would to movies on Lifetime. Those men who do read the instructions do so like they are cheating off of the smart kid's paper during a high school test. A few quick glances here and there, pretending like they don't actually need them. When the bicycle he is trying to put together begins to look like something from a modern art exhibit, a man will finally break down and read the directions.[168] If at that point he still can't figure out how to put the thing together, it clearly must be the fault of the person who wrote the directions. That person—whoever he may be—is a complete idiot who couldn't properly write the way to wipe himself, never mind how to put anything with more than six pieces together.

What happens if the wife offers her help interpreting the directions? The man would rather eat them than let the woman even be allowed to read them. If she gets a hold of them and is able to make sense out of them, then the man is wrong and the woman is right. Since putting things together is a "man's job" to many men, that third testicle known as an ego gets an uppercut that has it on the ropes begging for the towel to be thrown in. Therefore, the woman

---

168 It is a good realization with men that it may be important to put things together properly, as in a bicycle, where the handlebars may come off when the child is near traffic.

has about as much chance getting her hands on these directions once a man deems them hopelessly confusing as General Manuel Noriega has of landing a job as the next spokesperson of Clearasil.[169]

---

169 Manuel Noriega was the dictator of Panama from 1983 to 1989. He was notably known as the "Pineapple Dictator" because his complexion was so horribly bad. Using his face as a dart board would have only improved his looks.

Differences in Understanding the Rooms

or

Why Do They Call It Sharing a House When Everything Is Hers?

Each room in the house has a distinct meaning for each sex. It may be appropriate to quickly go through the differences so you'll know what to expect. We'll start with the bedroom. To the woman, this is her wardrobe room. If someone were to open up the bedroom closet, they'd find 75 percent of it devoted to her clothes and 25 percent devoted to his clothes…and the woman is eyeing that 25 percent with a gleam in her eyes. Her stuff has packed every ounce of available space. Meanwhile, he's got his one good suit actually on a hanger, while the rest of the clothes are usually lying in a crumpled heap on the floor with about as many wrinkles in them as the Dumpster behind a Beverly Hills plastic-surgery ward. The woman has also got bureaus of additional clothes and a vanity mirror in case she needs to apply enough makeup to get to the bathroom so that she can put her full daily ration of makeup on. And that is the bedroom. Oh yeah, and she sleeps there, too.

To the man, sleep is the first thing he thinks of when he thinks of the bedroom, or at least being in a horizontal position on the bed. However, the bedroom is much more to him than just this. For instance, it is also his laundry room. Usually his side of the bed is strewn with dirty socks, underwear, and shirts that he haphazardly kicks off at night as he climbs into bed. The pile is usually so large that one gets a nosebleed if attempting to climb it. He can claim it is a safety feature as it makes it impossible to fall out of bed and get hurt, unless you call what happens to your olfactory sense an injury.

What if a woman refuses to wash the clothes unless the man actually puts them in the hamper? No big deal for the guy. He'd walk around the house with no underwear and coffee stains on his shirt until his wife couldn't stand it anymore (or knew that company was coming) and she'd end up washing everything anyway.

The bathroom is another room that has multiple purposes. The woman does use it to eliminate her bodily wastes, if she would ever admit to having any bodily wastes. More importantly to her, it is like the Batslide seen on the old *Batman* TV show, dramatically changing her outfit and identity. She goes into the bathroom in the morning wrapped in a tattered robe thinking she looks like a gorgon[170] with an attitude and emerges like she is about to strut down a catwalk. You'd be amazed at the transformation, except that it took more time than it took Hollywood to transform Lon Chaney Jr. into the Wolf Man.[171]

The woman has been able to fit a small pharmacy in the bathroom by using every conceivable space. All drawers defy the laws of physics by holding two or three times their volume. No one can see counter space under the hoard of bottles. Luckily, they don't put makeup in bottles with suction cups, or there would be bottles stuck

---

170   The most famous Gorgon was Medusa. Basically, the Gorgons were hideous women with snakes for hair. One look at them would turn a man to stone. Legend goes that Prometheus went to her island that was full of statues of men and cut her head off by seeing her reflection in his shield. Why was the island full of guys who knew that they may be going to their death? Unfortunately, there was a miscommunication with the snake thing on hearing there was a lot of tail on the island when it came to women.

171   In the days before computer-generated special effects, things took a bit longer in the movies. When it was filmed for Long Chaney Jr. to turn into a wolf man, he had to sit in a chair for ten hours while they glued yak hair to his face one strand at a time, and they'd take film and splice it together so you'd see him get hairy. This time-lapse photography could work for all men—just take a picture year after year and splice it together, and you'll see hair sprouting in places you'd never imagine possible (while it is lost in the places they actually want it to be).

to every inch of wall space as well. She has got the medicine cabinet stocked with everything but medicine. The man will be allowed two square inches of space in the medicine cabinet—enough for under-arm deodorant, a razor, and shaving cream. But hey, that is all a guy needs. Any more room is as useful as additional butt hair.

So if the bathroom is akin to the Batcave for women, then for men, it is the Fortress of Solitude. It is where men actually read some-thing deeper than the *TV Guide*, not that anyone reads the *TV Guide* anymore. You used to be able to tell how long a guy was going to be occupying the room by the literature he brought in. If it was the expanded Sunday paper, then there would be other family members whose bowels would explode before they were able to see the in-side of the bathroom. With cell phones, all bets are now off.

There is one room of mystery to men. It is a place they have heard of but never seen, shrouded from sight like the mythic Shangri-la. Men believe in its existence, for they can see the miracles it creates. Naturally, the place I refer to here is the laundry room. Yes, most men couldn't find the laundry room with a map, flashlight, and pith hel-met. Meanwhile, women learn to despise the laundry room like there is an invisible chain always dragging them back.

Why don't women show men the secrets of this land so they won't be the useless sacks they naturally are when it comes to dirty laun-dry? Because like the secret of atomic power, it can be abused if it falls into the wrong hands. Any man's hands near a washing machine when a woman has her delicate clothes nearby can immediately be considered an imminent disaster. You may as well paint yellow lines down your body and lie down in the middle of a highway—abso-lutely nothing good will come of it.

A room that men and women can actually agree upon for its func-tion is the kitchen. The kitchen is for cooking, plain and simple. Men and women may disagree as to what qualifies as cooking (reheating something already prepared versus making something actually new), but this is the room they do it in. A significant amount of tension swirls around this room. In the olden days, a man really didn't enter this part of the house. He didn't do any cooking whatsoever. Heck, he'd yell to his wife to get him a drink if she was down the street at her neighbor's house and he had is carcass lying in the next room on the sofa. Women put up with this because the kitchen was the one place they could go without the guys trying to get their paws all over them.

These days, however, women do not want to be domestic slaves to the men. That means that men have to fend for themselves in the kitchen (sometimes). Women have to pretend they're OK with this, but after thousands of years of controlling the food-preparation area, they are just a wee sensitive about what the heck a guy is going to do in there and how much of a mess he can make that she'll later have to clean up. It is no secret that women have a particular place for everything in the kitchen. Each drawer has its own special purpose, and mixing of the drawers is met with the same trepidation as mixing heavy drinking and repairs to a running lawnmower.

The problem here is that the guy doesn't care about the order of the kitchen. He may place a sharp knife in the drawer with the spatulas. Then when the woman is cooking, she can't find anything and gets quite irate about it. But by the same token, doesn't it mean that the guy will also have trouble finding things and so will experience the same frustration and learn from it? Theoretically, yes. However, that theory has two dramatic flaws: (1) he so rarely cooks that waiting for him to get his posterior back in the kitchen to do more than nuke some pseudofood is like waiting for Arnold Schwarzenegger to win the Academy Award, and (2) when a guy can't find something within the first fifty nanoseconds, no matter if he is the one who misplaced it, he just calls for his wife, who then comes in and frustrates herself trying to find it.

The dining room causes some confusion for men. They never eat in there because it is difficult for them to grasp the concept of eating a full meal when not in front of a television. If men are forced to sit around a dining table to eat, they know they will be forced into actually having a conversation. Men don't want to have the brain engaged while eating. It is like trying to simultaneously pee and text with two hands—it can be done, but not without consequences. If the guy is concentrating on his food, his brain is throwing any random thought up to keep a conversation going. Eventually, he has said something ridiculous, like how thin his wife's sister looks when she is standing next to her or how tired he is lately because he, unlike his wife, has a *difficult* job. If his brain were fully engaged, then his self-censoring program would be up and those thoughts would never be uttered. Instead, she's mad, and he's left alone in the dining room without television or a conversation. If he pays attention to the conversation, then the food goes colder than a hockey puck (and about as chewy) so he doesn't eat it, and she gets in a tizzy for that.

So what does a dining room mean for a guy if it has nothing to do with eating? For some families, it is the place to show off the things that they never ever use and don't even want touched. They may have a china hutch where all their fancy plates are shown off like they are Van Gogh paintings. There can also be crystal candle holders with candles that never get lit. There could even be expensive family antiques set up for display here. The general idea is that when walking into this room, you immediately feel uncomfortable since you could accidentally bump into something and cause a maximal amount of damage in a minimal amount of time. Because of this, people spend as little time as possible here, and so its mission is accomplished—it is the one room that stays clean amid all the chaos everywhere else. If guests come over, they can have blinders put on and walked to this room as if all places in the house are this sterile.

Other families go the other way and use the dining room as a drop zone. The mail gets dumped on the table, homework for the kids gets lost under piles here, permission slips are hopelessly buried and unsigned, hats and gloves enter a black hole here, etc. Once the pile on the table gets too high, they can start using the chairs as satellite refuse collectors. For these families, the room is a scene out of *Twister*. The idea of eating in the room is a simple physical impossibility akin to having a bikini contest in Pakistan—theoretically possible, but destined to end in disaster.

The living room has become the central room of the household. Needless to say, it is because it has a television. The television is so important in today's society that it has made the living room the omnicenter of the house. People eat there, take naps there, fold laundry there, etc. I'm sure most men would throw a porta-potty in there if their wives would let them.[172] The main piece of furniture in the room is the couch. The only thing a man cares about when getting a couch is size: it must be long enough for him to fully stretch out so he can take naps or sleep on it in case he needs an early nap to store up the energy to climb the stairs to bed.

Any other furniture should also have a direct line of sight to the television. One may be tempted to get good furniture since so much time is spent in this room. Not a good idea. Since it is used as a dining room, there will invariably be food spills. Milk doesn't smell so good after the seventh spill on the upholstery in ten days. Then there are the kids tossing the cushions, jumping on them, building forts with them—everything possible to warp them into a ball-like shape. Therefore, the furniture should be near disposable since it will be beaten to death.

---

172   Not only would a porta-potty be a bit of an eye- as well as nasal sore in the living room (and yet another massive thing to clean), but you just know the guy probably still wouldn't close the door and miss those precious few television seconds—and no one should be exposed to watching that, especially if company is over. The aim may be bad already, but throw in the idea that he is looking over his shoulder rather than forward at the business at hand, and you'll have to wear a pair of galoshes to ever walk in the room again.

Differences in Compliments

or

If You Don't Notice the Haircut,

You Will Notice the Attitude

Most women love to be complimented—that is, by everyone but their husband. I'm not saying that a husband should not compliment his wife. According to her, she is the *only* person he should be complimenting. Not complimenting her will get him into the doghouse faster than a cheeseburger through a vegetarian's digestive tract. You see, women want compliments from their husbands, but they just don't believe them. If he says she looks thin, then she assumes that he usually thinks she looks fat, and he's only trying to atone for a horrible error he committed that she now has to find out about. If he says her outfit is nice, she'll ask how he can be any judge of fashion when he has about as much chance of matching one of his outfits as a blind monkey.

She'll either bat the compliment away or turn it against the guy. After years of this, most husbands give up even trying to compliment their wives. Big mistake. Huge mistake. One day he'll ask her to pass the salt, and the next thing he knows, she's trying to force-fit the shaker up one of his nostrils while screaming how he doesn't appreciate her anymore.

Not only does a husband have to remember to compliment his wife continually, but he has to make sure he gives her the correct compliment. Let us say, for example, that she gets her bangs trimmed about an eighth of an inch. To the woman, this changes her whole appearance, so the man should obviously notice unless he just doesn't care anymore and is now probably thinking about dumping her for his secretary. Meanwhile, the average guy really isn't particularly observant and so doesn't notice anything less significant than a loss of limb.

What does a guy do to stay out of trouble? He has to pick up on the clues his wife drops. When he walks through the door after work with his usual "Hi, honey," he's got to see what she does. If she stares at him with her eyebrows raised, then that means he's got to rifle through his memory to see if he was supposed to bring something home that he obviously forgot, or look closely at her and guess if anything is different. If he is not sure he forgot anything, he should hit the compliments as the backup. The key is to watch her eyes. If her eyes flick down, that means she is checking out her new outfit to see how the man could possibly miss it. If the eyes flick upward, she got her hair done. If they flick around the room, then she did some special cleaning. If they stare directly at the guy, then somehow he's screwed up. If the latter, you may as well spew out some more compliments anyway to soften the impending blow.

So what kind of compliments does a guy want? Actually, he doesn't need any since he makes them up anyway. Women start the day looking in the mirror and putting the makeup on. A man looks in the mirror, and whatever reflection he sees—overweight, bloodshot eyes, patches of beard missed by the razor—he's thinking "looking good!" and ambles out of the house. If he is at a restaurant and the waitress is being nice, he's thinking it must be his magnetic personality rather than her putting up with his inane comments for a better tip.

Household Chores

or

A Woman's Work Is Never Done...Since She Is Often Doing the Man's Work First

---

Two incomes are now usually needed to support a household, unless you work on Wall Street, at which point you have several hundred people supporting your household with 401(k)s hoping you don't rob them blind before they retire. For countless generations, only one person from the couple needed to go outside the home to earn a living. World War II rolled around, and when the men got sent off to war, the women had to not only keep up the households, but take jobs. When the men came back, the women realized that the concrete jungle that the men complained about to the point where women ran around getting their meals and slippers and back massages, etc., wasn't anywhere near as bad as the household bayou.

When the woman looked down and saw half a dozen whining children hanging off her body while she was trying to scrub the toilet, she had second thoughts about who actually received the short end of the stick (during the daytime, that is). She then thought about how she had to justify her expenses because it was his paycheck, while he couldn't even tell you the cost of a potato. At that point, more women found the thought of working outside the home more rewarding than ever. Even though the women got paid at a fraction of their male counterparts, it was a heck of a lot more than what they were getting paid before. It's like going from volunteer work at the insane asylum where the inmates are prodding you to join them to getting paid to push a pea around the room with your nose. It is certainly not nirvana, but it is a step in the right direction.[173]

When women went to work, it didn't take them long to figure out that it wasn't particularly fair that they did all the housework as well. They started looking over to the lump in the recliner and thinking that it would be nice to have an eject button installed. Women then realized that they were also "tired." When the couple would come home from work, he would retire to the living room, and she would head for the kitchen. When night rolled in, the man would strut into the room doing his best John Wayne impersonation looking for some action, while she looked more like Sleeping Beauty with fangs. Now this sat about as well with a guy as a habanero pepper sandwich washed down with grain alcohol on an ulcerated stomach. After all, his father and his father before him were treated like the king of the castle. Now he barely qualified as the duke of their dungeon.

If a modern guy wants a modern wife to be happy, the guy has got to help with the housework. End of story. A guy doing housework is simply the right thing to do. Men shouldn't act like taking out the garbage is moving a mountain or picking up his underwear is akin to slaying a dragon, albeit some pairs of underwear may be more hazardous to handle. Does doing your fair share mean that your wife should act indebted to you? About as much as buying a lottery ticket means you should call your boss a bag of boll weevil testicles right before you flood the company toilets and quit. However, not doing any housework is an ironclad guarantee that things will be chillier than Frosty the Snowman's testicles. Consider housework modern-day foreplay.

---

173 By Nirvana, I do not mean the band that sang "Smells Like Teen Spirit." Being the father of boys, if I use the word "smells," especially in the teen years, it is never in a good situation. The nirvana I was talking about was the Buddhist idea of a perfect state of mind free of worries or cravings. It is a pure, relaxed happiness. Modern Western societies do not have a similar concept, with the exception of when your kids finally move out of the house.

Grocery Shopping

or

Apparently, You Are Supposed to Buy Food That Has Some Mystery Quality Known as "Nutritious"

M any couples simply love to do things together. The time they spend doing the little things in life with each other can strengthen their bond. Take grocery shopping, for example—and remove it from this category. A woman, by default, is considered the shopping expert. Since she shops for everything else like clothes, household gadgets, Christmas gifts for her and his extended families, etc. (all things a guy doesn't care about), she naturally assumes she is better at getting the food (something the guy actually does care about).

If the couple goes shopping together, both her hands must be free. That means that the guy is always going to be relegated to pushing the cart. While the woman is analyzing various brands of pasta shapes, he is expected to keep both hands on the handle with the same intensity of driving an eighteen-wheeler down a mountain in snowy conditions. What if he makes the heinous error of suggesting his own things to put in the cart? She will explain to him why purchasing chocolate-covered doughnuts is unconscionable.[174]

For you men out there, did you ever notice the numbers on the side of the food boxes? Believe it or not, they are not just random, but have nutritional information on them that—and this is where it gets really crazy—some people (women) actually read and care about. Men who look at this information get about as much out of it as trying to decipher the bar code on the package or the instruction manual for building the space shuttle. Women actually look at them and plan their calorie intake accordingly. Unfortunately, none of those numbers are for tasting good, so allowing a woman to select food solely based on this strategy will actually result in the man *gaining* weight. How does this work? Because the guy will stop at a doughnut shop on the way to work and eat enormous sums of food for lunch and on the way home to survive the night.

So all he does is push the cart and keep it at an acceptable distance from his wife. It should be far enough back so that she doesn't get mowed down when she stops to evaluate an item, but not so far back that she can't grab something, pivot, and drop it directly into the cart. It doesn't take a lot of practice. What does take practice is slipping food items into the cart that your wife has not given express approval to do.

The man should know the layout of the store well enough so that when he is approaching items he would like to buy (Cheez-Its, beef jerky, Drake's coffee cakes,[175] etc.), the cart happens to be on the correct side of the aisle. Without stopping the cart, he nonchalantly knocks the item into the cart and then covers it up with other groceries. By the time they get to the cash register, there is nothing she will do about it because scolding the guy for buying something he wants to eat doesn't look good in front of other people. Sure, she wants

---

174 Apparently Devil Dogs to a woman are a sin against humanity, but they are oh, so good.

175 There is *no* substitute coffee-cake manufacturer. Little Debbie is an outclassed bimbo when compared to Drake's in this department. I am not being paid to say this, but I certainly would be willing to accept money for this, as well as a free lifetime supply.

him whipped to her bidding, but she doesn't want the welts to show where other people can see them.

Some women opt to go out grocery shopping alone. That makes most men want to cheer that they have (again) gotten out of doing something that involves leaving the house. Unfortunately, some women are always on a diet. They, therefore, grocery shop like they are dieting and so pick up only a few items that are low in calories and taste like Styrofoam. Is there any concern for the other individuals in the household who are not dieting? No. She'll come home with stuff for lean breakfasts/lunches/dinners, and there will be not one thing to snack on. Zip. Men don't do the "no snack" thing. If there aren't chips/pretzels/nuts/candy bars to eat, the man will just stand there staring at the cupboard hoping something will materialize out of thin air. His mouth is open. There is a frenzied look in his eye. He may teeter back and forth like he is about to piss himself. It's not pretty.

The man either has to learn how to eat healthy, which is about as likely as teaching a pig to use a fork, or do "underground shopping." He'll have to make up some lame excuse for leaving the house, go to the grocery store, buy the things he wants, sneak the stuff into the house, hide it in the cupboards, and then act like nothing's happening. She begins to think he's having an affair, and he's just trying to make sure he gets his daily requirement of lard-based products like Ho-Hos and Double Stuf Oreos. Because of all this, many men opt to do the grocery shopping themselves.

Unfortunately, we men have the short-term memory of a goldfish. Therefore, if a man is to go shopping, he needs a list to be written by his wife. Without this list, the man shops by going up and down each and every aisle, throwing in whatever takes his fancy at that time, and he ends up with unadulterated crap that is so artificial it doesn't expire this century, never mind having nothing suitable for dinner. Even a list doesn't fully guarantee that the man will get the right things. It must be detailed enough to include manufacturer and size. Otherwise, anything is fair game for the guy as he grabs the first thing that catches his eye that remotely looks like what is on his list. If she wants vanilla extract for a recipe and she just says vanilla, she could be getting vanilla pudding or vanilla cupcake, or maybe he'll actually get vanilla extract, but it would be in the industrial-use size meant for military bases and prisons.

When a man goes grocery shopping, there is little/no concern for meal planning, budget, calories, nutritional value, brand name, or whether there currently are fifteen boxes of the stuff at home because his wife refuses to cook it. Above all, there is certainly no concern about using food coupons. For some women, cutting coupons is as much a part of their day as brushing their teeth. She may not like Minute Maid frozen orange juice and certainly doesn't plan on buying four cans of the stuff to get the fifth free, but she's got that coupon ready just in case she changes her mind.

A guy just can't be bothered with coupons. He sees fifteen cents here, twenty cents there, and he just can't muster up the care to ensure that he buys the correct brands at the correct quantities. Even when his wife shoves the coupons in his hand, the man invariably puts them in his pocket, and his wife later finds them in the wash as crumbs of paper stuck to absolutely every piece of laundry there is. Now not only he has wasted all the time she took cutting and collating the coupons, but she has to pick all those disgusting paper bits out of the whole load of clothes she's just tried cleaning.

One week, a man may bring home snacks and all breakfast foods. The woman will be reheating frozen waffles for dinner because there is nothing even remotely considered a real main course. That is where the grocery list comes in. In essence, it is a "get out of jail free" card. If she complains about him screwing up by not buying something, he can just whip that thing out and plead ignorance—if he actually got what was on the list. What if the woman verbally told him /texted him /called him to remind him that there was a dire need of toilet paper, and he still didn't get it? Then he can remind her how often she claims his memory capacity is like trying to serve soup in a pasta strainer, and therefore she should have known he would fail at the task if it wasn't on the list. Not that this excuse works, but at least it catches her off guard. After all, if you give the car keys to a six-year-old and he gets into an accident, is it his fault, or is it yours for giving him the keys in the first place?

Cooking

or

Some Like It Hot, but Only

If It Is Microwavable

Men and women certainly have different ideas of what cooking means. If a woman spends two hours coming up with a six-course meal, a guy will think nothing of reheating some TV dinners the next day and claiming he has done the same amount of cooking as she did (one meal = one meal). Women also do something known as "balancing" a meal. To a man, a balanced meal is one that doesn't tip off the table. Women will try to make sure there is protein, carbohydrates, vegetables, etc., with every dinner. A man makes what tastes good. A single guy will think little of having a frozen pizza with a side of doughnuts for dinner. Maybe he'll even nuke it before he eats it (the pizza, that is).

If a man has run out of excuses and has to cook or risk a manual vasectomy, plan on making dinner. Why? Lunch is out since he is at work five out of the seven days. Telling his wife that he'll make two whole sandwiches and even throw some chips on a plate while she does the rest of the cooking will get him about as many brownie points as accidentally weedwacking her flower garden. Breakfast? Hardly. To cook the type of breakfast that would qualify as a meal would require him to get up around 4:00 a.m. and make dishes that are named after people like Benedict and Hollandaise. Even if he was actually awake at that time of the morning, he'd have about as much chance of putting those ingredients together properly as assembling a working robot from Legos and rubber bands.

The three-recipe repertoire that the average guy knows from his dating years is not going to cut it for a multiyear marriage. Does this mean the guy is going to actually have to work in the kitchen? Do bears shave? Luckily, we live in a space-age society where we can go to the grocery store and buy our way into a home-cooked meal. These days, you can waltz into a store and buy precut salads, frozen gourmet meals, and a loaf of fancy bread. Voila! Just throw the meal into the oven at the prescribed temperature and time, and it's done.

I probably have to mention a few words here about how a man interprets cooking instructions. Men do not like—in the least—any type of decision making when it comes to making food. They want to follow directions exactly. If something is supposed to be cooked for fifteen minutes, then fifteen minutes it is. So what happens in the instance when the directions give a range like "boil for ten to fifteen minutes" or "bake for forty to fifty minutes"? Simple. Men panic. What to do? They split the difference on the time and then cook it exactly that long. In other words, ten to fifteen minutes means 12.5 minutes exactly. So what if the spaghetti is so undercooked it tastes like pencil erasers? Serve it up anyway and maybe throw a bit extra sauce on it to cover up the texture. What if a man smells something burning in the oven but it is still not the prescribed time to take it out? Damn it, it's going to stay in there until that buzzer goes off.

If the woman complains about a charred coal that used to be a piece of meat, the man can always shrug and say that he did follow instructions and (more importantly) that if she cannot *appreciate* (she'll hate that word) his efforts, then she can just do the cooking herself. If you really want to throw a guy into total turmoil, then make him try to cook two different things in the oven that (1) require different cooking times and (2) require different heating temperatures. You'll see him break out the calculator, slide rule, and abacus and still burn all the food and sometimes hurt himself in the process.

Women, on the other hand, feel that they are free to take liberties with cooking; sometimes too many liberties. Rather than stick to a meat-and-potatoes type of theme that a guy loves, they try to spice it up with things that sound fancy like sweetbread and tripe. Unfortunately, when guys and kids find out that sweetbread is actually pancreas and tripe is stomach lining, then their adventurous appetite takes a nose dive. The woman, who has spent all this time making something special and finds no one willing to eat her masterpiece, now takes her vengeance upon all those who dare not eat what she has laid down before them. Imagine here the personality of a wolverine having been teased with a cattle prod and then let out of its cage.

I have been blessed with a wife who is a good cook. I routinely make it a point to compliment her meals. Now it happens that every so often she'll come up with a recipe that I don't particularly care for. My man's analytical brain will deduce that if I don't tell her I don't like something, I will most likely be seeing that meal again. Therefore, I feel compelled to tell her, in the nicest manner I can muster, that it may not be the greatest thing to grace my taste palate.

Now, my wife is a rational person. She can understand that as individuals, we all have different tastes and could not possibly be expected to like all the same things. Do you think that is going to help me in this situation? Sure, about as much as a fly swatter against a pissed-off killer-bee colony. She will take the rejection of the meal personally and therefore retaliate in a personal attack consisting of disparaging remarks against my personage and/or my masculinity. That is why some men will go thirty or forty years of marriage before finally building up the guts to say that they don't like their wife's special dish. Decades of resentment against meatloaf & broccoli surprise[176] will suddenly well up and set him off in a blathering tirade.

---

176 Let it be known to my wife that this is not some subliminal hint that I don't like her meatloaf. It is fabulous. If I accidentally got the meatloaf banned from the dinner selections, my children would never forgive me.

Dishes

or

It Doesn't Count as Two Chores When You Load and Unload the Dishwasher

Since women still generally take the role of primary cooker (having realized that the men are about as handy in the cooking department as a paraplegic tree sloth), dishwashing is a job that has now been passed to men for the most part. That's not such a bad deal when you think of all the time it takes to put a meal together. It's really not bad when you've got an automatic dishwasher or children you can pay off.[177]

It may behoove me to go over some dishwasher protocol here. For many men, "automatic" means that the dishwasher will do absolutely everything, so they don't even bother to scrape the food into the garbage disposal before shoving dishes into the dishwasher. What happens to those chicken bones when a man closes that dishwasher door is a mystery that he has no care for solving. So to those men out there, yes, the food should be scraped off the plates before said plates are inserted in the dishwasher. It does *not* magically disappear like socks in a dryer or promises after an election.

---

177 If you set your kids up with an allowance, you should make the payments contingent on chores. Coincidentally, those chores should have previously been in your camp to do.

The next big dishwasher hurdle is what to do with the stuff that doesn't easily come off the plates and utensils, like dried-on sauces. The problem here is that if you put the dishes in without rinsing them, rather than getting clean dishes, you get this hardened colored mass that is much harder to get off than had you rinsed the dishes in the first place. Many guys will not perform the appropriate quality control when putting these dishes away, and the wife will be absolutely disgusted when she pulls out a plate that looks like a Rorschach test made from spaghetti sauce.

A woman, upon finding these dishes in the cupboard, will not be particularly pleased. She will make it a point to tell him about each and every dish she finds below her standards in a tone normally reserved for talking to a naughty two-year-old. She'll then explain the proper way to wash dishes. Men *hate* to be corrected. They *know* the right way to do dishes. They just don't *want* to do them that way. After all, it is theoretically possible that those dishes may get cleaned, and then the guy would have done all that extra work for nothing.

So what does a guy do? Put everything in the dishwasher for another go-around. If a guy has been doing dishes long enough, you'll find dishes that have been in there a good dozen rounds. Does the term "let it ride" sound familiar? Some dishes eventually get cleaned, some of them do not. Eventually there is no room for new dishes with the old ones going round and round, and the guy has to come up with another option. He can admit defeat and take a butter knife to the dishes to whittle the crud off, or he can admit to nothing and bury them in the backyard.

So here the guy is with a pile of dishes. He has got to scrape them and then rinse them, or the wife will nag. If the guy just uses a bit of soap in this process, then it would be considered clean the old-fashioned way. So why the heck does one have a dishwasher taking up space in the kitchen if the guy has to scrape and clean them anyway? Because people now feel the dishwasher has this magical power to sanitize. They look over at that grubby old dishcloth or sponge that has that odd odor emanating from it and don't want that to be the last thing that dish touches before being put back in the cabinet. Generations have relied upon that dishcloth followed by a quick rinse, but now we're germ freaks. Keep this trend going, and in the end we'll all end up looking like Howard Hughes with the germ phobia, long hair, and long fingernails. Maybe he was just ahead of his time.[178]

---

178   Howard Hughes may be known for ending his life with a few extra jokers stacked in his deck while the sixes and sevens were missing, but he didn't start off that way. He was a famous film producer and aviator and was noted to be with many of Hollywood's most famous leading ladies at the time. He was one of the wealthiest people in the world. How you go from a daredevil breaking aviation speed records to obsessive-compulsive person is not quite well known. Maybe it was enhanced by addiction to pain-killers. Whatever it was, he did some odd things. For instance, he had an obsession with pea sizes and had a special fork to put them in order. One time, he told his aides that he wanted to screen movies in a film studio, so that is what he did—for four months without leaving. He lived on chocolate bars and milk during that time, relieved himself into empty bottles, stacked and restacked Kleenex boxes for hours on end. Oh, and was often naked. Money can buy a lot of things, but apparently it doesn't guarantee that bats don't take up residence in the belfry.

Cleaning

or

What You Should Be Doing

Instead of Sitting on the Couch

One of the big problems with men cleaning is that they physically cannot see dirt or dust. It is easier to be blindfolded and find a needle on an LA freeway than for a guy to notice that the reason the television picture looks so fuzzy is not because of bad reception but because there is a quarter-inch-thick dust layer covering the screen. In their previous solo existence of living with male roommates, a man's apartment was noted for looking like a demilitarized zone. You can't get to a single man's kitchen sink because there is a tower of leaning dishes that gets washed about as often as a new president gets elected. There are piles of clothes everywhere besides the bureaus and closets. The refrigerator is harboring Chinese food brought back by Marco Polo. The bathroom is so bad you can actually end up with more germs by taking a shower. And to top it off, most men are flabbergasted when they find out that they are actually supposed to wash their bed sheets.

Let's start with dusting. When a woman is doing this chore, she gets a dust spray, applies a one-quarter-inch layer of the spray on the table, and then wipes a dust cloth on it. She then goes to each and every thing in the room not made of upholstery and slathers it up and wipes it down. Guys claim they can dust, but it is like Mother Teresa claiming she was a good basketball player.[179] It's possible, but not bloody likely.

First off, a guy refuses to clean anything that is not dirty enough for him to deem it worthy of his time. How does a man determine whether a piece of furniture meets these criteria? If he can see dust on it, it is dirty. However, men's eyes just can't seem to see dirt until it is to the point where when something gets touched, it generates a dust cloud significant enough to start choking him. He then goes over and wipes his hand all over it. Granted, this certainly is the quickest method possible, but it may not be the most thorough. First off, the object now has streaks of dust on it from where the hand missed. Secondly, the net amount of dust stays the same when a man cleans this way; he's just transferred it from the hutch to the table or the table to the floor. Somehow, women don't see this as acceptable cleaning.

Instead, the man is supposed to get a dust cleaner, spray it on what he is about to clean, and then use a cloth to wipe it down. It boggles many men's minds to think of all this effort of finding the right aerosol can in the house as well as a cloth meant for dusting rather than just giving the object a quick rub with his shirt sleeve. It is somewhat important to keep cloths in the house separated to their individual purposes. After all, I may not know what chemicals make up dust remover, but if you then use that cloth to dry the dishes, I'm pretty sure you aren't satisfying one of the FDA food pyramids when you ingest them. Dust cleaners do help the dust stick to the cloth so that the particles don't go winging around the room making something else dirty. The only problem with a cleaner is that if a guy doesn't wipe well, it becomes a streaky mess, and that is as incriminating as leaving your fingerprints on the murder weapon.

So how does a man clean a bathroom? Only after he is forced into the room with a bazooka. A married couple's bathroom is never allowed to reach the state that a bachelor's bathroom gets in. Patience is not something that men have oodles of when cleaning. The idea of

---

179 Give her a hockey stick and put her on ice, however, and she was white lightning.

scrubbing the same spot with more than two or three swipes of a cloth just doesn't cut it for them. That is why bachelors head into the bathroom with an abrasive cloth on the order of steel wool and a cleaning solution whose primary ingredient is sand. Sure it will permanently scratch the living hell out of the tub, but he can finish the cleaning in a single commercial break. When men are married, they are not allowed to get away with this bathroom-cleaning technique. Instead, they are given a soft cloth and nonabrasive cleaner. You may as well send a man to the Grand Canyon with a pail and shovel and tell him to fill it. The only things this exercise will lead to are frustration and bad feelings by all. Men usually just can't clean a bathroom to a woman's standards.[180]

Am I saying that cleaning the bathroom is woman's work? Absolutely not. I'm pretty well convinced the sticky yellow substance surrounding the toilet bowl is the man's fault. I am, however, saying that if the woman wants to go into her bathroom and not care that it looks like it was used to gut deer, then it is perfectly fine to let the man clean it to his standards. The minor exception to this is that the man is supposed to clean any clogged drains, and that is just fine if that is all I have to do.

When I look at my wife and see that long brown hair that I love to run my hands through and then see the hamster-sized hairball I yank out of the shower drain every so often, I wonder how it can be the same stuff. Even though it is their hair for the most part, many women find that soggy hairball to be too gross to yank out. And yet these are the same women who will spend big bucks for a bath in mud.

---

180   Early in our marriage, my wife asked if I could clean the bathroom while our baby was napping and she went to work. I certainly wasn't going to deny her this. Sure enough, the baby dropped off to sleep hours later, and I trudged into the bathroom. I sprayed the whole thing down with bathroom cleaner, waited the appropriate time, and started wiping. The grime did not want to come off, so I did what every man does and scrubbed harder while swearing under my breath. I eventually finished up, and my wife came home. Later, she asked if the baby had been cranky, and I replied that *he* hadn't. I asked why she was asking, and she said that since I didn't have time to clean the bathroom, he must not have taken a nap. Yes, in her eyes, I not only didn't clean it to her satisfaction, but it was so inadequate that it looked to her like I had done nothing at all. Now, I don't want to sound macho, but I am a hell of a lot stronger than my wife. To this day, I don't know how she can clean the grime off a tub, while I can be rubbing like my life depended on it and still not get near the same results.

Taking the Garbage Out

or

Pretending the Trash Can Is Invisible

No matter how liberated women are, taking out the garbage continues to be a job that stays in the man's domain. Most men grudgingly accept this and even feel a modicum of guilt if they see their wife dragging the garbage out because they've been a bit lax. As with many other chores, men like to pace themselves. What does that mean when it comes to garbage? It means that a guy doesn't think it is necessary to take the garbage out as long as it is theoretically possible that another piece of trash can be placed on top of the mound without it collapsing on the kitchen floor.

The man can limit the amount of times the chore has to be done by first making sure that there is as much packed into the bag as possible. The way to do this is to shove it down with all your might. For the first step, you've got to pick some nongunky trash on top. Avoid anything that smells or has sauce on it. The guy then places his hands on the two "clean" pieces of trash and pushes down, putting all his weight on it.[181] If all works well, the trash compacts a few inches,

---

181 It is a rookie mistake for men to think they can accomplish this with one hand. You've got to use two—and use the wingspan of your fingers to really increase that mashing surface area. Sure, that will increase the gross factor when things are more likely to squirt up, but at times in life, you've got to be a hero. After all, the consequences of

and he may get another night out of it. If it doesn't go well, there is something like old spaghetti Parmesan underneath that goes squirting up and over, getting his hands smelly and slimy. You've then got to go running to the sink while you muffle a girly scream since it is so disgusting.

There comes a point where what is on top is too disgusting or the trash physically can't be mashed any more. That is when the mound starts to build higher than the edge of the trash basket. So what do people in the household do about this? Ignore it, for the most part. Besides the woman of the household, everyone else is fair game for taking out the garbage. Whoever "fills" it is the one usually responsible for taking it out, never mind that it should have been thrown days ago. It becomes a game of being able to toss things on the garbage without the pile toppling over. Whoever does have things fall is the one who finally has to take the garbage out.[182] Either that, or it is when the wife freaks out (rightfully) because it is too disgusting to be in the same room as the garbage or the smell from the rotting food makes it unbearable to cook.

---

not doing this are a waste of a trip outside, sometimes in snowy conditions, to put that trash out. Women can't even fathom the difficulty men go through doing this, as female chores, like cooking and laundry, are indoor chores. Well, come to think of it, they do have to go shopping for the food, and that does involve going outside. Women like to consider gardening as an outside chore, but men put that squarely in the hobby category, unless it is to put vegetables on the table since you aren't within two hundred miles of a supermarket. Having a garden with flowers in front is as important to a man as flossing a corpse before burial. If you want to do it, knock your socks off, but if not, it still doesn't matter at the end of the day.

182 Here is one good reason to have kids—the more you have, the less chance you have of being the one who loses the garbage game and has to take it out.

Decorating

or

Apparently, It Is Important for Women to Put Things on Walls

When a man and woman move in together, they are supposed to make their new apartment their own, an amalgamation of their personalities fused into one. What once had been two separate living quarters' personalities are now fused into a unique entity. What does that mean? It means that the guy's stuff ends up in the basement until the first available garage sale, and the woman's stuff is what is kept. Women hate men's furniture, and a woman begins to make plans for eliminating it immediately after the engagement ring has been slipped on her finger.

Why? For one thing, no piece of a man's furniture matches any other piece. Most men acquire furniture piecemeal; a relative was getting rid of it, they nab it at a garage sale, or they go cruising down the streets on garbage day hoping to find something that doesn't smell worse than what they already have. As the old adage says, beggars can't be choosers. It may take years for a guy to furnish his apartment this way. When it is done, not only does the furniture not match, each piece may have been made in a different decade. Even though the woman does not mention any difficulty with the man's furniture while dating, as soon as they become her furniture, the orange couch, green armchair, and blue rocker make her want to gouge her eyes out with a melon baller.[183]

It is phenomenally important to a woman that all the furniture in a room does not clash. So what happens to that nice, comfortable, hideously orange couch that he's loved all these years? It makes its way to the sidewalk to be recycled by the next generation of bachelors.[184] Meanwhile, another couch that is about as comfortable as sheeted Astroturf has taken its place. What if a man puts his foot down and demands that the comfy couch be kept? The woman will acquiesce, just as long as the guy enjoys sitting on it in a damp, cold basement.

There are some men who will insist upon keeping the couch in the living room. The woman then enters phase II of getting rid of the couch. Evicting the couch will become her obsession in life, and everything will revolve around getting it out of the house. She may end up doing her ironing on the couch and accidentally leave the hot iron on it while the bottle of charcoal lighter fluid that she had assumed was empty mistakenly gets dumped all over the cloth. She may invite her new friend who breeds pit bulls over to the house, forgetting that she was marinating steaks inside the cushions. No matter how much time it takes, that couch has a death sentence hanging over its head.

Women not only have to match colors, but stains—not pit or beer, but the color of wood. Not until a man is married does he realize that things made of wood aren't all just "brown." Heavens no. There are dozens of colors of stain that can be applied to wood. To a woman, having a light brown piece of furniture next to a dark brown piece of furniture is about as perverse as rearranging a blind

---

183   Yes, that was actually a description of my furniture. The first time I moved out of state, I packed the car with clothing and audiotapes (yes, I am dating myself) and didn't have one piece of furniture. I acquired the bulk from garage sales, and then that furniture traveled the country with me until I moved in with my wife. That orange couch was ugly as all get-out, but was it comfortable. The only other problem with it was, if you happened to sweat, the color bled, so you got up looking like an Oompa Loompa from *Willie Wonka & the Chocolate Factory*.

184   Please feel free to put down the book for a moment and sing a few bars of "The Circle of Life" by Elton John.

man's living room. A guy never notices these things until the woman hooks her index and middle fingers in his nostrils and drags his face just inches away from the first piece of furniture and then drags him to the second piece. Making a man actually care involves grabbing a completely different portion of the body in a vise-like grip and yanking him from furniture piece to furniture piece.

Not only do men and women disagree about the color of furniture, they disagree about what can even be called furniture. Take, for example, one of a bachelor's best friends, the milk carton. Upside down, it is a coffee table. Right side up, it is a storage unit. Sideways, it is a handy music CD library. Put two milk cartons together with a piece of plywood, and you can have shelving. Since they are stackable, they are the ultimate in rearranging convenience. Oh, praise the genius that is the milk carton. Women just don't seem to get this. A milk carton is made to carry milk and milk only. Having it for furniture is about as acceptable to a woman as asking her to pee in an alley.

And then you've got accents to the room. Women must have curtains. All a guy really needs is one shade to put up in his bedroom so he can sleep till noon because he was up till 3:00 a.m. playing Call of Duty[185] online. Maybe he needs two shades just in case the sun from the living room interferes with seeing the television. To a man, curtains are a needless luxury along the lines of a bathrobe that stays closed when he sits on the couch. Beyond curtains, women also like a valence. That is the cloth that hides the curtain rod. What is so bad about the curtain rod that it needs to be covered in a cloth? Maybe by this time in life, women have seen enough cylindrical things exposed (see bathrobe comment).

Once all the man's furniture is safely stowed away in the darkest, deepest parts of the house or on the side of the street, and the

---

185 At the time of this writing, Call of Duty is a wildly popular series of video games that have the player in various wars. They had a special Nazi zombie level that I particularly enjoyed, especially when I could find someone in the house to play with me. Unfortunately, I was not deemed a top-tier player by my older two, so it was always a struggle to get them to play with the "nube." Playing with my five-year-old would have been considered a bit of irresponsible parenting. What to do? Well, no one called child protective services yet. Then he hit seven and I was back to being a nube.

woman has matching colors/stains/theme furniture, then you'd think that would be the end of it. Let me clarify that last statement. You'd think that would be the end of it if you were a guy. Here comes the next problem: women get bored with rooms and like to rearrange furniture.

You can break women into two factions when it comes to the moving thing: the "I'm not sure" and the "covert ops." In the "I'm not sure" category, the woman will wait for a weekend when there is a good game on.[186] Minutes before the game starts, she'll announce, for example, that she wants to see how well the couch looks over against the opposite wall. He may complain about the timing, but all she has to do is explain that they can argue about it until and even during the game, knowing that at some point, she'll win the argument, or he can try to get it done before the game starts.

Women cannot just mentally picture what a piece of furniture looks like against the other wall. They *must* see it. She can't even visualize inches! If she is just thinking of the couch next to that wall, he'll be moving that thing back and forth at least a dozen times over ever-diminishing distances. It gets to the point where she says, "just a bit more" and he moves it about the width of pencil and she'll finally acquiesce that the spot is "not terrible." Heck, if the couch was to stay there, the first time someone sat in it, it would probably move that far.

Does that put a stop to the job of redecorating? Just about as easily as an eighteen-wheeler with low brake fluid hitting a marble factory. No, the woman then must see what the television looks like moved because it obviously can't still be in the proper position for viewing from the proposed new couch position. The guy will move the TV, then the bookcase, then the coffee table, then the bookcase, then the armchair, then the bookcase, then the coffee table (you get the picture), and then get back to moving the couch, which screws everything up yet again.

---

186 To be fair, a woman who is willing to wait for a weekend when her husband admits that there is no good game on may as well be waiting for world peace. If a guy knows it is a choice between sitting on a couch and chores, then he is going to develop a deep interest in professional toad sniffing.

Every time he moves something, his wife's face takes on the expression that would occur if she were trying to mentally move it with mind power alone. The Nazis didn't get so much scrutiny at the Nuremberg trials as does how that furniture looks in the new location. Once "she" is finally done moving the furniture, she may pass judgment that it suits her present mood. If it does, great, and if it doesn't, then it is time to move everything back to where it was originally. Either way, the game has started, and now the guy is frantically fiddling around trying to hook up the cable he had to disconnect to move the television so he can start watching. By the way, at any moment it will dawn on your wife how dirty it was under the couch, so if the game is still on, you'll still be moving furniture and trying desperately to hear over the vacuum cleaner.

Under the "covert ops" approach, the man will come back from work one day and the whole house will be rearranged. This approach is usually taken when the woman thinks she'll run into significant resistance on the part of the guy who is comfortable keeping the status quo. After all, most guys could live their entire lives being in the same conditions, keeping the same hairstyle, wearing the same type of clothes—a guy could be fine with eating leftover pizza forever if he had an infinite supply of it. Women, on the other hand, feel the need to keep reinventing themselves and their surroundings. If a woman wants a change of pace, she may get new furniture, dye her hair, or buy enough clothing to match the GDP of a small third-world village. If guy wants to make a drastic change, he'll switch from cans to bottles.

Once the furniture is set, then the fun really begins. First off the woman is going to want to hang art pictures. The only thing that men and women agree with about "art" is the spelling of the word. In general, women like pictures of fruit, meadows, or flowers. Since men are bored to tears with these things in real life, they certainly don't like looking at pictures of them. Some men care absolutely nothing about their domestic surroundings, with the sole exception that everything can't be pink and flowery, and only then because their masculinity can be called into question. Women could brick up the windows, and these men wouldn't notice. To these men, having these, for lack of a better expression, mind-numbingly dull pictures put up is no big deal. Some men, however, care.

Now the problem comes that the couple has to go to the art store and agree upon something. If you think this is easy, please stop by your local leper colony en route and cure a few of them, because that is considered a minor miracle compared to getting men and women to agree on a painting. My advice to men is to start with something that your wife will absolutely despise, like Marilyn Monroe with her dress blowing up in the air. This will help establish your baseline for a compromise position. If you were to go with a Dali or Escher, then by the time you compromised, you'd be back to a picture of fields of grain waving in the breeze. Sometimes, you'll end up with pictures by Ansel Adams that you'll both consider a bit dull but better than the alternatives.

So in the end, will a man get his way? That depends on how you look at it. He won't be allowed to pick out any pictures for the dining room, living room, bathroom, or even closet, but he will get to pick something tasteful (and small) to put up on his side of the bed. Maybe. If the basement is finished, he could get a picture down there as well. Maybe.

So now you've got the pictures. The woman's job is now to figure out the best position to place the pictures. Since she can *only* do this from a distance of ten yards back, she must rely on the guy to hold the picture up. Ever hear of the wind-chill factor? It takes into account not only the outside temperature but how much the wind is gusting so you know what temperature it feels like to be outside. Why do I bring this up? Because there is such a thing as the picture-hanging factor that works on the same principle. Sure, the picture and frame may only weigh a few pounds. Now hold it straight out for fifteen minutes above your head so that the blood completely drains from your arms as you move the picture ever so slightly from side to side.

With the picture-hanging factor, you feel like you are now holding up a flat bowling ball. If the man starts to complain, however, he is called a weakling for not being able to hold up a piece of paper (she'll somehow forget to mention that thick metal or wood frame and sheet of glass that may be adding a tad to the weight).

Sometimes, she'll want the picture up high. Since there is no ladder immediately available in the living room (go figure), the man finds himself with one leg on the arm of a chair and the other several feet away balancing on a bookcase. The man didn't think his legs were this flexible when he was on the ground, and now here he is high in the air with his hands trying to wield a hammer and nail. Therefore, when he eventually does fall, he has to take that split second to decide to sacrifice his back or the picture, never mind mentioning the ability to use his groin muscles for the next few weeks as they will clearly be out of commission.[187]

Now that the picture is in the appropriate place, it must get hung there. While keeping the picture in place (usually with one hand and the alternate elbow), he's got to take the free hand and make a mark on the wall with a pencil. While he's trying to do this, the picture inevitably slips. The woman has to then help realign the picture. That is why a man should leave the hammer in another room and ask his wife to go retrieve it. While she is gone, the man can then have the picture sliding all over the wall and have so many pencil marks that it looks like a three-year-old was trying to do a dot-to-dot picture. When she gets back though, the man can have the picture on the ground and pretend to have the situation well in hand and know *exactly* where his wife wanted it.

The man then experiences his next problem. He may now have a vague idea of where the picture was on the wall, but that in no way tells him where to hammer the nails in. The guy's got to look at the back of the picture and see if it is going to be hung on a wire or on clips on the edges. So after having to move that picture millimeter by millimeter to get it to his wife's specific spot, he's going to have to take a wild, ballpark shot at hammering that nail in the right place. His wife will *not* want to hear this. Therefore, the man has to pretend that he knows exactly what he is doing. If necessary, he may take out a tape measure and start whipping it around just in case his wife

---

187 A word of caution. If you pull your groin muscles, you will be walking funny for a while and people will inevitably ask what happened. Say you hurt a thigh muscle or some other excuse. Do not tell your coworkers that you pulled your groin, or there will be endless ridiculing. Trust me on this one.

looks skeptical of his abilities. He then takes his best guess and starts whacking away.

The moment of truth then comes as the guy has to hang the picture back on the wall. If it is slightly out of place, the man can try to pass the buck by emphatically stating that that is where his wife told him to put it. If it is wildly out of place, he's bagged. Then he's got to look for another reason why things went wrong. If the picture is hanging on a wire, he can say that the wire had more "give" than he originally thought. The guy is really not in the habit of stretching metal, but his wife may still buy off on this and let him do it again. If it has got those hooks in back, then the possible excuses get even slimmer.

Defective tape measure? Maybe he was doing inches on one side and centimeters on another? Maybe it has something to do with the tides (for those states bordering the Atlantic or Pacific)? Anyway, mumble a lot, and she may just leave you alone to try it again. By the time you are done and the picture is straight, the ultimate hope is that the wall does not look like it was propped up behind Sonny Corleone at the tollbooth scene in *The Godfather*.[188] If you do manage to get it right on the first shot, the wife may then compliment you on now having something well hung in the house.

Last but not least on this whole decorating-issues thing, men and women disagree on what even is a decoration. Picture of things? Sure. No problem. However, women tend to hang things on the walls and ceilings that men would never, ever do. Take, for example, a wicker basket. To a man, a basket has only one purpose: to put things in. If there is nothing in the basket, then the basket is useless. A woman, however, is quite different (how many times can I say that?). She looks at a wicker basket as art. Women can even go to basket parties to buy baskets with absolutely no intention of ever putting anything in them. They will get them and have them around the house as part of the décor. This makes about as much sense to a guy as soldering his ratchet set to his tool board for a display.

---

188   For those who haven't seen *The Godfather*, go rent the damn thing. In this particular scene, James Caan's character gets surprised at a tollbooth with more bullets pumped into him than a deer walking into an NRA meeting.

Then you've got other feminine decorations like scented dried flowers, scented candles, potpourri, and wreaths. Men find no sentimental value in flowers to begin with. The idea of taking flowers from an occasion, drying them down, and then displaying them makes about as much sense to a guy as duct taping his old jockstrap to the wall to commemorate the Great Game in his life. And the candle thing? A candle to a guy has only two values: when the electricity is out and when he is desperate to try to get a woman in the mood. Here a woman is buying something that is somewhat practical, but then she never uses it (it is for show and a few quick whiffs here and there), which puts it back squarely in the impractical category.

Potpourri? I didn't even know how to spell the damn word until I hit the spell check. What is it? It is a bunch of flower petals and spices that you hang up to scent the air. Where does this word come from? It is French for "a jar with rotting things," which is why I think women keep the word untranslated. Then you've got wreaths. Not only do women like Christmas wreaths, but they also like wreaths made of ribbon, patches of cloth, flowers, and any other garbage scraps left over from a crafts project that can be glued to something circular. To a guy, all this stuff is useless. So what does a guy like to accessorize a room with? How about the sports trophies he won from his glory days twenty years previous in games he can recite play by play, minute by minute even though he still can't remember his anniversary date.

Section 4

Becoming a Father

or

The First Part is Easy. After That? Not So Much!

Deciding When to Have a Baby

or

Well, It *Seemed* Like a Good Idea at the Time

There are many factors couples consider when deciding whether to have children. Some couples may opt to wait until they have a house, or they have gotten their career to the proper point, or they feel that they are emotionally ready. By the time a couple is truly ready to have a child, the woman has gone through menopause, and the man is so far past his prime that the only hard thing is his bowel movements.

No one is ever truly ready for a baby. How can a sane person say, "Yes, I just can't wait to be peed on, pooped on, puked on, and snotted on. I've had all this extra money that I needed to get rid of, so it will be nice to burn through it like a three-day-old taco through a vegetarian's intestinal tract. Besides that, people spend a third of their lives sleeping. If I have a child, I'll get so much more out of life by only doing five hours a night—not in a row, heaven forbid. And you know, I've got too much sick time saved up at work. It'll be nice to spend a day or two at home when the baby is sick and I have a project due. Since my sick time will be spent on the kids, I'll have to go into work with a raging flu. My coworkers won't mind me spreading my illness around. And another thing, those great adrenaline rushes must be so exciting when I get to see the baby try to swallow any small object that I carelessly left in her reach, or when I lose track of her for just a split second only to see her teetering on the top of a staircase ready to go barreling down. Yep, this baby is going to make my life so much easier and carefree! It's party time!"

So when do you try? Right away? After a few years of marriage? It is nice to spend some time together going out when you want, sleeping in on weekends, knowing what it is like to have friends/life/sanity before the kids come. Then years later, when you've just stopped your two-year-old from trying to snack from the litter box or your teen from thinking he can save time getting ready in the morning by blow-drying his hair in the shower, you can look back at this time to try to remember the sane years. The only problem with this is that one of you may decide freedom and cash don't suck. Then it is a test of wills where the couple has to debate the pros and cons of… Who am I kidding? If a woman wants a child and the man doesn't, all she has to do to win the discussion is lose clothing. By the time she is bare, a man would agree to raising piranhas in the bathtub.

What about having kids when the mood strikes? Many women pick up some other woman's baby, and it is like a virus that then gets into her pores and passes up to her brain that she wants one of these "things" too. Everything then reminds her of a baby. Anything she touches of a diminutive size and she'll give an "aw" and then look longingly at her husband. Any video, commercial, or even picture of a baby of *any* species and the woman starts choking up. The guy can eventually take no more of it, and then they decide to go for it.

How about deciding to have a kid when you finally get medical insurance? Now *that* is a must, or for the rest of your life, your credit score will be so low, you couldn't get a glass of lemonade by the side of the street on credit. If it is the woman getting the job, the *last* thing she will want to say during her interview is that she plans on getting pregnant. Yes, employers are supposed to ignore that, but some aren't excited about the idea of training someone, only to lose them six months later so they can start training another person, only to have them finally get competent in time for the woman to return from maternity leave. It is better in a job interview to act like the idea of having kids gives you the hives, and then later surprise them with it.

Quite often, you don't decide. The decision is made for you. Now, we are all rational adults, and most people know the ways to prevent pregnancies. However, many couples get a bit lax about the whole thing, and then a bun is in the oven. Let's face it—there are more methods of contraception than ever, and yet there are more unplanned pregnancies as well. That makes absolutely no sense. In the end, you just can't beat Mother Nature.[189]

---

189   Let's face it. Mother Nature is going to win and win big every time. It is basically in men's genes not to be able to keep it in their jeans when the opportunity arises to arise. If a guy doesn't want kids and so has put together a PowerPoint presentation along with flipcharts on how the financial impact would be too much to absorb at this moment, all a woman has to do is smile and walk toward the bedroom. At that point, there is no spreadsheet or compelling argument that is going to matter. The battle is over. You are General Custer whistling along as he skips his way into Little Big Horn.

Trying to Have a Baby

or

Sex without Begging or Alcohol...Really

T he most obvious way to have a baby you'd think would be to have a lot of sex. After all, you've spent years trying to prevent pregnancy. However, biology doesn't work that way, so you men out there can stop high-fiving your imaginary friends when a woman says she wants to start trying. If a couple has a lot of sex, the sperm count decreases per ejaculate, and it actually becomes harder to conceive. The odds of conceiving increase dramatically if a couple waits to have sex until the woman ovulates.

Therefore, it is imperative that a man does everything in his power to prevent the woman from finding this information out. For 98 percent of all men, this is the last time in their lives in which they will be getting any amount of sex to speak of. Men will want to stretch out this conceiving thing for long enough to get tons of sex, but not so long that she starts telling all your friends that she thinks your sperm count must be a tad on the low side. To a woman, talking about her husband's sperm count is on par with mentioning his cholesterol count. Not really that big a deal. To a man, his sperm count is a direct correlation to his manliness. If a man could be guaranteed a high sperm count, he'd have a doctor measure it and get the number printed up on a T-shirt for the world to see.[190]

When the couple decides to have a child, the man should say that he wants to do it "naturally" rather than start off timing the ovulations. Women have a tough time with this word since it is tied to things like "natural childbirth" and "natural breastfeeding"—things that she is supposed to aspire to these days. Therefore, she will give in at least for a few months. Her level of enthusiasm for this elevated sexual activity may be on par with having warts removed, but after what a guy usually goes through to get sex (lots of pathetic groveling and whining), just having the woman present and possibly awake is a mega step up.

The amount of time a woman takes to get pregnant is inversely proportional to how hard up the guy has been lately on getting any sex. If the guy considers himself lucky if his wife notices that he does indeed have genitalia, then it is a guaranteed bet that she'll be pregnant in the first month. Those few guys out there who get lots of sex will undoubtedly take a long time to get their wives pregnant and will try to lament to their friends how difficult it is servicing their wives so frequently. They'll get as much sympathy as O. J. Simpson will at his ex in-laws' family reunion.

If she hasn't gotten pregnant after a couple of months, the wife may want to get a little more proactive about the whole thing. First off, she'll end up buying an ovulation thermometer. Unlike a regular thermometer that is cheap and tells you whether you're running a fever, this is an expensive[191] thermometer that can detect small temperature differences. When a woman ovulates, her temperature

---

190 Here lies a conundrum. A guy always wants to be manly, so he thinks nothing of wanting a sperm count to be so high that he merely has to smile at ovulating women to get them pregnant. Yet at the same time, actually getting a woman pregnant is viewed on par with playing tag with a wood chipper.

191 This will not be the only time "pregnancy" and "expensive" are used together. For every other species on the planet, they somehow manage to produce offspring without spending any capital whatsoever. For humans, it is a small fortune to even get past the dating part, never mind the birthing part when we bring the woman to a wing of a hospital where she is waited on by an entire staff of people who have degrees in the whole baby thing so by the time you are done, if you ask for a bill to be printed, it will take about an acre of trees to make enough paper.

spikes a tiny bit. After a woman buys one of these thermometers, she will start charting her temperature on a daily basis. She'll get to know her ovulation cycle better than she remembers your birthday.

At this point, the guy's sex life is about as dry as a Mormon birthday party in Death Valley at high noon. The one exception is when that thermometer spikes. At that point, the wife acts like she is the sergeant on a paratrooper plane: "All right, hurry up and get into place. You've got one shot to get this right. Now move it! Move it! Move it! You're over the target! Launch! LAUNCH!" This may not sound overly romantic, but it's like a Club Med when you compare it to the rest of the month.

If this doesn't work in getting your wife pregnant, she may suggest going to the fertility clinic, which has about as much appeal to men as visiting a proctologist with mallet finger.[192] First off, the fertility doctor will ask every embarrassing question you thought possible in front of your wife like he were asking what you had for lunch. "Do you have trouble achieving an erection? Do you have a problem achieving climax during intercourse? Are you a frequent masturbator?" The proper answer to any question the doctor may ask you is "Hell no!" regardless of what the correct answer is. It also helps if you have a look on your face like he just asked you whether you like to parade around in your wife's underwear when she's off visiting her parents, unless you like that sort of thing, and then it is still "Hell no!"

You will then be required to give a sample only a guy can give. A man can "donate" there at the clinic or bring it from home. Because a sperm sample loses its oomph after only a few hours, the clinic

---

192 Mallet finger, not to be confused with hammer toe or especially camel toe, is an injury where the tendon in the top digit gets broken so that the finger can't straighten and so looks like a bit of a claw. Now, I am fully aware that making jokes at the expense of proctologists is something they are used to and have to deal with nearly every second of their lives. I'm sure they probably call home and their mothers still ask if they've seen anything new and then snigger. However, I feel it currently necessary to bring to light the plight of victims of mallet finger. When I originally wrote this, I suffered from that affliction—and yet with this disability, I garnered no sympathy. Sure, I got it during a company trip playing football on a beach in Florida while my family was freezing in a Maine winter. However, rather than come home to a hero's welcome when I arrived with a splint on my finger, I was still made to do dishes, etc. Are there any support groups for people trying to recover from mallet finger? Nay, not a one! Can I at least get a free trip to Disney? Not likely as the Make a Wish group seems to have monopolized that reward.

would prefer you to "donate" the sample there in one of the back rooms. As casual as a man may act when the doctor hands him a cup and a copy of *Nasty Naked Nubile Nymphos*, this ranks as the most embarrassing moment of his life. You might as well give the guy a public enema.

When you a see a guy carrying a cup in a fertility clinic, there is no doubt about what he is going to do, especially if he has a magazine nestled in his armpit. Even though the professional people who work at a clinic and the patients who are there because they too are having difficulty conceiving are not seemingly paying the man attention as he walks toward a private room, the man still feels like they are all inwardly laughing at him. That's because they are.

You then have to go into the room and somehow get that sample produced. That room is far from erotic, especially considering it isn't like you are the first guy in there. First off, the man should bolt the door and maybe even prop a chair under the doorknob so as not to be disturbed. The man should then examine the room to see if it is properly soundproofed. The room should be so airtight that the oxygen supply will be depleted within half an hour of activity.[193]

Actually, that becomes a serious problem for a guy—how long to take. If you try to "expedite" the sample so that you're out in a minute or two, people may jump to the conclusion that that is how long you last with your wife. If you take too long, they feel that you probably have difficulty achieving a level of attention. If you seem to have no problem and return in a reasonable amount of time, people will assume you are only too well versed in self-satisfaction. A no-win scenario if there ever was one.

Because of all these complications, many men opt to give the sample at home. The problem here is that the shelf life of sperm in a cup is just about as long as it took to produce it. Therefore, you've got to take chances on the road to make sure that you get that sample there promptly: tailgate, wing a few jaywalkers if necessary, but get the sample there immediately, or you'll have to do it again. Here

---

193 Heaven help you if it takes that long because you'll then have people banging on the door asking if you are OK, and that will make it soooo much easier to produce that sample.

you are running through the halls of the medical building carrying the sperm sample like it was a ticking bomb. When you finally reach the right office, you want to get out ASAP, and they'll want to keep you from leaving so that they can get the proper information. For some reason, the offices tend to frown upon jars of unlabeled sperm cluttering up the patient waiting room.

So what's the rush on getting sperm samples analyzed? First off, the doctors try to find out if you have an adequate number of sperm. A fertile male should have over one million sperm per milliliter of semen. Anything less and those sperm will have trouble "storming the gates" to get to that egg. To make sure that your sample is just not temporarily depleted of sperm, you should not have an orgasm at least three days prior to giving. How can a married be sure to overcome this problem? Just wear oven mitts continuously.

The doctor also wants to check the sperm for motility and morphology. Motility has to do with how well the sperm are moving. If you have an adequate number of sperm, but they don't move, they will be about as successful as a yo-yo without a string. Sometimes, men will give samples of sperm that don't swim around well. When this happens, the sperm are described as "poky." Doctors don't think much of saying this, but for many men, this is like having your mother make you wear a bicycle helmet when you play tag with your friends in case you fall down. Morphology has to do with the shape of sperm. If the sperm are all unusually shaped—no tails, multiple tails, multiple heads per tail, etc.—then they have as much chance of hunting down the egg as Elmer Fudd does of catching Bugs Bunny.

If you have a problem with your sperm, you and your wife may still be able to conceive a baby by artificial insemination. Under this procedure, a doctor first gives your wife drugs that make her produce multiple eggs by putting her in a continual super-PMS state. Picture Darth Vader mixed with an evil boll weevil and you'll start to understand what you'll be living with. The doctor then harvests these eggs by putting a tube up your wife's vagina, up her uterus, and down her fallopian tubes. The doctor then literally sucks the eggs out. And your wife wasn't excited about normal vacuuming.

The doctor places the eggs in a petri dish. She then takes a sperm sample from the male and concentrates the sperm.[194] Think of it this way: sure, it only takes one shot with a basketball to make a score, but the odds certainly go up if you have a fleet of blimps drop two or three million from above.

Once the eggs are fertilized, the doctor freezes some for later use. Now I don't know about you, but I pray to God that the doctors are able to keep better track of things than I do in my own freezer. More often than not, I forget to label things, and when I do, the labels fall off. Do the doctors have racks of embryos that they can't tell apart from creamcicles? And then there's freezer burn. What the heck does that do to fertilized eggs? Are these kids going to be born looking like someone that escaped from pro wrestling? When they have to defrost these freezers, what happens to those little embryos? Personally, I usually throw everything on the counter when I'm defrosting. Often, I end up finding something the next day I forgot to put back.

So back to your wife. The doctor then implants a few embryos in your wife. There are some doctors who implant multiple embryos. Doesn't that change the situation from the miracle of birth to more of something you read about in a Stephen King novel? Naturally. So why don't these doctors just implant one or two eggs? Well, the thought here is that implanting multiple eggs ensures that at least one will imbed itself in the uterus. Personally, I am a firm believer that any fertility doctor who implants a large number of eggs in a woman should be locked in a room with half a dozen newborns for about a month to see how his sanity holds up. If he's even capable of wielding a crayon object after this experience, then I'm sure he'll have a change of heart on how he treats patients.

If it is the patient who is insisting on a number more consistent with puppies than human children, that person should undergo a psych evaluation and be able to prove that they have the financial

---

194   To be as educational as possible, I could have looked up how they concentrate sperm and put the details here. Something about searching the web for sperm manipulation gives me the hives as I think the first million or so hits may not be exactly what I was looking for.

means to support them without having to go on the government dole or be signed up for a reality show.[195]

Unfortunately, this high-tech way of reproduction has other major drawbacks. First off, it's expensive. Each treatment is in the five-figure range. Combine that with the fact that the success rate isn't great, and it is not a relaxing venture to enter into. Now if you had $10,000 of work put in on your car, you'd expect to drive away when the experience is done. However, there are no guarantees in Fertilityville—except that the doctor is going to get paid.

So let's get back to talking about the more natural way of procreating: men begging for sex. So how do you tell when a man gets a woman pregnant? The biggest sign is a missed period. Are there other reasons that a woman may miss her period? Yep, several, and one of them is tension. Since your wife is trying to embark on the biggest change in her life, something that some women define as the essence of womanhood, you may say she's a little tense. That and the fact she has to have a lot of sex with you.

For a man, these are some of the greatest days in his life. Lots of sex and lots of...well, what the hell man needs anything more than that? He could have a job cleaning up after circus elephants that have some nasty intestinal parasites and still be smiling with a good sex life. Therefore, the man has no tension, and the woman is brimming over with it.

Because of this, the woman will want to take home pregnancy tests. You're supposed to do them when the period is late. However, many women are so anxious about getting pregnant that they damn near start peeing on these dipsticks right after coitus. The man figures that they'll need one to use about a week or two into the supposed pregnancy to confirm what they already believe; meanwhile

---

195   The ultimate example of poor decision making for fertility is the example of the Octomom, Nadya Suleman. Ms. Suleman had six children, was divorced, unemployed, and on public assistance when she thought it would be a fantastic idea to have enough more children to nearly form a baseball team. She found a doctor who implanted her with eight more kids. The public thought that this decision may not have been the sanest of choices and the doctor not the wisest of medical professionals. He lost his license to practice medicine, and she didn't get the reality television show she was counting on. Apparently she was able to find something people once thought as unfindable as the Holy Grail—a standard so low that even television network executives won't go there.

the woman is heading off to the wholesale store[196] to get pregnancy tests in bulk so that it feels unusual to pee unless it is on something.[197] You'd think that these women were trying to make up for the years of lost ground when boys could and would pee on all sorts of things.

If the pregnancy test is positive, the woman then has to make her first of around two hundred appointments with the obstetrician. What will this doctor do? Rather than go with something as unreliable as a home pregnancy test with 99.2 percent accuracy, she'll run a clinical pregnancy test with 99.6 percent accuracy. It's as if the doctor doesn't trust your wife's competency to follow instructions like (1) pee on end of stick, (2) wait five minutes, and (3) count up to two lines.[198] Let's face it, anyone who doesn't have the brains to run a pregnancy test correctly shouldn't even be allowed to operate a pair of scissors, never mind raise a child.[199]

The doctor will also want to work out a due date. The average pregnancy is forty weeks, but normal pregnancies can vary from thirty-eight to forty-two weeks. So how do you calculate the due date? First off, the woman has to remember when her last period was. She takes the first day of the last month, adds seven days, counts back three months, and then adds one year. Of course, that is if the woman has a normal twenty-eight-day cycle. If her cycle differs from this, she should do the above calculation, but take her normal number of cycle days, subtract 17.3, divide by pi, and use the Caesarian calendar rather than the Gregorian calendar to chart out the time. Isn't life simple with modern medicine?

---

196 The reader may think I believe it is a waste of money to buy pregnancy tests by the case. However, I heartily encourage it. In fact, you may as well have everyone in the household peeing on pregnancy tests just to make sure. This endorsement would have nothing to do with the fact that I work for the company that makes these tests.

197 There are types of jokes even below my standard, so I'll pass on this "golden" moment.

198 If a woman does feel worried about misreading the pregnancy test, she can get the one with a digital read which, coincidentally, is also made by the company I work for.

199 Unless you are smart enough to buy that amazing digital pregnancy test. Amazing technology.

Symptoms of Pregnancy

or

This is Natural?

A major symptom of pregnancy is tender breasts. Now when you try to grope your wife, she can say, "Don't touch them. They hurt," unlike what she has been saying for the last several years: "Don't touch them. I'm not in the mood." It's as if she would be in the mood, but gosh darn of all the coincidences, the time she would finally be willing to let you touch them, they hurt. Not only do the breasts get tender, but also there is a darkening of the areola[200] during the first trimester. What purpose does this serve? Don't ask me—I'd be happy if I just spelled "areola" correctly.

It is during pregnancy that a woman's breasts start to take a permanent vacation south. They shall be "perky" no more. There is good reason for this. As men, it may be hard for us to remember, but breasts actually have a functional rather than just ornamental use. They will

---

200 The areola is the colored skin around the nipple. During pregnancy, the color may darken. Not only does milk eventually come out of the nipple, but there are several openings in the areola itself. There are other openings known as Montgomery glands that give some lubrication around the nipple, which helps the breast pump and the baby suck on the nipple. Why do I mention all these things? To make men understand that breasts are functional organs rather than decorative items. A woman grows and carries breasts her entire life for the sole reason of dealing with these few months of a nursing baby. As such, you may not even get visiting rights.

produce milk for the baby to drink. If the breasts are hanging down, the mother can hold the child in her lap as the child suckles. If the breasts were still perky, she'd have to hold the child like she was doing dumb-bell curls. Unless your wife is built like a feminine version of Hulk Hogan, holding a child like this for an extended period of time would be a wee uncomfortable. Unlike Weebles, though, breasts don't bounce back.

Another major symptom is morning sickness. This name is a bit of a misnomer since some women with this condition feel nauseous twenty-four hours a day. For many women, this condition lasts for the first trimester, while other women can even be sick the entire nine months of pregnancy. It can be so bad that some women actually lose weight at the beginning of their pregnancy because they can't keep anything down. If this is the case, it is best to make sure the bathroom closest to her is always free, even if you have to drive to the local convenience store to relieve yourself.

So what can you do to help a woman in this condition? Remind her of the precious miracle of life and how this is a minor price to pay to bring a baby created by the love of the two of you into the world. Will this logic make her come to a deeper Zen understanding that will give her inner peace that will let her bear the outer discomfort? Hell no. However, it will distract her for a while as she is beating the snot out of you for saying something so ridiculous.

And yet another sign of pregnancy is food cravings. All of a sud-den your wife is going to want to eat strange things. The only guar-antee that you'll have about what your wife wants is that it will be something you don't have. Needless to say, it won't be her going out in the middle of the night or in a blizzard or miles and miles away to a particular restaurant for a particular dish to satisfy this hunger. She must have this food, and it must be immediately. If she wants Wendy's French fries and there is a McDonald's right on the corner, you are going to Wendy's. If you come back with Lay's potato chips and she wanted Pringles, you'll be putting the coat back on and rec-tifying this egregious error.

You may think it is a smart idea to stock up on said food-craving item so that you aren't trudging off to the not-so-local 7-Eleven at 2:00 a.m. Do that, and your wife will promptly change her desire. At this point, if she even hears mention of her previous food craving, she'll heave her cookies clear across the room. Therefore, anything you've stocked up on now has to be tossed, lest she happens upon it and the label alone makes her nauseous.

One way some women have of trying to control morning sickness is by using seasickness remedies. Because pregnant women are anxious about using drugs for fear of, I don't know, mutating their baby into a six-legged venom-spitting gargoyle, they opt for other treatments like the elastic wristband with a bead to put pressure on the wrist. Why does this work? I'm guessing it is based on the same principle chiropractors take. When I say this, do I mean that some methods of alternative medicine defy logic in their ability to heal ailments that modern medicine cannot fully address? No. I'm saying if you pay enough money, it fools your mind into thinking that you had best feel better, otherwise you're being ripped off.

Other women have success controlling morning sickness by eating continually. The theory here is that it is food hitting an empty stomach that makes some women nauseous. Therefore by keeping something in her stomach at all times, she won't be as sick. Unfortunately, women who need to use this technique will be in maternity clothing by the second month of their pregnancy—and remain in maternity clothing for the next decade after the child is born.

Besides the symptoms, there are many other woes that accompany pregnancy. Women are expected to gain twenty-five to thirty-five pounds. Gaining less weight may suggest to the woman that she is starving her child of needed nutrients, and adding more puts an unhealthy strain on her that may take months to years to never to eventually lose. There is stress either way for the poor woman. No one usually mentions the strain put on the father, however. The woman will look at her husband and say, "I'm fat!" in a way that implies he tried to get her pregnant just so he could satisfy his sick sense of humor as he sees her turn into the Goodyear Blimp. She may have begged for years to have a child, but "fat" is his fault, and he should pay for this transgression accordingly.

A vast majority of women have tried their entire lives to obtain an unhealthy weight standard, and because of something you did to her, she does not want to go to the beach for fear that Greenpeace members will try to keep pushing her out into deep water. If a guy tries to convince his wife that "pregnant" is different from "fat," he'll then find himself trying to convince her to remove his head from the waffle iron that she shoved it into. What to do? Just thank God he doesn't have one of those wives who has the opposite problem and refuses to dress like she is pregnant and so struts her ever-increasing stuff in spandex and tube tops.

Another woe of pregnancy is frequent urination. Men don't normally think of this, but a growing baby does some freakish things to a woman's body. The internal organs that were occupying that space before the ever-expanding child came along have to go somewhere, and there is very little place for them to go. Therefore, they end up getting squashed and distorted. In particular, the baby is going to be sitting right on the urinary bladder. Even before pregnancy, women were never known to hold their bladder as good as men. Tell a really good joke, and you could send a woman rushing for the bathroom with her legs locked at the knees. Take a cross-country trip, and you'll be pulling off highways and going down countless roads trying to find bathrooms that meet her standards.[201] Now with a baby sitting on top of it, a woman's bladder has the capacity of a tablespoon.[202] Pregnant women end up rushing to the bathroom continually only to have a few drops of urine dribble out. It's barely enough to moisten the toilet paper. This bladder matter is exacerbated at night as women find themselves getting up each and every hour to head to the john.[203]

---

201 Men are lucky enough that if they need to pee and the only place around is a gas station that looks like it hasn't been cleaned after being the primary spot for blind biker gangs to do their business for a decade, they can basically use their foot to open the doors, flush, and every last issue to keep themselves from being exposed. If a guy thinks he could get more germs by washing his hands and having to touch the sink, he can skip it. A woman has less luck with her anatomical differences. Once she is done, it is best not to discuss how she did what she did as she will more than likely immediately try to scrub it from her memory.

202 In the case of twins, it is a tablespoon held by a person on the Tilt-a-Whirl at the fun park.

203 Helpful hint: she will not find a bedpan to be a humorous gift. Trust me.

Now let me think…are there any other pregnancy woes? Oh yes, come to think of it, there are hemorrhoids, varicose veins, stretch marks, swollen and bleeding gums, fatigue, backache, indigestion, shortness of breath, various body parts swelling,[204] and maybe even a bout of gestational diabetes just for the hell of it. You'd think that after the millennia that women have been giving birth to babies, evolution would have the woman's body figure out what the hell to do when it gets pregnant. Instead, it is like putting an orangutan in charge of a nuclear power plant. Nothing—I repeat, nothing—about a woman's body is the same once she gets pregnant.

Mentally, her hormones have no clue as to which ones should be on and which should be off. It's like the pituitary gland is hopped up on speed and has the attitude of a drill sergeant to boot. This leads a woman's emotions to be about as stable as a three-legged cow in a hurricane. Not putting the toilet seat down may have slightly irritated her before, but now it may send her into a sobbing hysteria. Don't put the cap back on the toothpaste? That may be cause for her to attempt to dislocate your knees with a hot iron in a heated rage. Maybe this is nature's attempt to get men ready for the crying and temper tantrums that come along with the newborn baby. Maybe not.

Physically, a woman may have her hair and nails grow much faster or much slower than before. She may even have hair sprouting up in places she doesn't want.[205] While it is also not uncommon for the hair on her head to fall out, keep the remote control in hand and ready to change the channel should a hair-restoration commercial come on. If you aren't in time, do not dare look in her direction, or she'll be making your next meal with rat poison in it.

---

204 Not just the good parts. One really big problem is feet swelling. If she walks more than a quarter mile, her toes balloon up to look like link sausages, and the rest of her foot is so puffed you can't even see her ankle. The technical term for this is cankle, where you can't tell where her calf ends and her ankle begins. Do not utter the word "cankle" within six blocks of your wife, lest she teach you the word "emasculate."

205 It would be unwise to point out these new strands of hair. Do not even get caught looking at them.

Being Pregnant

or

Of Course You Don't Look Fat, but

I Still Can't See the Television

When a woman finds out she is pregnant, she is immediately thrust into a quandary. She wants to tell everyone, but is afraid to because she is fearful of having a miscarriage and then having to painfully explain to everyone what happened. Therefore, at the beginning, she'll only tell people on a need-to-know basis. However, with women, this list is still usually the size of a Manhattan phonebook.[206] So everyone will know, but nobody is supposed to let on that everyone knows. This conspiracy of silence is usually broken after the second to third month of pregnancy when one of the male relatives openly asks about the baby in a crowd of people because he is not familiar with the rules of silence, not that he or any other guy would understand them even if he did know them.

If the pregnant woman is not already worried, then the doctor will perform enough tests to get a woman into a full-fledged panic. So many tests get performed on a pregnant woman that it becomes

---

206 In ancient times, they had books that were just lists of phone numbers.

unnatural for her to pee without reaching for a cup.[207] Every time she goes to the doctor, she must provide a sample of this golden liquid. Quite often, the woman will have to supply blood samples as well. Things get bad enough that the doctors might as well install a catheter in her bladder and a spigot in her arm to make sampling bodily fluids that much easier.

So what do they test for? One of the things is alpha-fetoprotein from the mom's blood. Too much of this protein indicates a neural problem like spina bifida, and too little may indicate Down's syndrome. It is true that both of these conditions are rare, but by checking on them, the doctor draws the wife's attention to the possibilities and then makes her sweat, usually for the weekend, before the results come in so she can really be in a tizzy. Another blood test is to determine the baby's blood type. If the Rh factor of the baby is the same as the mother's, then there is no problem. If the baby is positive and the mother is negative, then there may be an issue for the next child as the mom develops antibodies that would attack the second child's blood. The mother's immune system is on watch against parasites. A child, although cuter than a tapeworm and a bit more wanted, is still, you may say, the ultimate parasite in a woman's body.

Another blood test involves the woman drinking this high-glucose drink. Just imagine taking about fifteen gallons of flat Mountain Dew and boiling it down to about ten ounces of a syrupy stuff. A blood sample is taken before the drink and after the drink so that the levels of glucose can be monitored. If the doctors find abnormal levels of glucose in the blood because the mother's body flips out with people trying to turn it into corn syrup, then that can indicate gestational diabetes.

Now, I know a tad about diabetes since my brother has juvenile diabetes. On a whim just to see if he is spontaneously cured, I wouldn't melt a Hershey's chocolate bar into a cheeseburger patty I am cooking him. That would be considered a bad thing. So why do doctors give tons of sugar to potential diabetics? That would seem similar to funneling Jack Daniels into a person to see if they are an alcoholic.

---

207 This comes just after you finally break her of the habit of needing a pregnancy stick to pee on.

Let's move to the urine tests. One of the things doctors check for here is hCG. Haven't you already done that, you say? Yes, that is the thing you checked for with those marvelous home pregnancy tests and were so happy to find. Now, however, a level that is too high may indicate Down's syndrome, and that will require yet more monitoring, testing, and panicking. They'll also test the urine for sugar. No, that doesn't mean she can put it on her corn flakes. It means that she has gestational diabetes. "Whoa, whoa," you say. Didn't we just cover that gestational diabetes thing with that supersugar drink and blood test? Why yes, but unlike the sugar drink, they can do this test each and every time the woman donates a urine sample. We've got to watch out for those schizophrenic diabetics, you know.

The doctors may even throw in a drug screen to make sure that the mother is not endangering her fetus with illicit drug use. Personally, I wish they could throw in a few other bad-behavior tests for prospective parents, like finding out those who park in handicapped spaces when their only malady is laziness, those who can't comprehend that the seven-item-and-under line at the grocery store could possibly apply to them, and those who think brushing their teeth every day is too "upper crust." Of course if they did that, the fathers would have to give a few samples to test as well. The ones who are willing to do so probably don't need it, while the ones who aren't willing probably think parenting ends when they put their pants back on after insemination.

The only fun test is when they do the ultrasound. This test will actually give you somewhat of a picture of the baby. To do this test, the woman lies down on a table. To ensure that there is good contact between the instrument and the woman, the doctor applies a two- to three-inch layer of goop all over the stomach. A flat probe is then applied. This probe emits an ultrasonic sound wave that penetrates the woman's belly, bounces off the child, goes back to the probe, and then makes an image of the baby on a screen.[208]

---

208 Didn't think sounds could penetrate a solid body? You haven't seen anything yet. Just wait until you are in the grocery store and your two-year-old child wants a bag of animal crackers and you don't give it to her. She'll emit a scream that will penetrate your entire being. You'll be feeling that screech reverberating in your bones, setting your teeth chattering.

A picture of the baby is then shown on the screen. Doing an ultrasound can help verify the due date, determine the sex, find out if there are multiple babies, estimate the baby size, check for malformations, and find out the position the baby is in. The information one gets is dependent upon when one takes the sonogram. Early on, all you can get is an accurate due date. The doctor will point out where all the baby's parts are, but to the untrained eye, the picture looks more like an inkblot test rather than your progeny.

In later months, the picture is a bit clearer. You still won't know what is what, but you'll use your imagination to think you can almost see something. Stare at it long enough like those 3-D pictures you find in the funny papers, and all of a sudden it will pop out at you. Either way, the doctor will usually give the two of you a picture to take home. That way, you two can point to various parts of the picture and argue about what the hell is what whenever you show the picture to friends and family.

The Don'ts of Pregnancy

or

Misery Loves Company, and She Is Going to Be Miserable

U nless there is going to be a star hovering over the hospital where the woman delivers the baby, chances are that she does a few things in her life that she will have to cut out or at least cut down on while pregnant. There are also things that she is supposed to be better at. If the woman is lucky, she'll have a partner who not only understands this, but makes sacrifices with her so she doesn't feel alone. Therefore, if your wife does not have a coworker or friend in the same position, buy her a puppy.

Let's start with the don'ts. First off, women should not drink alcohol. There is quite a bit of irony here because alcohol is the reason many women are even in this predicament to begin with. When pregnant women drink alcohol, it goes directly into their bloodstream, and from there, directly into the baby's bloodstream. The blood-alcohol level is dependent upon how much a person weighs and how much the person has drunk. Since the baby is going to range from a clump of cells to a six- to a pelvis-busting twelve-pounder, a few teaspoons of alcohol to them is like an all-night fraternity party.

Because the brain of a baby is busy forming billions of vital neural connections, it doesn't particularly need the additional challenge of doing so while plastered.

Certainly another don't is drugs. It is quite apparent that illegal drugs are a bad thing for a pregnant woman to take, but that is as self-evident as saying pregnant women should not bungee jump off bridges. That isn't the issue when we are saying that pregnant women shouldn't take drugs. If you are asking if heroin is OK for a pregnant woman, you are as ready to be a parent as Malcolm X is to be the grand wizard for the KKK.

The more difficult issue is with legal drugs, the kinds we take for granted, like headache medication, cold medication, allergy medication, etc. Most of these medicines people have taken their entire lives. Now, however, a pregnant woman must question any drug she puts into her body. Before taking even an over-the-counter medication, she should call her doctor to get permission, talk to the pharmacist to get details of how the medication should be taken, call the drug manufacturer to get clinical-trial information on testing of pregnant women, and maybe even check with the FDA to make sure there haven't been any recalls with this product.

Sound silly? Well, let's take a look at the most widely used medicine: aspirin. People take aspirin for nearly any ailment the body goes through, from headaches to fevers to even heart attacks (where aspirin is taken as a preventative). It also has been associated with extending pregnancy and labor, and even resulting in more bleeding during birth. All this from our little pal the aspirin? It's enough to give a pregnant woman a headache!

Therefore, most women end up suffering through all the minor ailments of life because they are petrified to take anything. You won't be saving any money on this front, because the amount of medicine a male needs during this time easily doubles as he is taking everything he can to put up with a pregnant wife if she is complaining about every single ache and pain—and there will be *plenty* of those.

What's the best way not to take medical drugs? Don't get sick in the first place. How is that for some lame advice? That is like telling a person who wants to lose weight that the only things she's allowed to eat are ice cubes and vitamins. Yes, it may be dumb advice, but unfortunately pregnant women have to follow it.

How do they do this? Pregnant women should avoid all sick people, no matter what the ailment is. As a rule of thumb, if a person coughs, just assume they have leprosy and act accordingly. To be on the safe side, your wife could become a neat freak. By continually wearing a surgical mask, avoiding places where people congregate, only breathing air that is at least 10 percent Lysol, and never actually sitting down on the toilet, your wife will maximize the chance that she will remain healthy. And that is when you get sick and have to sleep in the basement.

Another don't is cigarette smoking. No, that doesn't mean your wife should switch to chewing tobacco or light up a big stogie. Anything with nicotine should be considered a no-no. Nicotine has a way of permeating the entire organism, sort of like how seeing someone chew on aluminum foil can set off every nerve in your body. In women who smoke, you can even find nicotine in their vaginal secretions. Therefore, you can be sure the baby is getting a heavy dose of it. Cigarette smoking has been directly related to low birth weights. For those women fearful of the birthing segment of pregnancy, chain smoking to reduce the child's weight is not considered appropriate "preventative medicine."

Not only do women have to not smoke themselves, but they should avoid the secondhand smoke from others. There are two ways pregnant women avoid cigarette smoke. The first group of women always requests nonsmoking accommodations and actively avoids areas where they know there will be smoking, while the second group feels free to go anywhere, and if someone happens to be smoking around them, they threaten to extinguish the cigarette in the offender's navel if he doesn't immediately put it out himself.[209]

---

209 If there ever was a no-win situation, it would be getting into an argument with a pregnant woman. What can you do? It doesn't matter if she is saying she finds it perfectly acceptable to waterboard nuns. If people hear you saying no to a woman who is in the midst of creating (for the 13 billionth time in the history of humankind), the "miracle of life," they will look at you like you decided to gel your hair with dog droppings. In the cigarette scenario, maybe a guy had to leave his building during a break and walk several blocks to the corner of a yard that allows him the time for a single cigarette before he has to run back. If a pregnant woman happens to walk by and yell at him to put it out, what can he do? Not much. Of course if it is your wife and you are with her, there is nothing another guy can do *to her*…

A don't that many women have trouble with is caffeine. Most people in this society need to jump-start their day with coffee or soda and then need regular transfusions to keep from collapsing into a jellylike substance. However, caffeine, although not as bad as many things, is not the greatest thing for a pregnant woman to consume. First off, caffeine is a diuretic, which means that it makes you pee. Pregnant women do not need anything else making them pee more than they already are. Would you give a laxative to a person with diarrhea? Not only that, but women tend to pee out the calcium that is needed for healthy fetal bone development, and it is suggested that caffeine interferes with the proper absorption of iron. As if pregnant mothers don't have enough to fret over, the idea that a simple cup of coffee in the morning is sucking vital nutrients out of their starving unborn child should be enough to keep her wired without the caffeine.

A commonsense don't is for a woman not to overexert herself. She should not be lifting heavy things or working to the point of exhaustion. Unfortunately, pregnant women get this "nesting" impulse where they must get the domicile ready for the new family member. The two of you could have been living together for a dozen years, but when she gets into the latter stage of pregnancy, she'll "realize" that the basement has to be reorganized. It doesn't matter if your only visit to the basement is a yearly trip to drag in/out the Christmas decorations. If she says it needs to be done, then she will not change her mind. If you don't help her, she will end up doing it herself, and you will feel like the scum you find in a stagnant pond. During these nine months, every room is rearranged approximately seven times. Thankfully, the toilet, tub, and sink are bolted in place, so she can't do too much damage to that room.

There are two problem groups when talking about this don't. The first is the overzealous men who will not let their wives pick up anything heavier than a book. Life becomes quickly frustrating for these women who are told that they can't do anything that may cause the release of a single bead of perspiration. These women become so frantic for activity that you can find them slipping out of bed at night to bench-press engine blocks just to make up for the dulled-down days.

The other problem group is the women who feel that lifting anything more than the *TV Guide* is strenuous enough that they should recoup with a heavy dose of *Oprah* and bonbons. It is easier sighting dodo birds than these women doing anything more physical than blinking. These women sit around, expect to be waited on hand and foot, eat, drink, and emit various noxious gases. Who the hell do they think they are? Men on football Sunday?

One surprising don't that pregnant women should follow is not to listen to every freakin' person who comes out of the woodwork to offer advice on what a pregnant person is supposed to do.[210] For some reason, pregnant women work as magnets for attracting bad advice. When a woman is pregnant, everyone from relatives to absolute strangers feels perfectly comfortable giving their two cents about any issue they deem relevant. If a woman is carrying anything heavier than a loaf of bread, some people feel free to stop and scold her behavior. If she is—heaven forbid—exercising, you can expect cars to come to a screeching halt so their drivers can chastise her. You can expect this boorish behavior from the fifth month on until birth. Then expect the advice to double with child rearing.

What to do about this unwanted advice? Most people usually ignore it for the first two or three hundred times, but everyone's patience has a limit. I'm sure even the Virgin Mary felt like shouting, "Yes, I'm pregnant, and yes, I am traveling a lot by camel. God told me to travel, so I'm traveling. You got a problem with that, take it up with him. Now get off my ass!"

I feel like I have to warn you here about something else other people do when they see a pregnant woman—some people feel it is perfectly fine to go put their hand on a pregnant woman's belly to feel the baby move. Hello? Who do these people think they are to go over and grope someone else's anatomy? Would a man feel comfortable being crotched by a buddy asking about his hernia? How about a woman getting her buttocks grabbed because she has hemorrhoids? Quite often, the pregnant woman will give a fake smile when she is getting felt up, but often she is feeling like she'd want

---

210 Present company excluded.

to reach over and crush every last bone in the offender's wrist so that the next thing he feels is the inside of a cast. Therefore, be prepared for this to happen. At times, a husband may need to throw his body between his wife and probing hands.

One don't your wife will actually like is that pregnant women should not clean litter boxes. Some cats can transmit a disease known as toxoplasmosis. What is this dreaded disease? It's transmitted by *Toxoplasma gondii*, and the symptoms include a slight fever and mild malaise. Certainly not symptoms that should have a person shaking in their boots, but it can cause birth defects if the disease is transmitted to the baby during pregnancy. Greatest exposure to the disease occurs when dealing with old cat poop, hence litter-box duty is passed to the father. Chances are that a woman who has a cat with toxoplasmosis has already been exposed to the disease and needn't worry. However, why take chances?[211] Besides, the worst of cat poops is easier to clean than the best of baby poops. The only problem is that men never get to give this duty up once they assume full responsibility. Do you blame the woman for not taking that back?

Listing all the don'ts of pregnancy would make this section about as heavy as *War and Peace*, so I'll just briefly name a few more: hot tubs, horseback riding, skiing, tap water (that might contain lead), bottled water (that won't have the proper minerals), foods with too many preservatives, foods that aren't properly preserved, too much sun, not enough sun, and anything else she would find fun and/or tasty.

---

211 The guy damn well knows why—he doesn't want to be on permanent cat-turd duty. I adopted my wife's cat when we got married, and after the first pregnancy, I have changed that box ever since. Decades of sifting out little brown cat presents. The only blessing here is that cats don't have the muscles to be able to smirk when they stare at you with scooper in hand.

The Do's of Pregnancy

or

Do What the Pregnant Lady Says,
and No One Gets Hurt...Maybe

B elieve it or not, there are some things a pregnant woman is actually allowed to do. Unfortunately, most of them are about as fun as playing kickball in traffic. You see, the do's here aren't things she *can* do, they are things she *must* do. Why must she? Guilt. Buckets of guilt. Boatloads of guilt. A pregnant woman quite often feels like a human incubator who has to tailor her existence to the baby. She is a guilt machine. There are racks and racks of advice books telling pregnant women what to eat, how to work, how to sleep, ad nauseam, to the point where she is so stressed out that she could operate a jackhammer without turning it on.

The first major do is for the woman to eat a proper diet. If your wife reads all the pregnancy self-help books, she'll come to know that a pregnant woman's body should be treated like a shrine. Therefore, putting a Hostess Twinkie into it is about as sacrilegious as taking a whiz in St. Peter's Cathedral.

Let's start with sweets. Sweets are considered "empty calories." In other words, you get about as much nutritive value gnawing on Styrofoam as you do eating a box of chocolates. As a woman eats sweets, she is filling herself up and making less room for foods that can actually build a baby. Does that mean she will stop eating sweets? Absolutely not, but she will feel amazing amounts of guilt when doing so. You may have some women who enter more of a ninja mode where they sneak a bit here and there. No one may see them doing so, but the boxes of Funny Bones are not long for this world.

Another thing to consider is steatopygia. You, as a husband who has to live with his wife for the rest of his natural life, should warn your wife that she can acquire this dreaded condition by having too many unhealthy snacks. So what is this alarming malady?

"Steatopygia" is the technical word for having a big butt. By telling your wife you're worried she may acquire steatopygia, you sound like a loving and concerned partner in life. Telling her that you don't want her butt to expand faster than the national debt, on the other hand, will require her to sock you upside the head so hard that it will permanently erase any memory you had from the last ten years of your life.

Protein is important to a pregnant woman. She should have at least four servings a day. That equals out to a full cow and flock of chickens each week. Then there are your fruits and vegetables, of which she should have another three or four servings. This group provides a lot of vitamins, including folic acid. A lack of folic acid can lead to spinal tube defects.[212] Therefore, pregnant women should not be able to pass by some food-related item that is green without stuffing it in their mouths.[213]

They should also be sucking down four servings from the milk group. Milk is rich in calcium and vitamin D for strong bones as well as proper development of muscles and the nervous system. Unfortunately, her breasts are not open for business yet, so you'll have to keep buying the stuff. There is no cutting out the middleman,

---

212 Notice a pattern? Nary a day goes by where a pregnant woman isn't doing or not doing something that is theoretically possible to jeopardize the baby's health. It is a wonder that by the time the woman goes into labor she isn't in a straightjacket from the pressure.

213 There are many exceptions to this rule. If older bread has now taken on a green patchy color, that does not count. If you left raw hamburger on the counter rather than put it into the refrigerator, that would also not be appropriate to eat.

or middle cow or whatever you want to call it, for her to get her dairy requirements. Last but not least is the breads-and-cereals group. The thing to watch out for here is white breads. Instead, everything must be whole-grain fortified. If she can't taste the hay, then it isn't good enough.

Besides the basic food groups, her fluid intake should increase. Pregnant women are supposed to be drinking eight glasses of water each day. Considering that there are eight ounces in a standard cup and a pregnant woman's bladder can only hold three ounces at a time, you can figure that she'll be blowing more calories running to the bathroom than in any other activity.[214]

Another big do is exercise. That is, a pregnant woman should exercise once she gets permission from her doctor. As a general rule, pregnant women are advised to ask their doctor about any activity other than breathing—until time for delivery, at which point they'll even reteach her that! For many women, exercise is a vain attempt to keep the body in some semblance of order as all her parts are dropping, shifting, or widening. If nothing else, exercise will keep the woman in shape to carry all the extra weight that is going to be piled on her as well as keep her endurance up so she can get through a marathon birthing session.

Aerobic exercise is recommended, provided the woman prop-erly stretches out so as not to strain a muscle. In early pregnancy, standard warm-up stretches can be used. However, as a pregnant woman balloons, she's not going to be able to see her toes, never mind touch them. When about to exercise, it is best for the woman to wear loose-fitting clothing—*not* something she is excited to buy for herself. Usually, just putting on gym clothes is so cumbersome for a pregnant woman that it alone is enough of a workout.

Pregnant women even have their own sets of exercises. One of them is called Kegel. Exercise is often meant to improve muscle

---

214   Actually, that old rule of eight glasses of water a day for everyone is a bunch of bunk. All those years of health class telling you that were based on a scientific mistake. In fact, too much water can put a strain on your kidneys so you *don't* want to be doing that. Trust me, I'm a doctor, albeit one closer in range to Dr. Seuss than one you'd ask to inspect you for a medical malady.

tone, and this is no exception. It just so happens that the muscle in question is not available to be viewed by the general public. When a woman is doing this exercise, she is tightening her, well, her…Let's just say that she is trying to strengthen muscles for delivery. At least she doesn't need a piece of Nautilus equipment to do it. The other biggie is that after birth, this muscle is pretty much shot to hell. Men may pull a hamstring, but it isn't quite the same. One issue with women is that after childbirth, there could be some urinary incontinence, so her getting that muscle in shape may help keep you from waking to dreams of stepping in puddles.

Overall, the trick to exercising during pregnancy is to keep exercise as low impact and low excitement as possible. Light jogging is in, and kickboxing is out. If the mother is exercising dramatically and not eating right, the fetus may not have the nutrition it needs. If the mother decides the most exercise she plans on getting is lifting the television remote, the only figure she'll be getting back later is maybe a tax refund.

Believe it or not, another do is sex. Actually, it is more of a "pretty-please do" from the man's point of view and a "can, but do not want to do" from the woman's. The only medical reasons that should really prevent a pregnant woman from having sex with her husband are (1) if she has a history of miscarriages, and the doctor has warned that it may stimulate early labor; and (2) if she is already in labor. Besides that, medically speaking, husbands get the green flag. Meanwhile, your wife is waving the checkered flag because she thinks the race finished some time ago.

Therefore, it is the husband's never-ending job to convince her otherwise. First off, women in the first trimester are very tired. The energy it takes to build a placenta is equal to what is needed to climb a mountain each day. If the woman knows this piece of trivia, the guy can kiss any chance in the first trimester good-bye. A man will try to make some suave moves on his wife, who will then scoff at him, ask what the hell he did during the day, and compare that to that stinkin' hypothetical mountain she climbed, and that will be the end of that. A guy just can't compete. Throw in a bout of morning sickness accompanied by nausea and vomiting, and the guy's chances are about as good as the Chicago Cubs winning the Super Bowl, never mind the World Series.

In the second trimester, the placenta is formed, so she actually has more energy now than before. Her excuse then becomes "I'm fat!" The appropriate response is not "So? What does that have to do with me?" Never, ever give that response.. A man now must try to convince his wife that there is not only a difference between fat and pregnant, but that she is still attractive. It doesn't matter at all that her husband truly does find her attractive—a woman carrying the man's baby is an unbelievably beautiful thing to most men. As with every other opinion a man has that differs from his wife's, however, this one is treated like the rotting carcass of a rat found stuck behind the refrigerator and discarded as promptly as possible.

In the third trimester, the woman becomes so large that conventional sex becomes a bit difficult. The missionary position usually puts too much of the man's weight directly on her uterus. A man might think she's getting excited, but she's really gasping for her last dying breath as her uterus flattens out her diaphragm. Not comfortable.

Throughout the pregnancy, the woman may be afraid that sex will hurt the baby. It's not like the kid is going to be dodging an incoming Scud missile attack; he's in a different portion of her body separated by a mucus plug. However, the man shouldn't bother trying to explain this in too much detail to his wife because it's pretty hard for anyone to feel amorous after even mentioning the words "mucus plug," never mind discussing it.

The woman may also be unnerved in that she feels like she is having sex "in front of the baby." The guy has then got to convince her that the baby would have absolutely no idea what was going on. To any logical person, it is only obvious that the baby could not possibly have an inkling of what sex was, never mind that his parents were performing the act. However, we're not dealing with a logical person. We're dealing with a pregnant person. This is a person who may burst into tears if you tell her that her shoes are untied or may freak out and stab you if you cut her toast into rectangular pieces rather than triangular. Therefore, your chance of winning a logical discussion with her is about as good as your chance of winning an arm-wrestling bout with an enraged gorilla.

If the stars do align properly and a couple actually does engage in sexual intercourse, there are a few things to watch out for, namely breasts. It is no secret that men look at breasts with the same fascination that women would reserve for an extraterrestrial landing. To men, they are engineering marvels. Put a man in front of the great Pyramids of Giza, and then have a woman pull off her top—guess which one he will be looking at. However, during pregnancy, breasts are usually quite tender. Therefore, there is a strict "look but don't touch" policy in effect.[215] Most men find this cosmically unfair.

In short, sex during these nine months is going to be as rare as Amish hula dancers. To get through this time, a man must lower his standards for sexual gratification. Seeing his wife without her shoes on should now count as nudity. Being allowed to rub her back as she falls asleep is foreplay. And as for sex...well, hopefully you have some fond memories to fall back on, as well as high-speed Internet.

---

215 Actually, consider yourself lucky if you even get to look!

A Month-by-Month Review of Pregnancy

or

Out of the Frying Pan and...

By the end of the first month of pregnancy, the baby looks like a tadpole that is about the size of a grain of rice. The amazing thing here is not that this tiny little thing is going to become a full-fledged baby, but how much destruction it is causing to the mother's body. This once-graceful woman now pees every twenty minutes, vomits every thirty minutes, takes a nap every sixty minutes, has uncontrolled bouts of flatulence, loses her hair in clumps, and has moods that swing as often as Tarzan in the jungle.

A woman will not physically show signs of pregnancy, at least with her clothes on. The major thing to start changing is a woman's breasts. The aereolas start to get bigger and darker. Sometimes, blue lines appear on her breasts. These are veins getting bigger as the breasts need higher blood flow. Then sometimes the breasts will get little bumps from the underlying sweat glands. Sound bad? Don't worry—she won't let you see them anyway, as explained above.

Usually, it is the woman's diet that has to change. I mentioned earlier that she may need to eat a just a little, but constantly, if she has morning sickness. That way when she blows chunks, it doesn't have the volume to drown any small pets. However, even if the woman eats absolutely perfectly, it is still suggested that she take a vitamin supplement. Now, this ain't your usual pill. This thing looks like it is meant for horses. It's about the size of a cocktail wiener, and your wife is supposed to just swallow it down.

Personally, I'd think the vitamin manufacturers would do better by making six smaller pills rather than that mammoth one, but maybe they're just trying to get her emotionally ready to move something large down a passageway that just isn't used to such girth. If she wasn't sick before, this should do the trick.

By the end of the second month, the baby starts to look somewhat human if you cross your eyes and take a few hallucinogenic drugs. It's a bit over an inch in length and has arms and legs. At this point, the woman is probably having her clothes fit snugly. She will not be happy about this, especially because she knows she has seven more months to go, and she's going to expand like a mushroom cloud.

Just because she's gained a few pounds, a pregnant woman will start to fret about the impending meltdown of her figure, fearing that it will never return to its prepregnancy form. The real unfortunate thing is that the woman will usually blame the weight gain on the guy for eating all those chips and ice cream around her and basically forcing her to go off her diet. The way she'll describe it, you are basically shoving those Swiss rolls down her throat since you allowed her to find them hidden in your sock drawer.

Around this time, people will start to comment on how the pregnant woman is "glowing." People associate this glow with the overwhelming amount of love that the woman is generating for her unborn child. It sounds nice. Unfortunately, the truth is more akin to the woman's hormones going wacko and having her glands start pumping oil faster than a Saudi Arabian derrick. The glow is basically light reflecting off the oil slick that is now on her face. With that much grease, you could open up a truck-stop diner and still have enough to give your entire silverware collection a healthy glow of its own. It goes without saying that those "glowing" comments will dry up if her face breaks out like a pepperoni pizza. She'll think that her having her face look like those early awkward teenage years will be a laugh riot.[216]

In the third month, the baby is now almost three inches long and weighs about half an ounce. It now has a rudimentary circulatory system, and it may even be possible to hear the baby's heart. Because of this, it now exacerbates the "is my baby all right?" terror that women go through every time they step into the doctor's office as they wait desperately for the doctor to find the heartbeat. If the doctor has to move the stethoscope multiple times to try to find it, the wife's heart makes up for it by beating double time. Women would be more "calm, cool, and collected" while being abducted by aliens brandishing cattle prods than while at a routine prenatal visit.

By the end of the fourth month, the baby is about four inches long. It is capable of simple actions like sucking his thumb. Because of these slight movements, the expectant mother may actually be able to feel a slight fluttering in her stomach. When she does, you'll be able to tell because she'll freeze in midsentence or midaction and concentrate on trying to feel the baby move. Every essence of her being will be focused on trying to feel the miracle growing inside of her. Heaven help you if she's driving at the time.

About this time, the woman will have to succumb to the inevitable and buy maternity clothes. No longer can she walk around with an oversized T-shirt hiding the fact that she can't button her pants. The problem is that a woman must buy an entire wardrobe even though she'll only use it for a few months. Even if a woman does get pregnant again, it is destined to be in a different part of the year, so her winter maternity wardrobe will be useless in the summer when she needs it. Usually maternity clothes announce to the world that a woman is pregnant. They've got dorky bows, frilly lace, and all other sorts of nonsense. It certainly gets pretty tough for a career woman to plan a hostile takeover of a company when she looks like an escapee from the Ringling Brothers and Barnum & Bailey Circus.

By the time the fifth month comes to a close, the baby is now eight to ten inches long and actually looks human rather than like a

---

216 If you make a joke about her acne, she'll try to give you a matching problem by dragging her high heels out of the closet and dancing on your face while you sleep.

reptilian space invader you might find on the SyFy channel. At this point, it is easy for the mother to determine when the baby is moving. This month, feeling the baby move is still a novelty. The expectant mother will want to share this novelty. Therefore, every time the baby moves, the mother will go frantically searching for the father to put his hand on her abdomen. Here the guy is sitting there watching a ballgame when his wife comes storming into the room with her shirt half over her head. By the time he's figured out what the hell is going on, the baby will have stopped.

By the end of the sixth month, the baby is over a foot long and weighs almost two pounds. All the major organ groups are functioning normally, so it is possible that the baby could survive if born prematurely. About this time, the mother is considering that a viable option. In short, she is a tired, aching mess. Around now, the woman starts having difficulty sleeping. If the woman naturally sleeps on her stomach, she'll now have to give that up. Otherwise, that growing stomach is going to make her look like a seesaw. Sleeping on her back is also no good. The baby would basically be squashing all her internal organs.

So how does a woman who is not used to sleeping on her side now do so in comfort? Pillows. A pregnant woman needs lots of pillows. She needs pillows like Jerry Springer needs white trash.[217] She'll be propping pillows in front of her, in back of her, and even between her legs. You won't be able to get within a country mile of her—and don't think she doesn't consider that an even bigger advantage to tons of pillows. Thankfully, enough pillow manufacturers have realized the need for special pillows for pregnant women and have begun manufacturing and marketing them. They're usually

---

217 For those unaware of Jerry Springer, he was a former Cincinnati city counselor who got busted with prostitutes. He somehow got a talk show where they would find people who would utterly detest each other, like drug dealers and the parents of the kid who got addicted or seven women the same guy impregnated. They'd put them on stage and start asking questions until one person inevitably would jump up and try to attack the other while security then tried to pull them apart. It was Jerry's job to look appalled and disappointed that this behavior took place. It is kind of like going to a dog fight and being shocked that the dogs attack each other rather than sniff each other's butts like dogs do to get acquainted.

half the size of normal pillows, shaped for the specific purpose, and apparently stuffed with golden goose feathers. How else could they justify the ridiculous price?

Even if she is sleeping properly, a pregnant woman's back will ache like she's played nose tackle for the Denver Broncos. Actually, there is a valid biological reason a woman's back is in constant agony. The joints in the pelvis must start loosening up so that the baby will have an easier time getting out. Otherwise, it would be like trying to push a bolt through a nut rather than turning it. Combine this with an inflated stomach, and the woman's posture looks like she's about to enter a limbo contest. After going the full pregnancy and then lugging around a kid or two on her hips for a couple years, a woman's spinal column eventually looks like a telephone cord.[218]

Sometimes a man, sensing his wife's vulnerability, will offer to do every last thing for her. In no time at all, she feels smothered, and the next time he offers to pick up some groceries on the way home from work, she'll rearrange the living room just to show him she can move heavy things. I may add that by the time the second baby is in the making, a woman could be moving a grand piano and the husband may—if the mood strikes him—move his feet out of the way.

By the end of the seventh month, the baby is about three pounds. It now has a wide range of activities including sucking his thumb, and…well, OK so it could do a bunch of things if it weren't all cooped up. The baby can also respond to stimuli, like tastes and sound. The woman, on the other hand, is getting less responsive as she becomes more and more exhausted. Physically, she has had it lugging this full-time hitchhiker around, and mentally she is tired worrying about the baby's health, her health, the labor, the delivery, what type of mother she'll be, as well as a couple dozen other

---

218 OK, so this may be dating me as well. There used to be a time in the dark ages when a phone was connected to a unit that hung on the wall. You had a cord that was twisty and would allow you to talk only in a six-foot radius. Now, naturally you can talk to anyone anywhere, whether it is while you are driving distractedly down a highway at seventy miles an hour or when your boss is behind you while you and your BFF are sharing pictures of your drunken night out rather than working on the tight deadline you were supposed to.

concerns that are banging around in her head to such a degree that she has to look up a recipe to make a peanut butter sandwich.

At this point, the woman's body really falls apart. If a part isn't aching, then it's leaking. She'll have what is known as pink toothbrush. This is when her gums bleed. She may have hemorrhoids, which may be internal or external.[219] Throw that in with the hands and feet swelling, breasts leaking colostrum, flatulence, acne, back pain, dizziness, bloating, heartburn, varicose veins, constipation, headaches, indigestion, nausea, and you've got a woman who may be looking to give birth to a new life but may be so pissed she could end a few in the process. Ergo, stay out of her way.

One other note on this month. Your wife is going to be hot. By that, I do not mean sexy hot, I mean temperature hot. All the additional heat generated by the baby is going to make your wife about as comfortable as marathon runner in Death Valley. If she is pregnant during the summer, she'll want to spend most of her time poolside. Unfortunately, since she is still freaking about her weight, she won't wear anything that would allow her to actually get cool. The only bare skin she'll expose is her feet, which she'll dangle in the water, and her face under a large floppy hat. Everything else must remain covered, or she may have to kill whoever gets a good look at her present figure.

The worst part is that she'll be hot at night. If you try to cuddle with her, she looks at you like you want to shove a space heater under the blankets. You are now considered an incinerator in bed. Therefore, a man is only allowed to touch a woman's back and feet—and then only to properly massage them. Everything else is off limits.

Because she is so hot, she'll insist on sleeping with the window open, no blankets, with multiple fans pointing at her body. The average guy finds these conditions so cold that his testicles are doing everything they can to crawl back inside his body. A guy has to throw on several blankets and comforters if he has any hope of not freezing to death at night, but making sure they don't overlap his wife's body.

---

219 The internal ones can cause rectal bleeding. A laugh riot.

By the end of the eighth month, the baby is about a foot and a half long and weighs about five pounds. At this point, those exciting moments of feeling the baby move have become annoying times as the baby does bizarre and unusual things to a woman's body. It is sort of like the movie *Alien* in that the woman is just sitting there and an elbow or something else is trying to pop out the side. If it gets too uncomfortable, the woman has to try to poke the baby back into a more acceptable position. Sometimes, the baby will start kicking her mother's ribs, which is about as fun as being jabbed repeatedly with a pencil after swallowing it. Let's face it, the baby is bored and needs something to do. There's not enough room for jumping rope with the umbilical cord, and that thumb-sucking thing gets old quick, so a stretch of the legs is the closest thing a baby has to a party.

As long as it is not painful, a pregnant woman does enjoy the game of "What the Heck Part of the Baby is That?" That's when the women gets this large lump sticking out of her belly, and she'll sit there massaging it trying to guess what part it is. My wife would always sit there probing away before resolutely announcing it was the baby's butt. For some reason, it was always the butt. I didn't know whether I was just "lucky" enough to always be there during butt time, or if that was what my wife said every time. Whatever the case, I was a bit sick of my kid mooning me for a month straight.

Another joy your wife may experience is Braxton-Hicks contractions. This feeling is when a woman's uterus repeatedly gets hard and soft. It is basically the uterus starting to "practice" for labor. As far as I know, the uterus is the only major internal organ that requires any practice to perform its function. If these contractions get really hard, the woman may believe she is ready to have the child. This event is known as false labor. The man will then do his version of false panic. Everyone will run around for a while flailing their arms, and then the contractions will stop. The big trick here is trying to still act concerned during the seventh-plus bout of false contractions. By this time, the man has to *act* like he's been told that his mother has just been kidnapped by terrorists, while inside, he is feeling he's been told that there is a sale on kitten calendars.

By the end of the ninth month, the baby is, well, a baby. At this point, the child puts on weight quickly so that if your wife gets to be a few weeks past her due date, she'll give birth to what looks like a two-year-old child.[220] During the month, the baby will drop. By this, I don't mean that it will fall out of the uterus, so don't think you have to walk behind your wife with a catcher's mitt. I mean that the baby will go head down so as to get ready for birth.

The baby then gets locked into place by taking up every last bit of space inside your wife so it couldn't turn back if he/she wanted to. The good news is that this takes pressure off the diaphragm so that your wife can actually take deep breaths without looking like she's hyperventilating. The bad news is that every last ounce of the baby's weight is now resting square on your wife's bladder. Because of this now absolutely crushed internal organ, it cannot hold more than a thimbleful of urine.

Your wife now has to go to the doctor on a weekly basis. Every week, she'll hope that the doctor says, "Well, this is it. You won't be in next week." Doctors who do say this are lying. They see the look of panic and desperation on these women's faces and give them false rays of hope.[221] Many women even get quite calm as their due date approaches. This temperament dissolves like metal in an acid bath if the due date is missed. The woman figures that she has more than paid her dues and wants her tenant evicted. Now. Immediately. The idea here is that Nature wants your wife to be so sick of being pregnant that she'll gladly face the fear of delivery to get the damn thing over with.

---

220 My wife was two weeks late with our second. The baby was born eleven pounds two ounces and was a little over two feet long. It was the most unbelievable sight I've ever witnessed—breathtaking. My wife could also describe the experience as breathtaking, but in a somewhat different way. There were a few stitches with that one.

221 It is right up there with scenes from war movies where one guy has got his legs blown off and the sergeant is telling him that he's going to be just fine if he just "hangs in there." He ain't.

Childbirth Class

or

Getting a Degree in How to Breathe

E ver since the dawn of humankind, women have been giving birth. It has taken until the last century to actually have a class for doing it. It's kind of like giving a class in relieving your bowels: you are going to have to do it sooner or later, no matter whether you've finished your lessons or not. If you are pregnant, you *will* have to give birth when the time comes, childbirth diploma or no childbirth diploma. The mother should not go to these classes alone. She needs a "coach." In case you haven't figured it out by now, you are the coach. You will not be the Mike Ditka type[222] who has everyone do what you say without question. Instead, you've got to pretend you have some sort of authority when everyone around you knows you don't have the power to adjust the volume on the television.

For centuries, the man really didn't do much when it came to the childbirth experience. In the hunter-gatherer days, men were usually conveniently on a hunting trip when the blessed day came. However,

---

222   Mike Ditka was the coach of the Chicago Bears football team when they won the Super Bowl. Even though he was a "bear," people did not describe him as the warm and cuddly type of teddy, but more of a grizzly who would rip your arms off to use as toothpicks if you happened to fumble. Most of his players would probably have rather attempted to tongue kiss an actual bear than face Ditka after a loss.

when people became more civilized, the man couldn't use that excuse. Now he was stuck in the house and feeling about as useful as that red thing hanging off a turkey's throat.[223] Therefore, the doctor or midwife would tell the guy to go get hot water and plenty of towels. The guy would then go trotting off on his mission. For centuries, they never used the hot water and towels, but it did make the guy feel like he at least had something to do that was possibly helpful.

Eventually, couples started to go to hospitals to have their babies. Then for decades, the man was banished to the waiting room where he would have no idea what was going on. All he could do was pace around the room and read outdated *Good Housekeeping* magazines. Now, however, men are right up on the front line. They are at the childbirth classes and right at their wives' sides during the whole process. Unfortunately, men are still about as useful as that red thing on a turkey's neck.

Somewhere between the sixth and ninth months of pregnancy, most couples start the childbirth classes. Couples are required to bring several pillows to the hospital, where the class is usually taught.[224] During these classes, the instructor will teach women how to breathe (even though your wife has been doing just spiffy at it since she was born). The instructor will also teach her how to "relax" between contractions. That's like teaching a knife thrower's assistant to relax between throws when the thrower has just been visiting his dear friend Jack Daniels.

As an added bonus, you'll get to meet other couples in the same predicament you are in. The only bad part about this is that there will be one woman there who "just can't seem to gain much weight even though she's trying to eat all she can." She will be despised by every

---

223   The red thing under the beak is known as a wattle. The primary purpose is to cool the blood since turkeys don't sweat. However, it also gets redder during courtship. Men may scoff at the notion that a wrinkly colored thing could be sexy, yet they think nothing of strutting around the house in nothing but boxers with a beer belly hanging over the edge and expecting their wives to fawn over that figure.

224   I'm sure the hospital would give you a $200 rental fee (per pillow per session) if you asked. Since they are preparing you for the experience of childbirth, they may as well get you used to the financial gouging you are going to be receiving.

other woman in the room like she staples fur coats onto animals just to see them overheat.

There are several different childbirth classes that subscribe to different philosophies. The most widely used in the United States today is the Lamaze technique, which teaches a "psychoprophylactic method." When a hard labor pain hits, the woman is supposed to substitute a positive response rather than a counterproductive one.[225] In the Grantley Dick-Read philosophy, they combine birth education with relaxation techniques.[226] In the Bradley technique, rather than distract the woman's mind, they teach her that she should focus within herself. In this technique, they focus on deep abdominal breathing.[227]

So what technique is best for you? That is like asking which one of the Three Stooges was best qualified to be the president.[228] In other words, it just doesn't matter. Besides, whatever the hospital offers is what you'll end up taking. When the time comes and that first really hard labor pain hits, all that "education" gets tossed out the window. Do you really expect a woman—or a man—to approach a situation with thoughtful, contemplative logic when they are going to be put through a painful ordeal for God knows how long?

So what is the point of childbirth classes? The major reason to go is to get the couple emotionally ready to deal with the oncoming experience. During the classes, the couple will take a tour of the hospital so that they know where the maternity ward is. That comes

---

225   What a great idea! We should apply that to other cases as well. Maybe if you are the recipient of prison rape, you could instead be happy that they are serving strawberry shortcake for dinner. If you are a victim of identity theft, you can thank the heavens that you don't have to worry about all those banks bothering you by calling with credit card offers and mortgages you can't afford.

226   That is another fantastic idea. You don't even need a real massage—just imagining one can make a woman forget the vaginal tearing that occurs when a miniature human being tries pushing through one of her orifices to freedom.

227   Again, very good technique. If you are breathing from your abdomen rather than those silly lungs, you feel absolutely no pain. I don't understand why we even need anesthesia for operations when you should just be able to tell patients to breathe from the abdomen when you are slicing them open.

228   Curly may have been the best of the Stooges, but if you are picking a president among them, you've got to go with Moe for his domestic-policy experience. Besides, if foreign leaders gave him trouble, he'd give him the double eye poke.

in helpful so that the expectant father isn't dragging his laboring wife through every wing of the hospital trying to find the child-birthing rooms. It also lulls you into a false sense of confidence that you think you have an idea of what to expect. You'll need this false confidence to stave off the sheer panic building inside like the steam in Old Faithful. So have fun!

Labor Decisions

or

Plan Now as There Is a Whole Lot of Panic Later

Before the labor begins, many women nowadays plan out how it is going to go. They may pick out particular music that is soothing to them or have incense ready to burn. In the end, any decision dealing with any of the woman's senses besides pain are absolutely superfluous. The only problem with her wanting this stuff is that you've got to carry this crap with you to the hospital and then drag it all back home later.

There are some decisions that do matter. One of them is whether you want the birth videotaped. Not to offend couples who opt for this, but anyone who does this should have their head examined by a doctor who specializes in shrinking them.[229] Yes, it is a miracle. Yes, it is potentially the most awe-inspiring moment you'll ever witness. However, yes, it is also a close-up shot of your wife's genitalia for the world to see; and yes, your wife will be in a mood you once thought could only be obtained with her head spinning around and

---

229 I'm not implying that a person who wants to videotape the birth needs to go to a psychiatrist—I'm saying he should go to a guy that physically shrinks heads. *That* is how crazy I think filming the birth is.

puking green slime; and yes, the possibility does exist that she'll get so ticked off that the camera will end up taking footage of your prostate. Yes, your wife could defecate during the pushing, and yes, there may be vaginal tearing. A birth is truly a blessed event, but it is also pretty gross in some (most) regards. Not every important memory has to be a Kodak moment.[230]

One thing that really must be decided is who is allowed in the delivery room. Not only must this decision be made, but everyone must be informed of said decision. Otherwise, when the word goes out that your wife is in the hospital, close family members and friends think they can just ask for your room number, waltz in with a bag of popcorn, and get a ringside seat. For most couples, the moment of birth is supposed to be private. If those intentions are not made crystal clear, there will be an audience. When your wife is in the throes of pushing, it is not the easiest thing to take a break so that you can escort Uncle Jeb, Aunt Martha, and the kids the hell out of the delivery room and into the waiting area.

Sometimes, you even have to go a step farther and personally tell everyone that they specifically are not invited in. Otherwise, you'll have a few who think that you couldn't have possibly meant to include them when you said, "I don't want *anyone* not associated

---

230 In the old days, people took pictures with film that they then had to go get developed. Now, most people would think that is barbaric, but let's look at some of the positives of the old days, shall we? Back then, you had to plan ahead to bring a camera, so the event was probably at least theoretically interesting. These days, people take pictures of *everything*. I mean, really, you *don't* have to take a picture of your breakfast to post on Facebook. I don't care what I had this morning, and I *certainly* don't care what you had. Then you have people who feel they have to take pictures of themselves at every second. They can't pass by a mirror without whipping out their phone, putting a sultry look on their face, snapping a pic, and sending it to the world. They may never look sultry—or even happy—in real life, but you wouldn't know that by the thousands of profile updates they have. Then you have people who take pictures of their more personal areas. Really? Send that to a boyfriend or girlfriend, and when they later break up, they've got blackmail for life. Want to run for office later on? The congressional district may be able to access photos of "Mr. Happy" to see their "qualifications" for representing them. Taking pictures has even taken the place of normal human interactions. If an elderly lady trips and starts falling down an up escalator so she goes into a perpetual tumble, how many people, rather than reach for her hand, reach for the cell?

with the hospital staff to be in that room with my wife and me. No one!" For some people, that statement is simply too vague.[231]

Another decision an expectant mother may want to mull over is whether she wants drugs. We are not talking about crack moms here, but whether a woman wants medication to lighten the pain of childbirth. It will still hurt, but it is more like getting run over by a VW Bug rather than a semi truck. In this generation, many women opt not to have drugs. They want to have an experience that is fully natural. I'm sorry, but that doesn't make a whole lot of sense. A heart attack is "natural," but you want to stop the damn thing.

Many women don't want their bloodstream polluted by chemicals dampening their senses. They don't want to take the chance of any drugs making it into the baby's body. Of course they nearly all change their mind when the heavy labor hits, and then they are demanding every known drug to humankind, including horse tranquilizers, but that's beside the point. Heck, falling out of a tree and breaking your leg is also a natural experience, but you won't have to feel it in all its glory when the doctor is resetting the bones. How about a root canal? Want to feel natural on that one, too?

Let's dwell on this pain thing for a minute. Why is an act so natural also so painful? Well, for centuries, it was believed that a difficult labor was a woman's punishment for Eve making Adam bite the apple. Tell that story to a modern woman, and she'll likely take a bite out of your Adam's apple. Besides, if that were true, you'd think men should at least start taking some blame since Adam did eat the damn thing. No? Let's face it, a man will do just about anything a woman tells him to. I'll state this truism over and over: a man has two heads, and he only has enough blood to have one thinking at a time. If one is up, the other is out of commission.

There are several different types of painkillers. The most common type is the epidural. Under this procedure, a woman bends over as much as she can, and then a doctor inserts a needle about the size of a ruler between her lower vertebrae. DO NOT LOOK AT THIS. By this

---

231 I don't want to go so far as to point fingers at particular groups that ignore this rule so as to cause problems so the soon-to-be grandparents don't have to worry that I'm calling them out.

time, you are running on little food, little sleep, and even less nerves. Seeing a needle sticking out of your wife's back may be enough to make the toughest of men feel a bit woozy.[232] If, heaven forbid, you faint, everyone will find this out and make fun of you—forever. Nary a family reunion or birthday will go by when this story doesn't get told. Think I'm exaggerating? Go ahead, and you'll be having your first-grade teacher call you, your old football coach—heck, even your minister may jokingly ask the congregation for a moment of silence to mind the passing of your male pride.

Epidurals are popular because the compound does not make it into the baby's system and it does not make a woman feel all drugged up. However, the doctors do have a strategy they like to follow. The more of the drug they give, the less pain. However, less pain means that a woman will not be able to push as effectively. It would be like trying to run the hundred-yard dash with both of your legs in casts. Therefore, a doctor wants to give enough medication so that it deadens the pain during labor but is actually wearing off when it comes to the delivery. That's like wearing your football helmet during the warm-up but taking it off before going to play in the game. If a woman asks for an epidural when she is too close to delivery, the doctor may even refuse. Therefore, she should sign up early and often to make sure she gets one.[233]

The next step up is a general pain reliever known as an analgesic. That will knock out sensation all over the woman's body. The bad news is that it gets into the baby's blood stream, so the baby starts

---

232 Unfortunately, my wife was so huge with our mammoth second child that she couldn't bend over enough for the doctor to get the needle between her vertebrae. Now *this* was an example of natural childbirth that looked more like an alien encounter than a human birth. On the first child, however, they stuck the needle in, and I commented that it didn't look "right." They looked over at me and thought there was the possibility I'd faint and so put me on the floor with a cold towel over my head. To this day, I deny that I would have gone down. My wife tells a different story, but what do you expect from someone who clearly had lack of sleep and is in pain? No jury could call her a credible witness, and yet I am called guilty.

233 How should she get these drugs, you may ask? A woman should tell each and every person who comes into the room that she wants drugs *right now*. It doesn't matter if the person is just there to collect the dishes. Anyone the woman can intimidate is fair game. If no person besides you is in the room, she should yell it so anyone in the hall or, if necessary, wing of the hospital knows her preference on the whole drug /no drug issue.

off "sleepy." The good news is that it gets into the baby's blood stream, so the baby starts off "sleepy." Let's face it, you'll be hearing that kid crying for years to come. No sense diving into it immediately.

For the woman who can't even say the word "deliver" without passing out, she can have a general anesthetic. Quite often this technique comes in handier with Caesarian births. For some reason, most people can't get relaxed on an operating table when they've got a doctor fishing around their internal organs looking for a baby. Most women still refuse to be put under because they want to see the baby immediately after birth, usually fearing that they are going to miss that initial bonding period. Let me assure you all that we humans have evolved past the stage where the first person will always be "mom." Instead, the baby is looking for a nipple and a nipple only. Who or what is attached to the other end is irrelevant.

About the beginning of the sixth month of pregnancy, the mother starts deciding what she'll bring to the hospital in her suitcase. She'll certainly need a change of clothes. More importantly, she'll want to know what the baby is going to wear home from the hospital. To a woman, the decision as to the baby's going-home outfit is on par with purchasing a car. It must be studied. Pros and cons must be laid out. To a man, the decision is more on par with which sneaker to put on first. Unfortunately, the woman rules and will purchase a special outfit for this occasion. If left up to the guy, the baby would arrive home in stolen hospital clothes.

Besides the clothes, the woman will have to pack makeup, toiletries, a book, and enough other garbage to make it look like she is going to the Bahamas for a week. The suitcase will be fully packed and waiting by the door by the end of the sixth month, and you'll be tripping over it for the next three. Noah didn't have to do as much thinking about what to bring on his voyage as your wife will.

Labor

or

You *$&# Did This to &#$ Me and I'm in &#$! Pain While Your *%&# Ass Is...

So after all those Braxton-Hicks contractions, how does a woman know when the contractions are real labor? She doesn't, so you may end up taking a few extra runs to the hospital only to be sent back home empty handed and full bellied. Doing this is phenomenally embarrassing because the information network has been alerted, so everyone you've ever known is now informed that you are in the hospital giving birth. Your doctor may be dragged off the golf course, and you've got friends and relatives hopping flights to all converge on the hospital for the Big Moment.

Having to go out and tell your frantic in-laws who got up at 3:00 a.m., drove two hundred miles, and are still in their pajamas that it was a false alarm is not good. They will look at you like it is your fault. Does that make sense? No, but they sure as hell ain't going to blame their very pregnant daughter for anything. Don't expect any understanding from your own parents—they'll turn on you faster than a caged bear that has been poked with a stick for a week straight. They were expecting a grandchild, and you are sending them home empty handed. Therefore, a woman should wait at home until she's pretty sure. Of course if she doesn't make it to the hospital on time, the guy will be tarred and feathered—if he's lucky.

There are a few distinguishing signs of real labor. First off, the contractions should be somewhat consistent, with the timing slowly getting closer. It is a man's job as coach to time these contractions. A woman is too busy to acknowledge when and how long the contractions are. Therefore, the man has to look for subtle body cues to start the timer like shrieking, having the woman grab her stomach and fall into a fetal position, or the ever-popular deer-caught-in-the-headlights look. The guy can start calling time when one of these things happens and then when it happens again. If the time gets shorter, then it is time to get her to the car.

If the woman is walking around and the pains stop, then the labor is probably false. By this time, another false labor is the last thing a woman wants. So if the pains start slowing down, she may go out for a jog or horseback ride, jump rope, etc. Heck, she may be so desperate she'd even think about having sex to jump-start labor—"think" being the operative word.

Another big cue to real labor is the loss of the mucus plug. If that sounds disgusting, that is because it is. The mucus plug seals the opening of the uterus. It may drop out all at once or come out in separate smaller chunks, usually when a woman urinates. A man seeing this may feel the strong urge to add a few chunks of his own to the toilet bowl. Unfortunately, this plug can come out minutes before or weeks before the actual birth, so it is not the best predictor.

At some point, the woman's water breaks. This moment can happen while she is in active labor in the hospital or even when labor really hasn't started. Your wife may be doing some last-minute grocery shopping and—boom—her clothes and the floor are all wet. Hearing the intercom blurt, "Cleanup in aisle five," and knowing that it is her bodily fluid they are planning on mopping up is about as embarrassing for her as having her father congratulate her on her first period by posting a Facebook message to her. If she's a fast thinker, she'll throw a jar of pickles to the floor and pretend that is the mess. Meanwhile, she can make a quick getaway.[234]

When the time comes that the contractions are somewhere between five to ten minutes apart and are increasing in time and intensity, then it is time to mobilize. You should have a short list of people to call, usually not over two or three names. Time is now of the essence, so leave the responsibility of the major callings to these people. Needless to say, they should be somewhat dependable and not completely buckle under pressure.

A mother-in-law is not usually a good choice for giving responsibility because she panics like a chicken when a fox with a tapeworm is in town. Come to think of it, the grandfather-to-be usually isn't the Rock of Gibraltar either. You can't not tell the in-laws first, but that doesn't mean you then give them responsibility. After all, the father-in-law is still just coming to grips with the idea that his daughter is now very obviously not a virgin.

Many soon-to-be fathers completely crumble when the time comes and aren't even able zip their fly, much less drive the car. Unfortunately, the father has to be relied on because he is already there and the woman is going to need some help. It may be like putting Typhoid Mary in charge of the company barbecue,[235] but there's just no choice. Calling a cab is just not an option. You want to have your hands on the wheel so she does not feel the obligation to hurt you when the pains hit. If you two are sitting there waiting for a taxi, your ongoing health becomes less of an issue.

When the woman reaches the hospital, she first has to be admitted. In other words, some person at the front desk is trying to get the name of your insurance carrier on seven separate forms while your

---

234 Well, as quick as a very pregnant woman can waddle.

235 Typhoid Mary was a woman who loved to cook. Unfortunately, her gall bladder was chock full of the bacterium that causes typhoid fever, and she didn't think that washing her hands prior to cooking was overly necessary. In the end, she was responsible for infecting over fifty while killing at least three people. Eventually, she was arrested and put in quarantine. After three years, she was allowed to leave under the condition that she not take a job as a cook. She agreed, but couldn't help herself and was back on the range cooking at a hospital, where there was another outbreak and death. They say your job should be something you love to do, but this does prove that there are the exceptions to the rule.

wife is about to drop your firstborn onto the floor of the front lobby and you are having a difficult enough time just pronouncing your name. Try to calm yourself and work through this situation, because most of these receptionists were former female swimmers for the East German Olympic team and will put you in a headlock if you try to barrel past.

After getting admitted, the hospital will usually get a wheelchair for your wife and get her up to the maternity ward. You have to keep up by foot without being a nuisance. If the elevator is full, it is *not* acceptable to begin pulling other people out to make room for your wife. Trying to make people give way to your wife in labor may work as you are getting her to the hospital, but once there, she is another patient. The problem here is that she has been the center of attention and expects that to continue. You have run red lights and gunned down people in crosswalks to get her here. To her, if you were a real man, she *should* continue getting top treatment.

She may expect you to keep treating the outside world like paparazzi that you, as her bodyguard, are supposed to dispose of. If that person is having a heart attack or battling through cancer, knocking them up against the wall to make room for your wife's wheelchair will not win you any favors, especially as there will probably be healthy relatives who may want to have a word with you after. Yes, your wife will give you a dirty look if she experiences a delay, but labor pains every few minutes will interrupt her thought process.

When they finally get her settled in her room, you'll first realize that they have done away with what a hospital room usually looks like. Gone are the white walls and metal beds. Instead, hospitals want to give a calming atmosphere, so there are comfy chairs, paintings, etc., that make it look more akin to a hotel room. Yes, it is more like a Motel 6, but they will be charging you for the Waldorf Astoria penthouse.

When they first get her settled in her room, they'll give her an internal exam. What they are looking for is how thin the cervix is and how dilated. The woman isn't supposed to push until the magic number of ten centimeters' dilation is reached. Some women are several centimeters dilated before real labor begins. Other women may have twenty-four hours of difficult, sleepless labor just to get a couple centimeters. After hours of pushing and having the doctor say the cervix is only dilated two centimeters, the wife is about as beaten down as Mike Tyson[236] at a spelling bee.

Usually, the doctor will strap a fetal monitor to the mother's belly. By looking at the monitor, you can see the baby's heartbeat and the contraction before the mother feels it. It will also help gauge the intensity of the upcoming contraction. Try to be tactful when you see that your wife is about to enter a world of unpleasantness. Say things like, "Oh God, you pinned the needle on this one, honey!" or "This one's going to last forever!" and you best make sure all your body parts are out of lunging range, or you'll be joining her on that trip to Painville. This stage of pregnancy can last for hours or days, so buckle up.

Naturally, it is a bit difficult for a woman to relax or take a little nap when she has pain shooting through her body every few minutes. Besides that, anything she eats will most likely be heaved sometime during the labor or (even worse) jettisoned from the lower extremities in her physical exertion. However, it is still possible for the man to get a little rest and something to eat. Most men would balk at this suggestion, playing the martyr, saying that until his wife is able to relax, neither will he. Sure, that sounds good, but so does living at the Love Canal.[237]

In practice, it turns out to be a bad move for the long labors for a guy to have an empty stomach. Why? Well, a man is about to witness the most amazing event he'll ever see.[238] Here is the woman he has chosen to live the rest of his life with giving birth to a child of

---

236 In his time, Mike Tyson was a feared heavyweight boxing champion of the world. Winning the Nobel Prize, however, was not going to be in the works. His prefight talks were less eloquent speeches of "floating like a bee" and more the idea of eating the rival's children, whether they had children or not. After making over $300 million, he ended up owing over $30 million in taxes. I'd worry he would threaten me if he read this, but that would involve, well, reading.

237 The Love Canal may sound like a site for swingers. Well, it may have been, but it was also the sight where twenty-one thousand tons of toxic waste was buried. It doesn't do wonders for property values.

238 With the noted exception of some bachelor parties held in Las Vegas.

their making. Combine that with his wife in pain, blood everywhere, possibly seeing a doctor sticking an extremely large needle between her vertebrae, and maybe even his wife having an episiotomy, and you've got the recipe for an overly tired, overly hungry man fainting dead away at a critical moment. You will never, *ever* live that one down. You could jump in front of the pope to save him from a sniper's bullet, and you'd still be known as the guy who fainted at his baby's birth.

Keeping his blood sugar up by eating will help prevent this from happening. That doesn't mean he should go take a trip down to the local pub for a burger, fries, and beer while he watches ESPN. A quick check with the doc that his wife still has forever until ten centimeters' dilation means he has enough time to run down to the hospital cafeteria, blindly grab whatever his hand touches, pay for it, and snarf it down so quickly that he doesn't actually have time to taste it.

So the pressure is on for the man to both support his wife and simultaneously not humiliate himself, something many men find difficult even in nonstressful situations. Having said that, if you start to feel queasy, you should—nay must—admit it. Don't think that you can work through it like a hangover on Monday morning. A man admitting he is queasy is about as embarrassing as having his co-workers post naked baby pictures of him on the company intranet. However, it is not nearly as embarrassing as passing out and knocking over the doctor's tray on the way to the very hard floor. You don't want all the relatives to be visiting the baby in one room and you in the other.

Back to the mother-to-be. Lying there hour after hour strapped to a monitor loses its appeal for most women. Therefore, they can wander the halls trying to give gravity a turn to get the baby moving. When a contraction hits, she'll grab your arm for balance and proceed to try to rip it out of its socket until the contraction is over. During this time, a man can do absolutely nothing right. If you rub her back, she'll be annoyed. If you don't rub her back, she'll be annoyed. If you give her encouragement, she'll be annoyed. If you don't...well, you get the picture.

It is during these times that she may bring up subjects about you that have been secretly annoying her for years, and she'll yell them at the top of her lungs to make sure the ICU wing at the other end of the hospital knows you chew your food too loudly and scratch yourself a bit too often. Be grateful: she could be telling them how you like to be dressed like a schoolboy and spanked with a ruler, whether it is or isn't true.

Delivery

or

A Womb with a View

After hours of labor, your wife will be physically and emotionally drained. Now she'll have to work even harder. When the cervix is dilated ten centimeters, it is show time. Unlike the old days when a woman hopped up on a bed to deliver, she now has options. She can do the bed, or have a little help from gravity by going in a chair, or a lot of help from gravity by using a birthing stool.[239] Most people aren't sure what a birthing stool is. It looks like a walker made for midgets. The idea is that the woman can brace herself as she squats down and tries to deliver the baby vertically. It may not look particularly dignified, but at this point, a woman cares about appearances as much as the life cycle of fungi. However, she *will* care later, so you had best not be filming!

When the contraction hits, a woman is supposed to bear down and push as hard as she can. This part of labor can last for minutes or

---

239 Actually, there are more options than that. Some people opt to do things like give birth in a water bath. The thought is that women think that it may be less traumatic for the baby to go from one liquid environment to a second liquid environment. It is a brilliant point—if they were giving birth to a fish. However, we are mammals with lungs. I don't know of any other land mammal that thinks it is a peachy idea to go skinny dipping when they are giving birth. I don't get it. Beyond that, I'm sure the janitor isn't excited to be cleaning that up afterward.

hours. Believe it or not, a woman can get so exhausted that she may even take mininaps between the contractions, especially if labor has lasted more than a day. In quite a double standard, a man taking a nap now gets everyone so pissed off you'd think he just stole cookies from a Girl Scout.

So what does the coach do during the birth? He can stand at his wife's head and whisper encouragements while she uses profane language to describe his family heritage and cuss him out for getting her in this condition even though she had to beg him for years to start a family. If he wants, he can get a little distance so she isn't cussing directly into his ear and take up a spot more at her side. If he is within arm's reach, it is inevitable that she will drive her nails clean through his lower arm. Hopefully, she won't cut a major artery. He could instead go even farther down and help hold her leg so that he can be kicked as well as get a good view of several body fluids seeping out of her, or get nauseous enough to trot off to the waiting room and have the family make fun of him.

Eventually, after a significant amount of pushing, you will be able to see the top of the head crown. Usually, it pops back in when the woman stops pushing. What the woman has to do is pop the whole head past the pelvic bone. As a side note here, most men like to think of themselves as well endowed. No matter how many men have been before him, a man still likes to assume he was the most "gifted" when it comes to the woman he loves. However, seeing the size of the baby's head as she pushes, it is time to raise the white flag. Suffice it to say that it is a humbling experience.

Quite often at this stage, a doctor may have to perform an episiotomy. What is that, you may ask? An episiotomy is when the doctor first takes a needle of Novocain and sticks it into the bottom of the vagina to numb it. He then takes a scalpel and cuts the vagina[240] to make more room for the baby. Why do this? Because if the baby is large enough, it can tear the vagina all the way to the anus. Therefore, you may want to pull the doctor aside and inform him that he should warn you if he is going to perform that particular

---

240 Always cut down, never up.

procedure. Otherwise, when he starts cutting down, you may be heaving up.

Once the head is delivered, the rest is not so bad...at least compared to the rest of the ordeal. First off, they suction out the nose and mouth so the baby can breathe. That moment is one of the oddest sights you'll ever see—just having the baby's head sticking out. It's like a combination science fiction/medical mystery movie. Only a few more pushes and the baby will be born. The kid may get a bit stuck around the shoulders, but then he should plop right out. Naturally, everyone is focused on the genitalia for the big boy/girl answer. Don't be frightened when you see the genitalia. Quite often, there can be a significant amount of swelling, especially in baby boys. Don't naturally assume that the kid is going to rival John Holmes.[241]

When the baby is out, the umbilical cord is clamped. Many men even get the chance to snip the cord themselves. That way, the guy can think he actually did something useful somewhere during the delivery, even though that is akin to suggesting that the mayor who cuts the ribbon to open the new library actually had any part in pouring the concrete for the foundation or any other part of the manual labor.

Meanwhile, the mother has to then deliver the placenta. This stage can last from a few minutes to half an hour. After pushing out a baby, this is about as difficult as pushing water through a strainer. The doctor then has to do some repairing. Stitches are usually required when there was an episiotomy or tearing. Do not, I repeat, do not make a joke about putting an extra few stitches in when he is sewing her up. Usually, there is a lot of blood. For the joy the woman felt missing all those periods, it is now payback time. After birth, a

---

241 John Holmes was a prolific actor of the 1970s and 1980s. For those people who don't know his body of work, he made over 2,500 films. How, you may ask, can an actor make that many films? If you figure a generous twenty-year career, that comes to 125 films a year, or making a film every three days. The films were of the variety where there is a very cheesy soundtrack and there were no awards given for costume design as there was a dearth of clothing. Mr. Holmes was known to be a large actor—not in how tall he was standing up, but lying down. He had made claims to being with fourteen thousand women. Without taking vacations into account and, heaven forbid, being with the same woman more than once, that works out to two different women each and every day. Now that is the epitome of fear of commitment.

woman bleeds continuously for around six to eight weeks. Mention sex and you'll be bleeding six to eight months.

So back to the baby. Let's start off by saying that it ain't like TV. You are not going to be handed this cute pink little bundle of joy. The first thing you'll notice is that the head is in the shape of a cone, and a lopsided one at that. Rather than deciding whether he looks like you or your wife, you're going to see what looks like Zippy the Pinhead's illegitimate child.

You see, the bones in a baby's head are not fused at birth. Therefore, they act as joints and can bend. Otherwise, your wife would be walking around like she's riding an invisible pony for the rest of her life. It may take weeks for the head to take on some semblance of roundness, so make sure you've got those little baby hats, or the older kids are going to use him as a ring toss.

Secondly, the baby may have a bit of green on him. This green is called meconium staining. Doctors call it that because it sounds better than in utero pooping. Yes, sometimes babies can have their first "accident" in the womb, and when that happens there is nowhere for it to go but all over the baby. What a way to start life! The only good news to this is that the nurse will clean it up. For the next few years, every lower-extremity explosion is for the two of you to take care of.

Then you've got—believe it or not—baby acne. Many times, the child is born with immature skin pores. Therefore, the kid's face can be covered by itty-bitty whiteheads. Don't worry if this happens because it will go away quickly, albeit the first photo they take at the hospital is one you may want to bury deep in your wallet behind the blood-donor card. Don't automatically assume that the child is destined to become a pizza delivery guy.

The rest of the skin is pretty wrinkly. Just think how bad you are after a long, hot bath. The kid's been soaking for nine months, so the entire body initially has a prunish texture. Oh, and there may be hair in unusual places, such as on the shoulders. We're not talking like it looks like the kid is wearing a shawl, but be prepared for some of your buddies to ask if your wife had an affair with a Sasquatch.[242]

---

242 If the baby is even hairier, they'll suggest you can make extra money renting him out to the circus. Naturally, they will never have the guts to do that within earshot of the mother.

The first thing they do with a baby is put him on his mother's belly.[243] The baby will root around for his mother's nipple. Sucking is an instinct that children are born with.[244] The baby will root around until he finds a nipple and start sucking. Within minutes after birth, he'll easily get what you've been begging for months to even see. Don't get jealous, though. Now that a nursing baby is around, you'll at least get to see your wife expose herself since she has to continually feed the child.

243 That is, after they clean the kid up a bit. They don't want the mother's first hug to send the kid squirting off onto the floor.
244 Along with the uncanny ability to wake up crying whenever sex is theoretically possible.

Cesarean Delivery

or

No, This Isn't Getting a Salad
Sent Up from the Cafeteria

I f the baby is too big or the birth canal is too small, or if they have to go in and get the baby quickly, a cesarean section is performed. In the olden days, the doctor would open a hole in the woman big enough to pull out a watermelon. The medical establishment didn't particularly care that it left a woman with more stitch marks than Frankenstein's monster. Now doctors give what is called a bikini cut. To do this, the doctor shaves some pubic hair and makes a small perpendicular incision. That way, when the hair grows back, it will hide the scar.[245] Since the muscles will be cut through, it is not easy for a woman's figure to be as good as it was even with exercise, so the bikini may have gone the way of the dodo and lawn darts.[246]

---

245 Naturally, this assumes that she is not doing excessive "grooming" to get hair in special patterns or get rid of it altogether.

246 For those of you who don't remember lawn darts, picture a giant dart a few feet long. You'd then play sort of like horseshoes, lobbing the darts toward a plastic circle so they'd come down and stick in the ground. They were quite fun, unless kids decided to play catch or tag with them, which they naturally did. Eventually, they were outlawed and the world crisis was over.

If the doctor is performing a cesarean section, you don't want to be there for the actual surgery. The idea of you remaining emotionally calm while someone is acting like your wife is the Thanksgiving turkey is a bit farfetched. They'll put up a screen so the woman can't see the cutting, but they usually don't put her out because she'll want to see the baby immediately after birth. It is better for the doctor to do the initial work and then call the guy in. Otherwise, a lunatic husband running around the surgery ward tends to make the doctor with the knife a bit edgy. You want him to work like he's performing a cesarean section, not making a Caesar salad.

Now that you'll be in the surgery ward, you'll have to wear the surgical mask and gown. That way, you'll get to look professional to all the friends and relatives who have come to visit, when in actuality you're still about as useless as tinsel on December 26. Once you're in position, the doctor bursts the amniotic sac and sucks out the fluid. They then pull the baby out. Doctors who have done this procedure a jillion times are quite calm about the whole thing. They'll leisurely clean the baby up and eventually suction out the mouth and nose so the baby can breathe. You, on the other hand, are not experienced and presume that it is only proper to have the baby breathing sooner than instantly.

Therefore, your insides churn violently as the doctors and nurses seem like they take an eternity to get around to having the baby breathe on his own. He will, and then you'll realize that you yourself haven't been for the last fifteen minutes or so. It is a good idea to take a deep breath now before you acquire permanent brain damage.

After the mother has a few moments with her new baby, the doctors will want to take care of that gaping hole on her abdomen. Therefore, you get to bring the baby out to the waiting room to show everyone while your wife is taken care of. By this time, a man has usually regained his composure, so he can look pretty suave walking the baby out with surgical garb. Meanwhile, the real hero is finishing delivering a placenta and getting stitched up.

Wrapping It Up

or

Now It Begins...Unless You Are Talking about Sleep

The mother is allowed to stay in the hospital an extra day if she gave birth naturally or two days if she had a C-section. It is so "nice" of them to give the woman more time in the hospital since her abdominal muscles have been sliced open and it may hurt to pick up more than a loaf of bread. The hospital staff will keep smiling and being helpful until it is time for her to go, and then you are both hustled to the curb so fast, it is a wonder they don't melt the tires off the wheelchair.

During this time, it is up to a new mother and her husband[247] whether to have the nursing staff do a lot of the work in regards to the baby. If it is a first child, the new parents don't want to miss a thing. They will not think twice of changing every diaper and keeping the baby right at the mother's side so that every odd sound makes the exhausted mother awake in a cold sweat. You can tell parents that already have a child—they know the hospital is charging them for changing diapers, nursery time, etc., *whether it is used or not*. They

---

247 Who are we kidding? It is up to her.

are going to get every last ounce of relaxation they can. If the kid drops a deuce, they may as well have the nurse clean it. The thinking here is that there will be plenty of diapers for the next several years. And as for sleep—they're facing many upcoming weeks/months of missing that blessed state, so better to get a bit now because it just isn't going to happen when the couple gets home.

One issue is that everyone the couple has ever met now feels that they can swing by the hospital. The problem is that the mother is still, well, a woman. She is going to want to look good for people. So how does one look good with no sleep and maybe with just a sponge bath rather than full shower? Makeup. Lots of makeup. If the new mother didn't pack the industrial size in her bag, she may be sending the father home for it. Nearly every person walking in the door has got a camera of some type, so the mother doesn't want to come home and find a million pictures of herself looking like a bag lady plastered on the Internet.

When it is time to go home, some hospitals now actually check if you've got the right baby seat in the car. A regular car seat just doesn't cut it because the straps would be around the baby's neck/face so that a quick stop would result in the car turning around and going back to the hospital and the driver needing to post bail to get to spend more family time. They just aren't going to take the guy's word for it, but are going to have to see it. The baby seat for newborns faces the rear. Why does it do that? Maybe so mothers aren't looking in their mirror more often than the road to see what the new baby is doing.

As the family is leaving the hospital, they usually roll the new mother out in a wheelchair. There is every bit of TLC—until they hit the front door, and then the pampering is over. She's kicked to the curb so they can get the wheelchair free for the next one. However, that is usually OK. After all, there is big excitement to be starting a new life as a family. The guy is expected to drive home since, after all, the new mother has had major surgery. The drive home can go one of two ways: either the father could cut off trains and the mother won't notice because she is just enthralled in the backseat staring at the new baby, or she will notice if he is two miles over the speed limit for more than a nanosecond. That about sums up the next year's experiences—you will either be ignored or can do no right.

When the parents get home with the baby, the excitement hits fever pitch. They walk in the front door, take off their coats, pull the baby out of the carrier...and then it hits. Terror—sheer, unadulterated terror. Odd thoughts get uttered. How irresponsible could the hospital be to let two inexperienced people leave and go out in the world to care for this baby? Can they actually pull off this parenting thing? What the hell made them think that they were adult enough to be parents?

These thoughts are all natural. Parents should expect them. It is a very standard feeling being terrified that you are going to accidentally do something that may hurt your child. Relax. It will go away. How long will these feelings last? Until the children become snotty teenagers, and then the feeling changes to being terrified that you are going to do something on purpose to let them live!

Section 5

General Child Maintenance

or

Fatherhood: Now You Know Why Your Dad Went Gray

Breast Feeding

or

Thanks for the Mammaries

Babies are not born with any sense of time, which is quite evident if your wife gives birth at 4:00 in the morning after going into labor around 4:00 a.m. the previous day. The baby goes by his own schedule, and only his own schedule. If he wants to eat at 2:30 a.m. while you desperately want to sleep, he is going to eat at 2:30 a.m. It will not be 2:45 a.m. If he wants to be held when you need to get ready for work because you have a huge presentation to make to the boss, he is going to be held (and then spit up on your coat and tie). If he needs a diaper change in the middle of a football game, well, then you pretend you just don't smell it (until your wife yells at you to change it because she can near taste it even if she is up the stairs and down the hall).

The child will demand nearly every waking and sleeping moment of your time. You will become a semimindless zombie whose only purpose in life is to answer the calling of this two-foot-long master who makes multiple demands by just crying, and it's up to you to figure out which demand has not been satiated. It's like the baby has his own mini cult following, and you are the brainwashed servant who would rollerblade through the downtown area wearing only a pair of Depends if the situation called for it.

Starting at birth, babies want to be fed every couple of hours, twenty-four hours a day. Feeding will be the greatest time commitment a child demands of his parents. That's why it is absolutely imperative that you convince your wife to breastfeed. Work should begin on this project immediately upon finding out that your wife is pregnant.

Here's what you do: Pick up one of the baby books or magazines your wife has bought (don't worry about finding one—she'll buy enough so that one will be within arm's reach at literally any spot in the house, and you will be slogging through them knee deep by the eighth month). Flip to a random page and say something like, "Gee, honey, do you realize all the disease protection a child acquires from breast milk?" or "Hmmm, this article states that the fats in mother's milk promote brain development." Get your wife good and guilty over the belief that the child's future well-being rests solely on whether it was nursed as a baby. The screwed-up-to-the-absurdity-level hormones in your wife will aid you in this endeavor.

You can present several other reasons to convince your wife to breastfeed. The first is that it helps the uterus to contract. After something that is normally the size of an orange gets stretched out to the size of a basketball, with a child continually kicking it from the inside, the uterus will need all the help it can get. The second reason is that breastfeeding burns a lot of calories. After pregnancy, women *want* to lose weight, but they do not want to *hear* that they need to lose weight, so the best idea is to approach this reason with *extreme* caution (think "leaking plutonium reactor"). Do not make any statements whatsoever about your wife's current weight when introducing this incentive, or you will be gaining weight until the surgeons are able to extract the magazine from your esophagus. The third reason is that breastfeeding helps suppress ovulation and menstruation. Keep in mind I wrote *suppress*, not *stop*.

Breastfeeding should *not* be considered a reliable method of birth control. While breastfeeding, the woman should not take oral contraceptives, for they will find their way into the breast milk.[248] At this stage, the most reliable and practiced method of birth control is the woman's fingers: if a woman is in bed desperately trying to get some sleep—not action—before the baby wakes up, you may find those fingers closing around your throat.

If all goes well, your partner will agree to breastfeed at least in the beginning. There is something excruciatingly important to mention here: your child will be born with the natural ability to suck, but he does not yet really know how to suck on a nipple. The ability to breastfeed is a learning experience for the child *and* the mother. It's perfectly natural if things don't initially go well.

After birth, your wife will be extraordinarily tired, and her hormone levels—to put it mildly—make her sanity a bit questionable. Her first motherly job will be breastfeeding, and she may have trouble getting the baby to latch on properly. Consequently, on the first day of motherhood, many women of newborns will lose that thimbleful of mind they had left as they immediately feel like a complete failure and start thinking they should have never attempted having children in the first place.

When you try to convince the mother that this is not so, she will turn on you. She will ever so politely remind you that while *she* was reading book after book on motherhood, *your* reading during the pregnancy consisted only of *Sports Illustrated* and *MAD* magazine, and even that was only when you went into the bathroom. Expand those sentiments into a forty-five-minute diatribe, and you have an idea of what you'll be getting into. However, you still *must* try to console her, or you will be in for worse later. All you can do is just sit there and take it. It gives her a little comfort to think that even though she feels she is incompetent, she has at least more of a clue than you do. When your wife calms down and is finally able to get

---

248 Actually, nearly anything the woman consumes finds its way into breast milk. If the woman is drinking alcohol, it will make the baby a bit tipsy, which may make the baby go to sleep more easily. This is a very poor thing for brain development, but great if you enjoy visits from child protective services. Therefore, women have to be cautious with what they take, even prescription drugs. So if a woman has a headache because the baby has been crying, she can't take ibuprofen to relax enough to feed the baby to stop it crying. It's just part of the circle of life.

even minute amounts of sleep, she'll become more rational about the situation.[249]

When the child is first born, your wife does not spontaneously have milk. Instead, the child gets its nutrition from colostrum. Colostrum is a thin, yellowish fluid initially secreted by the breasts. It's rich in antibodies and minerals, and even teaspoon amounts can sustain a baby initially. Even though colostrum is quite remarkable, most men experience a medical syndrome known as the heebie-jeebies when hearing about it and refuse to deal with it until the milk comes in.

So the baby has got to eat no matter what comes out, and to do that, he's got to find the nipple. The baby is born with a reflex known as rooting. If stimulation is applied to the side of the mouth (usually by a nipple), the baby will whip his head back and forth trying to muckle on. This is where the learning experience kicks in. Your wife will put her nipple to the side of the baby's mouth, and the baby will start whipping its head around trying to get a good hold. The mother, trying to aid the baby's efforts, will chase the baby's mouth, nipple in hand, desperately trying to make the two connect.

This is a frustrating experience for a new mother, and a hilariously funny one for a new father (especially if the lady in question is not particularly top heavy). I suggest that if you have the urge to laugh, you find some way to stifle it. If need be, play bobbing for apples in the boiling water she is using to sterilize baby things. In the long run, this will be much less painful than a bassinet careening off your temple. Also, the woman does not find it humorous for you to offer to show the child how it is done, especially when that joke is repeated seventy or eighty times over the course of the first week.

Believe it or not, there is a plethora of positions to be tried when breastfeeding a baby. The basic position is for the mother to be sitting and the child to be lying across her lap. Mother and child can also lie down side by side. There's also the "football hold" (yes, that

---

249 Not to belabor the point, but "more rational" and "rational" are not the same. Ted "the Unabomber" Kaczynski may be considered more rational compared to Charlie Manson, but you still wouldn't want him babysitting the kids.

is its actual name), in which the baby's body lies next to the mother's side and the head is held like a football up to the breast.

If the woman has been having difficulty breastfeeding, and the football hold works, do not joke about spiking the baby as if she just scored a touchdown. A woman who has given birth and is now breastfeeding is *tired*. She has temporarily abandoned her life to aid a helpless new being on this planet. The only thing she wants to hear from the guy's mouth are things like "Can I get you another pillow?" or "Do you want something to eat or drink?" She simply doesn't want to spend the energy responding to jokes. If you tell her she's got the baby in more positions than a Las Vegas hooker, she'll ask her mother to beat you with a tire iron.

So why all the positions? Initially, breastfeeding is tough and uncomfortable. Not only does your wife have to try to find a position that works for the baby and her, but she has to deal with having her nipples abused. The nipples take quite a battering from a child constantly sucking and gumming them, not to mention the fact that old milk cakes on them, which makes the nipples dry out and crack, leaving them painful to the touch. Unfortunately for your wife, she has to work through the pain to feed the child when it is hungry. Unfortunately for you, she is not willing to deal with the discomfort of letting you touch them. So even though your wife's breasts are larger than they'll ever be, you are forced to live in "window shopping" mode—you can gaze upon the glory, but don't you dare touch.

Some babies/mothers have more difficulty than others in getting the hang of breastfeeding, and a lactation consultant may have to be called in. *I am not making that up—it's a real job!* As hard as it is for men to believe, there are even organizations such as the La Leche (Spanish for "The Milk") League that do nothing else but gather to breastfeed and discuss breastfeeding issues. Men cannot even begin to comprehend coming together and discussing a single issue like that. It would be akin to a group of sports enthusiasts assembling to talk only about bunting in baseball. Most women look forward to calling a lactation consultant with relief because they know professional help is on the way.

Men, on the other hand, now become embarrassed, especially if their child is a boy. Even though the baby is less than a week old, they do not want to admit that their son does not know what to do with a woman's breast. It's a sad state of affairs, but this is the point at which many men start living vicariously through their son's accomplishments. If it involves a ball or a boob, somehow men think their son should just know what to do. So why would men be this paranoid? If you bring another guy over, and the wife mentions she's having trouble making the child learn to breastfeed, the "friend's" natural tendency is to raise an eyebrow to the guy and make a comment: "Like father, like son."

Once proper contact is made between the baby's mouth and the breast, several more problems may be encountered. Large-breasted women may need to squeeze their breasts so as not to smother the child.[250] Also, some children tend to fall asleep before they are full. If your wife doesn't wake the child up, he will wake up sometimes minutes later and want to eat again. Rather than act as a chauffeur from breast to crib, your wife should try to keep the child awake, or she will be feeding literally all day long.

If the child dozes off during feeding, she should rub her nipple against his cheek.[251] If that fails to arouse the child, then she should tickle him. If that doesn't work, she may need to completely undress the child to get him uncomfortable enough to keep him awake (keep the diaper on unless you like to live on the edge). If that doesn't work, you can sometimes see a new mother partially exposed, baby muckled onto one breast, hopping up and down in front of an open refrigerator. After all this effort, hopefully the baby will get a proper meal and let the two of you collapse for a few hours until the whole process starts over again.

I should also mention that breast milk differs not only between women but even with the same one! We don't normally think of milk being different, since we are used to cow's milk. However, since cows have the second dullest of all diets—grass[252]—that is the only thing

---

250 That may be the number-one way a guy could pick to pass on from this Earth.

251 This would be the number-one wake-up call for a guy.

252 Vegetarians pull off the number-one position with tofu. Tofu for men is like grass with less sex appeal.

they make their milk from, and so it never tastes any different. A woman has a more varied diet (hopefully not as disgustingly varied as the fried clam/pickle/potato salad sandwich she was craving during pregnancy) that the milk is made from. If she has spicy foods, then the milk will be a bit spicy. She can have more flavors than a cappuccino bar, but it just takes too long to mix up the different brands.

Sometimes, the baby will even reject the breast if he finds the milk distasteful. A much more serious consequence is that the baby does *not* find the spicy milk distasteful. You see, a baby's digestive system is a somewhat fragile thing. Throw it a curve ball, and it may react violently. I remember my wife enjoying a cabbage dinner, and then my child ended up passing enough gas to refloat the *Hindenburg*. There was so much tooting in the house you'd think I was boarding Herb Alpert and the Tijuana Brass.

As with everything else to do with a baby, you must buy expensive items so that you can accomplish what should be a natural act. The first purchase is a nursing bra. This bra differs from other bras in that each breast can be independently exposed by unbuttoning a flap from the top. Most men think this is a wonderful invention and wish it would take off in standard women's wear.[253] The next purchase is bra pads that fit over the breast and absorb any milk that leaks out.

Leakage can occur for several reasons. If the mother has been away from the child performing some errand or (God forbid) actually enjoying herself, she may be late for a feeding. Excess milk will make her breasts painfully bulge out, and she will come home and even wake a sleeping child to make it eat to relieve the pressure. You will actually see the wife barreling into the house yelling, "Where the hell is that child! My boobs are killing me, and they're going to explode if this kid doesn't do some major eating!" This is not quite the picture that comes to mind when you normally think of a loving mother and child bonding through the quiet, intimate act of breastfeeding.

A second instance for possible leakage is when a nursing mother hears another child cry. A female's body quite often does not

---

253 Men would like it even more if it came attached to the Clapper.

distinguish between her own baby's cry and another's, so when she hears any baby cry, the milk lets down. Obviously I have no idea what this sensation is like, but women don't generally regard it as good unless a child is around to relieve this milk deluge. Don't bother to offer yourself in lieu of the child. You have a better chance of eating nuclear waste and thinking that you'll gain superhero powers from it.

So what happens if the baby is not there or the breasts just spontaneously leak? Well, as with any liquid on cloth, it leaves a wet spot on the clothing. At times as a husband, you will look over at your wife to find that she has one or two growing wet spots she is unaware of. Naturally, it is better for you to tell her than someone else, so as to save her some embarrassment. If someone else informs your wife first, she will not only be embarrassed, she will be mad at you. Now you *think* you've done nothing wrong, but her line of reasoning is that since you normally can't stop staring at her chest, this obsessive fascination should at least come in useful to her for the first time ever.

One problem that will pop up is how to breastfeed when not at home. There will come a time when your wife wants to do some shopping and doesn't want to send you because she doesn't trust your taste in, well, just about anything. Knowing she'll be gone awhile, she'll take the baby and maybe even you along. If the baby wakes up hungry and cries inconsolably about it, your wife may need to do some public feeding. As hard as it may be, you should try to find an out-of-the-way place.

Many bystanders are disgusted by the act of breastfeeding and will openly show their distaste as they walk by. Your wife, feeling uncomfortable to begin with, will want them dead and will expect you to perform the task. Therefore, you should try to minimize these minor confrontations by scouting out appropriate discreet places to minimize her discomfort and her anger at you for not being able to prevent people from staring. If nothing else, make sure it isn't outside a store frequented by men, as there can be serious accidents with men tripping over everything in sight as they are pretending not to look.

There are two basic tactics to public breastfeeding. The first is to be discreet. Your wife can wear loose-fitting clothing and a nursing bra. With a bit of practice, she should be able to slip the child underneath the shirt and begin the feeding process with no one seeing anything and the vast majority of people completely unaware of what she is doing.

The second way is for your wife not to care and let it all hang open. The second method may be a bit easier on the "docking procedure," but even if the woman doesn't care who stares, the husband does. Yes, breastfeeding is natural. Yes, breastfeeding has been done in public for millennia. Yes, breastfeeding is best for the baby. But even though the man may not get to use the breasts when he wants to, they are still his in that they are for his eyes and his eyes only. A guy doesn't want a video of his wife breastfeeding to be put up on YouTube for the world to critique. And as for the baby, he is only a temporary resident who must vacate the premises pretty damn soon because the landlord wants back in.

So how long should a modern woman breastfeed? The world average for children to breastfeed is four years old. Most men and women in the United States view this as a wee bit too long for them. There just seems to be something unusual with the picture of a four-year-old walking up to his mother and asking her to hike her shirt up because he's a tad parched. Also there is an issue with many women that comes up when the baby all of a sudden has teeth and has the ability to clamp down and gnaw on any object that comes within mouth range. Couples in the United States generally make the decision to stop breastfeeding because it becomes too difficult when the woman is trying to put some semblance of her former life back together.

If the wife goes back to work, the couple can decide to (1) collect and store breast milk for the husband or other caregiver to give to the baby when the mother isn't there, (2) supplement breast milk with baby formula, or (3) go straight to formula. Let us first discuss option one. As with anything new that you do involving a baby, you will need to make a major purchase. This time, you need to buy bottles, nipples, liners for the bottles (optional), ice-cube trays, and a breast pump. Breast pumps come in two basic types: manual and automatic. The manual works like a bicycle pump in reverse. A suction cup is placed over the nipple, and then the woman pumps it out and the milk collects in a container.

Although this, again, may look like a humorous sight as you see your wife getting a great arm workout, you should not poke fun. After all, between carrying the child around and working that damn pump, your wife has built up her biceps to the point that, if given the chance to put you in a headlock, she could crack your skull as easily—and with as much concern—as an egg.

Automatic pumps are usually battery operated. Not only are they good at sucking the milk out of breasts, but they suck the life out of batteries. If you've got your wallet out to buy an automatic pump, you may as well invest in a case of D batteries. Also, it is yet again amusing to look over at your wife, this time because she has a device pressed up against her nipple making her areola about five times its normal size while it hums "*rrRR**RR**RRRrrRR**RR**RRrr.*"

There she'll sit reading a magazine, acting like nothing is happening, and you'll have to pretend right along with her that it is a natural sight, not worth a second glance. Meanwhile, your internal guy humor nature is going to desperately want to make cow-milking jokes. You'll be tempted to say that the sight is "udderly" fascinating or what a "moo-ving" experience it is watching her produce food for your child. Pull together whatever self-control you have in your body and refrain from saying anything.

More than likely a woman has gained weight from the pregnancy, and even though cow jokes are not a comment about her size, she will take it that way. The next thing you know, she'll be calling the big guns in—her mother, not her breasts—who will give you a look that is so searing it can melt glass.

So what do you do with the milk once you have it? If you are going to use it within the next day, you can put it in a bottle—not just any bottle, but a sterile bottle. To sterilize the bottle (and nipples and caps and inserts) first boil water and then throw everything in for a good fifteen minutes. Now if you were to wait for the water to cool down, you could easily grab the bottles, give them a little shake, put the insert and cap on, and then wait for the milk supply to be ready before leisurely filling them. However, your wife will point out that as the water cools, it can then become contaminated. Therefore, you must do everything quickly while it's painfully hot. Here you are using tongs and other implements of destruction to bob for all this stuff so you can then assemble them right out of the scalding water. If your fingertips haven't blistered, you haven't done it quickly enough.

If the milk is not to be immediately used, it should be frozen. That is where the ice-cube trays come in rather than freezing the milk right in the bottles.[254] Milk should only be frozen once, so when it is thawed, it must be used or thrown away. Therefore, if you freeze a whole bottle and the baby wakes up slightly hungry, you would have to take the time to thaw the whole thing (meanwhile the baby is losing his mind crying because he sees the bottle and doesn't know why you aren't giving the bottle to him immediately). If he drinks only a bit and goes back to sleep, then the expiration on the whole bottle is coming quickly to an end.

If you have frozen milk cubes, on the other hand, you can pop out a few at a time to thaw and use, depending on how hungry you think the baby will be. But since you didn't boil the ice-cube tray, isn't that potentially contaminated, you may ask? Sure, but you don't have to mention that fact to your wife so she can fritz about that as well. Let that be our little secret. Also keep in mind that you should make milk cubes small enough to fit into the bottle. Otherwise you'll find yourself smashing them up on the kitchen counter with a hammer you just pulled from your toolbox, while lying to your wife about how you are doing so well keeping everything sterile.

Now let us move on to formula feeding. At this point, you should brace yourself (and your wallet) for a shock. Baby formula, even though it costs pennies to make, is phenomenally expensive—and you will be buying a lot of it. You can buy formula in one of three ways: ready-to-use, concentrated, or dry. Ready-to-use is by far the easiest. All you need to do is open the can and pour the formula into

---

254 Remember when you were a kid and you made your own popsicles by filling an ice-cube tray with juice? You put plastic wrap over the top and then stuck toothpicks in to make handles when the juice was frozen. Well, milkcicles may be a great way to promote strong bones and teeth, but anything that comes out of your wife's body is meant for the baby. Anything otherwise could lead to the forceful removal of teeth and crushing of bones where no level of milk could possibly aid in their recovery.

sterilized bottles. You need only lie to your wife that you thoroughly cleaned the can opener before using it. However, unless you are the president of a Fortune 500 company or are successfully embezzling funds from one of those companies, you will probably not be able to afford this option.

Concentrated formula is a tad less expensive but more difficult to use. Not only do you have to boil all containers, nipples, etc., but you must boil water. You must fill a sterile bottle half full, and when the child wants to eat, you then put in an equal amount of the concentrated stuff. If you decide on this route, you must always know how many bottles of sterile water are in the refrigerator at *all* times for *months* on end. Otherwise, you will get caught short. The baby will want to eat, and you will have nothing prepared. If the wife wants to feed the baby and making the bottles is your "official" job and they are gone, you will be in trouble. Think Terminator with breasts.

In these cases, try to get to the baby first so you can bounce him to try to quiet him down. That will usually give you an additional eighteen to nineteen seconds of peace before the baby flips out again. Patience may be a virtue, but the baby isn't going for sainthood at this stage in life. That's why babies are born cute; it helps resist the urge to drop them off at convents, which are a bit rarer to find these days. By the way, your virtuousness will also take a significant toll. Your first instinct will be to quickly boil some water. The old adage "a watched pot never boils" will never be truer than in this scenario. Besides, you don't want to quickly whip up a batch of scalding hot milk to feed the baby. Therefore, you should "find" a bottle of water in the back of the refrigerator that hasn't been used yet (pour tap water in a bottle when your wife isn't looking) and make the formula from that.

Powdered formula is much cheaper[255] and much harder to use. Again you'll have to have boiled water. You can bottle the water and then mix in the dry stuff or make it in one big batch and then pour it into several bottles (the batch way is easier if your wife lets you do it). This procedure wouldn't be so bad except that stirring formula is just

---

255 The only powder more expensive will get you five to ten years for possession.

a bit easier than mixing water and cement. Your wife will tell you that every speck should go into solution so that the child can have the optimum nutrition. If that were actually the case, your baby would have to chew his dinner earlier than expected.

The real reason you must get it all mixed up is that any formula that doesn't go into solution will clog the nipple. You'll be feeding the baby, and it will start to cry (yet again). You don't know whether he has gas or is tired or needs a diaper change or what. After checking everything, with the baby bawling the entire time, you'll realize he is crying out of frustration because nothing is coming out of the bottle. At this point, you usually feel like quite the slime ball because you've been growing more agitated with the baby because you think he is crying for no apparent reason while in actuality you've been slowly starving the kid to death while teasing him at the same time.

OK, so now that you have all your options, let's go over how to actually feed the child from a bottle. First off, the baby will start crying because he is hungry. How do you know he is not crying for some other reason? Simple. You don't. Women, on the other hand, will make outrageous claims as to be able to distinguish among all types of crying—usually when they are not there.

Let's say that your wife has gone to visit a friend. She will not be able to do this without calling you up periodically to make sure you aren't doing something wrong to the baby—i.e., you're not doing it *her* way. Let's say that the baby starts to cry during this phone conversation. You'll try to excuse yourself to attend the baby. But wait, your wife will ask you, "Why is the baby crying?" and "Is it a 'hungry' cry?" Being a male, you simply don't know, but at least you're willing to admit to it.

I have come to the realization that women cannot really distinguish among cries either. They like to think they do, not so they can more quickly aid the child, but to show their parental superiority over the men. Example: the baby starts crying and the father picks it up. The man will go through the checklist of possible problems—hungry, wet diaper, wanting attention, needs burping, etc.—even asking advice from the wife. They keep working at it until the baby stops crying or the parents give up in utter frustration because they can't figure it out.

Conversely, if a mother picks the baby up and can't immediately fix the problem, it is because the baby is "colicky." If you then solve the problem and make the baby stop crying by doing something like burping it, you are treading on some mighty thin ice. Do it quietly and don't mention it. Telling your wife how you solved the crying when she couldn't meets with about as much enthusiasm as explaining to a grizzly why it is morally unacceptable to steal food from your picnic basket and then hitting her on the nose with a rolled-up newspaper. When it comes to a mother's baby, it is best that she is right at all times, even if she isn't right—especially if she isn't right.

So now you have taken a bottle from the refrigerator. Unfortunately, you cannot just stuff it into the child's mouth. The milk must be warmed so that if you were to drop milk on your wrist, it wouldn't feel cold or hot. Your child, however, having seen the bottle and not having it immediately in his mouth, thinks you are purposely keeping the bottle away to taunt him and will cry uncontrollably. The quickest and easiest way to warm a bottle is to throw it into the microwave and heat on a medium level. This method is so quick and easy that you are not allowed to do it. Experts say that using a microwave may destroy some of the beneficial proteins in the milk, making it as nutritious as flat Coke. Instead most people put the bottle in running or stationary hot water. Yes, this method takes an inordinate amount of time compared to the microwave, but think of the health benefits your child is reaping by exercising its lungs so vigorously.[256]

Once the milk is adjusted to the right temperature (after the more than dozen attempts at putting milk on your wrist, you pretty much can't feel anything through the layer of sticky paste), you must then make sure that it comes out of the bottle at the right rate. If you

---

256 Considering it takes about seventy-five gallons of hot running water to get eight ounces of milk warm, it isn't the most environmentally friendly thing to do either. However, a woman who works at the EPA and moonlights at PETA would club baby seals to make sure her own baby is healthy. An art historian would wipe the child's butt with a Van Gogh if there was some medical advantage to it. All societal rules get tossed out the door when it comes to what is best for your own baby. If panda intestine was shown to increase a baby's IQ, pandas would be hunted down like a bingo game at a geriatric center.

gently shake the bottle on your wrist, several drops should easily come out. If you turn the bottle over and the milk gushes out, then you have the risk of drowning the baby, so you should discard the old nipple and get another. If you turn the bottle over and have to shake the living tar out of it to get a drop, then the hole in the nipple is too small, or you clogged it by screwing up the mixing (see above discussion). Your baby may know how to suck, but he doesn't have the sucking power of an industrial vacuum, so he isn't going to get anything out.

If that happens, get a "sterile" needle, stick it into the nipple hole, and rotate so as to widen it. Retry how quickly the milk comes out. Chances are the milk is now pouring out, and you'll have to throw that nipple out as well. Eventually, you will get a nipple that works properly.[257] Unfortunately, by this time the baby is so distraught from not being fed that it is crying so inconsolably it won't take the bottle.

Let us now suppose you have a hungry baby and a bottle that works. Find yourself a comfortable chair (preferably by the television) and sit down to feed the baby. One of the first difficulties you'll run into is that you have to hold the baby with one whole arm and the bottle with the other hand—which leaves you with no easy way to work the television remote control. Do not panic. Some men try to hold the bottle upright with their chin to free up a hand, but this doesn't work well as the bottle can become dislodged and swing down to bop the baby in the belly. It is far better to hold the remote in the hand of the arm cradling the baby. You won't be able to put the remote down the entire time you are feeding, but sacrifices have to be made. Also, your overall grip on the child is not optimal while you're holding the remote, so make sure you've got the ability to use your bicep as the last-ditch effort to clamp on to a squirming baby.

If all goes well, the baby will start to eat. You will have to pay a modicum of attention to the child. Sure, there is that whole "bonding" issue women keep bringing up, but you should at least make sure you're not so engrossed with the television that the nipple has now made its way in the child's nostril. Every so often, the baby will

---

257   It goes without saying that you should have a case of nipples under the sink.

need to be burped. How can you tell? If the baby screams when the bottle is taken away, then it is not quite time.

When it is time, meaning that the baby has a look on his face like he is trying to do algebra in his little head, make sure a receiving blanket is available. Put the receiving blanket on your shoulder, hold the baby up to it, and gently pat his back. Why is the cloth called a receiving blanket? Because when the child burps, you will be "receiving," along with the gas, anything from a little spit-up to an all-out puke-o-rama. Unlike adults, the act of throwing up doesn't faze children in the least. They'd just as soon kick back, eat some more, and maybe puke again if the urge hits. They're like midget bulimics. To you, however, it is quite repulsive to feel the wetness seeping through your clothing as you look at yourself, the chair, and the floor, all now garnished with baby vomit.

If your wife is home, yell to her to help you out when you are covered with puke. She may (will) laugh at you, but hopefully she'll take the kid long enough for you to scrub yourself down and get a clean shirt.[258] If your wife isn't home, you'll have to deal with the situation yourself. The first thing you'll have to contend with is a still-hungry baby. Remove your shirt and any other clothing that has been a target. If the chair is now adorned with vomit, you may want to move to another location. Begin feeding again. By the end of the feeding period, you may be naked and at a loss for furniture, but the child will be fed.[259] By the time a baby has gotten through the first six months, it is time to either buy new furniture or get your nose cauterized to help remove the sense of smell.

Another issue that comes up is that after the trauma of getting a bottle ready, a very hungry baby may gulp the bottle down and want more. If you see this happening, yell to your wife for another bottle when there is still a quarter left so that the baby's flow will not

---

258 If your wife takes the baby to allow you to clean up from being puked on, take your dear sweet time in case the baby happens to be in a puking mood. There is nothing like the joy of cleaning smelly curdled milk off your body only to be bathed in it a second time. Besides, my theory is that women go through morning sickness so they can get used to puke, so they are conditioned to take it. Right?

259 Did I mention you should have a case of upholstery cleaner under the sink next to the case of nipples?

be interrupted. If she is unavailable, you have two options: (a) the prolonged burping session or (b) getting a second bottle ready while still feeding the baby. In the prolonged burping session scenario, the child finishes the bottle and you start to burp him, simultaneously scrambling to prepare the other bottle with basically your elbows. After a few moments, the baby will figure out that this is no normal break and you are having some difficulty meeting his needs. Like a shark sensing blood in the water, the baby goes into a "frenzy" mode that will easily outdistance your patience, slowing you down further, which means the baby will cry more, which means your patience drops further…

In the simultaneous feed/make-new-bottle method, you will have to develop some skills you do not yet possess. First off, you must learn to carry the child while he is drinking with as little jostling as possible. Open the refrigerator with your foot. At this point, you must use your chin to hold the bottle with it still angled into the baby's mouth while your now briefly free hand takes out another bottle. The feeding bottle is likely to come crashing down unless you arch your back in a severe limbo position. Keeping your back in this highly unnatural (and painful) position, get the next bottle ready. Warm that bottle by the method described previously.

The problem becomes how to test the milk. You'll either dramatically lose accuracy and/or precision if you hold the bottle with one hand and try to shake it onto the wrist of that same hand (keep in mind that you've got to stay mainly focused on feeding the baby while trying to maintain your body in reverse Quasimodo fashion). Therefore you should free up the wrist of the arm holding the baby (without dropping said baby) and shake onto that wrist. Naturally, it won't be the right temperature, and you'll have to keep working on it until it is. The good part about this method is that the baby's eating is not interrupted, and you become close friends with your chiropractor.

After you've prepared the second bottle, more often than not, the baby will take only a few sips and decide he is full. Some books tell you that you shouldn't reuse this formula because multiple heatings and coolings will give bacteria a better chance to grow.

Speaking as a person with a doctorate in microbiology, I can attest to this. However, speaking as a nonrich person who had to shell out some serious bucks to get the formula, I'd be damned if I was going to throw it out. Instead I opted to segregate a bottle that had been used before in the refrigerator and make sure I used that one first when the baby had to feed again. If your wife doesn't like this, try building a wall of condiments in the refrigerator and hiding the semiused bottle behind them.

And then there will be times when you actually want to go somewhere with the baby. When the baby wants to eat, the baby wants to eat. You can't plan a trip farther than the mailbox without having bottles ready to bring with you. Leaving the house with a baby in tow should now be considered an ordeal.[260] Therefore you will have to plan ahead and have plenty of formula ready. I suggest for a two-hour trip you bring along enough formula for a day's worth of eating. Being away from the baby supply at home with a limited supply of food is an ironclad guarantee that the baby is going to go through some type of growth spurt and eat everything you have and freak out because you don't have any more.

Grabbing a few bottles as you head out the door is obviously too simple to ever work. First off, you must buy[261] a bottle bag. All this bag is is a cloth sack with loops in the bottom that the bottles fit into, leaving space for a cold pack. Way before you plan on going out, you should put the cold pack into the freezer so it becomes frozen solid rather than just a bag of warm blue Jell-O. Many a trip has been thwarted because the freezer pack has been found on the counter from the last trip rather than frozen again. Couldn't you just throw ice in a plastic bag to do the same thing, you ask? To a mother, this has about as much class as brown-bagging it to a wedding.

---

260 It is quite important to note that the word "ordeal" is never associated with the word "fun." There is no high-fiving or fist-pumping after an ordeal. Instead, it is a "finish and then crumple on a couch" sort of thing.

261 Imagine that—another baby purchase. The next time you actually have pocket money that can stay in your pocket any length of time, you'll be helped by a nurse in an assisted-living center.

When you are traveling with a bottle bag, you must find a refrigerator at your destination if one is available. If you are visiting friends who have a full refrigerator, you have two options. The first is to push as hard as it takes to squeeze the bottle bag in. Most products like ketchup now come in plastic containers that can be crushed much easier than the old glass ones. The second option is to remove enough stuff so that the bottle bag fits. If you think this is too forward, just wait until your friends aren't looking and then hide that egg salad on the top back of the refrigerator where it is out of sight.

Men, unlike women, will make scheduled trips even if the freezer bag isn't frozen. They will, however, pack the warm bag with the bottles so it at least *appears* that they are doing the right thing. However, having been threatened enough times, men actually become afraid of the milk instantaneously going bad if the bottles are not properly handled. Therefore, they will speed recklessly, passing stopped school buses if need be, with their child in tow, just to minimize the amount of time the milk is not cooled. It's as if men think the milk will spontaneously generate Ebola virus and subsequently wipe out most of Northern America if unrefrigerated for more than half an hour—and that's the way women want it, because it is our fault we didn't freeze that pack the way we should have in the first place.

Feeding a Four- to Six-Month-Old

or

Bobbing for Grenades, and

Other Messy Situations

E ventually, bottle-feeding will become easy and routine. This is when you know that you must move to the next level because *nothing* to do with raising a child should ever be considered easy and routine. At this stage, you will be supplementing bottle-feedings with cereal. We're not talking Captain Crunch or Fruity Pebbles here; we're talking rice mush. This stuff is so bad that you don't even get a toy in the box.[262] It is a major decision as to when the child is actually ready to start with supplementing breast- or bottle-feeding with cereal. Therefore, you will have nothing to do with it. One day your wife will make the grand announcement, and you will go along because you were told to.

---

262 Keeping with the philosophy that men never truly grow up, they just get hairier, it is my belief that men still look for the prize in the cereal box with far more frequency than they look at the nutritional value. Of course the big thing is flavor and, by that, I mean sugar content. Put a box of chocolate flakes with marshmallow stars that has 100 percent of the recommended lifetime arsenic intake next to a box of fortified rice patty wafers, and the guy's only hope will be that the milk turns chocolaty when he adds it to the first box.

Before this point, your child has become quite skilled at drinking milk: just muckle[263] on to some type of nipple and suck the life out of it. Now you are asking the child to learn a whole new set of skills. First off, you have to go buy a baby-feeding chair that you strap to a regular chair. But, you may ask, why would you need this when you already have a high chair that you bought for the sole reason of feeding the baby? A couple reasons. A high chair is meant for an older baby and so does not have the support a younger baby needs. Couldn't they make an adjustable high chair that could feed younger as well as older babies? Sure, but it conflicts with the second reason: the powerful Washington-based baby lobby has deemed it necessary that two-for-one items don't do as much for the bottom line as one-for-two or one-for-ten. If they could make a crib for napping and one for nighttime sleeping, they'd do that as well.

To prepare the cereal, pour some in a bowl. Thankfully by this time, women have dropped the notion that everything the baby contacts must be sterile. The cereal should be mixed with either breast milk or formula[264] and mixed. If the proportions are not right, the cereal will either come out too soupy and absolutely nothing will stay in the baby's mouth[265] or will be so thick the baby will choke on it. Achieving the right proportions is simply a matter of trial and error. If it is too thin, toss some more cereal in. Oops. Too much. Let's add more formula to get it to stick on a spoon and, dammit, it is soup again.

Now the cereal must be warmed—and you're even allowed to use the microwave! You still won't be able to warm up the bottles this way. Don't bother pointing out to your wife the hypocrisy that the cereal is made of formula, or you'll lose microwave privileges altogether.

---

263 Technically, "muckle" isn't actually a word. However, it so fits with what a child does to a breast that I have to throw it in. It is sort of a "manic suckle" that you'd need a crowbar to break.

264 Standard milk is way too inexpensive and convenient and so must be avoided at all costs.

265 It will, however, stay on the carpet and on the chair until it is chiseled off with a butter knife. If the walls of Jericho were plastered with this stuff, they'd still be standing today.

Now, you *must* test the temperature of the cereal before you give it to the baby. Those little amounts of cereal can heat up fairly quickly, and we don't want to be spooning liquid magma into our kids' mouths. Wash your hands (or at least tell your wife your hands are washed) and stick one finger into the bowl. If it is too cold, nuke it some more. If it is too hot, add some more cereal and formula.[266] Repeat this process until the formula is at the desired temperature. Usually this occurs about the same time that you have made enough cereal to feed an NFL offensive lineman and every finger has permanent damage.

Before the feeding process ever begins, make sure the straps connecting the baby chair to the regular chair are hooked up properly. The baby chair must be strapped to the bottom and back of the regular chair so as not to allow for even a fraction of an inch of mobility. Your wife will gladly check this out to ensure you've got it fitting tight and properly (you don't) and offer any suggestions (do it over and do it right).

Rather than having the straps buckle and pull to the correct tightness, the baby lobby determined that would be far too easy for the dads. Instead, that annoying inner buckle that slides to increase and decrease the overall length of the strap must be adjusted so that the seat is stuck to the back of the chair. Therefore you have to try to snap the buckle into place, see how much slack there is, unbuckle it, take the baby chair off, adjust the straps by a guesstimate, replace the baby chair, and try to snap the buckle, only to find that either you've overcompensated and the buckle doesn't begin to reach, or you've still got enough slack to hang yourself.

After several attempts, you'll finally get the strap to fit properly. Now repeat the whole process with the other baby strap to attach it to the bottom of the chair. See now why I suggest having this done beforehand rather than while the baby is crying to eat? Your wife may suggest that the baby chair be removed from the regular chair after

---

266 You may also want to run your finger under the sink to get the cereal off as it is blistering your finger. A simple shake won't knock off the sticky glob, so put it under running water to remove it and hopefully bring the third-degree burns back down to simple second degree.

each feeding because "it looks nicer if company drops by." At this point, either superglue or staple-gun the baby chair down to the real chair because you are not going to go through this hell every time the baby wants to eat.

Once the chair is in place and the food is ready, we can actually put the baby in the chair. As would be expected, there are more straps to deal with. This time the strap goes over one leg, a second strap with a loop comes up between the two legs, the first strap goes into the loop of the second strap, and then the first strap buckles into the other side of the chair. Meanwhile, you have to work this strap magic while your baby is either trying to be the human blob, oozing off of the chair, or is so hungry that it is flinging its little body around to the point where you'd think it would be easier to tie your shoes while wearing oven mitts than to get those damn buckles shut. Once you do get the baby strapped in, you must then further lock him into place by snapping the tray on. By the time you're done, you've got the baby in a position Houdini couldn't have escaped from.

Throw a bib on the baby before you start the feeding process. Don't think this will stop the baby from making a spectacular mess,[267] but it will at least cut down on it. Bibs come in two types: the cute cloth bibs with pictures of happy animals that all the relatives coo over, and the cheap plastic ones. Get the cheap plastic ones when it is your turn to feed the baby. Your wife may ooh and aah over how precious the baby looks in the cloth bibs, but cereal sticks to them like barnacles on a ship or hookers at a business convention. By the end of the meal, the bib (and the floor) looks like a picture of the lunar surface. After one meal, a cloth bib is completely unusable until it is laundered—and believe me, the laundry is going to be piling up faster than broken bones at a British soccer match. With a plastic bib, you can pretty much hose them down and be ready to use them again later. Cute, no; functional, yes.

You must then have a baby spoon. Baby spoons come in two different types: the short handle with wide bowl and the long handle with small bowl. As with most baby purchases, if there is an option

---

267 The baby can make a mess on the equivalent of throwing oatmeal, ketchup, and cheeseburgers into an industrial blender and hitting puree without the top on.

of which to buy, you must buy both. You'll be using the long handle /small bowl to begin with.

Pick up a partial spoonful of food and put it into the baby's mouth. The baby, who is only used to sucking, will try to use his tongue to take in the food. The tongue will knock a good 95 percent of the food out of his mouth. This extra food is smeared all over his face and bib—you hope. Otherwise, it is all over his clothing, your clothing, the nearby wall, the family pet, etc. You then use the spoon as sort of a food squeegee, mopping as much food as possible from the bib and face. In doing so, the actual mass of food hanging on the baby's face decreases, but you end up helping smear it over a larger surface area. At this point, you'll have about 50 percent of the food you started with. Repeat this process until the baby (and you) has decided it has had enough and raised the white flag.

By the time you finish, baby food is everywhere. You see, your child doesn't just sit there and eat—his hands are moving at all times. The baby will smear his hand all over his face and bib and then transfer the mess into his hair and clothing—and there is nothing you can do about it. You may try, but you'll probably end up in worse shape than you started. As you are attempting to knock away his little hand from crusting up what little hair he has, he is trying to knock the bowl of cereal off the tray with the other.

Here you are, trying to prevent having to give your child yet another bath, when you get too close and the baby's hand you weren't paying attention to whips out faster than a cobra strike and knocks the entire bowl of baby food into your lap or onto the floor. To the baby, this is the equivalent of nirvana. Not only has it made much more of a mess that you'll have to clean up, but you'll have to make the bowl of cereal all over again to finish feeding him.

When you offer any new food to the child, the digestive system stages a little protest in the form of a gastrointestinal explosion. The pooping will occur more often than a pitcher crotches himself in a baseball game, have the consistency of pea soup, have more volume than what you actually put into the child, and pack enough smell to drop a horse at fifty yards. When the digestive system simmers down to the point where it is not a Herculean effort to keep from throwing up when you change a diaper, it is time to add the jars of baby food to the cereal to give the digestive system its next challenge.

Jars of baby food have numbers on them ranging from 1 to 3 representing the stage of food the baby is ready for. In stage 1, the food is pureed to the point where the food loses all texture whatsoever. The only way you can tell the difference between things like peas and carrots is by the color. Stages 2 and 3 are much different—if you ask the mother. As far as I can tell, they just put the same bland stuff into bigger jars. Keep note of what your wife buys—if she gets stage 2, you get stage 2. Otherwise, she'll act like you're feeding him from the Hannibal Lecter cookbook.

Many flavors of baby food exist. At this stage, the baby will have even more variety than the parents, who will be confined to "take out" or any meal that can be made in fifteen minutes or less. Basically, you either don't have time to cook anything complex, or if you do have the time, you're too damn tired to spend it hovering semicomatose above a hot stove. My wife's and my standard of gourmet food was lowered down to Hamburger Helper when the children were young, and even then the noodles were a bit crunchy since I lacked the patience for them to thoroughly cook when it was my turn. People only have so much patience, and your child will suck down every last bit of reserve, so you find yourself doing things like eating undercooked food and wearing underwear that is slightly damp because you didn't have the time to put it through one more run on the dryer.

So what to pick for flavors? I recommend starting off with the vegetables rather than the fruits, even though the baby will enjoy the fruits more. This choice may seem antithetical to most men who (myself included) tend to parent by the path of least resistance. If the kid is going to cry about something for an extended length of time, men tend to give in to the child's whims. However, we do pay for these lapses in judgment in spades later on. Case in point—food. If you start your child off with vegetables, then the child does not know any better—i.e., that there are much tastier things in the world—so he ends up eating the vegetables. If you start them out with fruits and then go back to vegetables, he refuses to eat the tasteless plants.

You then give in and feed him the fruit. Congratulations! You are well on your way to developing a finicky eater.

Actually, all children are finicky eaters. It is just a question of degree. Finickiness starts out nearly immediately. One day, you feed the child a particular thing and he or she eats it ravenously and then signals for more. Having previously pushed aside the first dozen or so things you made because he absolutely refused them, you start to get excited about the prospect of something you can always have on hand that you could prepare with minimal hair-pulling.

After you rush to a store to buy a case of the same stuff, you find that the next time you put it into the baby's mouth, he or she will act as if chewing on salted Tabasco-dipped lemons. Unfortunately, this fickleness is a one-way street; the baby may like something at first and then decide later it is vile, but it will never not like something and then actually take the time to taste it before reconsidering. Therefore, the vast amount of choices initially presented to you in the baby aisle becomes ever more restricted by the day (and sometimes by the hour).

Most babies take on an act of not being interested in table food. Rather than having enough solid food stuffed into them to make them sleep through the night, they'd rather awaken every several hours and demand a bottle or breast. After several months of sleep deprivation, most parents no longer feel (if they ever did) that feeding the child at all hours of the day is a bonding experience. Parents can get so tired that they'd rather the child bond to a six-pack of Cheez Whiz if it gets them an extra twenty minutes of sleep each night, even if it means the baby will be so bound up that its colon will be slower than a turtle on valium. Therefore, if it is feeding time, most parents end up jumping through hoops to try to get their babies to eat solid food.

At the beginning of a feeding session, parents try to fool the baby by pretending as if spooning this slop is the most fun thing they've ever done, hoping that the baby will be dutifully impressed and open his mouth in some semblance of cooperation. Sorry. At best you get about two spoonfuls in before the baby realizes you're faking as badly as when a car salesman says he's going to go in to have it out with his manager to give you the best deal he can.[268]

The next step is to pretend the food is something that it is not, whether it is a train, race car, or boat, all of which are trying to "dock" in the appropriate port with the appropriate sound effect. If there is no "toot toot" or "rrrrooowwwrr," then the whole thing falls apart. The vehicle must also not drive straight into the mouth, but instead circle around so that the baby thinks he is accomplishing something difficult by actually capturing it in his mouth. This tactic will be good for a few more spoonfuls as the baby's mouth drops in awe of the stupid things parents are willing to do.

After that method wears out, parents can then adopt the "well, I'm going to eat it then" routine. The parent pretends to take a spoonful of the stuff and then mutters nonsense like "num num num." My question is whether anyone in the history of humankind has ever tasted palatable food and actually made this noise! I doubt it. Why do we then assume that making this noise will convince babies to eat something they were hesitant to eat before? Besides, further amusing the baby with how ridiculous an adult will act to make them eat does no good. That is why I propose the theory that babies feign noninterest in food—being hungry for a few minutes extra is a small price to pay for the entertainment in seeing how pathetically moronic adults will be to get them to eat.

As time passes, the percentage of food that gets from the spoon to the baby's mouth—and stays inside—reaches a high enough percentage that you can actually recognize the child once the meal is done.[269] At this point, the child will refuse to let you

---

268 As the car salesperson is paid a percentage of the sale, he is probably going in to the manager and begging him not to make the final deal too good. And while I'm on the subject, why in hell would anyone buy from a salesman who has an adjective in front of their name? If he is Crazy Eddy or Jolly Jack, shouldn't he be avoided if he is more on the mentally unstable side? Do you really want to buy an expensive item that has the ability to kill you if defective from a person who is a self-proclaimed lunatic? No other profession has nicknames. Do you pick your doctor by his nickname? I doubt you'd be signing up with Steady Hand Sam for a bargain-basement appendectomy.

269 There can be so much oatmeal on the baby's face that he looks like he has come out of some 1950s schlock horror film about mutant midgets from outer space trying to take over the world.

feed him. Now she feels she must feed himself. The earlier times you thought the baby made a phenomenal mess when eating will now be looked upon as fond memories as the child literally bathes itself in food.[270]

---

270 And now the child looks like a version of the Blob.

Feeding a Seven- to Ten-Month-Old

or

Patience Is a Virtue, but Unless Mother Teresa Is Feeding Your Kid...

A baby develops an independent streak long before he should. Around this time, the baby will want to do everything himself without possessing any actual ability to accomplish tasks. It is akin to kids playing with dump trucks in the sandbox and then wanting keys to the real thing. The baby will try to be independent, get frustrated when he can't accomplish what he wants to, and then sob vociferously. There is frustration, anxiety, and, yes, sometimes sobbing for all involved. Obviously, they have to learn for themselves at some point, but the baby wants to do it before any motor skills/coordination is there at all.[271] Rather than start with a spoon, it is difficult enough to put a cracker or Cheerio in front of him and see if he can eat that.

Have you ever played the crane game at an arcade? In this game, there are a bunch of prizes in a bin with a crane above them. Plunk in a few quarters and you are allowed to move the crane forward and backward above the toys, praying to get in the proper position.

---

271 The enthusiasm for the job is there, just not the ability. Think Congress, well, without the enthusiasm at least.

Once there, you press a button, and the crane falls down and clumsily closes. The (most often vain) hope is that the prize you were aiming for is now caught in the talons. At this point, the game is not over. Said prize must stay caught while it is delivered to the proper chute.

A baby learning to eat and the crane game have more in common than not, except that, unlike a baby, if you miss the object you are aiming for, you are not apt to lose your mind and try to obliterate the object of your frustration. Your child, after a dozen or so misses, will fling her arms around wildly in an attempt to knock every last speck of food from the tray. That is how a baby cleans his plate. Hand-eye coordination is not something a child is born with. If a child wants to rub her eyes if she is tired, she basically smashes her fist into her face somewhere and then mops it around until it finally hits an eye. Going for a Cheerio on a plate is about as difficult for a child as playing darts in the dark for an adult.

Eventually, a baby's aim gets better, and she is actually able to grab the food. As you've probably already surmised, solving one problem only means creating even more. The baby may pick up the food and have it completely enclosed in her fist so that when she brings the fist to her mouth, the food is not available to be eaten. She may try to shove her entire hand into her mouth up to her wrist to get the food in there. Luckily, the child does not have many teeth yet, otherwise she'd gnaw through her fingers to get to the food because that would be less difficult than trying to pick it up again. This scene repeats itself until the food is slightly sticking out of the fist, and the baby is able to get that scrap into her mouth. By this time, the food has been crushed in that baby grip to a point where it is utterly unrecognizable.

The next step for the baby is to get the food with a good grip, bring it to the mouth, open the hand, and shove quickly. More often than not, the food falls back into the tray or on the floor or gets further mashed into the side of her face. However, sometimes the baby does get a fairly substantial piece into his mouth. Unfortunately, the child usually gets so excited that she forgets to close her mouth, and the food topples out.

The grab-and-shove method is replaced by the pincer grip. The baby finally learns to use just her thumb and index finger to try to go after the food. At first she just pushes it all over the plate, snapping away at it like a lobster on crack cocaine, but eventually she gains the ability to come right down on it. Previously, the baby sometimes loved to mash food in her hand because she loved the feel of it squirting through her fingers. Now she has the added joy of seeing the food explode in his little squeeze. The peas and corn he had been shunning will now become favorites as he squashes them and sees the insides spitting out all over the high chair, floor, and herself. Sometimes, although not often, she'll get bored with this just enough to actually put some of this food in her mouth and swallow it.

Eventually, the child will grow somewhat tired with the pincer grip and want to emulate how the parents eat. Here's where the short spoon with the large bowl (the part of the spoon bowl, not a container bowl) comes in. If you gave the baby the long spoon with the small bowl, all the food he tried to scoop up would immediately fall out, and then the baby would proceed to poke his eye out with the unwieldy long handle. I'm not saying the baby won't have these same difficulties with the other spoon, but it will happen much less frequently (you go from the food falling off 99 percent of the time all the way down to 98 percent).

Watching your child learn to eat with a spoon, you feel that he is going to starve to death before he actually hits the target. He has to first hit the food, hopefully having the spoon right side up. He then has to get under said food and pull up at an angle that keeps the food on the spoon. Usually, this starts with him mashing the spoon down and assuming whatever food wasn't crushed should voluntarily jump onto the spoon for him to pick up. The really tricky part is that if he is excited that something is on the spoon, he has to keep the damn thing level all the way to his mouth. The closer he gets to his mouth, the more excited he is, so the spoon starts shaking more and more. Of course, he then has to hit the mouth as opposed to bonking the spoon off his nose, which then knocks half of the food off and clogs his nostrils with the other half.

I'm sure many more calories are burned up flinging the food around than are actually consumed. That is why the baby still needs bottle-feedings. If it weren't for the nutritive value still supplied from bottles or breast milk, the poor child would not have the energy to trash your kitchen every time he ate.

And then there is drinking (the baby's, not yours). Besides still demanding tons of the expensive formula, he's going to want a little variety. Luckily, the people who are fleecing you for the baby food are once again there to fill in the gap. Because of them, you are able to go to the supermarket and purchase juice made just for babies! How do they make this juice, you may ask? Simple. They take a bottle of the adult stuff, dilute it with water, pour it into a bunch of tiny bottles, and then price each of those tiny bottles at the same amount they charged for the original adult bottle.[272] Naturally most people buy these baby juices because they feel that these companies can do something magical to apple juice to make it more palatable for a baby's digestive system and anything else would result in his small intestine twisting into a sailor's knot. Don't you love capitalism?

You now have to buy a special baby cup known as a sippy cup. Not only will you have to purchase many so that there will be at least a couple clean, but there are even several stages of sippy cups.[273] That way, if you actually have an adequate number of cups, they will become inadequate, and you will have to move to the next stage. The first sippy cup is based on the Weeble principle in that it wobbles but shouldn't fall down. It has a weight in the rounded bottom so that it rocks into an upright position when tilted, preventing juice from pouring out—the whopping assumption here is that the baby hasn't turned it completely over so that the cup cannot right itself. Watching juice spill everywhere is high entertainment for a child, on

---

272 My lawyer here wants me to add that I don't know for a fact that there is an all-powerful baby lobby or that they make juice for babies by diluting the adult stuff. It may be up there with my guessing that the sun will rise in the east tomorrow morning...

273 You should have enough sippy cups that you can't put all your regular cups in the cupboard easily anymore. It should reach the point where you'll need to catch a falling glass every now and then when you open the cabinet door.

par with a night on Broadway for a woman or a Three Stooges marathon for a guy.

When the baby first tries this cup, he pretty much nearly drowns himself. He's used to having to work to get liquid in his mouth. Now he just has to lift up. When he does so, juice shoots into his mouth as well as down his neck, under his bib, through his clothes, and (whatever doesn't saturate the clothing) onto the floor. At first, the baby does a lot of gagging, but does eventually manage the swing of the cup. As mentioned, the baby realizes that *not* trying for the mouth can be quite amusing. However, the large humanoids tend to get peeved when he does it and will even take the sippy cup away as a punishment if he is seen doing it.

Therefore, the baby has to lull the adults into complacence. Whether he is trying to drink or maybe making a play for the Cheerio, the adult eventually has to avert attention at some time—hell, you've got to at least blink—and that is when the previously uncoordinated baby can snatch the cup, spin it, and start making a puddle. The baby is moving along at sloth speed and then instantaneously can have ninja reflexes kick in.

Puddles. Puddles. Puddles. Children *love* everything about them; they love creating them, touching them, making them larger, and transferring them to other places. The split second you turn your back, the child is commanded by destiny itself to turn that sippy cup over and watch that glorious liquid pour forth onto the tray and/or floor in an attempt to create a masterpiece puddle. As soon as you realize a puddle has been created, you must clean it up quickly. If you wait until the end of the meal, assuming that one big mess is easier to clean up than the multitude of smaller messes, you will be wiping up juice from *every* object within six feet of the high chair. You see, once a puddle is created, the baby feels he *must* play in said puddle. The best way to play with the liquid is to put both hands in it and whip them around as quickly as his body will allow. There will be times when you'd think a mask and snorkel are required feeding-time equipment.

Once your child is used to feeding himself baby food, the next step is table food. By table food, I mean food you would—at least theoretically—actually eat yourself. In the area of knowing what to give the child, the father is horrendously inaccurate. Let's say you want to give the child a little fruit mixed into the cereal with some milk. Where did you get this crazy idea? You got this inspiration because you saw the mother give a little fruit mixed into the cereal with some milk earlier that same day. However, when *you* do it, the mother will act as if you are trying to kill the child off, even though you saw her give what you perceived to be the same thing earlier. Perception here is the key. Let's dissect the event to see how the husband was wrong.

First off, he probably made multiple mistakes just by picking up the piece of fruit. The husband, wanting to give the child what he believes to be the best fruit, reaches in and grabs the nicest-looking fruit. Unbeknownst to him, he took a piece of fruit that was nonorganically grown. Unfortunately, many child-rearing books[274] instill an irrational fear of what you are supposed to feed a baby. Many new mothers are terrified of artificial sweeteners, flavors, colors, and preservatives—as well as pesticides that are sprayed on most fruits and vegetables to keep the bugs off of them. Serve a baby the wrong food, and the mother will freak out to the point where you'd think you had just scraped lead paint off your house, thrown it in a bowl, poured some Jack Daniels over the top of it, and served that up to your child.

The fruit you *should* have served is the organic one with brown spots, tiny insect holes, and exorbitant price tag.[275] If you are not

---

274 It is a misperception among women that men simply don't care about raising their children the right way. Men care very much. However, this caring doesn't go to such a drastic step as having to read multiple books on the subject. Are we just lazy? That is slightly the reason, but it is more that we feel that raising a child is a natural thing that has been done for hundreds of thousands of years successfully without the need for experts constantly telling us how far short of the mark we are when it comes to our parenting skills. Who is to say the experts are really right anyway? Case in point, when I was raising my kids, a popular video series was called *Baby Einstein*. The idea was that they were DVDs meant for babies to watch. Anyone else remember that one? They were so popular that Disney stepped in and bought them for millions of dollars to increase their brand. Then a study came out that showed that, not only would these videos *not* make children smarter, but may actually have the *opposite* effect! Maybe we men know something that the women don't. I'm guessing the women will stick with the "lazy" theory instead.

275 Please don't send the hate mail on the organic thing. I can accept that organic fruit doesn't have the pesticides that other fruit may. I'm not saying it isn't better that way; the only thing I have a hard time swallowing on this food is the price.

married to a woman who insists on having everything organically grown, be very, very grateful. Even if you are not married to one of these women, you still will make a mistake choosing the fruit. At this stage, most men know you at least have to mash the food up. However, you can't (according to women and the books they will gladly throw at you) just mash the damn thing up. First off, you must wash it (not just the quick rinse, but the whole scrubbing procedure). Depending on the fruit or vegetable, you'll then need to peel off the skin you just scrubbed clean. Make sense? No? Too bad. After all that is done, then you can mash the thing up.

Ready to plop it into the cereal or serve it up a la carte? Of course not! First you have to give it a visual inspection to make sure there is nothing wrong with it. For example, let's take the case of the seemingly friendly banana. You think, great fruit, easy to peel and mash up—no problem. But wait—sometimes bananas have that stringy part on them. I'm not sure what mothers think—whether they believe the child can tie these strings together into a noose and hang himself—but I do know that mothers believe the string is a *bad thing*. The president would not have as much attention paid to his food even if the Taliban did the cooking.

The next mistake men make is in the selection of the milk. Men, again assuming incorrectly, believe that since the mother is so health conscious that 1 percent or skim milk is the best for the baby. At this point, mothers will gladly share their knowledge that the baby needs the fat in milk for energy and normal brain and body development. The man—simply by pouring a tad of 1 percent milk into cereal—is jeopardizing the child's chances of being a Rhodes scholar or ever being able to walk on his own. At this point, the man is ready to use heavy cream the next time he makes a baby meal; however, women have been known to gut men for lesser offenses. The key is to watch the mother meticulously—taking copious notes if you have to—and try to repeat as identically as possible what she does.

The next question will be when to start the child on more solid things like crackers. For the first time, it is not the wife who makes that decision. Ha! Ha! No, it is not the father either. You're still not even allowed to choose the brand of toilet paper, never mind anything that actually matters. It is the baby himself. One day, you'll be relaxing somewhere, and you'll realize you haven't been paying attention to the baby. You'll run over to find him gleefully eating out of the dog or cat bowl.

It seems babies have a propensity toward those crunchy little treats people leave out for their animals. You can dig the remaining ones out of his mouth, but you know the kid has been snacking for quite some time. If you don't have a pet, you may visit a family who does, and the child will be magically drawn to the bowl. The Pied Piper of Hamelin wouldn't be able to do any better at gathering children than a good ol' bowl of Friskies treats.

At this point, the child's menu resembles that of a dieting woman: bread, crackers, rice cakes, cottage cheese, etc. Even though to real men this food is as dull as a Hallmark card for a cat's birthday, babies with inexperienced taste buds will actually enjoy this new diet—for at least three or four days. After that, the baby realizes that what is on your plate is one hell of a lot more interesting than the stuff you served him and will refuse to eat it.

Eventually you will serve the baby more and more of what the adults are eating. The big problem here is that you have to cut all that food up so the kid doesn't choke on it. Unfortunately, the baby usually hasn't matured past the point where he's losing his little mind because he's hungry. Therefore, you have to hold him to console him. Have you ever tried cutting food with one hand? The plate moves back and forth while the food gets dented rather than cut. At this point, you have to decide whether you want to hold the baby and take twenty minutes to cut his food while he is whimpering or put the baby down and cut the food while he is bawling at the top of his lungs.

Later on in the feeding evolution, the baby will remember that awful rice-cake diet and will assume he is still getting the shaft with the real food you are now serving him. He will want what is on your plate and only what is on your plate. It doesn't matter that the only difference between the two plates is that his food is cut up. It doesn't matter if you show him the two plates so he can see the food is identical. It doesn't matter if you scrape food off of your plate and put it onto his. To him, it is all a conspiracy to get him to eat crummy food. The only way he feels he can be sure he is getting the good stuff is to have your plate sitting in front of him.

You have two choices. If you give in, you then have to cut up the food on your plate, and then you'll eat the nibbles of food you had made for him earlier. If you don't give in, the baby will cry, but you won't set a bad precedent. This second method is hard because when it comes to issues that an adult considers trivial, a baby's will is actually much stronger than an adult's. However, short-term triviality can easily become a long-term nightmare when you find yourself actually looking forward to seeing the bunny at the bottom of your plate when your food is all gone.

Feeding a Ten-Plus-Month-Old

or

Feeding a Child in under Forty-Five Minutes and Other Fantasies of Nature

T he big problem at this age is that children become better at voicing their displeasure with what they are supposed to eat. Now they can use words like "yucky" and "no want that." Here is where the patience of parents can really become taxed. One day, she may ask for second portions of a dish that, if you serve it at a later date because you do want him to eat things she likes, the child will not only insist that she does *not* like it and *never* has liked it but also hold her breath for fear of even smelling something so repulsive. Your first instinct is to reason with the child, pointing out that she previously did like the food. Unfortunately, reasoning only works with reasonable people. Children are about as reasonable as the Iranian ayatollahs[276] judging a wet T-shirt contest.

---

276 The ayatollahs in Iran are not particularly keen on equal rights for women. The only body part they want shown by women is their eyes, and that is only so they can see so they don't get hit by traffic and dent poor men's fenders. The only positive to this is that they will never be able to successfully challenge the US women's soccer team if they are in full burkas.

The only thing you are going to get from arguing with your child is an ebbing of your sanity. You find yourself yelling things like "you eat see bunny" or "no yucky food yummy." Your wife will walk in, and you'll find yourself continuing to talk this way: "She no like. No eat bite."

Rather than eat what is put in front of her, your child will say things like "I'm not hungry. Can I have some candy?" Don't bother pointing out the inherent contradiction in that statement to your child. All you'll end up with is years of frustration, in addition to teaching the kid to lie a bit better by waiting at least fifteen minutes before asking for candy after snubbing you on the dinner thing. Better yet, the kid learns to receive the buy-off from one parent that she is done eating dinner, maybe feigning a stomachache, and then goes to the other unsuspecting parent for dessert permission.

Kids, unlike adults, decide what foods they like not by taste, but by sight. Just by looking at the food for 0.18 seconds, the child can decide if she likes it. Some children have even evolved to the point of developing superhuman extrasensory powers. You'll call them to dinner—without telling them what you've made—and they'll yell back, "I don't like that! Can I have ice cream instead?" Pretty impressive, huh? If you press the point, then they not only don't like it, they *hate* it. If you make them eat whatever it is anyway, they actually develop hand tremors so bad that the food can't stay on the spoon and falls off before hitting its target. Most adults develop tremors of their own as they see the food they labored to make continually falling back into the plate rather than into the little darlings' mouths.

Another problem is that kids will comment on how bad the food is by saying things like how it tastes like smelly puke or slimy poop.[277] These insults further tick off the wife to have her food denigrated, and if, heaven forbid, you lose your appetite because of the comments,

---

277 Children can be quite impressive with the combinations of words they can put together to make an insult, even at an early age. Basically, they can put any negative adjective next to any negative noun, regardless of whether they have anything to do with each other—stinky booger, stupid butt hair, fat fart—and they are good to go. As a parent, your job is to scold them for this practice without laughing at the idiocy. If you show any slight sign of approval, it will only increase the activity, which can be phenomenally embarrassing if you are in places such as a grocery store or church.

she'll staple-gun your stomach so you don't need to worry about eating her "awful" meals ever again.

If you do convince the child to eat, whether it is by bribery or threats, you will then go into the "bartering stage." Your child will ask exactly how many bites she needs to eat before she is done. With his attitude of "what minimal amount do I have to do to be considered adequate," you'd think she'd just started a job at town hall.. The only other analogy I can offer is that of a convicted felon asking how many years until she is set free.

To that child, the dinner table is a prison cell, the food in front of her is hard labor, and she's looking for any and every way to escape from it. If there is a dog, it brings up the complication of the child getting rid of the food by feeding it to their pet, who is more than a willing accomplice. If there is not a dog, you have the potential problem of later finding rotting food that was successfully hidden.

If you answer the "bite question" with phrases like "a lot" or "keep eating, and I'll tell you when you're done," you'll only make the child cry as she looks at the plate of Spaghettios like you were telling her to climb Mount Everest during a blizzard in a Speedo. Most parents break down and give a number. The first thing you've got to watch out for is selective eating. If you say ten bites, they'll usually leave the entrée and have ten bites of French fries and then prance off to watch cartoons. Therefore, you must be specific. You will have to give the amount of bites for the entrée, vegetables, etc.

The next thing you have to be wary of is bite size. If you do not watch the child, she will get the smallest shred of matter that can be seen with the naked eye onto the spoon and count that as one bite. Let me assure you that it is not fun to inform your child that the bite she is so proud she took was too inadequate to count toward his parole. A third problem that comes up is that no matter how intellectually advanced your child may be, she will "lose count" of the number of bites. She may count the spoon going toward her mouth as one bite and away from her mouth as another or may skip numbers altogether. Now you can be assured that if you promised her an exact amount of candy and you shortchanged her, she will let you know exactly how much more candy she thinks he's entitled to.

So what does your kid actually want to eat? Prepared meals, sugarcoated cereal, and fast food. If it can't be gotten in a drive-through or doesn't come in a can or box ready to heat up and serve, the kid is just not interested. My wife *used to* make a special macaroni-and-cheese dish involving multiple cheeses with a breadcrumb topping, etc. It *used to* be delicious. After years of children acting like we were forcing arsenic down their throats, my wife gave up. If the kids want macaroni and cheese, that means they want the highly processed stuff with the fluorescent orange color. If the food looks like it can glow in the dark or is coated with enough sugar that it glistens in the light, then that's for them!

Let me go further in the category of sugar-coated cereals. You ask the child what cereal she wants when shopping, and she'll go for the sugar-frosted glazed crisps. Wave this box in front of a diabetic, and he'd just about drop into a coma from smell alone. Yet there are times when you just don't want a fight and will give in to the child's demands. At this point, naiveté usually takes over, and you assume that since you are giving the child what the child wants, there should not be a problem. This little bubble of happiness will quickly be dashed on the rocks of good intentions. You see, here you are pouring a bowl of cereal that your child has asked for, and when it is delivered, the child starts crying like he's watching Barney the Dinosaur being roasted on a spit.

Why is the child crying? Maybe you put the cereal in the blue bowl when the child wanted the green bowl. Don't bother just transferring the contents of the blue into the green because the food has already been contaminated by the mere essence of the blue bowl. Maybe you put milk in the cereal (because the child asked for milk in the cereal), and the child has changed her mind and does not want milk. Maybe the child wanted the milk poured into the bowl first, followed by the cereal, so only the bottom half of the cereal nuggets would be soggy while the top remained crunchy. The only guarantee here is that you didn't do it right—and you thought that only happened with your wife!

Every now and then, you'll treat your child to a fast-food restaurant. Children love this. They may not know the names of their uncles, aunts, or cousins, but they sure as hell know who Ronald McDonald and all his friends are. Fix them a cheeseburger at home, and they act like you just served them head cheese, head included.[278] Serve a cheeseburger from McDonald's, and they think it's manna from the gods. So what do the kids love so much about fast food? Is it getting out of the house? Not really. Is it that same stale, limited menu of choices? Somewhat.

What really gets them is that cheesy three-cent toy they throw in the bag. The kids *love* this toy. Unfortunately, they love this toy so much that they forget to eat their meal—which is why you brought them to the restaurant in the first place. Here you are at the restaurant, begging them to eat fat-enriched grease-saturated food, because at least that is fractionally healthier than eating no food at all. The meal ends in frustration as you threaten to take the toy away unless they eat enough to clog at least seven adult-sized arteries and drink enough soda so that the caffeine will keep them awake until at least 2:00 a.m.

So what is a parent to do if the child is a finicky eater at home? First off, cut out the snacking between meals if they are doing so. If a child promises to just have a little snack without spoiling her appetite, that is akin to Hitler promising no further aggressions after he takes over little ol' Poland. If the snacks are cut out and the child still does not want to eat dinner, that throws many adults into fits of hysteria as they continue cooking until the child does eat. Wrong. The thing to do is *not* panic and *not* continue making food.

If the child does not want to eat, then that is fine. No problem. Send the child off to play. However, when the child comes back for that snack, she gets that same plate of food. Consider it optional if you want to heat it up in the microwave. This tactic may sound

---

278 Technically, head cheese is not really cheese. Instead, it is meat jelly made not only from the meat from the head, but feet, tongue, and heart. Now, one normally does not think there is much meat on the head of an animal or, if there is, that it is something that makes one salivate. To go further, one usually doesn't put the words "meat" and "jelly" next to each other without thinking about upheaving. So how does one go about making head cheese? Just boil these select "meats" together, and the natural gelatin in the tissue should make them congeal when it cools down. Mmmm, finger-licking good! I bet you didn't know that this was part cookbook!

heartless as your child is begging you not to make them eat something she hates rather than the Captain Crunch they like. However, parenting is *not* a popularity contest. The object of parenting is not only to raise children to become responsible adults but to also *retain your sanity*. If you're making a dozen or so different meals a day, you'd better plan on eventually living in a facility where the walls are padded and visitors can't have anything sharp in their pockets when they visit you.

The corollary to this problem is that if you have two or more children who are finicky, they cannot agree on what they'd like to eat, which increases the number of different meals exponentially. You also don't want to raise spoiled brats who know that they can get their way if they complain enough. Do that, and these are the kids who grow up into adults who don't know how to cope in life when their job makes them actually work or their landlord, for some cruel reason, wants them to pay rent.

Another food-related problem at this age is that children now like their food "customized." Everything must be done a certain way, or the entire meal is ruined. Even the simple task of making a peanut butter and jelly sandwich can be a chore. The child will want it on a particular type of bread, probably with the crust cut off, and the sandwich cut in half. If you cut the sandwich down the middle and your child wanted a diagonal cut, the child will act as if you just hacksawed the head off her Elmo doll. Sometimes, the child will cry so hard she can't even tell you why she is so upset. Japanese restaurants take less care serving up puffer fish than you will need to cook for your child.[279]

Yet another problem is that kids at this age try to progress too quickly in some food-related areas while they tend to backslide in others. How do they devolve? They could decide that chewing with their

---

279 For those of you unaware, puffer fish is a delicacy served at some Japanese restaurants—only *some* since it is phenomenally toxic, so if it isn't prepared correctly, it can kill the person eating it as it contains one of the deadliest toxins known to humankind. Correctly prepared, the fish should make your tongue and lips a bit tingly as they go numb. Personally, I'm not a fish person. Apparently, I'm also not a person who is going to put my life in the hands of a chef I haven't met, hoping he is sober or didn't just break up with his girlfriend.

mouth closed is too much hassle. They could decide that using utensils is passé. They could challenge themselves to see if they can fit their entire dinner in their mouth before starting to chew. Heck, they could ask you to start spooning the food into their mouth if they are lazy enough.

For an example of trying to advance too quickly, your child says she wants some juice. Fine. You go to the cupboard and grab a cup. The child then bawls because she wanted to get the cup from the cupboard. She feels she is a big girl, and so she must assume the awesome responsibility of getting her own juice. You put the cup back. The child continues to cry hysterically. After minutes of calming the child down, you find out she is crying because you (heaven forbid) left the cabinet door to the cups open and she wanted to open it. You close the cabinet door.

She then acts like the last ten minutes of anguish never happened and happily starts to get her own cup. The child has to get a stool, climb to a precipitous height (usually standing on top of the countertop), back up toward the countertop edge as she opens the cabinet door, grab a cup (hopefully not glass that can shatter on the ground if dropped), and then make it down with the one free hand. Meanwhile you must act nonchalant about the whole mountaineering escapade while you brace yourself to dive between the child's falling body and the floor.

She then has to get juice from the refrigerator. With luck, she won't decide to pick the juice bottle up by the cap that may or may not be tightened if she is the one who insisted on putting it on the last time. If she does grab it by the top, you have to yet again dive for the juice before the bottle hits the floor while the child is still holding the cap. Quite the mess. Unfortunately if you do make it to the bottle, the child cries hysterically because you have just "impinged upon his drive toward independence." She'll be inconsolable for at least twenty minutes. I'm not sure what is worse—the physical labor of cleaning up the mess or the emotional wracking of hearing the child sob for that long. When it comes down to it, it's cheaper to keep grabbing the juice and a heck of a lot nicer not sticking to the floor every time you walk by the refrigerator.

If your child does not grab the juice bottle by the cap, you are not out of the woods yet. Your child must then transport the bottle to the kitchen counter. At this stage, children have not yet learned the rule of keeping things upright to keep from spilling. Therefore, the bottle is usually swung sideways as she is hefting (throwing) it up on the counter. If she insisted on putting the cap on the last time, you best hope you remembered to sneak into the refrigerator and tighten it when she wasn't looking. Fixing it to your satisfaction after the child is gone gives the child the illusion of independence when she really doesn't have much to speak of.

If they do manage to get the bottle up on the countertop without incident, you can be near guaranteed that your good fortune will change. Part of the problem is that the only way they know how to aim the juice into the cup is to start pouring and then direct the flow (akin to how boys learn to toilet train). If they are a bit better at aiming, they usually hit the side of the cup with the flow so that it knocks it over. Hopefully, they'll realize sooner rather than later that if the cup tips over, it is a good idea if they stop pouring.

If they manage to pour the juice into a cup, yet more danger lies ahead. There is a host of other ways children have found to spill. First off, they like to pour until the juice is near/at/beyond the brim of the cup. It doesn't matter whether they have a little baby cup or a large mug—they are going to fill that sucker to the top. That cup in a not-too-steady hand is a better recipe for disaster than hash brownies at an all-you-can-eat buffet.

Secondly, even if the cup isn't brimming, it still has to be transported. When they grab the cup of juice from the counter, they then have that recurrent problem of keeping things upright. If they manage to keep it upright, they usually don't keep close tabs on it when they are carrying it, so they swing their arms as they normally do. If—miracle of all miracles—they do get the cup to the table, then a random elbow will eventually knock it over.

Then there is food. Food is continually being dropped. When food hits the ground, it doesn't make nearly as much mess as a drink.[280] Other problems exist when it is food that hits the floor. The

---

280 There are clearly exceptions to that rule. A popular child dinner is spaghetti. It not only tastes good to them, but the sauce stains everything around them, and the spaghetti feels good being mashed into their hair or into the carpet.

first is that the food may be "irreplaceable." What do I mean by that? Say you've got two hotdogs left in the package. If you cook them both and give one to your child and keep the other to eat yourself, your child will promptly drop hers. You then have the choice of the child going hungry or you going hungry.

This scenario is why the five-second rule was developed. How does this work, you may ask? Simple. If the child drops food, and either you or the child picks up the food before five seconds has elapsed, the food does not count as "officially dropped." The child can continue eating the food like nothing has happened, with maybe just a quick dust of the hand to get off any visible hair or chunks of dirt. Many adults object to this rule and are morally outraged when parents incite its use. However, when you think of how many filthy things the average child is stuffing into his mouth to suck on during a day, from the dog's chew toy to the old pacifier she found buried in the cushions on the chair, you realize that a child's mouth is a virtual cesspool of microbial activity. A little bit more is like adding a rock to Mount Everest and claiming it is now bigger. So don't forget to ask for that kiss good night, especially at this stage when they only know the open-mouth kind!

When it comes down to it, it is just easier to accept that you will never be able to get through any meal without someone spilling or dropping something. There are no exceptions. Because you don't have time to clean everything thoroughly after each and every spill, the floor quickly becomes pretty gruesome. You'll be walking past where your child eats, and your shoe will be wrenched from your foot as it gets stuck to the floor. Escape becomes more difficult than what the dinosaurs faced in the La Brea tar pits. By the way, the one time you lose your patience and yell at the child for spilling, you'll be destined to knock the next cup over yourself, making you feel lower than a snake's butt.

Feeding Older Children

or

A Box of Devil Dogs Is Not Supposed to Be Considered a Single Serving

Anything goes. Chaos reigns. Many kids have to wear a sweater in the summertime because they live in the refrigerator. They can be eating machines. Usually at this time, most parents have to give up any semblance of control besides what is served at the main meals. Most children cannot walk by the kitchen without opening the refrigerator and looking into every single cupboard. I'm talking every time! If they have to walk by the kitchen to go to the bathroom, they will check all places where food can hang out *both going to and coming from*. I don't know whether kids think adults can do an entire grocery-shopping run undetected within minutes, or they think they can actually spot something new on the seventy-second look of the day that they didn't see on the seventy-first.

Also, no food is considered "sacred." If you buy a particular item because you like it, the children are guaranteed to eat it before anything else. As mentioned in the title, an entire box of Devil Dogs can be considered a single serving. To a child, it had better be a single serving lest, heaven forbid, someone else could get a chance to eat one.

Threats to stay away from your food rarely work. All a threat does is alert them that there is something delectable in the house. At that point, they will eat most of whatever it is, leaving the last of something so they can honestly claim they didn't eat it all (only 97.7 percent). Usually what is left are the crumbs that you would have in previous years thrown out. Now they are precious little morsels.[281] If you really want something, you have to hide it in your underwear drawer. That is the only safe place that a man has in the house.

Remember all those troubles you had with children trying to do things before they could? Luckily, those days are (somewhat) behind you as the child has (nearly) developed the coordination necessary to find what he wants to snack on/drink without your continual supervision. Unfortunately, your child has moved to the next stage, which we shall affectionately refer to as "regression." In this stage, your child realizes that he can have food whenever he wants, and now the possession of this ability becomes no big deal to him. In fact, now your child considers this ability a hassle. He'll be a vegetable out on the couch watching cartoons and yell for you to get him some juice— even if you're sitting next to him. He used to beg to do it himself, and now he can't be bothered.

Before getting upset, most men should think from whom did he learn this one (if you need help with this question, ask your wife). You can either acquiesce to being his slave or battle it out with him. You'll find yourself doing a bit of both. Unfortunately, if you do more of the former than the latter, the child will sink further into his blissful regression. He could be standing next to the utensil drawer and still call upstairs for you to come down and get a spoon. Keep going and you'll find yourself dipping his French fries into the ketchup for him and then hand-feeding him.

Because the child can get his own food, you have to watch for the snacker. This is the kid who has a few chips, some yogurt, a couple pieces of cheese, maybe some Slim Jims, and then is not hungry for dinner. You pretty near have to put a padlock on the refrigerator, or he'll never be eating a meal with the family again. Restricting

---

281 If you can find potato chips left in the bag that are larger than snowflakes, consider yourself a lucky man.

food from your child, however, can be quite entertaining. He'll act like his life is ebbing away because of malnourishment, but there is the slightest chance he may survive if he can get his hands on some popsicles since dinner is still thirty minutes away.

You will also get periods of regression in general eating habits. Early in life, the child struggles to use silverware. Later on, he decides that it is just more fun to go without utensils. So after years of mastering the art, you'll look over and your five-year-old is eating macaroni and cheese with his hands. He'll be dropping food left and right, but you can tell by the look in his eyes that he is not going to be losing any sleep over it. He may regress in wearing clothing as well, so that would at least save on laundry, but less on embarrassment if you have surprise guests. He may also be wiping his hands on his clothing or at least walking away from the table touching everything humanly possible so that you'll be cleaning cheese sauce from the walls, floor, furniture, siblings, etc.[282] Your job is to rant and rave about it enough so that he does care. And he will care—as long as there is a commercial on the television, but after that, he's likely to remember it about as well as he remembers to put down the toilet seat and flush.

The big challenge here is teaching him how to use a napkin. It is as simple as teaching him how to program the DVD player to land the space shuttle. He'll have the napkin in one hand, and he'll still wipe his mouth on his sleeve. Every shirt will eventually have permanent stains on the arms. Somehow, he'll even be able to manage this with short-sleeve shirts! Why use a shirt sleeve when it is as simple to use the napkin? You may as well ask your dog why he licks himself.[283]

He may also get bored with the eating process. That repetitive "scoop up food, bring to mouth, put in mouth, chew/swallow" may seem too inefficient to that five-year-old. That's why you could look over to see that he's eliminated the middle steps and has his face in the plate. After the initial thought of, "Well, at least he is

---

282 Maybe that is the reason Velveeta made their mac & cheese with fluorescent-orange cheese—you can at least see the trail the child has made, so it is easier to spot and clean up.

283 And the answer is…because he can.

finally eating," you realize the inordinate mess this new technique will make, so you eventually have to scream in a shrill enough voice to penetrate through the sauce-filled ear canals so that some sort of signal reaches his brain that a parent is indicating dissatisfaction.[284]

All of these relapses become magnified in difficulty if there now is a younger sibling around. Younger children emulate older children. More than that, they idolize them. If a younger child sees an older child with his face in the plate, then the baby is going to be doing some bobbing for cereal as well. The baby will make more of a mess than the older child could even dream of. It can even become sort of a competition—there may not be a winner, but there is certainly a loser.

Another thing you'll notice at this stage and until the children are kicked out of the house is that your grocery bills will be enormous. Years ago, you were able to go shopping every other week, but now you find yourself going multiple times a week and getting cartloads that are brimming with food. Even if you cut coupons[285] or buy generic food rather than brand names that contain "taste," it isn't going to be pretty seeing that register tally up. For men who aren't used to doing the grocery shopping, it is safer to ask if there is a defibrillator on the premises before checking out.

I recommend getting a lot of easy-to-prepare dishes for when your wife is away, even if that type of food is more expensive. If you have one or more children, it is not the easiest thing to cook and watch them at the same time. Come to think of it, though, boiling water in an empty house is a chore for most men. If your wife is going to be gone and you will actually have to feed the children something, it is handy to have the little jars of nuke-and-serve food or chicken nuggets that you just quick bake. Don't fret about that nutrition thing—that's for your wife to worry about—or just serve a Flintstone chewable vitamin as the vegetable.

---

284 The exception here is when you are in a restaurant and you can't scream. In these circumstances, you have to rely on a modified Vulcan pinch as you grab his arm or leg in a way as to cause minor pain that signals the brain that something is awry, but the grip can't be so hard that the kid screams himself or yells out that you are hurting him for all to hear.
285 Men don't cut coupons.

Most men take the easy road and cook the children something they like. At that point, everyone is happy. You don't really have to cook; just heat it up and the children get something fun to eat. That is until your wife then puts all this effort into making some difficult-to-prepare well-balanced meal with multiple things on the plate and the children snub it and ask if daddy can open them up a can of Winnie the Pooh–shaped pasta and curly fries. That will get you in trouble. What will get you into the next level of trouble known as "hell's fury" is when the kids actually ask that mom leave the house so dad can cook them good stuff rather than what she serves.

Bathing a Baby

or

Urine Trouble Now!

After a baby has spent nine months completely immersed in amniotic fluid, the last thing he wants to do is to be plunked down into more water. That is why the child will scream as if you were shoving bamboo strips under his toenails when his naked body first contacts the water. Unfortunately, society frowns upon parents who decide not to bathe their children on a regular basis, and so you must go through this grueling torture on a rather periodic basis. Besides, it is somewhat of a relief to have them not smell for at least brief periods of time when you are holding them.

When to give a bath? I suggest nighttime. Some people claim baths may soothe children and better enable them to be put to sleep. The fact is that they scream and kick so much that they (and you) are left at the extreme end of exhaustion while your face and clothes are soaked from the bathwater that the baby has inevitably peed in. By the time you've finished and have the baby dressed, the only thing you want to do is hand the baby off and drag your sorry carcass to the bed, whether or not the child is going to sleep as well.

So what to do? First you must buy a baby tub with all that extra money you have left over from paying the hospital deductibles. While you're at the store, you might as well get the baby towels, baby washcloths, baby soap, baby oil, and most importantly, "no tears" baby shampoo. The only tears you want will be your own when you see that bill ring up! You see, many companies specialize in putting out lines of products meant solely for the gentle needs of babies. What does this mean? As with the case of baby juice, they probably dilute their standard adult stuff by half and then triple the price. It's either that, or they are testing these modified products by injecting them into the eyes of baby bunnies to see if they tear up. But considering rabbits don't have the biological capacity to cry, pretty near anything, including onion extract, should pass that test.

Getting back to the chore at hand, you must then fill up the tub with water. Sound simple enough? Sorry, but the word "simple" by this time in your life has disappeared from your vocabulary, along with words like "recreation," "solitude," and "kinky"—potentially never to return. It will not disappear from your wife's vocabulary with quotes like "How could you mess up something so simple?" By the way, that is a rhetorical question, so she doesn't want an answer. When the judge says "Guilty," he is not looking for you to come up with excuses at that point. He wants to hear *nothing*, and neither does your wife when she passes sentence on you.

Everything—and I mean everything—now has become a *big deal* when it comes to the baby. How could a chore that sounds as pathetically simple as putting water in a plastic tub possibly become a big deal, you may ask? Because you have a wife, and anything involving children must be done *her way* and only *her way* because she considers your judgment when it comes to child maintenance about as valuable as hygiene tips from New York City bag ladies.

Naturally, you would first bring the baby bath over to the kitchen sink or the bathtub and turn the water on. The ultimate goal is to fill the bath with the appropriate level of water that must be at body temperature give or take 0.0023°F. You may first be inclined to add cold water and then bring it up to the right temperature with hot water. Resist this temptation even though it is based on a fundamentally sound thermodynamic principle.

You see, your wife has the uncanny ability to sense any water in a one-hundred-meter radius that has the potential to either freeze or scald the child. She will whip into the bathroom, thrust her hand in the running water, and then berate you on your inability to perform the "simplest" of tasks. Don't bother trying to explain what you are doing. She either won't buy it or will try to convince you that even though the final average bath temperature may be adequate, there will be pockets of hot and cold water swirling around trying to injure your child.

Therefore, you must continually adjust and feel the water with a finesse that is usually reserved for someone trying to cut a diamond. Once it is at the appropriate temperature, you must rush it out to the area where you are to bathe your child and quickly strip your child from its clothing. Why so quickly? Because the water that was at the correct temperature is now slowly dropping and—believe me—your child will let you know this if it gets too cold. You must also make sure there are no wind currents of any sort—an open window, a fan, etc. Passing wind (pun intended) of any type will make your naked child uncomfortable. To ensure your child's ease, I suggest pitching a pup tent in your kitchen and giving your child a bath in there.

It should be noted that with all that you have to keep in mind, you still must remember to take the diaper off of the child before plunking it into the water. If not, the diaper will expand to unbelievable proportions as it tries to suck up every ounce of liquid in the tub. Will this hurt the child by squishing it? No. The disaster occurs when your wife sees this faux pas and then runs off laughing to call her mother, your mother, her friends, your friends, your neighbors, ad infinitum. If her phone is readily available, video of the event will be posted on every social media site available for everyone to see and comment on. Rest assured that if at any time in the future there is any gathering of women you know who are laughing, it is likely to be about your mistake(s). In such areas, women do not take pity or spare the dignity of a man.

Besides the frantic kicking and screaming when entering the water, your child is likely to have another biological response affectionately known as the "golden fountain." If you have a boy, you are in a crisis situation the entire time the diaper is off. *Do not forget this* lest you accidentally lean into range and find the yellow spray hitting your body and clothes. You must remain on constant vigil—even if the child has already urinated seconds before! Now I don't know whether it's a biological throwback in our genetics, but babies possess the ability to pee more times than a greyhound locked in a fire-hydrant factory.

You may also suffer from the misconception that since a baby boy's equipment is small, he's not really going to be able to get much distance out of the thing. That would be a mistake. People don't saw off a shotgun to make it safer. As it turns out, their equipment is perfect for a parental strike. Since it is small, it can only point straight out to where you are standing. The best thing to do if your baby boy starts to pee is deflect the stream down. My personal favorite was to just throw the washcloth over his privates. That way, you can limit the amount of floor/carpet washing you will need to do later. Do not attempt to grab a soapy baby and spin him around to point the action somewhere else. In your attempt to get a good grip, you wouldn't be able to get the kitchen wetter if you had set up a sprinkler system in it.

At this point, many of you may be relieved you have a baby girl. Sorry. The fear may have changed, but a different danger is present. A baby girl has the ability to pee in the bathwater without you knowing it. Why is that a big deal? Because your baby girl is anything but immobile. Never mind the fact that you are continually plunging your hands into the water, she is splashing you to the point of drenching your entire upper body. It may not be until the end of the bath when a big wave hits your face that you realize the water is a bit saltier than it should be. If this should happen, calmly finish giving your child a bath, dress her in the appropriate clothing, and hand her off to your wife before you run screaming from the room to strip the clothing from your body, shower, and brush your teeth.

Now we come to the actual technique for bathing a baby. The first thing that should be washed is the face. The reason for this should be clear—if the child has a "mystery pee," you don't want to be rubbing it in her eyes and mouth. By doing the face first, you can at least cut the odds of this from an absolute certainty to a mere high probability. You'll want to gently wipe the face clean. However, "wanting" and "getting" are worlds apart. You see, during the day your child has built a hardened crust of eye goop and nose gookies (my apologies for throwing around those technical terms) that are about as easy and fun to remove as superadhesive Band-Aids on your hairy chest.

Even though your child may not be able to hold her head upright, she will find the strength to whip her noggin around enough to make your job more challenging. Your child will also object by voicing a complaint loud enough that the neighbors will be tempted to call 911 for fear you are trying to do her in. After continuous rubbing and swearing under your breath (and not so under your breath), you will get the eyes and nose fairly clean. At this point, you'll have a fairly disgusting washcloth. You may ask yourself whether you want to discard it for a fresh one or whether you should plunge ahead with the same one. If you have successfully managed to convince your wife to do the laundry duty, then you might as well find a new one. Otherwise, you'll want to minimize disgusting laundry and keep using the same cloth.

You should then shampoo the head. I found this mildly amusing since for the first year of their lives, my children had as much hair on the top of their head as Michael Jordan with a five o'clock shadow. However, you still have to do it no matter how much hair they have—even if a peach has more. Why? Because your wife says so. Even though the shampoo says "no tears," the child will object if any liquid gets into her eyes, and there will be oh so plenty of tears. Therefore, you must one-handedly massage the scalp while keeping the other hand free for mopping up any drops of water that begin heading for the eyes. One errant bit of liquid, and she'll scream like she's in a vat of acid.

Once you think you're done with the shampooing, carefully rinse every last bit of suds off their head—and I do mean every last bubble. Now I'm not sure what would happen to the child if any suds were left on (I've never heard of unwatched suds penetrating the skull and leading to brain damage), but I can guarantee that if your wife saw them, it would be a *big deal*. If you do accidentally finish the bath, take the child out, and then realize that you missed rinsing major portions of the head, make sure your wife is not around and towel them up before your crime is detected.

The next area to be cleaned is each and every chin.[286] Make sure to lift and clean under all of them—otherwise the milk that has dribbled down during feeding times will ripen into an odor that will singe your eyebrows when you try to pick the child up. Make sure you get under each and every fold—and do they have folds: belly fold, arm folds, leg folds, and even back-of-the-neck folds! Continue cleaning your way down until only the child's private parts are left. Sure, their ever-active butt has been immersed and contaminating the water all this time, but at least you can pretend the water only becomes a minicesspool at the end.

I should caution here that the baby may be squirming around a great deal, and it may be difficult to hold him down. Now that you've soaped him up, it will be impossible as he will easily slide out of your grip. Luckily, he'll have few places to go in this tiny tub, and so you will catch him eventually. Getting him cornered and eventually pinned to one of the edges seems to work the best.

At the end of the bath, pick your child up and start drying him off with a baby towel. The only difference between a standard towel and a baby towel is that the baby towel is thinner and has a hood on one end. The purpose of this hood is to put it on the baby's head and then wrap the rest of the towel around the body so as to keep him warm. Most babies don't like it and will shrug it off. You will find this hood comes in useful only in later years as older children use it after their bath as a cape and run around the domicile pretending to be a naked superhero.[287]

---

286 As the old joke goes, you could find more chins there than a Chinese phonebook.

287 For boys when they are mobile, they put the hood of the towel on their head rather than tie it around their neck, put their hands out and run, acting like they are flying. Apparently, they do their best justice-fighting in the buff. You may be tempted to videotape that for posterity, but avoid doing so. He could never run for office if that footage made it onto YouTube.

Bathing Older Babies

or

The Last Hot-Tub Party You Will Ever Be Invited To

Once your child no longer fits in the baby bath, you must transfer the child to the standard tub. As you should begin to expect, doing anything new with a baby involves a financial transaction of some type. This time, you will have to buy a baby bath ring. The purpose of this device is to hold the child in a sitting position while in the tub so that (a) he or she doesn't flop over and drown, and (b) the child can no longer directly urinate on you.

This ring has suction cups on the bottom that hold the device in place and a ring on top that holds the child upright. Naturally, the top ring has to have a small diameter so the kid won't slip out. The unfortunate consequence of this design is that you must now bend your child's body in unnatural angles to get her into the damn thing. Luckily, children's bones are a lot more pliable than adults' and can achieve some unusual angles—not that I recommend anyone testing this theory![288]

---

288 Testing this theory would rightly get a person an all-expense-paid trip to a federal "resort" where all your meals are taken care of. Of course you may be traded around by the other members for a pack of cigarettes, but that is another issue.

By this time, your wife still thinks you are a clod when it comes to child rearing but now trusts you to be able to keep the child alive with minimal supervision. Therefore, she may only check the water temperature on every other bath, compared to the few dozen times on every bath when the baby is first born. The water temperature standard will also be relaxed, allowing for 98.6°F ± 0.7°F.

You must then purchase bath toys. Heaven forbid that the child not be within arm's reach of a toy at any second. Enough toys should be placed in the tub so that you can't actually see the water underneath. At this point, wedge your child into the bath ring. Try to wash the child in the same manner as before. You will notice that the bath ring makes many baby folds nearly inaccessible. At this point, you have the option of pretending that you did them or making a mental note of doing it when you pull him out, forgetting after all the tugging and screaming getting the kid out of that ring, and then pretending that you did them later when you do remember.

Being a proper father, you will try to entertain your child while she is in the tub. Sounds nice, but again, not a good idea. The major ways your child will play while in the tub are to (a) get you soaked or (b) get the rest of the bathroom drenched. She can accomplish this either by the direct splash or throwing one of her wet toys out of the tub. You will actually begin to feel like a goalie as you begin blocking shot after shot trying to deflect the toys back into the tub. Needless to say, don't wear anything that you plan to keep on after the bath is done, unless you are going scuba diving. Actually, you may as well plan to change clothes altogether unless you think damp socks are comfy.

Please note it is usually torture to get your child to drink water rather than some other beverage. Put them into the tub, and you can't stop them! The child will either try to plant her face directly into the tub or use one of the toys as a cup. Knowing how filthy she was before you put him in the tub, you will try to stop this practice—to no avail, I may add. All you'll do is teach her to be sneaky about it. If you knock the toy he is using as a cup out of her hands enough times, she will adapt to alternative methods such as pretending to wash her face with the cloth while secretly sucking the water from the cloth. Children have such developed sucking muscles that you can take one of these sucked cloths in your hands and it will feel bone dry!

Some children actually start to enjoy the bathing experience. This is also not good. If they are having a good time, they will start to want to spend longer and longer periods of time in the tub. Longer times mean that the chance of an accident grows exponentially. As the child plays by herself, you will not help but become lax in your overseeing. After a couple minutes of letting your mind wander, you'll look back to see poop floating in the tub. Your first instinct will be to vomit from the sight. I recommend first calling for your wife and *then* vomiting. If you time it just right, your wife can see you upheave and then you may be excused from cleanup detail.

When a number-two accident happens in the tub, everything in it, including the tub, should be sterilized. Bleach works the best, followed by a thorough rinsing.[289] I'd give you more details here about the proper cleaning process, but my revulsion acts have been so convincing that my wife has taken care of all decontamination situations. Therefore, be ever vigilant when your child is in the tub. If any facial features show even a hint of wanting to "push," be ready to grab the child and yank her out.

The only other significant concern is that it is more difficult to shampoo the child's hair. Not only do they have more of it, but they are no longer at an angle that makes it easier to wash the suds out. At this point in the bathing cycle, you can't help but get soap in their eyes. The child will let you know if the slightest sud has slipped past your wary view by screaming, "MY EYES, AAARRGGH, MY EYES!" oh, about seventy or eighty times in succession. Your wife will assume you have poured the shampoo directly into the eyes and commenced vigorous scrubbing with a Brillo pad.

The most effective method to keep the soap out of their eyes would be to have the child lie back with its head resting in one of your hands while you use the other hand to pour the water back over the head. It goes without saying that this option will not be available

---

289 Removing the child before addition of caustic cleaning chemicals is advisable.

to you. You see, your child views this situation the same way a man would being marched in front of a firing squad without a blindfold. Any sanity and decorum the child currently has quickly slips away when she thinks of lying back and looking up at a cup of water about to come tumbling down on her. I'm sure you'll want to try to reason with the child about this approach to comfort her and assure her that this is the best method. I certainly did. Alas, children don't reason, just react—and they will react badly. And since they do squirm, water will undoubtedly get into hher eyes no matter how careful you are, and then the child will look up at you like you just traded mom for a six-pack as they assume you lied to them as it couldn't possibly be their fault.

The average child usually assumes the position of head down with their face buried in their hands when you tell him that the time has come to remove the shampoo. You have no choice but to pour away. The child will begin panicking, so be quick and have a dry towel ready. She will take the towel and try to gouge her eyes out in the attempt to dry them. Let her. You have no choice, and at least she is the one inflicting wounds, so she won't turn you in later.

So why is it that adults can jump into a pool and swim underwater with their eyes open and not complain about water in their eyes, while a child can feel the mildest drop and believe they are going blind? Why does wiping a towel across a *closed* eye make it feel all better for a child? These are among life's many imponderable questions, like "If love is blind, why are there stores like Victoria's Secret?"

As children get older, they want to take on more responsibility. This independence includes bathing themselves, which for most men is a peachy idea. The problem comes in that when they think they are ready is completely different from when they actually are. When you first plop them in the tub for independent bathing, children believe in the slow-dissolve theory, which basically states that even though they have been working hard to grind dirt deep into each and every pore of their body, just by being wet they will become magically clean. After you persuade them that this theory stinks as much as they currently do and they cannot get away with not scrubbing, they become believers of the magic-cloth theory.

Under this philosophy, any part of the body the cloth barely touches, including surrounding areas, is now considered clean. When I say touch, I mean that the cloth need only slightly graze a body that was previously doing a commando crawl through the local cow pasture. To the child, her body is so clean after the magic-cloth treatment that she doesn't even have to look. At this point, you'll have to convince the child to abandon this theory by pointing out the various clumps of grass and dirt still clinging to her body. Finally, she will get to the point where she will understand that she may need to scrub a little bit. So how long does it take to convince them that you actually know more about bathing than they do? With continual monitoring and patience, you should be able to whip through the whole process in just under three to four years.

During this time of self-bathing, you'll run into other difficulties (naturally). The first does not seem difficult, but still happens each and every time the child steps into the tub. Let me repeat that—each and every time. How often? Each and every time. The child will get into the bath, look up at you, and say, "Do I have to use soap?" After countless baths asking the same question over and over and getting the same answer time and time again, you'd think the kid could figure this one out. I'm sure that there are some fathers out there who are puzzled by this because their child in the years of bathing has never asked this question. In these instances, it is because for years, this child probably hasn't been using any soap whatsoever or does the initial dab on the cloth and expects it to last for the entire bath on the entire body.

So there you are, sitting down watching television, comfortable in the thought that your child is finally getting the hang of washing in the tub. Then you hear your child complaining that his or her pajamas don't fit any longer. As the child turns the corner, you can see why there was so much difficulty putting them on. Your child did not towel dry, and the pajamas are now soaked through. You'd think that there would be somewhat of a light bulb going off in that little head when she is soaking wet yanking clothes on for all she's worth.

Apparently not. You then have to nearly pull their limbs out of joint trying to get these water-sodden clothes off before you really towel dry and put fresh pajamas on her. Believe it or not, this mistake happens. Do not assume that your child has the IQ of Forrest Gump even if this mistake becomes routine.[290]

---

290 But, then again, he may.

Bathing Multiple Children

or

Does Flood Insurance Cover This?

L et's face it—you're not going to have the energy or patience to give two completely separate baths when you have two children. At this point, you should throw both kids in the same tub. Naturally, there will be several unique problems you will need to attend to.[291]

First off, it usually takes the older child several months to build up a complete repertoire of things to do in the tub that annoy you to no end. A child learns through standard trial and error which noises reverberate off the tub walls in the most irritating acoustical manner and what toys carry the most water with them when thrown out of the tub. It takes many months of begging and yelling to break them of these habits. Now when a second child comes along, they need not go through this elaborate period of hit-and-miss learning since the first child is more than willing to share this hard-earned knowledge.

The first child often teaches the younger child these actions *hoping* to get the younger child in trouble. That way, the older child can accomplish the two most important objectives in his or her life at the

---

291   Naturally, this rule doesn't apply when the children are older or from a previous marriage. We don't want child protective services to come knocking at the door with lots of pesky questions.

same time: annoying you and getting their sibling in trouble. The amazing thing is that even if the younger child doesn't yet speak or understand much English, and the older child's English can only be understood by his or her *extremely* patient parents, the lessons are still effectively taught at near the speed of light.

Obviously, two children in the bath will eventually try to annoy the vinegar out of each other as well as bother you. It may start with a bit of friendly splashing, but it will quickly escalate into one child trying to drown the other. You'll try to separate them into opposite ends of the tub, but then you'll have problems with one kid sneaking over the imaginary boundary line, or a particular bath toy that both children simultaneously decide they want is floating in the demilitarized zone, and they both go for it. You have a choice to make. Either you can let them annoy each other, or you can let them gang up and annoy you.

Much earlier in life, the older child has discovered that it has genitalia. If it is a boy, then by now it has become the Greatest Fascination in His Life. Not to worry; this is a stage boys grow out of, oh, soon after death. But you wouldn't think that at this stage of the game a penis would be any more important to them than, say, an elbow. Alas, it is, and you'll have to deal with it. The problem, when it comes to the bath, is that they love to show It off—and now there is an audience.

The boy will also want to see what the sibling is bringing to the party. Therefore, you have two children staring at each other's privates. Most men tend to put up with this for fear of making a big deal out of it and thus accidentally encouraging it. The line, however, gets drawn when one child reaches for the other. At that point, most men pretty near drown themselves throwing their body in between the children trying to prevent any contact.

When your children get a bit older, there is a brief respite where bathing is actually easy. You toss the kids in the tub and sneak off to watch TV (volume turned down so your wife doesn't hear) or read a book. When the kids are done, they'll call for you. Rush in so that your wife doesn't get wind that you haven't been in the room with them. Take them out and dry them off. You may then want to cover your tracks by wetting the soap and a few clothes (chances are the kids haven't touched them) and maybe splashing your own clothes a bit. If you find this risky, luckily you now have tablets and ear phones to keep you busy in the bathroom. The only problem with that is electronics and water. To properly defend your possessions, you can reverse-straddle the toilet and hunch your back over your device. Think of it like taking a bullet for your best buddy.

Older Children Bathing

or

Cleanliness Is Next to Godliness, but What the Devil Is That Kid Doing in There?

There comes a time when kids should go from bathing once or twice a week to bathing every day. When a child goes through puberty, his/her skin gets oily. It is obvious to most adults that it is a fairly hygienic thing to take a shower each day.[292] A preteen first balks at this idea, even if he is on a junior high sports team and comes home with his clothes weighed down with an extra pound or two of sweat.

Trying to convince these kids to shower each day is a constant struggle. You could point out the plants that wither when they walk by, and they'd still be unconvinced. Every day you don't force them to take a shower, they will conveniently forget, and then you've got

---

292 Unfortunately, there are adults who think they are exceptions to this rule. It is often confusing because these do not seem to be the most socially connected people, so they should have more time for things like bathing. Friday and Saturday nights are certainly free for them.

to put up with their aura until that night when you barricade them in the bathroom.

Another big problem with these kids is that if you enter the bathroom after they took a shower, it looks like their clothes exploded off their body. You can find them everywhere—under the sink, behind the toilet—if you have any lighting fixtures, you'll find them hanging off those as well. The question is why? Why does a preteen feel the need to make the bathroom look like a typhoon was able to miraculously arrive from the toilet to decimate the room? Because he/she can. If you have a hamper in the bathroom, that is about as much guarantee that the clothes will find their way there as Hansel and Gretel finding their way back by laying a trail of Twinkies through a junior high. These kids want to get out of every ounce of work humanly possible. When you point out that you want them to put the clothes in the hamper, they then give you a look showing how lazy *they* view you since you obviously were in the bathroom to notice and couldn't do it yourself.

As kids at this age can sweat playing video games, these clothes will stink to hell and back. Just on the off chance that the odor won't rip the nostril hairs out of your nose and whip you with them, the kids will make sure not to hang their towels up so that they will get good and rancid on the wet floor along with any clothes. If they have their own bathroom, this pile can become quite deep. Will this bother your child? Of course not. Just as long as they are able physically shove the door open enough to shimmy in, they are good to go.

I should also mention something that has boggled the minds of kids the world over. It is a challenge on par with doing a Rubik's cube blindfolded for these poor souls. What is this Mount Everest task that even a few men never master throughout their lives? I speak of being able change the roll of toilet paper. If my kids run out of toilet paper, they simply don't have the mental capacity to figure out what to do in this situation.

I can bring them over and show them the inner cardboard tube. I can ask them if that is acceptable for wiping, and they will correctly answer no. Good! I can then ask them what they can do about this. Maybe I need to give them a hint that it involves something white and soft—and that it is not a marshmallow. With enough prodding, they can figure out that they need to get toilet paper. Now, my wife and I often keep toilet paper right under the sink. I do not consider this "hidden."

If the toilet paper is gone from under the sink, we have a stash in the basement. Again, this stash is *not* hidden. It is in plain view. Do they ever go get this paper? Why the hell would they do something as silly as that when they can steal it from their parents' bathroom and that is far easier? Well, apart from me screaming when I realize too late that my bathroom no longer has toilet paper.

So if they run out of toilet paper, the kids now have the ability to reach under the sink and put the new roll…on top of the sink where it can get nice and wet since they apparently don't know how to wash their face without creating a splash zone larger than what you'd expect if you threw a grenade in the sink. Of course if the paper is significantly wet, they aren't going to want to expose their delicate derrières to a little moist chill. So their solution is to throw the whole thing away and put another roll right back in the same spot of water rather than pick one of the seventy-five towels on the floor and give the spot a quick going over.

So wouldn't they *want* the roll of toilet paper to be changed? Absolutely. As long as it is not them doing it themselves. You can show them how to do this multiple times, stressing how easy it is to squeeze the rod with the spring in the middle. They will nod right along like it is the simplest thing in the world. Yet the next time you go into the bathroom, you can be guaranteed that the toilet paper will be anywhere else but on the roll.

There will magically be a day when the kid starts taking showers without being asked. It may even be that there are multiple showers in a single day. You can bet that when this happens, it is because hormones have kicked in and he is now interested in the opposite sex. Now you may wish/beg he'd go back to smelling.

Actually, when it comes to boys, they go from smelling like they are shoplifting socks and underwear from the Pittsburg Steelers locker room to something much, much worse. How is this possible? This is the horror you get when you mix hormones and commercialism.

There is a thing known as Axe body spray. In the commercials, a guy sprays it on and women are hurdling over each other to get to him. OK, so I don't expect truth in advertising. The problem I have with Axe is that they go one step farther and suggest that the volume of the stuff you use is directly proportional to how attractive you will be. When they say body spray, they apparently mean that the entire body must have every pore saturated with the stuff to get the desired effect. Therefore, each can is considered single use.

I'm not saying it is all bad when a son enters the "Axe" stage of life and you are willingly rubbing snotty babies against your face in the hopes of catching their colds to clog up your nose. So what could possibly be the "pro" to this? Well, you know if he is anywhere in the house no matter what floor. Secondly, I can't imagine this technique works too well getting girls close to them as it should nearly blister their skin to make contact. It is when they learn to throttle back that you should be waking up in a cold sweat.

So what happens with girls and bathrooms? The simple advice here is to take a picture of what the bathroom looks like so you have a chance to remember it and go build yourself an outhouse if you don't have a second bathroom. If it was ever possible to wear out a mirror, young girls would do it. They will change their hair, then their makeup, then their hair to match their makeup. You may toss in some jewelry and then start the whole process over. How can you tell if a young woman lives in a house? Just look for the claw marks on the bathroom door as people are begging to get in.[293]

---

293 Boys can also take a long time in the bathroom. Don't ask.

Diaper Duty

or

Poop Happens...a Lot

First off, babies pee and poop a lot. That's because they are good at it. Michelangelo had his paint, Rodin had his sculptures, and babies have their excretory system. Besides that, it's one of the only things they can do themselves. If they eat, then they need to be burped. If they want to sleep, they usually need to be rocked. But if they want to pee or poop, they can just let it fly without a care in the world. They also do this with no rhyme or reason. They may skip a day's bowel movement or poop so much you'd think the breast milk was liquid Ex-Lax.

No man in his right mind looks forward to several years of changing diapers. Actually, a man in *any* state of mind does not like changing diapers. Throw a dirty diaper at Charlie Manson, and even he would probably get a bit squeamish. Years ago, men were not required to do diapers—it was basically considered a woman's job. The belief was that a man who puts in a hard day at work is entitled to come home and get the rest he deserves. However, if given a choice, most men would gladly put in a few extra hours of work each day to get out of diaper duty.

Today's men (unfortunately) are supposed to be *liberated* from these old stereotypes. Now in my dictionary, to liberate means to "set free from oppression, confinement, or foreign control." Women's lib set women free to vote, pursue different careers, etc. Men's lib has done the exact opposite—we now have no choice but to do things we don't really want to do. This is why real men don't talk about being liberated—it is a brilliant female invention to make men do some of the work they should have been doing all along. Any man who calls himself liberated might as well use the more accurate description of "whipped" because not only is he doing things he'd rather not, but he is proudly exclaiming that fact to the world. Be that as it may, most men in today's society have to change diapers—it doesn't mean you have to pretend it is a badge of honor.

Diaper duty usually begins in the hospital. Your wife, having gone through a somewhat exhausting process, barely has enough energy to feed the baby and greet the endless throngs of people coming to see the new baby. Therefore, when the baby poops, she may give him to you to change the diaper. Emotionally, most men have been preparing for this time. However, the visualization in their mental preparation was always of a small brown lump of poop that should be removed, and then the baby's bottom would be wiped. Throw a new diaper on and you're done. Easy? Wrong as usual.

The Essence of Poop

or

This Used to Be Milk?

The first few messy diapers that you'll be expected to change have a stool that is a quite remarkable and disturbing shade of a greenish black. Your first reaction will be that something must be terribly wrong with the baby to get poop of that particular shade. The color can vary from a swampy-green to a metallic-green sheen. This phenomenon is normal, and the poop even has its own special name. It is called "meconium," which comes from Latin meaning "gag me with an eating utensil."

The color of poop then turns to shades varying between French's yellow mustard to Gulden's brown mustard. If it weren't for the smell, you would swear someone is playing a practical joke on you and keeps rubbing condiments on your child's bottom. This is the natural state of affairs. Over time, the color will change to the standard brown/black we know and "love." However, there are exceptions to this rule. Some things your child eats or drinks will change the poop to that color. For most parents, this is quite disconcerting since they don't instantly put together the arrival of red poop and the previous day's introduction of beets into the child's diet. They are ready to ship the child off to the Mayo Clinic thinking there is blood in the stool when it is just that wonderful immature digestive tract trying to figure out what the heck to do with the new food.

The color of poop may be difficult to deal with, but the consistency is much worse. Since the baby is first on a liquid diet, all the baby will poop is liquid. Solid poop may cause a horrendous mess, but it can't get into the multiple nooks and crannies that the rolls of baby fat create. You think that you're all done, and when you move a leg to stretch out some skin, a couple more brown creases appear. Then you have to break the wipes back out and finish the job properly. Unfortunately, your wife doesn't give partial credit for doing a diaper change nearly right.

If she happens by when you are finishing up a job and she still sees a bit of poop, she will assume that every diaper you've ever done has been slipshod. She'll then make it a point to inspect your later works. I'm not saying she'll drop the baby's drawers every now and then for spot inspections, but she'll coincidentally be looking over your shoulder every time you are changing a diaper. For most men, this is a blow to their egos. Men—as if I am telling you something you don't already know—hate to be told that what they are doing is wrong or that there is a better way. Therefore, avoid this scenario. How? The easiest answer is to run to another room and hide if you smell that your child just had a bowel movement. Unfortunately, your wife will catch on to this rather easily and will do nearly the same thing to you when you get in an amorous mood.

Let's discuss another thing about consistency. Imagine, if you will, mixing up a batch of Rice Krispies cereal complete with milk. Now pour it into a flat plate and run around the room. Chances are that you are going to have milk and Rice Krispies everywhere. The same scenario basically holds for a child who has pooped in his diaper. It goes without saying that diapers are wonderful inventions. However, they do not always adequately contain poop from escaping. I'm sorry to say it, but poop can escape from a diaper easier than Houdini could have gotten out of a paper bag. This leakage is especially true of younger children with liquid stools.

I'll start with the basic design of the diaper. The diaper wraps around from back to front and then secures itself around the legs.

Disposables, unlike cloth diapers, have a bit of elasticity around these legs so that poop doesn't just fall out the gap. Instead, it falls out more by an oozing action. You see, the elastic can't be made too tight. If it were, you'd see the baby's little legs turning blue. I may not be a medical doctor, but I can tell you with a fair amount of confidence that anything that doesn't start off blue on the baby should not become blue during any point in time.

Either way it goes, liquid poop cannot be contained. "Born to Run" is not just a Bruce Springsteen song. There is another hole from which poop shoots out, and that is right up the back of the diaper. Now I don't know how much force it takes for a baby to expel feces from his body so that it has enough velocity to hit the bottom of the diaper and ricochet upward, but I can tell you it happens quite often. I do not expect you to believe it until you see it, but it is absolutely true that a baby can poop all the way up to his shoulders![294]

Consistency can also be a problem if it is too hard. Here you have a baby that you are trying to clean, and you gently run the baby's bottom only to find that the fecally encrusted bum is not getting any cleaner. You take another wipe and try with a bit more force and meet with the same amount of luck. You can't just throw up your hands and say, "Oh well," and throw another diaper on—you must remove every last molecule, or you will certainly be in trouble. So here you are scrubbing away while at the same time trying not to hurt your child. It will start coming off in flakes, but there will still be some left. The baby will lose patience and start wailing, and all you can think about is how much easier it would be with just a few swipes of low-grit sandpaper.

No discussion of baby poop would be complete without mentioning smell. Smell can vary from mildly disgusting to a room-clearing fetidness. The purpose of smell is to alert someone that a diaper has been critically soiled and is in dire need of replacement. I guess if

---

294 When the shoulder poop happens, it isn't the explosion one would think, but a straight line of poop that goes from the diaper right up to the shoulder. How this happens in this way is far beyond my expertise in physics. Is it all one giant poop that takes a sort of landslide approach pushing the other poop up? Is it a series of poops that keeps pushing the older poop ahead?

nature had made poop with a more appealing aroma, it would have led to not getting the diaper changed as quickly or letting the diapers pile up in the corner of a room, both of which would constitute a health hazard.

Smell, however, is not consistent in poop, which makes it even more insidious. For example, you cannot accurately judge the amount of poop to prepare yourself for by the intensity of the smell. Therefore, you find yourself getting into the frame of mind and clothing one would associate with the Centers for Disease Control (CDC) setting out for an Ebola outbreak, and when you get the diaper off, you find a little brown lump that is easily wiped away. Much worse, you think you are just changing a wet diaper, so you don't take the necessary precautions. In this case, you end up with poop on your hands, your clothing, the baby's clothing, and everything else in a six-foot radius. You then have to pull a Lady Macbeth before you even feel close to normal again.[295]

Diarrhea is often the exception to the rule of smell not being a giveaway clue as to what awaits. As your nose goes through every traumatic assault, you will develop the ability to guess when the baby has had a bad bout of diarrhea. On the smell scale, diarrhea is comparable to sticking your head into the engine of a Boeing 747 on the noise scale. You can refer back to my discussion of consistency to know that no diaper made today truly contains diarrhea, so when you smell it, you know you're in for a real treat.

Therefore, you should memorize a list of potential excuses that will extricate you from the situation in the instances when you get the first smell and the aroma hasn't traveled far enough to reach your wife. Try things like "Gee, honey, I heard your car brakes squeaking. I won't be able to sleep unless I get the brake

---

295   For those not up on their Shakespeare (it is usually in the classics section where this book will naturally end up), Lady Macbeth pushed her husband into killing off his political rivals. She later went crazy, trying to cleanse her hands of blood that wasn't there as the guilt made her believe that she could never fully get it off. The baby will have messy poops that require nearly a package of wipes, and they end up falling all over the floor, spilling poop, getting it all over the changing table, etc. In the end, after one of these poops, you'll understand the mental state of Lady Macbeth more than you could have ever imagined.

pads checked out because I don't want you and the baby to be unsafe." You can then go crawl underneath the car until the danger has passed. This type of excuse works best because you feign superlative concern for the baby's and her health. Make sure to have a mental list of excuses. If you write them down and your wife finds it, where she puts said piece of paper will coincidentally make it so there will be one less person's poop you need worry about.

The next sense experience to discuss is sound. Obviously, the poop itself doesn't make sound, but the body certainly does when it is trying to get rid of it. If you can imagine, it sort of sounds like Jell-O being squirted out of a syringe. You will quickly learn to hate this sound. Here is this baby, the product of your loins, lying in your arms. The baby looks up at you, smiles, and then you hear this gushing sound. Since the poop is still in the liquid stage, the act of defecating takes no real energy or concentration. The baby will continue smiling and pooping, pooping and smiling.

The other sound that needs mentioning is gas. Men have, in general, come to terms with their own gas. They have also come to terms with other men's gas. Women, on the other hand, would rather do the lambada on broken glass than be witnessed passing gas in public. Naturally, babies are not going to care and let it fly often and loudly. This can be embarrassing for parents in the case where someone else is holding the baby. After all, does this person acknowledge the gas? The person probably wants to toss the child back to one of the parents and run away before the smell hits, but thinks that would be impolite. As with a soldier who jumps on a live grenade, the closest parent is obligated to take the child back so the other person is free to make a hasty departure.

As amazing as it may seem, the frequency and volume of passing gas is not related to body size. There are some men who take pride in their gas and take great happiness seeing how many rooms can be rendered unlivable to other people from ground zero. All of a sudden, this little newcomer is able to challenge him effortlessly. Unfortunately, there is a bit of sexism in this arena. Some slightly insane fathers may actually take a bit of pride if their sons can bring tears to another person's eyes from fifteen feet away, yet feel uncomfortable if their little daughters can do the same.

The last sense to discuss is the sense of touch. Most parents don't mean to touch poop, but it is going to accidentally happen over and over again. There will be times of daring (you can substitute the word "stupidity") when you are carrying a naked child, as when you are transferring to and from the tub, and the child will poop. There will be times when the child has pooped up the back of the diaper so much that it is seeping through the back of the clothing and can even seep through your clothing if you are carrying the child. There will be times when you may playfully scoop the child up, causing poop to jettison out the leg holes. There will be times when you are wiping the baby's bottom and realize the wipe you just folded over to get a clean spot is one you had already folded over so that you are holding poop. There will be times when the diaper is so bad that there is no good place to grab it, yet you must because the squirming child is about to put his foot in it if you don't. There will be times you think you are doing your wife a favor by picking up extraneous clothing you found, only to find out (rapidly) that she purposely segregated it because it was pooped out.

So what is the consensus on touch? I can honestly say that after myriad times handling the stuff, I still don't know. You see, the sensory part of your brain immediately shuts down to divert energy to the "oh, gross, get this off me!" part of the brain. Therefore, you aren't really "feeling" anything. Instead, you are hopping up and down holding the exposed part of your body up in the air so as not to touch anything else while screaming for your wife to help. As soon as she does and can watch the baby, you set off to clean every last molecule off of you. The funny thing is that you near give yourself a second-degree burn with hot water when the poop wasn't actually hurting at all.

Unfortunately, if you are at home alone and the baby is high up on a changing table, you will not be given the luxury of panicking. Running around the room may result in the unwatched baby rolling off the table, which would launch you into a different stratosphere of trouble and pain. Oh yeah, and the baby could get hurt too. In these instances, the mind is able to blank out the feeling of poop for longer periods of time so that you can finish the job and put the baby in a safe place before completely wigging out.

Changing a Diaper

or

The Gift That Keeps on Giving

First off, you have to remove the baby bottoms. If your wife got him a fancy outfit, it may have buttons, suspenders, Velcro, etc., so you are flipping that body every which way trying to get the damn things off. If your child happens to be in full tantrum mode, that just adds to the thrill of it all. That is why I always picked the pants that looked like they'd be better for Chippendale dancers—snaps on the bottom for quick exposure.

After the bottom clothes are off, you then need to remove the diaper. What you *don't* want to do is remove the diaper totally. If you do, the poop that was on the baby's bottom will be transferred onto whatever you were changing him on and then get transferred back to the baby in a plethora of places since that flailing body has not stopped moving. You then have to clean up the baby *and* what you are changing the baby on. If you don't, the poop that was on the changing table will then get on all the clothes that the baby is wearing. If that happens, you then have to either remove the soiled clothes without letting the dirty side touch the baby or go clean the baby yet again. You then have to watch where you put the offending clothes and what they touch because all of that can be easily contaminated. A parent who has successfully handled a child's diapers and training is fully equipped for a job handling nuclear waste.

With all these things getting contaminated, the chance of getting poop on you has now increased exponentially. As of yet, you will probably still be a bit naïve as to how very *very* often in the next several years you will have feces smeared on your body and clothes. It is a lovely experience when a coworker asks, "What's that?" and you realize you've had a poop stain on your shirt all day long. Therefore, you will end up using a lot of baby wipes at the beginning so that you don't get the poop all over you. So let's get back to the baby...

Here the baby is lying down screaming with the diaper half off. If it is a boy, he is now to be considered armed and dangerous. Be ready to whip the diaper back in place if a golden stream of liquid begins to head your way—or any way, for that matter. You must now survey the damage. By lifting up on the baby's legs, you can see how far back the poop extends. Your first job is to separate the diaper from the baby. That way, you can throw the dirty wipes into the dirty diaper and have one mess to clean up. Otherwise, it is akin to a person wiping him or herself, dropping the toilet paper all over the floor, standing up, and then putting the toilet paper into the bowl before flushing. Yes, that is disgusting, but the point here is to minimize what is disgusting in the actual act of changing your first of *thousands* of diapers.

So again, you lift up on the baby's legs so that you can now get in with the free hand to start cleaning the poop away. If it is a large poop and you need a lot of room to maneuver for cleaning, be careful that you don't pull up high enough on the legs that the baby is standing on his head. Women tend to be a wee paranoid about that soft spot. If it happens that it is a large poop, you'll have to rock the child to the side and venture in that way. As you go along, each wipe can then be thrown into the dirty diaper.

Once you have cleaned enough of the bum that the poop won't hit the changing surface, you can put the baby's legs down. The problem here is that baby's legs love to move in ways you never thought possible. No matter how far you pull that diaper away, that foot somehow magically finds a way to plunge into the poop and then leave several fecal footprints on the changing surface. You'll think there is no way it could stretch that far. Maybe the baby will distract you with a kick in the opposite direction. Maybe the baby will pretend he is falling asleep. No matter what, as soon as your guard is down, that foot will find that diaper, and then that foot becomes bionic with speed. You'll be trying to corral that sucker while not getting tagged yourself.

Once the diaper is moved to a safe distance from the baby but still within *your* reach, continue cleaning with the wipes. When you get to the genitalia, you then have another problem. Wipe poop away from the genitalia rather than toward, especially in the case of baby girls. Otherwise, the baby could get a urinary tract infection. If you are not sure if you are wiping the child correctly and your wife is in the room, simply listen for the ear-piercing shriek followed by being called names that would make a Hell's Angel wince.

The tendency here is to first clean up so you aren't being visually and aromatically challenged before proceeding. Suffer with it. Put another diaper on the child *immediately* before doing anything else. Just because the baby may have just had a bowel movement of epic proportions, that doesn't mean he can't give an immediate encore presentation. If the child starts pooping again when the diaper is off, things simply don't get pretty. The new diaper is usually a bit out of arm's reach, so you end up whipping one arm around trying to grab it while the other arm is kept near the child to keep him from thrashing around too much and so spreading the poop over the largest surface area possible. Meanwhile, keep your eyes peeled on the baby so you can (a) make sure he doesn't roll off the changing table and (b) keep a running list of all the things that are becoming contaminated.

When you are done, you'll see an extraordinarily large pile of wipes in the diaper. The original thought was to just roll up the diaper with the wipes in it and have one contained biohazard to throw out. Now since the pile is so high, you've got to do a balancing act as you hold the diaper and slowly lift up so that the feces-laden wipes aren't dropping all over the floor and over you. You then have to open the diaper pail. Fortunately, most of them have a foot pedal to open the cover. Unfortunately, there is another plastic insert that you then have to push the diaper through to get to the bag. This plastic insert helps to cut down the smell that emanates from large numbers of aging diapers. It also acts to make you have to push the diaper to get it through so you can be guaranteed you'll either accidentally touch poop directly or push on something that can cause poop to squirt out at you.

At some point, you will have to throw the diaper bag out. Most men tend to avoid this until you physically can't close the diaper pail anymore. Since the plastic insert is now jammed into an open position, it doesn't do much good containing smell. To throw the bag out, you must first remove the insert, which is covered with dried poop after having multiple diapers shoved down the middle of it. The plastic bag is supposed to be held in place in top of the pail so that you have something supposedly clean to grab on to. In the real world, however, all the shoving of diapers usually stuffs the bag to the bottom of the pail. Not only do you not have a clean spot to grab on to, but you may have to work your way through the diapers to get to the bag. At this point, some men just get another plastic bag and dump the pail into the new bag. Other men are so thrifty (tightwads) that they'd rather endure the nauseating experience of retrieving the old bag than waste the nickel the other bag costs. Either way, this bag must get out of the house.

If it is garbage day, you can bring the bag to the curb. If not, keep it in your garage. Whatever you do, DO NOT leave it unattended outside with your other garbage. Otherwise, animals that are trying to find a little snack in your trash may rip open the diaper bag and strew diapers and wipes all over your and maybe your neighbor's lawn. You can try to convince your neighbor that you are actually helping by providing fertilizer for his lawn, but chances are that he won't buy it and you'll be picking it up, potentially seeing it for yourself on YouTube later.

Choosing the Right Diaper

or

Sooner or Later, There Is

Going to Be a Jailbreak

One of the big decisions is cloth versus disposable diapers. Being a respected scientist,[296] I decided with my wife to try the reusable cloth diapers so that we too could do our part to protect the environment. If you decide to go with cloth diapers, you then have another decision to make. You must either get a diaper service that cleans the diapers for you, or you[297] must clean the diapers yourselves. Let's start with the worst scenario first: cloth diapers that you have to clean yourself.

As with anything to do with a baby, the first thing you must do is make many small purchases. You may notice by this time that your Visa card is taking on an unusual shape. That is because the continual swiping at stores is generating enough heat to warp the damn thing. This time, you will need diapers, safety pins, plastic pants to put around the diaper, talcum powder, diaper-rash ointment, air freshener, and a myriad of other products that *Homo sapiens* were able

---

296 No, really, I am a respected, well, a scientist at least.
297 Meaning your wife.

to manage without for hundreds of thousands of years but are now considered indispensable.

So here you are feeling good about yourself because you are using cloth diapers. You go to pick up your child from the crib only to find that someone must have snuck into your house carrying a large pail of urine and dumped it into the crib without your child waking. If you were physically able to wring out the blankets, sheets, mattress pads, and mattress, I'm sure you could easily come up with a volume of golden liquid equal to or greater than the size of your child.

I cannot stress this enough—your baby will pee a *lot*! More technology has been devoted to building better disposable diapers than has been put into the creation of the space shuttle. Therefore, there is absolutely no way a cloth diaper can compete on an absorbency scale. You then have to figure out that environmentally you are wasting a hell of a lot more water with cloth diapers because you are continually washing bedding and the baby's clothes, as well as your own clothes that become soaked every time you pick up the baby.

Cloth diapers are also more apt than disposables to leak poop since there is no elastic. Therefore, by the time you smell something, the child has already soiled his clothes, your clothes, and/or a major piece of furniture. If the baby is older and mobile, he may even leave a trail for you to follow. You don't know whether to change the diaper or call in a hazmat team.[298]

And then there is a thing called diaper rash. I am not saying that a baby that has disposable diapers won't get diaper rash, but the intensity and frequency is less severe. Diaper rash with cloth diapers is akin to how your face would feel and look if you shaved with the same disposable razor for three months straight. Oh, and use that razor to peel a bag of potatoes and leave it outside in the rain before you apply to your face.

---

298 Dangerous goods are also known as hazardous materials, or hazmat for short. If there is a spill of things like radioactive waste, concentrated acid, biological pathogens, etc., then people in what look like space suits can come in to get things cleaned up. Getting one of these suits is a near necessity if you go the cloth-diaper route.

To clean cloth diapers, you first have to go to the bathroom and toss any poop into the toilet.[299] You then flush the toilet containing the poop and the remnants of whatever meal you ate last that you just upheaved. You then put the diapers aside in a diaper pail until you have enough to do a significant load of laundry or the stench emanating from the pail is too awful to stand. You then, well, you then…Actually, I'm not sure what to do then. I know it has something to do with the washing machine, but I never wanted anything to do with it. The thought of putting a mass of diapers into the washing machine and then in the next load putting my bed sheets or any of my clothing doesn't seem particularly appetizing.

Naturally someone has to do this rather unpleasant job, and then the washing machine will be used for other things after (like all your shirts, underwear, socks, etc). That is when I go to a very "happy place." It is also known as the State of Denial. Yep, as long as we men don't have to do the dirty job ourselves, we have the wonderful ability not to think about it at all. We'll blow our nose with that freshly washed hanky or rub our entire bodies dry with the freshly washed towel and blissfully not care that pounds of runny, multicolored poop have made their way into the same washing machine.

Now I guess I could have asked my wife how she did the diapers and reported her answer to you, but she had no interest whatsoever in washing cloth diapers either. Therefore, we opted for the secondary approach of a diaper service. With a diaper service, you need not touch the dirty diapers at all. The delivery guy will come to your door, take the diapers away, and give you fresh diapers. Besides the obvious benefit, a strong feature to this service is that the diapers are cleaned properly. It seems some household washing machines won't hit a high enough temperature to kill all the germs present in poop. Therefore, you keep putting soiled diapers onto a sore diaper-rash bum, which makes the problem worse. After all, you wouldn't think it appropriate when you cut your finger to first rinse your hands in the toilet before applying a Band-Aid.

---

299 Sometimes the poop is a little lump that rolls off into the toilet. Sometimes, it is a smeared mess that acts like it is superglued to the diaper.

As I said, my wife and I decided to go the environmentally friendly route with those cloth diapers. We were shocked at how soaked the baby would get during the long naps. Tired of the diaper rash and continuous laundry, we decided to go the hybrid route. We kept the baby in cloth diapers during the day, but put disposable diapers on at night. That way, we wouldn't have to change the bedding every few hours. This approach lasted for almost a week. When we had to do a running jump to get over the massive pile of laundry that now spilled into the hallway so we could get from one part of the house to the other, my wife raised the white flag, and we went to disposable diapers totally. It also happened that if the baby had an unusual look on his face, you were tempted to run him over to the tub in case it was a loose bowel movement that was going to be slipping down his leg as fast as it came out.

Disposable diapers are going to be a major expense in your life. At first, it doesn't seem so because they cram a lot of those diapers for newborn babies into the package. This is to get you hooked. The problem occurs when the child grows and keeps needing bigger and bigger diapers. Therefore, the company puts fewer and fewer diapers into the same-size package. The price per package doesn't go up, but it will now only last a minor fraction of the time. You are now a diaper junkie. You can't go to cloth because you are too lazy at this point to deal with them, so you are stuck. It would be like throwing away your television remote control so you can get more exercise running back and forth from the couch. For most men, this is nothing short of sacrilege. If it came down to it, you'd rather rent one of your internal organs than give up disposable diapers.

Training

or

The Real Question Is Who

Is Training Whom

The first decision to make about potty training is when. This decision is quite difficult to make. In previous generations, the child was extraordinarily uncomfortable in wet, smelly diapers and so fussed to get out of them. Now that the disposables are so much better in absorbency and comfort, the child can be quite content sitting in his bodily waste for extended periods of time. Originally, the child used to be thrown on the toilet at around the age of one and kept there until he got the knack of it. Now psychologists say that the child should be emotionally ready and be part of this decision-making process as to when he is ready to potty train. Therefore, each kid now goes through five times as many diapers as babies used to.[300]

---

300 Personally, I would not make the suggestion that there is an *ongoing conspiracy* in that the *American Psychiatric Federation* is being *paid off* by a confederation of *diaper manufacturers*. No, that would certainly not be my style. However, if other people drew this inference from the overwhelming and patently obvious clues before us, then I would not stand in the way of these clearly intelligent, intuitive, insightful, and highly attractive people.

When many toddlers are into potty training, parents switch to Pull-Ups diapers. Rather than having tape from the back to the front, the diapers can be pulled up like underwear. For added incentive to train, Pull-Ups are supposed to stay a little damp to help remind the child that he wet himself. In actuality, the diaper manufacturers probably had a few warehouse loads of old-model defective diapers that didn't meet the quality control for absorbance, so they reformatted them, jacked up the price, and sold it as a *plus* that they weren't as good. Being the dutiful US consumers we are, when we are told that we should buy a new product for the baby, we now act as if it is a necessity of life.

Let me state a few problems with Pull-Ups. First off, if you pull the Pull-Ups down and there is a poop that didn't smell, you now have smeared feces all over both of the child's legs, your hands, and undoubtedly on the child's clothes as well. It will be *everywhere*. The problem is that 95 percent of the time, if there is no smell, there is no poop, so you get lulled into forgetting to check. Disaster is then allowed to strike.

Another problem is that since Pull-Ups are meant for the toddler to pull down, then that is exactly what the toddler will do—at any time of day or night whether he has had, will have, or hasn't the slightest urge for a bowel movement. Children go through a stage where nudity is a wonderful thing. By putting him in Pull-Ups, you are encouraging your child to bare himself no matter who is around. He could be at home, at day care, at the mall, etc., and all you need do is turn your head for more than thirty seconds and he will be showing his wares to anyone within eyeshot.

One of the best ways to get a child interested in potty training is by him seeing others do it. If the child goes to day care, it is not a problem coming up with volunteers. Go into any day care and you'll see a wide range of kids in various stages of potty training. One kid will be shuffling around with his pants around his ankles asking the day-care workers if his bum has been adequately wiped. Another kid, who according to her parents is "fully trained," is having all her clothing changed for the third time that day because it is soaked through since she can't be in diapers anymore. There will be lots of kids traipsing in and out of the bathroom. Few of them have the modesty to close the door.

If your child is not in day care, then his source of observation is much narrower—namely you and your wife. Most adults consider bathroom time as alone time. For the past few years, the bathroom has been the sole refuge of solitude, a place where there can be a brief interlude of peace and privacy. It is not uncommon to find a parent handing off the child to the other so that he/she can go to the bathroom even though there is no real biological urge to go. This is usually accepted unless one of the parents is going in with a long novel and snacks.

Now to help your child train, you are being asked to open up your intimate sanctuary. The idea of keeping the door open and having the child studying you *in the act* can be most unnerving. It helps to act like you are having a good time so the child will be more interested in starting this process for himself. So here you are on the toilet trying to smile, laugh, and sing, praying that the child will not remember this quite embarrassing portrait of you.

This experience can be especially uncomfortable for you if the child is of the opposite sex. If you do feel uneasy being an excretory role model, then just don't do it. It may not seem like it, but your child will eventually work his way out of diapers whether he sees you posing like Rodin's *The Thinker* on a less-than-flattering throne or not. A word of caution: peeing standing up may not be the greatest idea. If the child is a girl, she can try to be just like daddy and will end up peeing all over herself and her clothes. If the child is a boy, he probably won't be able to reach and will end up peeing all over everything.[301] Also, if the child is trying to push out pee in the front, he may push something worse out the back. If you twist him around, you may get the poop in the toilet, but then the baby will pee on everything in a 180-degree arc.

Training to pee in the potty is a matter of exhaustive repetition. Every time the child moves, you try to sit him on the potty. You can sit him on the potty each hour, before a meal, after a meal, before a drink, after a drink, after anyone in the house was running water, if he

---

301 Here is where many women ask what the difference is between young boys and adult men.

walks past a waterbed, if he fingerpaints with watercolors, if you've got waterfront property, if the History Channel mentions Watergate or Waterloo, or any other reason. For every hundred times you throw him on, he'll pee in the potty once or twice. Hopefully, he'll eventually be so bored getting dragged to the bathroom every few minutes that he'll get himself trained.

If you are teaching a boy to pee while sitting on the potty, then you must teach the child to aim down. At this age, a boy's "equipment" is, shall we say, less than intimidating. There is simply not enough of him to be able to naturally hang down. Unless the penis is pushed to angle down, he will be peeing straight out onto the back of the toilet, which then sprays on you and you the floor. Getting peed on multiple times a day gets old quickly. Here you are trying to act exuberantly happy that your child is learning to pee on the toilet, and you keep taking a golden shower. Freak out and he could get scared, setting his training back months.

Training to poop on the potty, on the other hand, is a matter of precision timing. You basically have to watch for "the look." If your child is happily playing and all of a sudden gets a look on his face like he's trying to understand Einstein's theory of special relativity, that means he is pooping. At this point, you should jump up and ask him if he wants to go to the potty like you were asking him if he wanted to go to the zoo. You should jump up and down like it is a wonderfully exciting experience. Most of the time, the deed has already been done, and he's packing a load. However, there are times you can catch him and spirit him off to the magical land of Pottytown where he can be seated on the throne.

At first, the whole experience will be unnatural to him. After all, there were times when you let him run around without a diaper or when you were bathing him and he pooped. What did you do? You freaked. Plain and simple. You were either carrying him off the shag rugs or whipping him out of the bathtub while screaming for your wife to help. Now you actually want to child to poop when the diaper is off. Such a drastic change of attitude may be confusing for a child. Maybe he'll try magic markers on the wall again since you now seem to have had a change of heart.

If your child shows reluctance to defecate on a toilet, the standard advice books tell you to apply no pressure and give up. The child simply isn't ready and shouldn't be pushed. Sources say that forcing the child may lead to constipation and anal fissures.[302] Meanwhile, (1) you are being forced into bankruptcy with these diaper purchases; (2) your back is breaking because everywhere you go outside the house, you have to carry extra clothes, diapers, and wipes, not to mention the toddler; (3) changing a large, messy child is not as easy in restrooms and other public places as a little baby; and (4) you are just freaking tired of such an intimate relationship with what comes out of that child's butt.

Besides that, as the child gets bigger, their poop gets bigger, and the potential for disaster expands. It is not like, after years of changing diapers, you get used to it. You don't. Ever. If someone were to leave a flaming bag of dog poop on your front doorstep every day and you had to stomp it out, you would not simply come to accept it as a natural part of your daily life. You would want it stopped as soon as possible before every last remnant of your sanity was sapped away.

Alas, you are supposed to sit back and wait for the child to express the desire to toilet train. The child may start and then decide it is not worth the effort. Nearly all children go through the stage when they know they are supposed to poop in the potty but simply don't want to. When the urge strikes, the child casually walks into another room or behind a chair and grunts away until the job is completed to his satisfaction. Now you have to watch for your child disappearing and coming back packing heat. When you do realize he is out of sight, you'll end up frantically looking for him only to find him with (pardon the expression) a shit-eating grin knowing that he's gotten away with it yet again.

To make the child want to potty train, feel free to do something all child books and child psychologists said you shouldn't do to teach a child something—try bribery. Whether it be a simple little stamp that the child can wear on his hand or maybe a special snack, get

---

302 OK, so I'm not exactly sure what anal fissures are, but it sounds bad enough that I am going to go out on a limb and say that it is not a good thing.

the child to buy in. NOTE: If you wait too long to begin bribing, then the toddler is a bit older and has much more savvy. The child can see your desperation and take full advantage of it. When once he would have been tickled pink to have a sticker that cost a few pennies, he may now hold out for an action figure or Disney movie. Think loan shark with a diaper rash.

The other problem with bribery is that you can have a child who can manage to squeeze out a few drops of urine every fifteen minutes and then expect candy for it each and every time. At that point, it is like taking a dog for a walk: you can't pass by anything without the child peeing. There's not much you can do but be glad they're not humping your leg as well.

The child can either learn to pee on a potty chair or on the regular toilet that has an insert on it so the child does not fall in. Your child will definitely prefer one over the other. However, you will not be able to intuit which one he'll prefer, so you'll have shell out money for both. Since most places don't take kindly to returns on something you defecate in, you'll probably have to write off the unused or semiused item as yet another loss.

The potty chair has both a significant pro and con versus an insert that goes onto the seat. The potty seat is nice in that the child isn't taking his life into his hands trying to climb up onto an adult toilet and hoping someone put the insert in. Otherwise, he is going to learn diving at an early age. Sometimes he may try to grab on to something for leverage, say the toilet lid, which can then come swinging down to clock him good, which can then, again, end in a splashdown. The alternative is the chair. The child can fairly easily get himself on and off it. The *massive* drawback is that the child is going be moving his bowels in it, and then it is up to you to transfer said waste into the real toilet. It is not pleasant as each time is its own surprise—urine, feces, a combination event? Maybe it is loose or sticky. So which one do you hope for—the one easier for you or for your child? If you think I'm going to put the answer to that one in print, my lawyer would advise otherwise.

Some of these potty-training items have a splash guard. It's a little piece of plastic that comes up in the front to knock down the urine stream. The good news is that it helps you from continually getting sprayed. However, there is some bad news. As all parents who have children at this stage are painfully aware, children are ferociously independent. Heaven help you if you walk into the bathroom and turn the light on when the child wanted to do it. He'll cry like he just saw a mafia-style execution of Barney the Dinosaur. Since he is independent, he'll want to get on and off the potty chair himself. However, if he doesn't do it with the proper amount of clearance, he risks leaving his genitalia behind on the splash guard. If he does this once, he'll now regard the entire potty experience akin to that laugh-a-minute circumcision you probably already put him through. Getting him back on the potty now meets about as much enthusiasm as the joy he experiences when you have to Roto-Rooter his snot-encrusted nose.

One of the (only) things the child will love about the potty experience is toilet paper. With a simple flick of the wrist, he sees gentle cascades of never-ending white sheets stream down to the floor. The experience for them is near religious as they go into a semitrance. Your child's hands will move as quickly as possible to get the paper blazing and also to cause as much mess as possible before you realize what he is doing and break him from his trance so that he'll actually stop.

Your dilemma then is what to do with all that toilet paper that has been lying on the bathroom floor. Do you throw it all away or roll it back up to use later? After all, most men would at least have to admit that it is theoretically possible that "the shake" lets a few drops hit the floor rather than the toilet. Women in the house are usually adamant that most men don't have the William Tell marksmanship they think they do and much more than "the shake" ends up on the ground. If the toilet paper is on the ground, it could come in contact with urine or some other thing. So does this mean that you should rewind or not? That directly depends on whether the wife will find out or not. After all, the worst it is touching on you is your butt, and that isn't known as the cleanest thing on the planet when the toilet paper is needed.

Not only do children love unrolling the toilet paper, they love using it. If one drop of urine trickles out of a child's body, they want to start whipping off the toilet paper. They will wrap their hand multiple times before they shove all that paper into the john. If left to their own devices, they will use enough toilet paper to fully mummify a human body and then stuff it all into the toilet so that when they flush, it clogs and then starts backing up and pouring out onto the bathroom floor. Therefore, you must always be present in the beginning and monitor their use. Don't let them get away with unchecked amounts of toilet paper, or you'll be wading regularly through a flooded, feces-infested bathroom trying to get to the toilet to unstuff it.

There will be times when you turn your back and sure enough the toilet overflows. At this point, you'll have to use the plunger to fix the problem. Children will look at the act of plunging a toilet as an absolutely fascinating feat. It's as if at the tender age of two, they have already realized that their life's goal is to become a plumber so that they can do what daddy (who is now swearing profusely) is doing all day long.

When you are done fixing the problem, you most likely will want to get away from the bathroom. If you do this, you can be guaranteed that the child will pick up the plunger and start playing with it. You'll come in a few minutes later, and the plunger bowl will be over the child's face as the child laughs from all the fun this new toy is bringing him. Needless to say, you'll find this act more than a bit repulsive.[303] Therefore, you must hide the plunger in a very safe place. Expect, however, that no matter how much caution you take, there will be a time when the broom closet is left open a crack, and the child finds his way into it and uses the plunger as a teething ring.

When a child finally does learn to do poop on the potty, he should not have the full responsibility to wipe himself. He can start, but you should finish the job to ensure it is done properly. Even with the independent streak, he'll accept this in the beginning and proudly bend over for your inspection. Moments like this are when you realize how far down you've sunk to become a butt inspector—and you wouldn't give it up for anything in the world.

---

303 You may not want to mention this whole scene to your wife as she is kissing the child good night.

You'll be amazed at the learning curve that is needed for a child to learn to wipe himself. The first big decision he has to make is how much paper to take. The child takes enough paper until it is approximately the size of his fist. He then packs this paper into the size of a grape. Therefore, when he wipes himself, he is using a lot of toilet paper yet still manages to get poop on his hands. Besides that, the surface area of the little ball is so minimal that the child ends up wadding up at least a dozen or so to finally get to the point where no more brown is being wiped. By this time, he's managed to get poop from his fingertips to his elbow. He'll then forget to wash his hands before he runs out and gives you a hug.

No topic about toilet training would be complete without mention of teaching the child about the sanctity of the toilet bowl. Your child will think nothing of touching, taking things out of, or putting things into the toilet bowl. Being the responsible parent that I am, I try to handle these situations in the appropriate demeanor: if the child is trying to extract something from the bowl, I freak like he was about to plunge a screwdriver into an electric socket. By the shrillness in my voice and having my arms and legs wildly flinging around, I hope to garner his attention long enough to get to him before he reaches into the toilet and proudly displays to me what he's produced.

Children have no fear of germs. You can easily realize this for yourself when they eat those soggy Apple Jacks at dinner that they happened to find from breakfast.[304] Children just don't care. If they want to eat a dog biscuit, they'll take it out of the dog's bowl. Heck, they'll take it right out of the dog's mouth and eat it if they get the chance and the dog is one that doesn't snap.

Another thing children do is touch the rim of the bowl when the seat is up. The rim of the bowl usually is not a pretty place. It's covered with short hairs and hardened yellow splotches. Most men have never noticed this mess before, but you will when you see your child's hands and face leaning up against it. Even though women don't need the seat lifted—or want to see the seat lifted—they know

---

304   Not necessarily that day's breakfast.

what lurks underneath that seat and have an uneasy feeling that those germs can penetrate straight up through that piece of porcelain to contaminate them.

Men, on the other hand, won't realize that under the rim needs to be cleaned until the seat refuses to come up because it is stuck to the multilayered urine that has now taken on paste-like qualities. Now that you have a child, you are going to have to watch out for this. I am not saying—heaven forbid—that you actually have to clean the toilet, but that you just have to make sure the child doesn't get a chance to get his hands on it.

The other sanctity issue is that nothing goes into the toilet that isn't supposed to. The problem is that most children have a fascination with flushing. If a child is able to pee a few drops, then he is determined that he must flush that toilet. You'd have better luck persuading Rush Limbaugh to have Bill Clinton as his child's godfather than you would trying to convince the child to save water. Because of this compelling urge to flush, some children go one step further and drop nonflushable items into the toilet to see what happens when you flush. Whether it be items that potentially could fit down the drain (e.g., your car keys) or items that don't stand a chance of fitting down the drain (e.g., your phone), you will not approve of this trend.[305]

Once your child is excited about toilet training and it becomes part of his daily routine, he then enters a gray zone of being considered partially potty trained. Having a child who is partially potty trained makes you feel about as comfortable as hitching a ride home

---

305 Not too many years ago, there was an actual toy on the market in the shape of a toilet bowl. The object of the game was to keep shoving into it until it exploded—sort of like a plumber's version of hot potato. Without a doubt, this had to be one of the stupidest games ever created. I struggle to think how this game got made. There had to have been a guy who originally thought it was a good idea, maybe even got encouragement from family members whom he mentioned it to. Then he told his boss, who must have somehow thought this was a winner and brought it to the planning committee, who agreed, and the marketing people must have said they could sell the damn thing, so they sent it to production. It is off the market now. I can only hope that not only was every person associated with this abomination fired, but that every parent who had their bathroom flooded by a child who not only played the game but saw the commercial and thought this was a fun idea be tied up on their bathroom floor as their toilet is used until it overflows.

from a party with a partially sober driver. At this point, the child is rewarded by getting to wear underwear rather than diapers. That means that if there is an accident, there is no real containment. It's like living next door to a nuclear power plant that's got huge cracks down the side of it. Any accident not only makes a mess of the child's clothes but also leaves an unsanitary version of a Hansel and Gretel trail around the house.

One of the big problems with this period of being partially trained is that the child literally forgets to go to the bathroom until the urge to go is overwhelming. Up till now, pooping and peeing in a diaper has now been the status quo. After all, the child hasn't minded letting it fly without a diaper many times in the past, and you responded in kind by acting like there was a zombie horde banging at your front door. Now you have to have the child unlearn that response and think you are now happy about it. You now have to keep reminding the child to check how his body feels to make sure he's not forgetting.

At this stage, you see the child rushing up to you with a frantic look screaming "Potty!" You've got to pick him up, hurdle over any furniture in your path, dash into the bathroom, and—here's the tricky part—get his clothes off before the bowels lose that last bit of control. It is a very good idea to have simple clothing on the child. Parents who think their children look cute in sailor suits that have seventy-two buttons, sixteen snaps, and five ties to undo before the child's bare butt is exposed had best not wonder why their child has accidents. Heck, at that point most adults would have to question if it is worth making it to the bathroom.

It may not seem like it at times, but your child will eventually be fully potty trained. There will be the random accidents, but that is about as unavoidable as bird droppings on a newly washed car or babies unwilling to go to sleep on the one night your wife is in the mood.[306] You can then concentrate on other matters that come up. One of these issues is, when your child moves from a potty chair to the toilet, he is going to have to remember that he needs to put in

---

306 OK, so "in the mood" may be a stretch as the more appropriate words are "finally willing."

the adapter seat. If he doesn't, he may be going for a little swim. I'm not saying the kid's got to walk around the house with water wings on, but it is not a pretty picture to go into the bathroom and see the child's legs and arms sticking up in the air and his butt wedged underwater in the toilet.

As mentioned umpteen times already, many children want to act like adults well before they are ready. Because of that, many do not want to use the adapter. For some children, this is like trying to use the cork from a wine bottle to plug up a pitcher of beer. To have any possibility of working, the child has to be fairly acrobatic. He's got to be able to swing his legs far out to both sides so that he can perch himself in the middle of the toilet. If he needs both hands to balance himself, he won't be able to hold his penis in the appropriate direction, and he'll end up peeing up and over the front of the toilet. If he sits off to one side to free up a hand, then he may/will poop on the seat.

Because of these problems early on, you may try to coax your child to staying with the potty chair (even though that means you have to keep cleaning it). However, if he puts up too much resistance, he may regress in his toilet training altogether, and you'll be worse off than when you started. As a general rule, if you're sick of changing the potty chair, your child will demand to still use it, whereas if you're afraid you have to keep fishing him out of the big toilet, he'll insist on using that.

No potty training would be complete without teaching the child to wash his hands when he is done. This may sound easy to do, but in practice it is about as difficult as teaching a basset hound not to drool. A child's mind works a fair amount like a pinball machine. Focusing on completing a task is about as successful as bailing out the *Titanic* with a colander. Therefore, once the child has finished his business, he is off to the races. You'll see him bebopping around the house sticking his hand into the big bag of chips, wanting to wrestle with you, etc., and since you know he's been to the bathroom recently, you ask him if he remembered to wash his hands. Nope. He'll trot right back into the bathroom and finish the job. Meanwhile, you have to decide whether to throw out the rest of the bag of chips he just shoved his entire arm into.[307] After enough harping, your child will learn proper sanitation techniques. Of course by then, you'll be teaching him to shave.

As boys get older, they tend to get a bit lazy with the peeing thing. Lifting up that seat is just way too much work for them. Men don't notice much, but it is a little difficult to ignore crusty pee on an area you plan on sitting on in the immediate future. For boys, they don't see too much of a problem not lifting the seat because their aim is good enough to get 95 percent of the pee in the toilet, and they figure that that is a whole lot better than what they were doing before. However, eliminating your bowels is something that people should strive to get as perfect as possible. It's like an airline pilot who hits the runway 95 percent of the time upon landing probably should pick an alternative occupation.

---

307 The other decision is whether to tell your wife or to keep her in a blissful state of snack ignorance.

Potty While Traveling

or

Now? Are You Sure This Is a Superemergency? The Bathrooms Here Are Repulsive and...OK... Just Try to Touch Nothing!

Once your child gets used to the toilet, there will come times when you are out at public places and the urge will strike him. You've then got to bring him to a public restroom. As an adult, you find a public restroom to be a bit unsanitary, something to be avoided unless your bowels are about to explode in a particularly heinous fashion. Your child, however, will look upon it like a visit to the Emerald City. To him, it is a whole new experience of wonder and marvel. Because of this, the child is going to want to take his time so he can absorb the ambience of the situation.

When you first start bringing your child to public restrooms, you'll have to go into the stall with him. The big problem here is that the child's feet do not reach the floor. To passersby, it looks like you've got a guy pacing around in a stall doing heaven knows what. The child will sit there and let nature slowly take its course while you are locked into a little box with him so you can experience each and every moment of the entire process. Let me forewarn you, it doesn't make for a compelling drama to watch.

Then if you have a boy, he is going to notice the urinals. He'll act so excited, you'd think you brought him to Disney World. He'll have a tremendous urge to go over to the urinal, grab the sides, and stick his head into it so he can fully capture the magic. You've got to drill it into him that he is to never, ever touch the urinal, not even to balance himself when he is pulling up his pants. He will want to use the urinal badly, and that's how he will use it. Urinals are built for adult men. As so, they usually come up to the chest or head of a child. It goes without saying that it wouldn't be a good idea for the child to try to arc his urine stream up and into the urinal. Therefore, he will pull his pants down and you will have to pick his entire body up and aim him like a tiny garden hose. You'll feel pretty strange doing this, but not half as strange as when a stranger walks in and sees what you are doing.

When your child gets older, he is going to want to go into the stall by himself. You'd think this would be easier, but this is where you can really get into trouble. When the two of you enter the restroom, he'll trundle off to one of the stalls. Since he is small, no one can see his legs when he sits down. Therefore, to everyone walking into the restroom, it appears as though you are an individual who is standing there for the sheer enjoyment of hanging out next to public toilets. People will acknowledge you with the same enthusiasm as they would if the grim reaper were knocking at their door.

To allay people's fears, many men will try talking to their child in the stall. "How are you doing in there?" is the usual chant of men with children in stalls. Unfortunately, many times the child doesn't answer. Most of the time, you can't get the kid to stop babbling, and for one of the few times you want him to talk, you get nothing. To strangers, you've now gone from a sicko who likes hanging out in bathrooms to a psychopathic sicko who talks to himself while hanging out in bathrooms. By now, others in the bathroom are avoiding you like you've got dynamite strapped to your chest and are dousing yourself in gasoline.

Waiting for your child to be done in a public restroom can feel like waiting for water to boil.[308] Restrooms aren't built to entertain people, so there is nothing to do but wait. There are no benches to relax on or magazine racks to peruse the latest sports trades. There may be the occasional magazine or paper on the floor of the stall, but most people like to pick that up just about as much as used Kleenex.

Once your child is done, he may ask you to inspect his work. Most men prefer to do this in the closed stall for more than obvious reasons. If the work is deemed satisfactory, the child pulls up his pants and is ready to go—almost. Now you've got to have your kid wash his hands. In a public restroom, it is possible that touching the sink to clean your hands is where you'll actually come into contact with some of the most repulsive things. At least with your own junk, you know where it has been!

Quite often, the sink will be too high, and you'll have to lift the child. The soap dispenser is usually difficult enough for an adult to handle, considering it is usually clogged so bad it squirts out at a right angle. Alas, your child will insist he get his own soap. First off, he'll have to learn whether to pull the lever, push the lever, twist the knob, whatever. He'll then have to learn to keep his other hand still while the first hand finagles the dispensing unit. The soap dispenser is like a child's version of a puzzle. It's best just to distract the child and squirt some soap on his hands. You'll then have to try to brainwash him into believing that he actually did it, but that is easier on the nerves than yet another twenty minutes in the bathroom with a now frustrated child.

Hopefully the bathroom has the automatic faucets. Otherwise, the child then needs to turn on the water. Either the faucet is too tight to turn or the water comes out too fast or the temperature is

---

308   If the bathroom has a particularly bad odor, it is like waiting for water to boil while heating it one match at a time.

wrong or...[309] Once the hands are washed, they've got to be dried. If they have the air dryers, your child is in for another thrill. He'll try to put every area of exposed skin under the dryer, especially his face. He may even want to wash up again so he can reuse the dryer. The irony is deep that the only time you want him to hurry up with hygiene is the time he is as thorough as possible.

If this public restroom scene has taken place in a restaurant, you can bet that your food is stone cold. The only thing colder than your food is your wife, who was waiting for you two at the table. She's going to be mad at *you* for taking all that time, not the child. That's like blaming the Americans for Pearl Harbor because they had all their ships docked at a place where the Japanese were coincidentally bombing.

If your child is of the opposite sex, you may have a bit of a quandary. Do you take the girl into the men's bathroom past all the men with exposed genitalia at the urinals or take her into the women's bathroom where women do not expose themselves outside of the stall so that you would not see anything. Easy choice. Go to the men's bathroom. A man entering the women's bathroom is about as safe as crashing your car into a busload of lawyers.

---

309 In the biblical story of Job, his love of God was tested in multiple ways. Everything he owned was stripped away from him. He had boils break out all over his body. His address was given out to Jehovah's Witnesses in a hundred-mile radius. Terrible things. After an unexpected thirty-minute stop in a men's room bathroom with your child, you'll wonder why God went through so much effort with Job when all he had to do was have him switch places with you.

Sleeping

or

Unless You Have Ninja Qualities, It Is Inevitable You Will Wake the Child

---

"**S**leeping like a baby" is a common phrase in the English language. The words bring up the picture of an angelic face peeking up out of her blankets. Perception and reality are two very separate things, however. A sleeping baby is like a time bomb. It is going to explode. The only questions are when and how much collateral damage (loss of nerves, loss of sleep, loss of hair, loss of sanity) it is going to cause.

A sleeping baby is a conundrum. You could be on the New York City subway during rush hour in the dog days of summer, and the baby will sleep peacefully in your arms. You could have that same baby sleeping in his crib, and the act of dropping lint several rooms away will wake the child up. As much as parents try to modify the baby's schedule so that he is sleeping more during the night than during the day, the baby will be about as willing to adapt as the dinosaurs when the Ice Age hit.

As with anything to do with raising a child, absolutely nothing is easy. Even the act of putting a sleeping child down is fraught with uncertainties. Some doctors believe that sudden infant death syndrome may be related to the position in which the child sleeps. As any woman who has given birth naturally will attest to, a baby's head is vastly out of proportion with the rest of his body when compared to an adult human, often looking more like a Mrs. Potato Head rather than a member of the human species. Combine that with flabby neck muscles, and the baby has about as much chance of moving her head in the appropriate direction as an adult does of pushing a rock with a piece of cooked spaghetti. Years ago, they thought that it was safer for the child to sleep on her stomach. That way, his head could be lying flat rather than twisting around, considering the baby's head is 95 percent of his body weight and his neck can barely support just a few of her chins. Also, doctors were afraid that if the child ever vomited, she could choke. As if they don't give parents enough to worry about!

After years of preaching this advice, they decided to change their minds and have the child sleeping on his back to avoid the possibility of carbon dioxide buildup that theoretically could happen with the face right next to the mattress. Now, they don't know what to say, so many doctors are compromising and telling parents to put their child to sleep on their sides. Naturally, this position works about as well as trying to balance a pen on its point. Therefore, parents who go for this position have to roll up towels and place them in front of and behind the baby to keep him propped up. You may not think this looks comfortable, but don't forget that the baby's previous sleeping place was a wee bit more cramped.

Early Infant Sleeping

or

Got a Minute?

W hen the baby comes home from the hospital, he does little else but sleep, eat, and poop—usually in that order of volume.[310] You'd think that with all that sleeping, life would be fairly easy. Believe that, and you probably also think that Elvis is alive and well and working behind the deli counter of your local supermarket. Since the baby is expected to eat every few hours, the only undisturbed sleep you can possibly get is at work. That may be well and good if you are employed as the ethics advisor on Wall Street, but most other employers tend to frown upon drowsy employees, especially if you are operating heavy machinery or driving school buses.

The baby starts off in a bassinet. The bassinet is then placed next to the parents' bed so that it is easier to grab the child when he/she wants to feed or be held. There are two thoughts on whose side of the bed the bassinet should be on. The first is that since the mother by default will be doing the breastfeeding, it only makes sense to have the bassinet on her side. The second way of reasoning is that both the mother and father should live all the joyful experiences of

---

310 Heaven help you if the order is reversed!

childhood, and that includes an ebbing of one's sanity due to the lack of precious sleep. Therefore, the least a man can do is drag his carcass the few feet out of bed to pick up the baby and deliver him to his wife's bosom before lapsing back into a coma, only to be awakened minutes later when he has to transfer the child back.

When looking at this situation objectively, there is no good reason why two people should suffer when only one has to. Indeed, according to a utilitarian moralist standpoint,[311] it only makes sense that just the breastfeeding woman should get up with the child and leave her husband to his much-needed sleep since she is going to be awake anyway. Why impact that man's entire day, including his employment performance, when his wife's performance won't get any worse for the simple act of reaching over to grab the baby?

Looking at it logically, it only makes sense that the bassinet be on the mother's side. However, postpartum women are not known for rational objectivity. These women are more than happy to take a chainsaw to a bottle that doesn't open properly or adjust their husband's tie by restricting the circumference of his neck. There is little doubt Genghis Khan used a steady supply of postpartum women to train his barbarian hordes in the acts of unspeakable violence to win battles.

Even if the man is given the responsibility to get the child from the bassinet and accepts said duty without complaining, he will still be on his wife's defecation list. Once the baby is eating, the man is able to go back to sleep. At this point, he can usually sleep through anything, even if the baby has been crying uncontrollably for hours on end. The guy will usually be able to doze there in blissful ignorance. Women hate this more than high heels on a waxed floor. Most women go one step beyond "misery loves company" into the realm of "misery better get company, or there will be a hell of a lot more misery dished out."

---

311 As an undergraduate, I double-majored in biology and philosophy. I'm glad to say that, because of this comment, I have now finally used my philosophy degree nearly twenty years after receiving it. And those crazy parents of mine wondered why I was going through the trouble of the second major!

If the man is lucky enough to escape being awake during the breastfeeding process, he may not escape the nighttime diaper change. It may not be convenient, but it makes for many less odor-induced nightmares when the changing table is not located in the parents' bedroom. Therefore, the person changing the child is going to have to fully wake up and make the appropriate trek to the diaper-changing area. That may not sound so difficult, but when it is 3:00 a.m., you've had about six minutes of REM sleep in the last three days, and the house has got a chill to it, that walk is looked forward to about as much as walking the plank into shark-infested waters.

What a man really has to hope for here is a woman who gets slightly bored during breastfeeding. If the child is eating for twenty minutes, and the woman is bored sitting there in bed, she may opt for going to another room and watching television. If it happens that she is already up and about, she will be more likely to change the nighttime diapers and leave you to sleep. After all, it then may be more of a chore to carry the child to your bedroom and prod your woeful sack of skin until you come back from the sleep of the dead. If the woman chooses to stay in bed to breastfeed, and the child does experience an "explosion south of the border," you must not only change the child when asked, but must not complain about this chore unless you want to risk finding the diaper in your briefcase.

The baby isn't going to cry in the middle of the night just because he is hungry or because he wants his diaper changed. If he wakes up, he immediately becomes bored and has little else to do but cry. If you pick the baby up each and every time he makes a noise, the only benefit you'll get is bigger biceps. By getting into the habit of grab-bing the child when he peeps, the baby will come to expect it and literally forget how to fall back asleep by himself.

So how do you know when the child needs to be picked up when he cries at night versus when not to pick him up? Women will tell you to listen to the cry. Is it a "tired" cry? If so, the baby will more than likely fall back asleep on his own. How the heck can you distinguish a "tired" cry from a "run of the mill" cry? Easy. If your wife jabs you in the ribs and yells, "What the hell's the matter with you? Can't you hear the kid screaming? Get your lazy butt out of bed this instant and get that kid—my boobs are killing me!" chances are that it is not a "tired" cry.

If you go to get out of bed so that your wife can have an extra precious few moments of sleep, and she whips around and says, "What do you think you're doing? Can't you hear how tired that kid is? I just fed him forty-five minutes ago, so he sure as hell ain't hungry! You think I'm a friggin' milk factory? Maybe you think my body makes so much I should give you some to put on your Frosted Flakes in the morning? Get that baby out of bed now, and you'll really wake him up and I'll never get back to sleep," chances are that it is a "tired" cry. Some men will try (in vain) to distinguish between the two cries, but that meets with about as much success as trying to tell the difference between ball bearings.

The big, Big, **BIG** problem at this stage of a baby's sleeping is that it becomes very convenient to let the baby sleep in bed with the two of you. That way, the mother can actually doze a bit while the child is feeding. When the child wakes up to feed again, the mother can drag the kid over and have him muckle on to her breast. Babies get very comfortable with this scenario and then will *only* sleep when with an adult. If you try to lay him down at night in his bassinet, he'll lose his little mind. You'll have to lie down with him and try to escape when he finally nods off—which is about as easy as escaping from a German POW camp with a butter knife and hall pass.

You have no idea how much a bed creaks until you try to quietly crawl away. It's about as quiet as tap dancing on Rice Krispies. On the extremely rare occasion that you do make it out of bed with the child still asleep, you then have one more difficult maneuver to perform. Even though the child has never turned over, theoretically it is possible that he'll get up, do a few somersaults, and end up falling off the bed. Therefore, you've got to build a wall of pillows around him. Do that and you just have to get out the door and close it without making a whisper of sound. Naturally after all this work, you'll probably walk over to the couch and collapse of exhaustion, so you may as well have stayed in bed in the first place.

Not only will the child not sleep alone at night, but he will want to sleep with someone for his naps as well. At the beginning of life with baby, the idea of taking a nap is not so bad since both parents are so sleep deprived that they can find themselves carrying on conversations with the television and trying to brush off the little green people crawling up their clothes. Later on, however, parents realize that naptime is the only time any significant chores get done. It is the only time laundry can be folded without it being knocked over or spit up upon. It is the only time the crust-laden dishes can be scraped before a dishwasher can even think of cleaning them. It is the only time formula can be made without the child going into a psychotic frenzy. It is also the only time you have to either think about yourself, such as whether you have been following any course of personal hygiene, or choose not to think at all.

If a child has become dependent on sleeping with an adult, the only exception comes when the child is in constant motion. One way to achieve this motion is by buying a baby swing. Many parents use this apparatus as a crutch to parenthood. They crank up the device one notch below the baby-whiplash setting and go about their business. Since the swing usually has a little tray to keep their toys on, the parent need only return every one to two minutes to put back the rattles, pacifiers, etc., that the child throws off. That may sound like quite a bit, but two minutes of semirelaxation is next to heaven for the brain-fried parent. As a general rule, the moment a toy is thrown by the child is the moment the child realizes he does indeed want that toy and only that toy. When that toy is returned to him to appease his crying fit, he will then immediately forget how much he wanted that toy and toss it again. Sometimes it does help to throw as many toys on the tray as possible so the baby has plenty to toss, but usually he wants the particular toy he threw and will accept no substitute.

The other way to achieve continuous motion is by driving. Many babies blissfully nod off when in the car—and only when in the car. If this is the only way a baby falls asleep, you're in more trouble than a paraplegic at the running of the bulls. Many parents cave in and drive around at night to put the kid to sleep rather than face the hours of crying that it takes for a child to collapse in total exhaustion before he goes to sleep.

Why is that trouble? Because there is no way to get the baby out of the car seat, into the house, and into the crib while keeping him asleep. If you have to keep driving to keep the baby asleep, that gets awful expensive and awful dangerous when you get drowsy as well. At some point, you have to just give up and let the kid cry so long that he exhausts himself to the point where he doesn't have the energy to stay awake.

Now there are a slight few babies who, once you drive them around, fall into a sleep deep enough that you can take them out of the car. For most other babies, you'd feel more comfortable transferring Agent Orange in a sandwich bag during an earthquake—and not those "yellow and blue make green ones" either. These parents are bitter people. You can see them unshaved, with greasy hair, wearing a bathrobe while they drive around with a cup of Dunkin' Donuts coffee glued to their hand for hours on end. Most likely, they are the ones flipping off the clerks who say, "Have a nice day." Mention the problem of the greenhouse effect with all the gas they are burning, and they'll say they'd gladly allow the melting polar icecaps to submerge the state of Florida for a single night of uninterrupted sleep.

Baby in a Crib

or

To You, a Safe Place to Sleep, to the Baby, a Prison Complete with Bars

After several months, it comes time to transfer the baby to a crib in her own room. Many parents look forward to this as a slight sign of getting part of their lives back. In the scheme of things, it is akin to a prisoner in solitary confinement getting a picture of someone lying on the beach; it may help him remember freedom, but he still ain't going anywhere.

When the baby is in the bassinet, a mother has this uncanny ability to hear the baby move about throughout the night. She does this either by waking up in a "is the baby all right" panic every ten to fifteen minutes, or her subliminal mind goes into hyperdrive and monitors the baby continually. Either way, this lack of a decent night's sleep will manifest in her nerves being in such a state that she'd rip out your spinal cord just as easily as pass you the salt shaker. Don't think she doesn't see you sleeping all cozy on the other side of the bed and wish ill things to happen to your body involving sandpaper, fire ants, and agitated tree shrews.

You'd think that moving the child to another room would calm your wife down. That's like saying a Christian should be calm in the

Colosseum when the lions are released if he's got a blindfold on. At first, your wife will be even worse in trying to sleep since she now has to trundle off to another room to see if her baby is OK. Not only does she have to see the body, but she must see the baby move or breathe. Unfortunately, the mother sometimes gets impatient waiting for the baby, so may actually give her a bit of a poke.

Luckily, modern technology has prevailed to make the baby easily heard from any room in the house. A baby monitor is now standard issue as much as diapers for the baby and Advil for you. A baby monitor is basically an expensive walkie-talkie system that isn't as good because you can only send voices one way. Don't get me wrong—pumping all the sounds a guy can make (especially when trying to be quiet) into the baby's room would be enough volume to wake the dead, and so can be deemed a bad idea. However, you'd think that taking out this feature would not enable the manufacturers to charge more.

So now all parents are equipped with baby monitors. That way, the mother can continually know what state of sleep or nonsleep her child is in. Yes, that is stressful, but it is actually less stressful on the woman than having no immediate information on the baby. Heaven help us if they develop easy-to-use baby heart monitors so that every time there is a slight skip, the wife can skip a beat right along with it. Now when I say most parents have these monitors, I do mean most. During my early years, my wife and I were students and so could only afford a small apartment whose walls were made of what appeared to be a heavy-duty cardboard. Hearing anything from one side of the apartment was about as challenging as not trying to fly off the face of the planet when I jump. Yet, we had to have a baby monitor. That makes about as much sense as wearing a Miracle Ear to a rock concert on the bizarre chance that the band forgot the amplifiers and we are in the nosebleed section.

When the baby first goes in the crib, the mattress can be raised high enough so that you can gently lay the child down rather than leaning over and dropping him in.[312] It is also mandatory that each crib have a colorful stuffed-animal mobile that plays music. Personally, I don't think having a pink elephant and blue lion dangling and

---

312 And if you are short, you really don't want to be tossing the child in the crib as you would move a bale of hay.

swinging around ready to pounce on my head would induce me to sleep, but mothers are determined that children need this visual and auditory stimulation. God forbid that the child has to look up at a white ceiling for a few minutes a day—she could go blind and deaf.

Many babies do end up liking the music that a mobile plays. Unfortunately, if this is the case, they listen to the music rather than sleeping and then cry when the music stops. You then have to keep going in and cranking the mobile back up every ten minutes until they eventually fall asleep. By performing this act for several hours, you can see where we got the term "cranky." Of course if the kid wakes up in the middle of the night, she won't be able to put himself back to sleep without music, so you'll be making the trip back and forth to his room. You'll get so you don't know if the music is on or you are hallucinating it.

As the child gets stronger and is able to pull up on things, the mattress will have to be lowered farther down past the crib railing. Since the baby is putting on some tonnage, the once-simple act of picking him up gets harder and harder to do. You may think that you are getting a little exercise "clean and jerking" the child in and out of the crib so often. Au contraire. When you are doing this, you can't help but lift with your back rather than exercise any arm muscles. Therefore, the only body sculpting that you do molds you more into the form of Frankenstein's assistant Igor than any other shape.

The baby will continue picking up strength and will eventually reach the stage where he can stand up in the crib. Naturally by this stage, the mattress will be at its lowest point compared to the railing, or the child will be doing a Greg Louganis[313] impersonation on a routine basis. Children at this age often have no fear of the consequences of their actions, so gravity is something you worry about, not them.

After a child gets bored with the standing thing, it may then occur to the child that she can escape. By pulling up on the side and flinging one leg over, he can get his body to tumble to the floor. The first time this happens, I don't know who is more scared, the baby who has just fallen

---

313 Greg Louganis was potentially the most famous American diver ever. He won medals in two separate Olympics. It can be very riveting watching a world-class athlete jump from a high board into water with precision. Seeing the baby take a header into the floor is more heart pounding, but not in a good way.

several feet, or the parents who are tripping over each other racing to the bedroom after hearing a dull thud followed by crying. Usually, this first escape is enough to scare the child into not doing it again for a few more weeks. However, once a child realizes he has the power to escape, she treats the crib as if it were a POW camp. Concurrently, she'll treat you like a Nazi commandant who is always recapturing him and sending her back to the brig. An escape-artist child is usually not successful since her landing is about as graceful as a drunkard rollerblading on a buttered hardwood floor. That body crashing to the ground usually sends enough of a shock wave through the house to topple any china that you may be displaying. When you go in the room to throw the child back in the crib, she usually acts surprised that you could figure out that she got out without actually seeing her escape. She is far from ninja stealth at this age.

There are two scenarios once you have a child who learns to escape. The first is that every time the child gets out, you are terrified she is going to snap her little ankles or neck from the fall. You can't put plywood on the top of the crib weighed down by cinder blocks to keep the child in. Child protective services tend to frown on this, even if you are doing it to supposedly prevent injury. The second possibility is that the kid actually gets good at it. Some kids can shimmy down the side, and you'll never know that she got out. However, it is inevitable to have a child out of bed.

At this point, or just when the kid gets big enough that he keeps rolling into the bars and waking himself up, you then have to go out and buy a real bed. To a child who is used to sleeping in a crib, the idea of sleeping in the wide-open space of a bed is like asking an adult to sleep high up on a branch of a greased redwood. Fear of falling is pretty hefty with a child.[314]

---

314 You may think I just contradicted myself by saying they have fear, while a few paragraphs ago, I said that they didn't. Au contraire. What I said initially was that they don't have fear when *they* are responsible for the action. If they try do dive off the changing table or try to swallow a marble, that is within their right. However, they are less trusting of your judgment. After all, it is *you* who put them in that big bed. Come to think if it, it was *you* who decided to leave him unattended for the 0.6 seconds on the changing table to so carelessly look away when the phone rang and *you* who placed that delicious-looking marble in the house years earlier in such a convenient spot to find, like under the refrigerator.

Therefore, you can go and make another purchase for bed guards. These guards go on either side of the bed and have netting between them so that the child can't roll off the side. Unless you have a hyperactive child who tumbles head over heels in her sleep, the child should stay in bed. That is, she should stay in bed when she is asleep. When she is awake, she can now get up whenever she wants. It'll be three in the morning, and you'll awake to see these little eyes staring right at you. Nothing like a heart attack to make you feel alive.

The only thing worse than her scaring the holy tar out of you in the middle of the night is when she realizes that if she wakes up, she *doesn't* have to go get you up. Instead, she has free rein of the house. No parents, no rules, no problem eating the cat food, no screaming parents when the iPhone is being dunked into the commode, no freaking out when he tries to plug the Erector set into the wall plug.

Usually, however, the child opts to try to crawl in bed with the parents. In the beginning, you will be awakened no matter how deep your sleep is since the child has the stealth of a rhinoceros in heat. However, you may be too tired to actually get up and return her little body to her bed. If you don't, this will reinforce her efforts to get in bed with the two of you. She will then try her little commando raid into your room multiple times every night.

For those people who aren't sleep deprived, returning a child to bed sounds like it would take less than a minute. However, when you've taken more laps than a NASCAR driver to and from the child's room, it is pretty damn tiring. The easy way out is to not return the baby and just go to sleep. A problem here is that as a baby grows, so does her ability to hurt you. She may roll over and end up punching you in the face. Sure, it is a tiny little hand, but if you are asleep, it is quite the surprise to get bopped in the nose. Another issue is that if the child wakes up, she may become bored and do things like try to find your eyeball by poking her little finger where it usually is.

Of course if you think putting a child back is tiring, that is nothing compared to getting her in the first place when she is inconsolable for some reason. One of the big things is for both you and your wife to fake sleep and see who cracks first from the crying. If you don't get up and your wife believes it is your turn, she may take a more active approach by kicking at your spleen as a nonverbal attempt to get you to understand that it is *not* her turn. You then have to summon up your will to dredge your body out of dreamland and figure out what the child wants.

The child may then ask for a glass of water or maybe needs a potty trip. Sloughing off to the kitchen is bad enough, but potty breaks can be a real nightmare. Quite simply, the child's bowels are in no rush to produce anything. It's not like you can ignore potty requests because you obviously want to stop hemorrhaging money to diaper manufacturers. Besides that, if there is a bowel blowout from the diaper in the bed, you can kiss off a good half hour of sleep for both parents. One parent has to bathe the child while the other breaks down every blanket and sheet. The dirty set has to be sanitized while another set has to be placed on. By this time, the child is fully awake and ready for party time. Meanwhile, the parents are looking for a bottle of chloroform to babysit the child so that they may return to their own blessed bed.

As the child gets older, she may start sneaking into your bed if she is lonely—and now she may be very good at it compared to before. She can crawl into the room, head to the foot of the bed, untuck the covers, and shimmy right up into place. Eventually, you'll wake up and realize you are sleeping on a six-inch-wide strip of bed as the kid is camped out in the middle. Again, the big decision then is to fully wake up and move her or try to go back to sleep. After around the fifth time waking up and realizing my back felt like it had a metal rod shoved up the spinal column, I'd usually decide I'd had enough and move the kid back. Personally, I'm still somewhat amazed that a child who usually couldn't walk from one end of the house to the other without crashing into at least three things could crawl between my wife and me and get under the covers without us knowing.

When the child is big enough, a new problem enters the picture. The child may be so big that her body stretches down a little below your waist. If that is the case and you flip around during the night, it becomes inevitable that you'll be kicked in the crotch. Now that wakes you up faster than a double espresso!

My first kid wasn't too bad. I'd usually just realize he was there, decide how uncomfortable I was, and eventually move him back to his own bed. With my second, I wasn't so fortunate. For some reason, he had to be touching both parents. Meanwhile, we would subconsciously keep moving away. If he woke up, he'd reposition himself to again be touching. It wasn't long before he was perpendicular, and my wife and I were both teetering on the edge. Needless to say, I got the feet in my face, while my wife got the head.

There are other odd sleep patterns to be wary of. There will come times when you are on the move with the child and he'll skip a nap. The very logical assumption is that the child will be groggy and maybe a bit cranky. You'd expect him to fall asleep early and get caught up on sleep. That may well be the case. However, many children go into hypermode when they miss sleep. Somewhere in the child's body is an untapped source of energy that gets dredged up during times of sleep deprivation. My theory on this is that in caveman times, if the parents didn't have time to give the kids naps, there was something serious going on like being chased by a pack of saber-toothed tigers that were looking for a salty-flavored snack.

There comes a time when the child is going to bed so late that you want him to drop the nap so that he'll dial back his final hurrah. If the child is up too late before nodding off, the only thing you are capable of is dragging your body into your own bed, and that isn't good for your sanity or your marriage in the long run.[315] Your brain needs a bit of time at the end of the day to stop working and unwind. If you are forced to hear about SpongeBob Squarepants[316] and there is no time to put another thought in your head before you fall asleep, you are going to be getting some pretty freaky dreams. If your child

---

315 Luckily, your wife has enough energy to get the dishes done and start a load of laundry. Feel free to ask if she has a teeny bit more so she can give you a back rub when she finally crawls in next to you.

316 Mr. SquarePants is this generation's answer to Bugs Bunny. He is an overly enthusiastic sponge that has a job as a fry cook. No, I'm not kidding. His best friends are a starfish in Bermuda shorts, a squirrel in a space suit, and an octopus who thinks he's a squid. You may scoff at the idea of watching *SpongeBob SquarePants*. However, the alternatives are much, much worse. When my oldest kid was young, Barney the Dinosaur was popular. He was a purple dinosaur on Prozac. For the second, there were Teletubbies that were weird little creatures that had televisions on their stomachs. With the youngest, there was a show called *Yo Gabba Gabba* that was a guy weighing about 110 pounds dressed in orange dancing around with weird creatures he kept in a box. Just when you think it couldn't get worse, television producers find a way to dig lower. SpongeBob is the equivalent of Shakespeare to the rest of this drivel.

then makes you start your day by talking about his absorbent pal,[317] you run the risk of starting to talk like that, and you really want to talk to bosses/customers like they are five-year-olds.

So when the day comes that you are going to have him drop his nap, the first problem is that you have to keep him awake. There are three categories of children when it comes to sleep depriving them. The first is the coma babies. Their eyes just simply glaze over, and they collapse. You could blare a foghorn in the child's ear, and there reaches a time where there wouldn't even be a flinch. With this type of child, moving his nap time can only be done painfully and gradually.

The second type is the evil baby. He is going to cry over nearly everything when he is tired. What he doesn't cry over, he is going to scream about. If he wants juice, you'll get him the wrong type. If you get him the other type, it will be in the wrong cup. He will make your life a living hell until you let him nod off. The third type of child is the one who, the more tired he gets, the more hyper he gets. That may sound like an oxymoron, but they end up getting boundless energy. You can turn around, and they are climbing up the counters or chasing down the household pet with a blender in hand. These kids could hit the final bedtime and *not* want to go to bed. Therefore, you end up running around trying to capture and secure them with bungee cords to the bed.

Eventually, the naps do go away for the most part. However, there are times where the child will end up taking a nap. He may be in a car and nod off or just fade away while watching television. Once a child goes down, it may be virtually impossible to get him back up. With my third child, I had the situation where if he fell asleep for literally one minute and I woke him up, that qualified as a full nap, and so he'd be up till all hours of the night. I wish I was exaggerating.

As a quick note, when kids become teenagers, there is no problem getting them to enjoy sleep. Sure, it is absolute hell getting them into bed at night as they'd rather be playing video games, texting, or watching television. Try getting them up in the morning for school,

---

317 Although it is far more exciting than your wife talking about her absorbent friend.

though. That is when sleep is their best friend. On the weekend, they will sleep past lunch if you let them.

To finish this section, I believe that the greatest sign of maturity is not when a child gets a driver's license or when he's got enough money to post his own bail, but when he can actually admit that he is tired and will put himself to sleep. When will this happen? Usually around the age of twenty-five or so. Before that time, kids won't go to bed unless they are expressly told to go to bed. It doesn't matter if their bedtime is 10:00 p.m. and has been for two years. The child will try to blend into the background so that you may miss him and he can stay up.

What is so exciting about not sleeping? For kids, I think they believe they are going to miss something. It is as if there is a party waiting right outside the front door. After all, they don't see their parents do too much that's fun while they are up, so they must do something—anything—later. For the parents, they know that the party was over long ago. For teens, they do come to understand that their parents are as dull as dirt. You may try to convince them that at one point, your life did have a pulse, but they are not overly likely to believe you.

.

Section 6

As the Beatles Sing...
"A Day in the Life"
or (More Likely) "Help!"

Starting the Day

or

After a Good Night's Sleep, Well

It May Not Be Good, but It Is

Better Than Your Wife's

T here are multitudes of examples in nature of biological clocks: flowers know what season to bloom in, cicada bugs spring out of the ground every seventeen years,[318] and every four years, politicians tell us why *this* time we should believe they'll keep their promises. The most amazing of all biological clocks belongs to young children. Now, one would not normally assume this to be the case. After all, if you were to tell a child to come in the house when it gets dark outside, the child will assume "dark" means that you can't see your hand in front of your face. Therefore, you have to scream their name out the door like a banshee caught in a bear trap for them to come in every night. However, these same children down

---

318 The cicadas are interesting insects. They spend the majority of their life living in an adolescent form where all they do is stay underground in the same spot eating. After seventeen years, they finally mature into adults and emerge from the dirt, where all they want to do is mate before they die. How do you distinguish a cicada from the average guy? The cicada has wings and doesn't ask if he was better than the other cicadas after being with a female.

to the age of three months instinctually and inexplicably know if it is a weekday or weekend day even when they don't go to school. If it is a weekday, getting them moving is like reanimating Frankenstein's monster, but if it is the weekend, it is time to get you up early and play, play, play![319]

On a Saturday morning, there is nothing the average adult likes to do more than cozy up under those warm blankets and sleep in. After a hard week of work, it is a guiltless pleasure to let your brain take a few extra moments in the morning to relax and play hooky. You have as much chance of achieving this dream as regaining the metabolism of your youth when you could eat everything without gaining an ounce (unlike now when anything besides a salad goes right to your butt, giving it the look of a bag of marbles). Instead, your child's pituitary gland has spent the night storing up high-potency adrenaline. It keeps the adrenaline in that part of a child's brain that later gets converted into the portion that later learns that not everyone on this Earth was put here to serve their personal whims. At 6:00 a.m., the pituitary gland releases the floodgates in a biological version of Niagara Falls. That much adrenaline poured into an adult's bloodstream only occurs in extremely stressful situations like wartime or when your wife decides to check out your website browsing history.

The child, now a nuclear reactor of energy, jumps out of bed, runs out of his room, and plunges headfirst into your bed. If the child gets it just right, he is able to head-butt you squarely in one of your kidneys. To the child, it is now party time. Break out the tunes because it is time to rock and roll! Needless to say, you want to try to change the child's mind about doing this. Trying to convince the child that he'd rather play with mommy right now will result in the

---

319 Please note that this is for young children. When it comes to teenagers, it still may be difficult to wake them up during the week, but it takes lobbing grenades into their rooms to get them up on the weekends. (Lawyer's note: I am not recommending this practice). I am not making this up—studies have shown that when smoke detectors go off that only 42 percent of kids wake up! Even if they do wake up, it would take them twenty minutes to get out of the house as they are posting to Twitter, "I'm hot and not in a good way right now. LOL," and posting pictures to Facebook of their pajamas igniting off their bodies.

immediate loss of the other kidney as your wife plunges her heel into your lower back.

Another option is to send the child downstairs by himself. Of course then by the time you get up, you'll be spending the rest of the day trying to remove the creative art he has drawn on every wall and the gallon of milk he has poured all over the floor trying to make himself a bowl of cereal.

The final option to trying to get those precious few more minutes of sleep is to have the child crawl in bed with you to see if he'll doze off for just the few minutes you'll need to regain your foothold in humanity. This technique used to work when he was a baby, but now is about as likely to work as splitting an atom with a ball-peen hammer. It may start off nice enough. You drift back into a peaceful slumber as your child lies next to you. Since he has no plans whatsoever for going back to sleep, he's going to get bored within minutes. So there you are sleeping, and he may decide to yank out one of your nostril hairs or open the lids covering your eyeballs just to make sure you are *really* sleeping. Eventually, you'll realize that the only way you're going to get sleep is to get up, put some cartoons on the television, and hope that he's distracted enough to let you doze in a chair.

Now if it is a standard weekday, the situation is entirely different. You've got to go to work, and the child usually has to go to day care. That means that both of you have to get ready and get going, a feat comparable to what Admiral Peary had to do to get ready for his trip.[320] First off, you've got to get your own body out of bed much earlier than usual. Before children, a guy could get up and be out of the house within half an hour. Sure, he may have little bits of blood-stained toilet paper hanging from his face, but the point is that he

---

320 Admiral Peary was the first person who supposedly made it to the North Pole, although that is now in dispute. He learned from the Eskimos to build igloos and dress in furs. He took many runs at the pole, risking his life more than a few times. He did get fame and fortune for his efforts. Oh, and he ended up losing eight toes due to frostbite. Personally, I'd rather be working the night shift at 7-Eleven and keep the toes, but that is me. You will also *not* find me climbing Mount Everest, where the air is so thing that you can get brain damage without a respirator, running with the bulls in Spain, or attempting to teach my grandmother how to program the DVR.

can sleep in until absolutely necessary to get up, whereas it takes a woman half an hour just to lay out the makeup to get ready.

Now if it is the man's responsibility to get the child going in the morning, he should conservatively tack on an additional hour or two of preparative time. Still, only with a significant amount of cursing (under his breath so the child doesn't hear) will he have a shot of being remotely on time for work. Even then, the odds that he'll have remembered to brush his own teeth after struggling with the kid's are even at best.

Once the man has finished taking a shower, he must now wake the child. Previous showers usually involved not a whole lot—just making sure you don't smell. Now, you end up finding things on your body and you can play the quick game of "what the hell is that and how long has it been on my body?" Maybe you see something that looks like dried cereal, and you think back to the last time your child had that, which was breakfast the day before. Maybe you have a sticky glob in your hair, and you are wondering if that was why your boss was giving you that odd look.

Usually, the child wakes as if he had consumed a six-pack of Milwaukee's Best the night before. The child is groggy, incoherent, and prone to collapsing back to sleep once your back is turned. So why is the child in such a sad state? Because the night before, the child insisted that he was not tired and fought going to sleep every step of the way. There will be more on that later.

Once he's up, you've then got to drag the child's limp body to the kitchen or television room. First off, he must be fed. Will he want cereal or toast? The time of decision is directly proportional to how desperately you need to be at work. Rather than taking the time to use actual words when his brain isn't working, you may need to pick his body up and bring him around physically showing him the food choices. Once he has the food, he still has to actually consume it. If you're in the kitchen, your child may have nothing to focus on to help get his mind in gear, so he sits there not eating. If you prop him in front of the television, then he'll become so engrossed in watching it that he'll forget to eat.

Either way, day after day, you end up begging him, waving the food in front of his face, imploring him to eat faster. Eventually, he usually complains that the cereal has become soggy because he has taken so long. That's when it is easy to lose your cool as you try to explain to him that if he ate the &*$#ing food when you first put it in front of his @+!*ing face, then it wouldn't be so %&*!ing soggy. That is when your wife walks in and crushes your %*$& voice box so you'll never make that mistake again.

While the child is eating at the same speed at which snails mate, you've got to eat your own breakfast and get dressed. Quite often, time has now become tight enough that you need to do both at the same time, so I hope you like cream cheese as underarm deodorant. After the child finally pronounces that he is done eating, then you've got to get his clothes on. By the way, it *should* go without saying that dressing a child comes *after* he eats breakfast. If not, then once he inevitably spills the milk down the front of his shirt, you've then got to decide whether it is worth it to change him or just have him smell like cottage cheese gone bad for the rest of the day.

The first problem to getting a child dressed is what to put on him. Men barely know how to dress themselves, so they have little to no idea how to dress children. Women may somewhat give up on having their husbands going out dressed like colorblind geeks, but they'll be damned if their child's outfit isn't going to match each and every day.

Therefore, the child's outfit has to be approved by the wife, or it risks getting rejected, at which point the guy has to go back to the drawing board. Rather than drag the child in front of the woman for sentencing every day, the guy can either try to remember what outfits go together or have the woman lay them out the night before. Of course, it is not quite that simple. You do have to not only match the outfit, but have the outfit appropriate to the weather. Sending Junior to day care with that cute shirt-and-shorts outfit your wife loves isn't going to gather you any brownie points if he has his extremities subject to frostbite.

If the child is young, you'll have to dress him yourself. With those flimsy arms and legs, dressing a child is like trying to thread a shoelace through a shoe by holding the back of the lace. Without getting the limb bent at too strange an angle, you've got to feed it through to the other side. Difficult, but not impossible. But wait. What if your child does not want to go to day care? Then he's got those little arms and legs flapping around like a kite in a wind tunnel. You've first got to trap one of the wild appendages and try to stuff it into the correct hole while the other three appendages are working to thwart your efforts. If that is successful, you've then got to grab a second appendage and try to accomplish the same with that. Meanwhile, the child could be trying to stop you from doing that or squirming out of what you've already accomplished. By the time you're done, both you and the child should be ready for a nap, which is the last thing you are allowed to do.

If the child is older, he will be able to put his own clothes on. Theoretically, this should be easier. However as with most elegant theories, they tend to get crushed with the ugly facts. These children like to claim that somehow during the night they have forgotten how to put clothes on their own body, and so you must do it. They will claim this for months to years even though you used to have the opposite problem when they would put their shoes on the wrong feet and insist on going to school that way since they wanted to do everything themselves.

That must have been quite the night to wipe their memories clean like that. Were the covers over their heads so tight that the level of oxygen was depleted? Maybe they are part of some alien abduction/experimentation scheme that erases vital information from their little brains each and every night? Or possibly, just possibly, they are lazy little slugs who would ask you to chew their food if they could get away with it.

Somehow, the child's memories become clearer when your voice gets so loud that he knows your patience is in tatters. For those adults who think yelling at children doesn't work, they either don't have children, will be canonized after their passing,[321] or they are

---

321 No, being canonized does not mean being shot either at or from a cannon. It means that a particular church declares the person to be a saint sometime after they are dead. A lot of the saints become what is known as patron saints and people ask them for favors. For instance, St. Michael is the patron saint of accountants, and St. Genesius is the patron saint of dances. So if you lead a life without sin, you get to do more work after you are dead? Makes you think doing a bit of jaywalking may be worth it.

getting Prozac at a volume-discount rate. Even when the children suddenly remember how to put their clothes on, they are sometimes not particularly successful at it with lack of sleep. They'll be complaining that their shirts don't fit them anymore, and you realize they are yanking their heads through the armhole. The old "both legs through the same leg hole with the underwear" is also a popular move. It goes without saying that all clothes can be worn backward and/or inside out, and yet the child looks at you like you just told him he was adopted when you try to correct him. How the child gets it into his head that his mistake must be somehow your egregious fault is beyond me; unless, of course, he's copying his mother.

The final difficulty for the child to put his own clothes on is the socks and shoes. You wouldn't think socks would be too bad, but they are the *New York Times* crossword puzzle to a child. Getting the heel of the sock to match up to their own heel is met with more frustration than an amorous dachshund in a crowd of greyhounds in heat. If it isn't perfect, he'll complain that it won't feel right when he puts his shoe on, so he'll keep ripping it off his foot—and often tossing the shoe down the hall. Why not just twist the sock a bit to line it up? Because kids usually have it lined up so poorly that twisting the sock till it is in the correct position will cut off the circulation to their toes, and they'll turn blue. Why not just line it up correctly before putting it on? Sure, and if you can actually do that, why don't you trot him into the bathroom and see if he can better line up that urine stream?

Now come the shoes. The major problem with shoes is that they are nowhere to be found. Your child will usually approach you like you got up in the middle of the night and hid them (yet again) so that he would have such a hard time finding them. Does he actually think you have nothing better to do? He'll do this even if his shoes are right next to the door right where they should be. Of course, "where they should be" is a rarity on par with finding an albino squirrel—being eaten by an albino bear.

When the shoes are missing, you have to try to remember what the child did the night before. Was he using them as pretend bombs as he tossed them at you while you were relaxing on the couch?

Were they part of the pirate's treasure loot that is now hidden God knows where in the house? Naturally, you'll question your child. You may as well ask him what the gross national product of Mozambique is. He'll look at you like he doesn't even recognize the language you are speaking. You then speak slowly while enunciating. "SHOES," you say slowly, pointing at your feet. After a moment or so, a dawn of recognition will come over your child's eyes, and he'll know what you are talking about. He'll then shrug his shoulders because he stored that data with other nonimportant issues like telling you he volunteered you to chaperone is class field trip today.

You then have to find the shoes yourself. Are they in the toy box? The bathroom? The oven? If you're late for work, you'll be guaranteed not to find them for quite some time. Once the shoes are found, the child has then got to put them on. Younger children have to ask each and every day what the correct foot is. OK, I can understand that. Then they put the shoe on and pick up the other one and ask which foot that one goes on. That's where we get into the problem. Now, I'm not expecting my kid to be the next Einstein (Edison maybe), but I am hoping his powers of deductive reasoning are a bit beyond this.

Tying the shoes is also a problem. Early on, you have to tie them yourself. The child doesn't want them too tight or too lose. Don't worry—he'll let you know if it is wrong, usually either by yelling "ow, ow ow!" for too tight or "ew, ew, ew!" for too loose. When the child gets older, he'll have to learn to tie the shoes himself. At first, he feels that this is quite an accomplishment. After he gets over that feeling, he usually loses interest in tying. He'd go around all day with his shoes untied if you let him. Usually, if you do force the child to tie his sneakers, he ties them so poorly that they are undone nearly instantly. Naturally, he'll be giving you a look like you secretly untied them with your mind.

When the child is done getting dressed, he is supposed to put his pajamas in the hamper. Even though he is told to do this every day, he will forget every day well into and sometimes past the teenage years. When do they learn? Never—they just stop wearing pajamas eventually and go to shorts. Each day it is like telling him something he would have never considered in a million years on his own. Maybe he feels there are laundry fairies that magically come in and pick up their clothes and transport them to the laundry basket. Silly, isn't it? The fairies are far too busy picking up adult guys' clothes to ever get to the kids.

Ready to go to work? You're not even close. Now you've got to get the child washed up. Brushing the teeth is the worst part. It really stinks if the kid hates the taste of toothpaste. He'll be whipping his head around while you are trying to plunge that bristly stick into his mouth. It looks more like scenes from *Psycho* than a loving parent just trying to promote a bit of dental hygiene. Somehow, you've got to hold the child down, pry both hands away from his face, and open his mouth with only one hand because your other is holding the toothbrush with toothpaste. With any hope, you'll have broken his spirit by then and he'll allow his body to go limp and you can finish the job. I had no such luck with my first child. He would make these primal gagging sounds as he continued to fight. By the time you're done, you are such an emotional wreck that you'll have trouble inserting the key into your car's ignition.

Many other kids simply love getting their teeth brushed. Actually, they love eating toothpaste. As soon as the brush is in their mouth, they try sucking the paste off the brush. Since their sucking muscles are still pretty strong, the brush is dry before they ever get to the first molar.[322]

Later on, the child has to brush his own teeth. Day in and day out since he has even had teeth, you've been brushing them. So after thousands of times, you'd think he might have picked up something of a hint on how to do it. Right? That is like teaching a worm to bait itself on a hook. You've got to hold his hand and scrub each quadrant of his mouth. When it is his turn to try, all he'll do is brush the

---

[322] I had to do quite a bit of babysitting for one of my cousins. If I ever lost sight of him, he was inevitably found in the bathroom sucking on the toothpaste tube, which made it ever so hygienic for the rest of the family to use after. The problem—and you really may not believe this—is that fluoride in higher concentrations is a toxic poison. Yes, I know you probably don't believe me, so go ahead and google it. Don't worry…I'll wait. (Key theme music from *Jeopardy!*) So, you're back? Believe me now? So you want to use toothpaste to keep teeth white, and if you eat it…it makes brown splotches on them! Sorry for the bad news, there. Kind of like getting word that too much toilet paper causes uncontrollable flatulence.

front four teeth for about as long as it takes to sneeze, and he'll think he's done. You then have to explain to him that that was not nearly enough. He'll reinsert the brush in his mouth and go for another two or three seconds over the same teeth.

After your eighteenth time telling him it was not enough—pointing to the sections not touched, putting the toothbrush in the right position so all he has to do is move it, telling him that it doesn't count if the brush side isn't in actual contact with the teeth—the vein on your forehead is standing out a good quarter inch. Either you yank the brush out of his hand and finish the job, which is what he wanted you to do in the first place, or you keep making him do it until you are so late for work your boss is launching signal flares out the window, or you give up and allow his teeth to discolor to the point where they look like candy corn.

Eventually, your child will get better at brushing his own teeth. Keep in mind that I didn't say he'd be good at it, just better. After years of practice at it, you may feel that the child is now capable of brushing his own teeth without constant supervision. Children are known to regress once parental supervision is removed. Therefore, you've got to apply the sniff test here. Have him breathe in your face, and if the aroma doesn't make you lose consciousness, then he probably has done a moderately successful job.[323]

So once his teeth are brushed, he then has to have his face washed. Even though I do technically have a biology degree (from an Ivy League school, no less), I have no idea what to call that crusty stuff in their eyes. I don't know about you, but my family refers to it as eye goopies, not the most scientific of terms, I know. Anyway, the goopies have got to go. Again, when the child is young, it is your job. Take a cloth, rinse it in warm water, and, starting at the bridge of the nose, gently try wiping them away.

---

323 A child will do more work getting out of work than just doing anything right the first (or seventeenth) time. Why they would actually want to go out with breath that makes people think they gargle with toad urine is beyond me. Maybe it is the game of getting away with it. So if you spot-check the breath, one of their tactics is to breathe in rather than out so you don't smell it. I don't know if that has ever worked in the history of our species, but they all give it a shot. The good news is if they do that, you know they didn't brush, and so you send them back in—no need to demand they breathe on you at that point and make you wonder what water they are rinsing their toothbrush in.

Are they gone? No way in hell. The goopies are a yellowed version of Elmer's glue. Therefore, you've got to get the cloth hotter and scrub a little harder. Unlike with the toothpaste thing, your child is going to have a right to complain. Your sole agenda is to get every last goopie out of his eyes so he looks somewhat presentable when he gets dropped off at day care. However, the child has an alternative agenda. He wants to walk away from this episode without having one or both of his eyes gouged out of his head. Naturally, the rest of his face has to be washed afterward. If he's nice, maybe you should use a different washcloth.[324]

Later, the child should be on his own in the face-washing department. A child, in the name of efficiency, will think that the only thing that needs washing is the part that is visibly dirty. That might mean nothing or the area immediately around his mouth. He will also think that white lump on the counter you so affectionately call soap is optional. After all, if he scrubs hard enough, won't the majority of food crumbs come off without soap? Heck, the sleeve may be good enough all by itself without wasting time on that "water" thing.

So how do you check to make sure your child actually did wash his face? Well, you could ask him, but this is the same child who lied about eating the entire bag of Hershey's kisses you so neglectfully left in the cupboard without a watchdog or silent alarm system. He would lie to you even if his mouth was full of chocolate, chocolate was smeared all over his face and clothes, and there was a circle of crumpled foil around him.

So to really determine how well he did, you must first start with a visual inspection. If he passes that, then you sneak into the bathroom and do some behind-the-scenes investigating. Is the washcloth wet? How about the soap? If not, walk out, wait a minute or two, and then ask him if he washed his face. If he claims he did, tell him you know when he is lying and send him back to the bathroom.[325]

---

324 If your wife finds out you've been removing the goopies with her washcloth, she'll rub your face hard enough to take off any freckles you may have.

325 It is good to foster in your child a belief that you are omniscient so that he minimizes what he tries to pull over on you. *Do not* let on to your child any of these secrets. Otherwise, he'd know how to plant the evidence and look like he did what he was supposed to rather than just doing it. It is like children are in training to become master criminals, and you have to be the detective and stay one step ahead.

The next part in getting your child ready is, in some ways, the worst part. He has to have his hair combed. For some children, this is no problem. Break out a comb, run it under the water, zip it over his head, and he is finished. Not that it was my first child's fault, but I hated combing his hair. He had a big cowlick in the back that I couldn't get to stay down until I drenched the washcloth and mopped it down. Of course, the water would go coursing down his back, and my wife would ask what the hell happened in the bathroom that made it look like he had been hit with a hose. I'd just shrug my shoulders in a way that suggested I must have looked away, and the child somehow got himself turned around and splashed himself.

Even after the cowlick was down, I still couldn't get the rest of the hair to look right. I didn't know what I did wrong, and I certainly didn't have an idea of how to fix it. I just knew it didn't look *right*. Sure enough, when the child and I walked out of the bathroom, my wife and child would be walking right back in. Eventually, I just stopped trying altogether. If the child had been a girl, I probably would never have attempted the whole thing in the first place. So what if your wife is away and you must fix the hair? That's where baseball caps come in handy.

Now the child is almost ready to go. A key point to remember here is that he must go to the bathroom before leaving the house. Otherwise, you'll have him strapped into the car and be out of the driveway when he announces that he has an emergency situation on his hands and will *not* be able to hold it. Looking back, you'll see that the emergency situation is literally in his hands and he is in the process of holding it quite tightly.[326] You've then got to get the car turned around as witnessed in *The Dukes of Hazzard*[327] and get that

---

326 Even though I'm a biology major, I've never seen any studies that support the idea that crushing one's penis does help prevent the urinary bladder from letting go. Once the flow starts, vise clamps ain't going to stop it. Note: that is *not* a challenge, and no one should attempt to prove me wrong on that part. Heaven knows, there is enough in this book to prove me wrong on far easier issues than this.

327 *The Dukes of Hazzard* was a show about some country boys who liked driving a car very fast to get away from the local law enforcement. Why the sheriff even attempted to catch them when he could have far more easily driven over to their house in the middle of the night and pistol-whipped them is beyond me.

child back in the house before he wets himself. If you do not make it in time, you then have to remove all his clothing, give him a quick rinsing off, and then put a new outfit on him. By this time, your boss will have given you up for dead, or at least you will be by the time you get into the office.

How do you find out if your child has peed already? Again, asking may not give you the correct answer. Unfortunately (actually it is very fortunate), there is no test on this one to find out if the child is lying. What to do? Ask another dozen times and see if he'll crack. If he doesn't, cross your fingers and get him back into the car.

Now that the child is ready, are you? If you are bringing him to day care, does he have his necessary lunch? What about his snacks? Should he bring a raincoat? If you're in a cold winter climate, what about mittens, boots, snowsuit, etc., so he can traipse around in the snow with the other kids without getting pneumonia? If you are waiting until now to get things packed, you may as well save your money, stay home, and read the help wanted section. You (preferably your wife) have to get everything ready the night before and have it waiting by the door so you can't forget it. The only thing that can't wait by the door is the lunch, and that is something that you will then have to go back for when you are six blocks away from the house.

So you are ready. You put the appropriate outside-weather gear on and then head outside. You've now got to get the child in the car. When he is young, it is easy enough to open the car door, throw him in the car seat, buckle him in, and then he ain't going anywhere. When he gets older, he is going to want to be independent. He'll have to open the car door himself (no problem), get in the car himself (minor problem), close the car door (big problem), and then buckle himself into the car seat (huge problem).

Opening the car door is fine if he is physically strong enough to do it. When he tries getting in the car, however, he usually likes to take his dear sweet time. You're tempted to give his bottom a little nudge, but then he'll turn around and try to explain that he is a big boy and can do it all himself—and that will take even longer. Therefore, you're left with only offering him verbal "support." A more accurate word for "support" is "begging" as you try to get him out of slow gear. Once he is in the car, he'll want to close the door. With his weight and strength, he'll only be able to manage to get it partially shut. However, it is not acceptable for you to think that is good enough and drive off. There are safety issues here.[328]

If you open the door and reclose it, you'll end up getting him crying, which will make it hard for you to get him in his seat and buckled in. If he sees you helping him close the door, you're liable to provoke the same reaction. That is how I became a master of helping close the door with my knee. When he starts closing the door, give the outside a little knee nudge for momentum. He'll never see it that low, and he'll think he accomplished it by himself. Now the tough part comes. He's going to want to buckle himself in. If he is not good at it and you help him, he is going to start crying again. However, this time he is immobile if you force the situation, and you can drive off, as long as you can stand the ensuing wailing protest.

Now you have to drive to the day care. Take it as a compliment, but your child would much rather stay home and play with you. Therefore, he may start making up excuses why he doesn't want to be left at day care. He could feign illness or just start crying. You'll try to explain to him that you would rather stay home with him, but that you have to go to work so that you can get money. He'll then ask why you need money. Paying rent or mortgage is a concept that is usually a bit advanced for him, so you've got to get more practical. You can tell how money buys food and toys. That will perk him up, but then you have to explain that you are not picking up a new toy that day or taking him out for ice cream, which will then get him crying again. What did you expect—to be able to make a child understand economics when he can't even remember if he has emptied his bladder or not?

When you get to day care, you've then got to get him in. If you thought he was dawdling when getting into the car, then you'll think he is wearing cement shoes getting out of the car and into the day-care building. My child, like many other children, was pretty shy. As

---

328 Besides, that red light on the dash will drive you nuts eventually. You can put duct tape over it so you don't see it, but that doesn't stick permanently and tends to cover up the light for an engine problem as well.

soon as we entered the day-care center, he was attached to my leg in a way that would make a leech take notes. I would literally have to pry him off my leg and hand him over to another adult as he screamed. It is moments like that that make you feel like you are a lousy parent.[329]

You then have to sulk out of the building feeling like you've been kicked in the stomach. However, if you were to peek into the window of the day care a few minutes later, you'd see him playing trucks with another child. It is moments like that you should seize and run away with. Otherwise, if you wait too long, you'll see one of the two kids not sharing quite as well as he should and bopping the other kid on the head with the truck. Then you're back to feeling guilty again. Hopefully, you don't return to the car to find the child's lunch sitting on the seat and then have to go back into the day care and start the leaving process all over again.

---

329 It isn't uncommon at this point to have thoughts about whether this is what Hitler's parents did to him to make him turn out the way he did. Rational? Absolutely not. However, when this little body that you love more than anything is upset because he wants to spend more time with you, you feel as crappy as the porta-potty at a construction site two hours after the taco cart rolls by.

Working Hours

or

If You Have an Office, a Nap

Is Oh, So Tempting

U nlike single people, many married people arrive at work with a smile on their face. That is until the boss arrives and notes that you are a tad late for work *again*. Don't try to assure him that it won't happen again, because unless he is in a later Alzheimer's stage, he's going to notice the very next day. Many working parents vow that to get to work, they just need to start the morning earlier. They should get the kids into bed earlier, wake up earlier, and then they'll be on time. Somehow, and I'm not sure how, that never works.

I don't know what type of quantum-mechanic time shifts are involved here, but no matter how early you wake up, you end up being the same amount of time late. Maybe it is because you get more relaxed, complacent even, when you think you've got all the time necessary. Then you're not barking like a drill sergeant trying to get the child or children moving, and then he takes longer and the both of you are late again.[330] All you end up doing is losing more ever-

330 If you give your child a cup of juice in the morning, you'd expect that the child would drink it, especially if he asked for it. However, his brain isn't fully engaged, so if you

precious sleep for yourself and your children. Now, when you are at a sleep loss, you are not as efficient at work. That is just what you need: getting a reputation for being late *and* lazy. You can just feel your hair blowing in the breeze as you fly up the corporate ladder.

Even when you are at work, you are not fully at work. Family comes foremost there as well. For instance, your day care could call and say that your child has thrown up. According to most state laws, if your child is sick, she is not allowed to be in day care. That means that someone has to go pick her up immediately. You've then got to go to your boss and explain that you'll be leaving a tad early, like before the first coffee break. As his knuckles get white as he grips the papers he was holding, quickly take leave of his office and hope that he wasn't holding your annual evaluation.

On your way to day care, you may wonder how your child became so sick so quickly. Although, how do you tell if a kid is getting sick if he normally is irritable and whiny when you drop him off? When you arrive to pick him up, she may already be over her "illness" and be happily playing with the other children again. So is she really sick, or did she just spontaneously puke for no reason? With kids (and fraternity brothers), you can never tell. However, it doesn't matter because you've got to take her home anyway. When you get home, you may find an entire empty box of Oreo cookies that may have something to do with the mysterious illness.

Luckily, kids grow out of sporadic puking. That doesn't mean that you won't be getting calls about them at work, though. Once they enter school, you may have teachers or principals calling you. Rarely, if ever, will it be good news if you get a call at work from the school. You will *not* be getting a call saying how little Susie aced her big test. You *will* get a call if little Susie coincidentally has the exact same answers on her test—including misspellings—as the child in front of her. Needless to say, they will not be complimenting her on her wonderful eyesight.

---

don't remind him that he needs to actually raise the cup to his lips to get it into his body, you'll come in to get him dressed and he won't even have started. If you get upset at him, he'll remind you that you didn't tell him to drink it, so he didn't know if he was supposed to. This is the same child who will go around drinking the liquid out of any cup in the house left unattended for more time than it takes for a hummingbird to flap its wing.

Even if you don't hear from or about your child during the day, you may still have to deal with some child matters. One of the worst times is with fund-raisers. Whether it is to make money for an athletic team, a field trip, or bail for a favorite teacher, kids now are trained to be used-car salesmen.[331]

In previous generations, they'd put a can in the kids' hands and send them out in front of liquor stores to guilt adults into coughing up their spare change along with the other vagrants. These days, most of the fund-raisers are in the form of catalogue sales. One day the kid comes home and he has got a fund-raiser book with him. Not so bad, you think. You'll pick out a couple cheap things and at least get something for your money. You then open the catalogue and your heart starts palpitating like Miss America has just offered to give you a sponge bath. However, as you read the catalogue you realize the experience is more akin to giving the sponge bath to your Great-Aunt Gertrude with the giant hairy mole bulging out of her neck that everyone is supposed to pretend doesn't exist.

On the first page, you see a few sheets of wrapping paper being sold for twelve dollars. At those prices, the wrapping is more expensive than the gift! You may as well just keep the gift and just give them the paper. Maybe on page two there will be a tub of popcorn—for about eighteen dollars. That about covers your year's popcorn budget in one whack! Of course that prepacked, old, preservative-laden popcorn does taste so much better than anything fresh.

So here the kid comes home with this catalogue that would make Donald Trump wince.[332] What happens now? You are responsible for bringing it in to work so you can show it to your coworkers. Now you are making your coworkers feel like cheapskates for not helping children. As you walk down the corridor with the catalogue, you

---

331 Do *not* get me started on how used cars aren't called used cars anymore—they are preowned—or even more confusing/obnoxious, pretitled. I've even heard the horrifying phrase "new to you" rather than just saying what it actually is. Just because a car is used doesn't mean it has no value. It isn't like you are selling preowned condoms or anything.

332 Although not as badly as Barack Obama's birth certificate or hearing what people actually think of his hair.

have people diving under their desks and picking up their phones pretending to talk to somebody, anybody but you.

There are some fund-raisers that aren't too bad, like Girl Scout cookies. They aren't too expensive, and they taste pretty good. The issue here is that many kids are in Girl Scouts, so each business gets flooded with order forms. As a parent, your only hope is to get in first. People are OK buying the first box or two of cookies. It's when they get asked for their eleventh and twelfth boxes that they start getting a little testy, especially if they are diabetic and were only doing it to be nice in the first place.

So let us get back to "work" while at work…Quite often, job projects have deadlines. Believe it or not, most bosses don't put arbitrary deadlines on projects just for giggles. Deadlines have consequences. Sometimes deadlines are difficult to hit, especially when one or two of the coworkers is late coming in so that other workers need to pick up the slack. If the deadline arrives and the project doesn't, that means a call goes out for some late-night work.

It always looks good to the boss when you volunteer for special assignments at work. If it is your responsibility to pick the child up from day care, you really don't have the ability to volunteer. It is not an option to leave your child at the day-care center like you'd leave your car in overnight parking. In fact, many day-care centers have a late policy in which each *minute* you are late, you get charged a dollar. Loan sharks don't have late fees that strict. Anyway, you've got an excuse as to why you absolutely can't stay late. Your single coworkers, however, can only offer up a lame excuse of ever trying to have a social life. Therefore, they will "gladly" offer their services so you can get out of work.[333] After all, they know that you would stay late if you could. Besides, in another dozen years or so, the kids will be old enough so that you can stay late again.

---

333 Remember the camaraderie that used to exist between you and your coworkers? For some reason, they seem to have gotten a bit bitter ever since you reproduced. Don't worry about it—it is probably just jealously.

Late Afternoon

or

There Is No Place Like Home...

Besides a Zoo at Feeding Time

My biggest problem when I would pick the kids up from day care was that I'd forget to do the debriefing. The guy is supposed to ask the day-care providers if the child had a nap; if so, how long; how much the child ate at lunch; if there is anything in particular the child will need to bring the next day; and if there is something special the child did that day. Not only do men have to ask, but they have to remember the answers. I always got in trouble with this one.

"How did the child sleep?" the wife would ask.

"Good," I replied.

"What does 'good' mean? If it was only an hour, we should get Junior into bed at a reasonable time. If it was more than two, then we're never going to get him down tonight and there is a show I want to watch. Does 'good' just mean that he stayed in bed this time, because the other day, he got up, woke the other kids, and the day-care people found them destroying the room. So what exactly does 'good' mean?"

"Two-hour nap?" I'd reply.

"You're lying to me," she'd state coolly.

"Yes…yes, I am."

As she let out an exasperated moan and ran her fingers through her hair, she'd then ask, "So how did he eat? Do I make something quick for dinner so that he isn't freaking out, or do I have enough time to make a real meal?"

"He ate…fine?"

That's when she'd stomp off to the next room muttering things I had every reason to believe were unflattering curses about my attention to detail, among other things. I'm sure she'd tell me if I asked, but if I was in the mood to ask questions, I should have done that with the day-care workers in the first place.

So now you're home with the family. If you watch any 1950s sitcoms, you'll see the father come home from a hard day's work and collapse in the chair. He'd then have time to decompress with the newspaper,[334] oblivious to his surroundings, while his wife finished making dinner and simultaneously dealt with the chaos around him. That still can happen! All you have to do is stay up late enough, and I'm sure one of the cable channels will have old sitcoms for you to watch again. If you think that you will be relaxing when *you* get home, then you probably also believe that yetis are in cahoots with aliens from Venus to fix the World Series playoffs.

These days, the job of a father when he gets home from work is to do whatever it takes to keep the children away from their mother. That is, if he wants her to cook anything better than macaroni and cheese.[335] For most families these days, both parents work. Therefore, the woman comes home, everyone is hungry, and she hasn't given the first thought to what she'll make for dinner. Meanwhile, the kids

---

334 In the old days, people transmitted news by printing it on paper and distributing it around the country. Somehow, they were able to get the news of the day written up, go to a printer, make copies, and mail them all over the country at night so people could read it in the morning. Of course, these days, any news that isn't received instantaneously is barbaric. Could you imagine going back to the old days where you had to wait so they could actually check for accuracy and whether it was deemed worthy of being considered reportable? Heck knows, if someone had a dream that a Kardashian was impregnated by a cross-dressing alien, that should be tweeted and liked instantly.

335 After a hard day's work, having both macaroni *and* cheese now counts as a two-course meal. Do you want more than that? No problem. Pour yourself a glass of milk and look under the couch cushions for some pretzels that had gotten lost.

are running in and out between her legs asking if they can have a snack. If you or she gives in, then there is no way that the children will eat dinner. They may promise and/or beg, but if you give them so much as a single Cheez-It, they won't do much more with their dinner plate than look at it with a mixture of apathy and disgust. Having them groveling is not going to help your wife decide what to make. Therefore, drag them out of the kitchen and try to preoccupy their little minds. Let them play with matches if you have to, but keep them away from your wife.

Meanwhile, your wife goes frantically searching through the cabinets trying to come up with something to eat. When you hear the rattle of pots and pans, you'll know that she now has a plan of action. This is where your job gets trickier. Your children also know that she has decided on something, and they want to know what that is. Therefore, they will try to slip in a few evasive maneuvers and bolt toward the kitchen. Your wife will be none too pleased to see their faces so soon after getting rid of them.

If they make it to the kitchen, the children will then ask what she is making. Naturally, she'll tell them. Unless she is making something like chicken nuggets with French fries or another item of little to no redeeming nutritional value, they will start complaining that whatever she is making is *yucky* and then offering up their own suggestions. They may go so far as to make barfing sounds at the thought of what your wife is cooking, and she'll just think that is *so* funny as she is trying to feed the ungrateful cretins!

Your wife has had a hard day. The last thing she wants is to be taunted by little beings that only come up to her waist. Will she be mad at them? Nope. It is the man's fault for letting them escape. Therefore, he should expect a cold glare from his wife usually reserved for passing judgment on animal abusers. That glare means that he had better get those children out of the room now, or the pan she was cooking with will become a blunt, but effective, weapon.

If you are successfully able to thwart the children's advances to the kitchen, then they will hit their backup plan: screaming at the top of their lungs asking what she is cooking so that she could hear them if she were cooking in the house next door. She may yell back the proposed menu. Knowing that they are out of effective arguing range, the kids will vent their displeasure over the meal selection by yelling things such as "gross" and "boogers." Your wife will not find it amusing for the children to make an analogy between her food and any liquid or semisolid that leaves the body through any orifice. Before she gives up in frustration and makes you cook *and* watch the kids, you've got to get them silenced. Wrestle them to the ground and gag them if you must, but don't let them keep talking.

When dinner is finally ready, then it comes time to choose where to eat it. If the children have their say, they will be in front of the television watching cartoons. If you have your say, you'd probably vote to be watching cartoons as well. However, many women consider mealtime to be "family time." In other words, do what she says. Of course if you really want to watch television, you can egg the kids on when your wife isn't looking by softly humming the *SpongeBob SquarePants* theme song.[336]

After all, a guy figures he already lived his day, and reliving it orally at a table just isn't worth the effort as it wasn't that exciting the first time around. What is more tiresome for a guy than living a day yet again? Hearing about someone else's day filled with people he doesn't know and doesn't want to know. Gentlemen must remember that talking is exactly how many women decompress, and since her day is usually harder than the guy's, he had better do as told.[337] Besides, if you get to the dinner table first, you can take the seat that gives you a peripheral view of the television.

After dinner, you'll then have to check with the kids to see if they have any homework. The children are about as effective at lying

---

336 Who lives in a pineapple under the seas? SpongeBob SquarePants! Absorbent and yellow and porous is he. SpongeBob SquarePants! If nautical nonsense is something you wish…SpongeBob SquarePants! Then drop on the deck and flop like a fish! SpongeBob SquarePants!

337 Don't believe me on that one? What does a guy do during lunch? More often than not, he sits down and eats. Simple. Many women use every last period of free time as errand time, so lunch for her may mean eating a yogurt while running to the bank, swinging by the grocery store, going to the doctor to get a copy of vaccination records to then drive to the school even though all the $&#@ doctor does is hit the "send" button on the computer, but that would be way too hard for his %*#! finger, etc. Get the picture? If women didn't keep running all over the planet, life would cease to function as we know it. So when your wife starts talking, open the ears and nod the head.

about this as you are telling your wife how they did at day care. The difference is that many men don't push the children for the truth as hard as they should because that would be yet another delay in getting to your close friend, the television. Very bad idea. A precedent of not caring about homework now can lead to less caring later, which means that your child will be fighting you for television time until he leaves the house for college—if he ever leaves the house for college...or any job.

It is now time for that hyped-about elusive thing that all the talk shows and books bemoan the lack of: Quality Time. Yes, you spend time with your children in the morning and night, but during that time you are pushing and prodding them to do your bidding while they attempt to thwart your actions simply because they have nothing better to do. Now after dinner is the only time when you aren't battling time or each other.

What to do? Usually you want to try to get them outside. Why? Is it because sunlight is a perfect source for collecting vitamin D for their growing bodies? Is it to strengthen their muscles and agility? Or is it to have them expend their energy running around the yard rather than trashing the living room that you then have to clean up? You be the judge.

If your children are too young, they cannot go out by themselves, so you must join them. They'll want to do fun things such as attack you with squirt guns, throw balls at you, and try to run you down with their tricycles. If you have more than one child, each will want your undivided, unwavering attention. They get that by trying to be the one who yells "dad" the loudest. To make them stop yelling, you have to yell even louder to have a chance of being heard. And you wonder why you aren't more popular with the adults in the neighborhood.

I am a parent who likes playing with the kids outside even though they are old enough to be out there alone. As such, I have noticed an unusual phenomenon. Neighborhood children can smell from blocks away when there is an adult willing to play games. Within minutes of going outside, I've attracted neighborhood kids like ticks on a dog. Here I was planning to spend quality time with children whom I personally have sired, and now I can't even see them over the sea of children all screaming, "Watch me! Watch me!" Naturally, the favorite game becomes "Smear the Old Person."

Whether you are out with just your own kids or surrounded by a horde, you will quickly realize that children are an endless source of energy—and you are not. They are figurative volcanoes spewing lava, and you are the people of Pompeii, staring on in amazement and fear with nowhere to run. At no time are the kids not racing, rolling, and flapping their arms about like they are trying to take flight. Unfortunately, putting them on the dog runner is not looked upon as using appropriate parenting skills. Meanwhile, just watching the kids is enough to get you winded.

When you are out there with a bunch of kids, your basic job is to act as a referee, not that they'll be playing any formal games. Instead, you'll be assessing when the kids are playing rough enough where someone (possibly you) is going to get hurt. Whether they are playing dodge ball with a chunk of concrete, playing catch with a younger child (as the object being thrown), or playing keep-away with a child's inhaler, you've got to step in and correct the action. Otherwise, other parents will be ticked off when their child comes home with a gaping head wound. Of course they are not so concerned as to actually take time out of their "busy" day (filled with thinking about getting around to fixing their car that has been on cement blocks for the last seven years) to spend time with their own little monsters, not that they'll complain about the free babysitting they get when you are doing it.

Early Evening

or

Vampires Aren't the Only Things to

Worry about When Night Comes

O nce it gets a bit dark, it is time to come in and probably relax. Maybe you want to watch the news to catch up on the world or a sitcom to unwind. Maybe you'd like to take a quick ride in the space shuttle. You've got the same chance of doing either, so you may as well dream big. Once in, the kids rule the television. Now technically it is true that you pay the cable or satellite bill (and mortgage and electricity and phone and…), so you can pull rank and watch what you want. The problem here is that if kids really want to watch something, they are going to keep asking so that you cannot possibly enjoy your show.

"Is it over yet?" "Noooow can we watch our show?" "This show is soooo boring. When is it going to be over?" With all the arguing, you are bound to miss 75 percent of the dialogue, which is fairly infuriating unless you are viewing *Baywatch*.[338] However, with young

338 *Baywatch* was a television show about lifeguards. They'd sit around in skimpy clothes and go run in slow motion after people drowning. The women lifeguards were never in fear of drowning themselves since they were so artificially inflated that they couldn't sink if they wanted to. The show was so bad that the network cancelled it pretty quick. Usually,

children about, you have as much chance of your wife letting you watch *Baywatch* as a show about how they kill chickens and end up with the chicken nuggets they love so well.[339] If you demand that they stop asking you questions, then they just talk loudly to each other (or mumble at a ridiculous level that strains the entire definition of "mumble") about how unfair life is that they aren't at that instant watching a *Barney & Friends* episode they've already seen eighteen times.

It may be that there is a show that you really want to watch, so you order the children to stay away from you. If children can literally see your eyes bulging out of their sockets in frustration/anger, they may sense that you are actually serious and truly leave you alone. That's when they have a sword fight and are running around obscuring your vision. Eventually this will get on your nerves, and you'll order no more running around for the children. Then they'll break out some action figures and feel the need to supply boisterous sound effects that will have you straining to hear the television no matter how fast you're clicking the remote to crank the sound. You can then order the children into silence. Now, you are thinking in the back of your head that you are paying a mortgage on a house that is larger than the television room, and your kids could be in any other part of the house, but that would be far too convenient. You could throw the coolest toys in the world in their room, and they still won't tread near it as they don't want to be near a bed at bedtime.[340]

Children are not physically capable of remembering to be quiet for more than forty-six or forty-seven seconds. Their voices will slowly creep up until they are again at a level that would have the neighborhood airport complaining. You've then got to order them out of

---

that is the end of the story. In this case, the show syndicated itself and became the most popular program in the world. No exaggeration…*the world*. I don't even know if they bothered translating the dialogue into the native language of other countries.

339 Personally, I'd be far more horrified about all the nonchicken things they do to make those nuggets.

340 This reverses during the teenage years when they only come out to be fed. If you get mad at a child this age and send him to his room, you may as well be sending him to a party. Between Facebook, online video games, and the phone, his room is the *best* place to be.

the room to have any hope of watching the show. When they are out of sight, it is inevitable that they will pick on each other, and a fight will break out. You've got to then go in and referee. Naturally, they will have widely different stories of what the heck precipitated the fight. If you take the time to work through the details so that you can confer the proper justice, then the only chance you have of getting back to catch the tail end of the show is if it is the Jerry Lewis Labor Day telethon.

In the off (way off) chance that they actually do remain quiet in the next room, you know that is going to be even worse news, whether they have found creative new uses for scissors or have managed to get your work briefcase open. Eventually, you'll realize that it is just not worth the effort to try to watch something for yourself beyond recording it and trying to save up the energy to watch it when they are asleep, which then would cut into the minimal quality time you and your wife attempt to have.

At some point, you are supposed to get back to that quality-time mode. First off, you can attempt to engage your child in conversation.

"How was school today?" you ask.

"Fine."

"Anything new?"

"No," the child says with a look suggesting you are asking him what toe cheese tastes like.

"What did you learn today?" You keep prodding, hoping at some point to get even the semblance of a conversation started.

"I don't remember." He shrugs.

"So why is it that we send you to school if you can never remember anything when you get home?"

"Dunno. Why do you?"

It is easier to get information out of mobsters than get any pertinent details out of a child. Throw in the bright lights, and he still won't crack. You'll get more information from staring at wallpaper.

Eventually, you'll have to abandon the whole conversation angle with your child when it comes to daily life. All that happens is both of you end up getting frustrated. Unless little Jimmy in his class was eating paste and had to be sent to the nurse's office, you won't be hearing a thing about his day. Whatever you do, don't complain to your wife about how poor a conversationalist the child is. She may have some prime examples of where he possibly would have gotten that trait from.

Evening

or

"Good Night"...Yeah, Right!

Every evening, you'll have to announce that it is time to get ready for bed. Every evening, the children will act surprised that they would actually have to do such a thing as willingly lose consciousness. At this point, the children go into ultraslow motion. They want everything dragged out so that they can delay the inevitable bedtime as long as humanly possible. The only things that will come fast are the excuses. This is usually when the child's mind clears, and he remembers that he *does* have homework that is due the next day. My absolute favorite is when it is a project that requires supplies, so you are off to find an all-night supply store.

There are many types of children when it comes to homework. The first group is the Incapables. These children, who may have been playing chess online minutes ago, now act like they can barely remember how to blow their own noses when the homework gets pulled out. They are constantly whining for help for each and every little question. At the top of the page where it says "Name," they'll look at you with a querying frown like they are wondering what on Earth they are supposed to name. After telling your child that the blank is for his own name, you may even need to prod him as to what that would be.

When he gets to the first problem, he'll attempt to solve it by staring it down. Several minutes will pass, and then he'll finally realize that the problem will not after all disappear from the page or spontaneously combust, so he will call for your help. Usually, you want to give him just enough hints so that you can get the wheels turning in his own head and he can figure the problem out for himself. I say "usually" because if *Monday Night Football* is going to be starting, you want that child in bed before kickoff. With the Incapable, the hints keep piling up until you're reduced to saying something like, "It's a number rhyming with 'seleven.'"

Once you help him with a problem, you hope that the wisdom you have imparted will give him the clarity of mind to easily work through the rest of the problems that are mainly just rehashes of the same one you did. No luck. The minute you leave the room, he'll be begging for you to come right back in. Technically, he wouldn't even have had time to read the next problem, never mind take a second to see if he could figure it out. If you erased the first answer, he'd stare at the first problem like he'd never seen it before in his life.

What the Incapables are actually trying to accomplish is to get their parents to do all the work for them, even if it is *more* work to actually get you to finally break down and do it. By continually looking like they have been asked to solve global warming supplied only with a ball of string and Q-tips, the kids make the parents keep on giving hints to the correct answers until they physically have to move the child's hand to put the answer down on the paper.

Then you have the Flashes. These kids are going to put down some answer—any answer—so that they can get back to doing something more engaging to their intellect like teasing the holy tar out of a younger sibling. To these children, homework is like ripping off a Band-Aid—if you've got to do it, get it done in as little time as possible so you suffer as little as possible. Whereas the Incapable looks at the homework like it is printed in hieroglyphics, the Flash writes in what looks like hieroglyphics.

Unless you have your own child's Rosetta stone to crack the code on what the heck he's incomprehensibly scribbled, you wouldn't know if he were doing algebra or a report on Brazilian cockroaches. If the Flashes were asked to do a book report, they'd be satisfied doing it on *Clifford the Big Red Dog* for any grade up to and including junior high. The minimal amount of effort is what they are going to do each and every time. To them, a D stands for "Done," and that is certainly good enough.

The Blamer is quite the fun child to have when it comes to homework. Nothing *ever* is his fault. This is the child who believes that for some reason unbeknownst to him, the teacher has singled him out of all the children in the classroom to torment. Yes, she spends two hours each day after school correcting everyone's homework.[341] She then stays up the rest of the night thinking of devious ways to make his life personally miserable. Quite often, the "diabolical" teacher will somehow be able to tell the entire class about an assignment without him knowing about it so that he'll not know he's supposed to do it.

"How's the homework?" you may ask the Blamer.

"Rotten," comes the reply. "That stupid Mrs. Crabtree is giving us a test on things that she hasn't even taught us about. On top of that, I've got a major project due the same day." Now that doesn't seem particularly fair, you think. You may even be tempted to call Mrs. Crabtree to find out why she would do something like that to your poor child. However, you will find out that your child's version of events is missing some critical components. The test may be on a subject the teacher hasn't personally taught him because he was busy drawing rocket ships in his notebook rather than paying an iota of attention. However, the rest of the class is more than ready. Meanwhile, he has had a month to finish the project and is now working on his second extension.

There is an excuse every day for everything. Year after year, for some reason, the teacher singles him out to torment. Somehow the child has become involved as the center of a conspiracy hatched by

---

341 The child would have you believe that the first hour is for everyone else's homework in the class, and the second hour is just on his and trying to find any reason to mark him down. "But the answer you put down is wrong," you might add. Then the child may suggest you are in cahoots with the teacher to make his life miserable.

the National Education Association to test the sanity of a single child over years of persecution. If you were to believe what the Blamer tells you, then the only thing missing from his life is the crown of thorns.

A small fraction of children belong to the group known as the Overachievers. These are the kids who, when given a page to write a report, write as small as possible on the front and back of the page to get every last bit of information that would be remotely pertinent in there somewhere. If they have to pick a book for a book report, it is something like "G" from the *Encyclopedia Britannica* set.[342] You'd think these kids would be an absolute joy, but they have their difficulties as well.

First of all, when they don't understand something the first time, they panic. Beads of perspiration start pouring down their faces as they start taking it personally that they must not be particularly smart if they can't intuitively know how to do something before they've learned how to do it. They get so frustrated that they can't settle down and listen long enough to get it. You're trying to explain to him how to set up the problem, and he is hyperventilating over the thought that he's going to have to repeat the grade or have to start taking the short bus into school because he's having trouble remembering to "borrow from the tens column."

No matter what group your child is from, Quality Time dictates that you should go over the homework with the child when he is done. If you have an Incapable, then you've really already gone over every last detail. So now that you have done his homework rather than helping him do it himself, you can either let him off the hook or ask him how to do it again.

"Do you know how to do this now?" you ask.

"Sure," comes the hesitant reply.

"OK, I'll make up the same type of problem, and you show me how you approach it."

---

342 Believe it or not, encyclopedias used to be printed on paper and come as an entire set of books. There used to be people whose sole job was to go door to door selling these large volumes. They were written by people who were paid to try to get the facts correct rather than by anyone with an attitude, a bottle of Jack Daniels, an agenda, and access to a computer. Barbaric times.

"I said I know, so shouldn't you just believe me? I don't think the teacher would like you assigning me more work she didn't. Isn't that some sort of child abuse?" he admits in defeat. At this point, it is a question of who has the endurance to last the painful process of going through yet more problems.

With the Flash, there is going to be a lot of eraser time if you are reviewing his work. Forget that little eraser on the head of the pencil. He's going to need the industrial-sized one.

"What does that say?" you may ask, looking at one of the answers. The Flash's first reaction is that *you* can't figure out the problem, and so you are asking for *his* help. You've then got to make him understand that his answer is indecipherable and hence unacceptable.

"I'm not sure," he may eventually reply. "Maybe the Bill of Rights?"

"Great. But you are doing math, so that can't be right. Well, erase it and do it over."

"But I already did it!" he gasps.

"But even *you* can't read it! How do you expect your teacher to read it?"

"That's her job! You can't expect me to do her job for her."

With the Blamer, you have to hunt down his assignments. To him, starting to study for a test or work on a project any earlier than ten hours before it is due is about as incomprehensible an act as sticking a drink umbrella up your nose and opening it up. Therefore, you have to go through each and every class to find out what needs to be done. Unfortunately, that still usually doesn't work because the textbook he needs will always be accidentally left at school. More things disappear in this kid's locker than in a magician's hat.

The Overachiever will actually search you out for approval. Not only will he show you his answers, he'll explain how he arrived at them. One by one. You'll actually find yourself hiding under the kitchen counter when this kid's homework is done.

When homework and other chores are done, you announce that it is now definitively time for bed. That is when your child remembers that he is hungry. You remind him of the plate of food he left in the dining room. If it is still there, then you can make him eat it quickly. It is only at this time that your child believes in actually chewing his food for proper digestion. Any other time he is like a snake swallowing his prey with one gulp.[343]

If the dinner is gone, then you've got to get him something else to eat. Grab the nearest processed-food bar (unwrap it for him because it will take him several minutes just to get it open) and encourage him to eat it as quickly as possible. You basically feel like a cross between a cheerleader and a prison guard trying to get your child to get the food down as soon as possible and then off to the next activity.

And that next activity is washing up. That may mean anything from washing his face, hands, and teeth to a full shower. No matter what activity it is, he will take a long time. You will find yourself banging on the bathroom door asking if he needs a life guard. For years, you've demanded privacy for yourself when you are in the bathroom. The observant child will be more than happy to point this irony out.

In the morning, you could barely get him to pass the toothbrush in the vicinity of his teeth, and now he is brushing each and every one individually, or he takes forever, and when he comes downstairs he *still* hasn't brushed his teeth because he forgot (as he forgets every single night). You then have to remind him each and every night to pee. He will not do this voluntarily. Why, you ask? Because he is going to store up any excuse he can muster to keep getting out of bed. The bathroom excuse is a pretty good one. After what seems like decades of potty training, the last thing you want to do is start cleaning up one of his accidents.

One of my children had the uncanny ability to store his bowels all day long so that there would be a marathon pooping session at night. Since he was in no hurry, he was content to just sit there and let gravity do the work for him rather than muster up any physical

---

343 A snake is able to unhinge its jaw so that it can open its mouth wide enough to eat its prey. For instance, a boa constrictor can eat an entire goat in one swallow. With children, they'll down an entire Twinkie in one bite or a hot dog in two. You'll look over in disgust as his cheeks are bulging in a way you never thought possible for a human. The only good news here is that if you want to diet, watching your kids eat will help you lose your appetite.

effort to speed the process along. I used to beg for him to grunt just a little bit to show he was making some sort of attempt at getting done. Even when the child was finished with his "work," he would just sit there on the toilet rather than go to bed. Therefore, I had to ask him if he was done every few minutes since he was not going to volunteer that information. Eventually, he would finally have to admit it out of sheer boredom or because his legs had fallen asleep.

When he is done washing up, it is then time to actually get the child into bed. Time for sleep? No. Time for books. When the child is young, in yet another sacrifice on the altar of Quality Time, you are supposed to read to your child each and every night. The big fight here is on what to read. Your child will usually have a favorite book that he wants read night after night, over and over. I don't have any clue how many times I read *Goodnight Moon*, but I was baying at it by the time I was done. I was begging for Dr. Seuss—or absolutely anything other than that freakin' moon.

Usually, the parents take turns reading to the kids. Then you've got the problem that one parent reads the story one way, and the child wants it read only that way. Maybe you don't make the right voices or don't pause at the right places, but your child will point out that it is wrong and should be tried again until it is correct. My only advice is to be the one who reads it with the most entertainment value so that it takes your spouse, rather than you, forty-five minutes to read *Curious George*.

After the stories are done, then it is still *not* time for sleep. Many children require a song. Some not only want a song, but they want to be rocked while singing the song. Therefore, you've got to lug him around like a large sack of potatoes hoping not to throw your back out in the process. You need to carry the child because you want him calm. If you let him go between the bed and the rocking chair, then he is likely to run/bounce/cartwheel over to the chair so that his adrenal gland goes into gear and he starts waking up again. It is amazing, but kids can actually expend so much energy between the bed and the chair that they'll break into a full-blown sweat.

After that point, you are ready to tuck the child in. Usually, this tucking has to be in a specific way. Heaven forbid the scratchy blanket is touching his delicate skin at all. Also, the child may always sleep with a particular stuffed animal. The big problem here is where could the stuffed animal be? It may be hiding under the covers, in the toy box, in the car, in the hamper, still at day care, temporarily transported to a parallel universe...wherever. The point is that, without that particular stuffed animal, the child is starting to get as tense as Bill Clinton at a high school cheerleader camp. He could have several dozen more animals piled up all over the room, but he will need that one in particular to go to sleep.

You therefore have to traipse around the house looking for the errant animal. If you find it, great. If you don't, then you've got to convince the child that there is nothing you can physically possibly remotely do about the situation, and so he must go to sleep. Only when he realizes that there is no way he will get that particular stuffed animal will he go to his second choice. You've then got to repeat the process, hoping to have a bit more luck finding this one than you did with the first.

So after all that, you give the kid a kiss good night and head to the television. I wish I could say that this was the end of the nightly ritual. However, many children like to sneak out of bed every several minutes just to keep you on your toes. I'd be watching television, and I'd hear a slight sound coming from the kitchen. When I'd go in, I'd see my son crouched there. Realizing he was caught, he'd offer up some lame excuse like he was still thirsty or had to go the bathroom again. I was never happy with these excuses as I don't usually leave glasses of water under the table, and I don't want him sneaking under there to do his duty.

I certainly didn't want to give him yet another final drink lest he have a vivid dream about playing in the sprinklers. I also didn't want him to go to the bathroom again because after he sat on the toilet long enough to pose for Rodin's *The Thinker* just a half hour ago, I didn't think he could even theoretically squeeze another drop out of his body. I then found myself becoming the Potty Police, checking to make sure the water was somewhat discolored so that I knew the child wasn't lying to me.

The other lame excuse is the "I forgot to tell you I love you" excuse. It is about as convincing as Tammy Faye Bakker's[344] tears or Anna Nicole Smith's[345] breasts. Whatever the excuse, you've got to get rid of it and get the kid back in bed.

If you have more than one child, you have to watch that they don't keep each other up. Sometimes, I'd hear noises upstairs, and so I'd go to check. By the time my foot hit the first step, there would be a flurry of motion, and both kids would be back in their own beds with their eyes closed. Did they think I was so stupid that after hearing the thundering noise of their running footsteps I wouldn't know they were carousing around upstairs? Actually, yes they did.

I then had to give my "stay in bed" speech to two children faking that they were already asleep. My big question here is how they were able to hear me quietly coming up the steps in the first place. All day long, I would have to say things at least three times (the third one none too softly) before they would even register that I was present in the same room with them. Now at night, they somehow had acquired bionic hearing.

---

344 Tammy Faye Bakker was the wife of a televangelist. They had a program together called the *PTL Club*, in which they would cry for things like your personal financial success—and then ask you to part with as much of it as possible to send them. Unfortunately, not only would she cry to beef up the prayer, she would wear a lot of makeup so she'd end up looking like a zombie raccoon by the time she was done.

345 Anna Nicole Smith was a plus-size model who decided that the love of her life was a billionaire sixty-two years older than her. She was twenty-six and he was eighty-nine. Some people may say love is blind, but there are four other senses, and more than a few suggested her sense of smell (of money) just may have been the overriding reason.

Things to Do in Playtime

or

Adult Knees Are Not Meant to Do This

Performing a family activity is what life is all about—doing what somebody else thinks is fun and having to go along or suffer the consequences. When your children ask you to do something with them, you rarely actually have a choice. If you say no, then you can expect your wife to say the same thing later. Of course she'll be saying no either way, but at least she'll do so less emphatically. Besides that, it is highly important to spend this time connecting with your child. It will save loads of money in therapy later on.

When your children are younger, many of their games revolve around fantasies or physical activities. Men can only wish that their own lives were the same. Stereotypically, you will have to endure pretending to enjoy tea parties with your daughters and wrestling with your sons. If your son likes make-believe, you may have to pretend you are a superhero or supervillain of some type. Now I am not saying that these activities are not enjoyable. I am saying that there are aspects of each that make it somewhat unpleasant.

Let's take the tea party example first. A tea party with your daughter is a wonderful chance to relax and bond with your daughter. Everything, however, is on the daughter's level, including the furniture. The furniture a father is supposed to sit in would be uncomfortable for Tom Thumb (or Tom Cruise), never mind someone of average to large stature. When a man sits down in one of these chairs, his back takes on a shape that would make a camel blush, and his knees are hovering in the vicinity of his ears. Drinking imaginary tea and conversing with several of the privileged stuffed animals who are also invited is all well and good. It is when the hamstrings start giving out from being in such an awkward position that things get a little touchy, and you find yourself rubbing your legs briskly in a vain attempt to force much-needed blood to the lower extremities.

When the party is over, you end up walking away like you've just returned from a cattle drive. That wouldn't be so bad, but the older you get, the less tolerant your body becomes of discomfort. If you go into work the next day limping because of an extended tea party, your coworkers will never let you live it down. There will be more "old man" comments than at a Rolling Stones concert. As years pass and coworkers come and go, rest assured that the story will pass to succeeding generations (usually at Christmas parties). Better to tell them you hurt your back clubbing baby seals than say you hurt it at a tea party.

Most men would assume that wrestling with their sons is a lot of fun. It is. Few days passed that I did not wrestle around with my boys. That actually became our primary means of communication. We couldn't pass each other in the hallway without taking some jab at each other or going for a headlock. The issue here is that as years go by, men are on a steady decline in their strength, whereas boys are on a stratospheric incline. One day you'll be playing around and they'll take their usual jab at your ribs, and you'll realize that you are truly in pain. Gone are the days that you can take everything they can dish out. Now you've got a decision to make. Do you let it be known to your child that you are indeed mortal? That you can be hurt?

Any rational person would agree that you have to tell your kids to tone it down and start pulling their punches. Of course when it comes to issues relating to masculinity, men are about as rational as

Sybil[346] on psychedelic mushrooms in a fun house. It took me several years of having one child trying to choke me into submission while the other boy was rapid-firing his fists into my spinal cord until I eventually let it be known that I indeed had a pain limit. My kids took this news not with a sigh as they realized that their father's figure could not be found among the statues of the Pantheon, but as a challenge as to when they could legitimately take out their old man. How lucky I am.

If it is a make-believe game, many kids love superheroes. They love to pick their favorite. You then become the oversized sidekick. The two of you run around the house pretending to stalk villains. Maybe it is OK if you are a young father, but men who are older have far less enthusiasm for running and crawling around the house with a towel tied to their neck for a cape. The younger fathers can tuck and roll around corners to get the jump on the evil villains. The older a guy gets, the more he offers to protect the reach (and his knees) as the kid plunges ahead and he catches up eventually.

I would like it to be known that even though a lot of what I've written has involved the usual stereotypes between boys and girls, it is fine to mix it up. Do what the kid wants to do, not what you think he or she should do. After all, you've had your childhood. It is their turn.

So let me go through a list of what boys and girls generally like for toys. One thing boys like is trucks. Get them a bulldozer, a loader, and a paver, and they are set for hours. That also means they will be providing sound effects for all the possible movements a truck can make. The truck will not be able to move more than a few millimeters without some serious engine noises. I'm not sure where kids pick up these sounds, but they usually can be heard at least two rooms over and come with enough spit flying that you can't keep any electronics within a six-foot radius.

---

346 Sybil was a girl who suffered a psychological trauma as a child and because of that developed multiple personalities—sixteen of them, to be precise. Most people would find that absolutely amazing. Well, at least guys who hope some of them may be naughty cheerleader, sultry French maid, or lonely librarian.

Another thing boys love is building stuff like Legos. Actually, it is usually not so much the building that they like but the destroying part. Boys can spend an hour trying to build a little city. They'll then build a killer space robot and lay waste to their creation in seconds. Was all that effort worth it? Considering they start rebuilding their little empire minutes later, I guess so.

Many boys also like action figures. But aren't these just dolls for boys? Sort of. However, you never see girls imagining Cabbage Patch Kids battling to the death over a lava pit. That is about all boys do with action figures: fight to the death. Naturally it goes without saying that like the trucks, these battles come complete with sound effects that spray enough saliva that you have to watch that he doesn't drown the family pet. Now, I am not one who is crazy about guns in my house, nor am I one to watch violent shows when my kids are around.[347] However, my boys managed to come up with approximately seventy-two different noises signaling gunshots, anywhere from bazookas to machine guns. Where did they learn this? Probably the same place they learned the twenty-three different ways to make noises that sound like farts.

Girls' toys are worlds different. I have already mentioned the dolls. However, that is merely the tip of the iceberg. These dolls, much like the real adult versions, must accessorize. The doll can have outfits for anything from a night on the town to going out on a safari. She'll also have campers, dream houses, and luxury boats at her disposal, not to mention a boyfriend to tag along. Combining all the materialistic goods these dolls command and their anatomically gifted bodies that make them look like they should capsize at any given moment may in hindsight not be the greatest message to implant in little girls' brains.

Girls also like dressing themselves up. When I go visit my nieces, they go through as many costume changes as a Rockettes chorus line in the course of an evening. Most of the time, they come out looking like princesses, but they'll throw in the occasional bride or Dorothy from *The Wizard of Oz*. They love these clothes. They love

---

347 Naturally, when the child is asleep, a show basically has to have violence, sex, or, hopefully, both.

the costume jewelry (the gaudier the better) to the point where they look like they'd break into rap at any second. Shoes are another big hit, especially tap shoes. One time my brother was mystified that his little daughter was able to put on her shoes all by herself for two days straight. It was only by cross-examining the older daughter that he realized the younger daughter liked them so much she was sleeping with them on.

The one unifying thing about girls' and boys' toys these days is that they come in countless pieces that are destined to be lost or stepped on. When you used to buy Legos, you'd get a box of random sizes and shapes and just start putting them together in any willy-nilly shape using a little imagination. No longer. Now many Legos come in sets with instruction booklets (not pamphlets) that take as many steps as you would estimate it would take to build a nuclear submarine. Many children get excited about building these sets, but as the enthusiasm wears off, you are supposed to step in and "help." This help starts off by you trying to get the pieces in some sort of order for them. It ends up with the kid sitting in front of the television and you building the set while mumbling profanities loud enough to make you feel better, but not loud enough so that your child can understand and tell on you. Once done, the kid then has a fun time playing with it all over the house. Needless to say, pieces are falling off here and there, so that by the time you get it back into the box, you'll never get it assembled again. Ever.

Playing Games

or

Throwing Games to Keep Him

from Losing His Mind

When children get older, toys start to give way to games. Board games are particularly popular in my household. The first board game that a kid usually gets is Candy Land. The object of Candy Land is to get to the Licorice Castle by moving ahead on colored spaces. Interspersed with the colored cards are special cards that can leap you ahead or throw you back. It is in playing these games that children learn valuable life lessons, such as trash-talking your opponent when he is losing and vociferously whining about the unfairness of life when you're not winning. Yes, kids of any age hate to lose and, yes, most men mentally still are kids.

Be that as it may, most parents have to throw the game to ensure that their child wins on a somewhat routine basis. Otherwise, you'd think the child just lost a limb in a grain thresher with the way they act. Most parents feel they should sneak in a win or two to teach the child about fair sportsmanship. Sure. Once they are done with that, they can teach piranha the benefits of vegetarianism.

A bigger problem comes when there are two children involved and they both hate to lose. Seldom do these games end without a fight. If one child is significantly older than the other, I have found it helpful to bribe the older one with candy to throw the game. Naturally, this only works if the older child can keep a secret. If he later tells the younger child he got candy *and* could have won the game, the younger child will head out on a warpath that leads right to you. You've then got to double him up with sugar so that he can lord it over the older sibling. Isn't family dynamics fun?

Candy Land is also usually the first time children learn to cheat, or at least try to cheat. If they get a card that will send them backward, they immediately get a look of panic on their face. They may try to stuff it back in the deck or somehow claim that what they are holding isn't actually the card they picked, so they have to grab another one. Throwing the game is one thing, but it never sits well with parents to let their children think that rules don't apply to them since cheaters never prosper, except in the cases of lawyers, businessmen, politicians…Huh, now I'm just trying to think of a high-paying job that *isn't* associated with cheating. Maybe I should have tried teaching the kids how to put cards up their sleeves!

Video games are extremely popular with most kids these days. My children find it fascinating that there actually were no home computers and game consoles when I was young. To them, these things are about as essential to daily life as automobiles, electric lights, and potato chips. We have a game console in our house. I was playing a game and was quite pleased with myself when I finally managed to battle to the end of a level and then beat the bad guy. My seven-year-old takes the game and is able to beat the same thing the next day. OK, that's difficult for the ego when I finally realize that something challenging for me can easily be done by a child who claims he doesn't have the hand-eye coordination to wipe his mouth with a napkin.

The next week, I come home from work and see that my four-year-old can now routinely beat it. Ouch. Now my kid is giving my ego an atomic knee drop in the technological arena. No longer do I have to throw games. It is to the point now where I can barely follow what he is doing on the screen as his spaceship nimbly avoids asteroids while wiping out armadas filled with thousands of ships. He goes into a semitrance when playing, to the point that I can only get his attention by leaping up and down frantically waving my arms while shouting his name loudly enough that a normal person could hear it even if a Harrier jet were landing. Wherefore art thou, Pac-Man?

I am now officially an embarrassment when it comes to games. There is now a popular game called Call of Duty. It is a war game where there are tons of guns. If I see an enemy, I have to stop, line it up, and then fire. As in regular war, I would have been dead by step two. Kids can jump from a building, spin, and fire backward with unbelievable accuracy. Meanwhile, I sit there spinning in a corner wondering from what angle death is going to drop my guy. I can sit there and play with a machine gun while my kid has a knife and *still* lose badly.

Everyone knows that games can be played on many devices. No longer do you have to worry about conversation in the car, at the dinner table, or for that matter whatsoever if your child has his hands on these things. He won't even acknowledge your existence on the planet when that thing is on. You could come out dressed as the queen of England doing a number from *Riverdance* and not be noticed by your child. Some parents view this as a problem since they used to like talking to their child. That's because they don't remember the conversations that usually began with phrases like "Put that down," "That's not supposed to bend that way," "No, that is not something you are supposed to put in your mouth," and the ever-popular "And you thought that was a good idea because..."

Computer games are also popular with my kids. For those adults who are afraid of computers, it is quite terrifying to see three- and four-year-olds turn on the computer, start their program, and get it running all by themselves. By the time these kids are in their teens, they'll have the capacity to take over the world with their computer expertise.[348] Our only hope is that there will be enough illicit sites on the Internet that they are continually sidetracked.

---

348 Or at least your bank account and identity.

The big problem with computer games is that they involve the computer. Unlike a game console, there is much you can do to mess it up. With a computer, they can change internal settings, wipe out the hard drive with all your files on it, or somehow turn the whole system into an expensive paperweight. Many times, my son has asked me to come in the room, and I have no idea how he has gotten the computer to do what it is doing and no idea how to get it back to the way it was. My only hope is to reboot and pray while it is coming back online that nothing done was too permanent. One time, he had somehow gotten the display to be upside down. We had to turn the screen downside up so we could search the Internet for a way to reverse it.

Section 7

Holidays

or

Are There Any Days
That Aren't for Kids?

New Year's Eve

or

A Night of Partying...Is What You

Remember This Day *Used* to Be

H ere's a holiday that really isn't a holiday as much as it is an excuse to drink.[349] The pressure used to be on to find out the cool thing to do. Where was *the* place to be? Who was going to be there? What was going to happen when everyone got there? Who was going to vomit first? Would they make it to the bathroom, or would the event be on display for the enjoyment of the entire gang? These worries are all behind you—way behind you. In years past, you could party all night and sleep all day. With children, you may want to party like the old days, but then when you think about paying babysitters, how bad you'll feel after too much to drink, and that sleep is now something to cherish, you will happily opt not to go wild.

So what are parents to do on this holiday? If they're like us, they'll most likely plunk in a movie and switch over to see the ball drop in Times Square. We'd then give each other a quick kiss and collapse in bed. It didn't take too many years to realize that seeing the ball drop

---

349 I won't even remotely get into St. Patrick's Day, which is basically a holiday to get completely obliterated while wearing green.

was about as exciting as pumping gas. Besides, trying to get the kiss earlier in the evening could at least theoretically lead to popping the champagne cork later.

If you want to celebrate with the children, then you certainly don't want them staying up till midnight. Kids are grouchy if they lose an hour of sleep. Let them stay up to see the new year, and they would be evil incarnate. Therefore, you've got to make them *believe* that they are staying up late. I know this sounds unimaginable, but there are some holidays where you try to deceive your children about some aspects of the celebration. The easiest way to fool the kids is to turn the clocks ahead by about three hours. Just remember to turn them back the next day, or you'll find your kids drinking soda and eating chips because they think it is past lunch. One other thing that is "cute" to do for the kids is to get some ginger ale and tell them it is champagne so you can all toast together. It is "cute" until they tell neighbors/teachers/clergy that you let them have alcohol, and you have to explain yourself.

Valentine's Day

or

How Many Kids Are in Your Class That We Have to Make Cards For?

Here is a holiday that isn't so much a celebration but a dilemma. What does a man have to do for his wife to prove his love on this day? Does she want chocolates, or will she not like that because she is watching her weight? Does she want flowers, or will she think this is too common and a sign that you aren't willing to put any thought into pleasing her? Does she want jewelry, or will she think it is an expensive waste of money? OK, so she'll want the jewelry, but it doesn't mean you have the cash to fork over. You can either do the cooking—and it had best be a damn sight better than microwaved hot dogs with chips[350]—or take her out to dinner and spend several hours in line at the restaurant, and then wait another hour or two for your food with the other slobs trying to remember how they romanced their wives into getting them to agree to marry them years ago.

So what about the kids? Schools usually have a Valentine's Day party. Now, it does seem a bit peculiar to get kids under the age of

---

350 Grilling them is much classier.

ten interested in the opposite sex. Usually, schools these days are doing everything humanly possible to dissuade this sort of thing, including zero-tolerance sexual-harassment policies where if kids hold hands in the playground, they basically get labeled as sexual predators and have to wear a shock collar that goes off whenever they are within ten feet of another kid during recess.

Schools don't want to have the kids show favoritism or in any possible way have any child's feelings hurt, so the rule here is that every kid has to get a valentine for every other kid in the class. So what is the whole point of a holiday about that special someone when no one is special? As far as I can tell, it is an excuse for one of the parents to make cupcakes to bring into the class.

As a parent, you may think this all sounds easy. Silly, silly, people. The first big problem is that a kid wants "cool" valentines to give out. If you wait until the week before to buy cards, the only thing left on the shelf is cute little bunny ones, and if you have a boy, that will *not* do. He may as well be handing out "kick me" cards. Therefore, you had best be in consultations with your kid on what counts as cool or not. Get his top choices and head off to a pharmacy or box store in January. If they have them, you are all set. If not, you could be hitting each and every store that *may* possibly carry them hoping to find something acceptable.

Once you do have the cards, the next big issue is that you have to get your kid to address them. He has to fill in the "To" and "From." This act could take anywhere from hours to days. First off, he or she has to select the card for each kid. If he has a pack of superhero cards, should they give the Wolverine to Billy, or is he more of a Spider-Man? If she has famous princess cards, then Billy isn't going to like it no matter what he gets. Then it is time to write their names.

Kids are notoriously bad spellers, and in the early days of writing, often get their own name wrong. You will either have kids who try to do this at a blistering speed so you would think their name was written in a code that could not be broken by top CIA specialists, or you get those who cannot abide a single mistake. Trying to spell correctly is normally a good thing, but let's say there are twenty-six kids in the class, and you have thirty cards. There are only four mistakes possible, and they can do that with the first name only.

It was bad enough when a kid's name was Bob, and they would make the letters backward and get Bod. Now, however, parents have decided to get "creative" with spellings. By creative, I mean downright ridiculous. If you have a name like Cindy, there used to be one spelling. Piece of cake for the world. Now, they can spell it Sindee, Cyndie, Syndy, Tsindea, etc. For the rest of the kid's life, she now as to spell it out for each and every person who ever has to write her name down. Painful for all involved.[351]

So you set your child up on the kitchen table with the list of names and the cards. If you walk away, you may as well drive to the store to get more cards because they will be unsalvageable. The whole "To" and "From" thing is the first thing to stump kids. They are used to school where they put their own name at the top of the paper, so that is how they will start doing the valentines. They then have to erase them or start over. Your child wasn't excited to do this the first time. Doing it again will send him into a sobbing rage. You would think writing names on cards is on par with performing an appendectomy on yourself...with kitchen utensils...that haven't been washed.

As kids will hate this task, they are easily distracted. Turn around, and they are at the television, in the fridge, hiding under the table—anything but writing. If you hover above them so that they can't leave, they go into slow motion. Kids don't understand the Band-Aid principle: if you go slowly, it is far more painful. So what should take twenty minutes is now two hours. You are feeling anything but love doing these $&# valentines!

Once they are done, the valentines need to go into envelopes. The sheer terror part here is that your kid stuffs the cards in, seals them, and then no one has any idea who they go to. If you rip them

---

351 The most painful thing in this process is parents who somehow get this ostentatious attitude like other people are dimwitted when they don't know how to spell their child's name properly. You'll get that "no, it is Jason with a 'y.'" A "y"? Where the heck are they sticking that? Just because they decided to be ridiculous with the spelling doesn't mean the rest of us should...Hold on, my editor is saying something...insulting readers... alienating...As I was saying, what a lovely, uh, gift it is to give your child a creative name.

open, you are screwed. You can try to steam them open or give up and stuff them into whatever envelopes you have around the house.

Personally, I am ready to give up at this point on the whole venture. If Cupid were in front of me, I would rip that diaper off his bottom and make him wear it as a hat. When you think this whole thing is done, when you have lost every sense of reason you once possessed and it is hours past your child's bedtime, only then will he remember that he signed you up to make the cupcakes for the party tomorrow. "Love" is in the air!

Easter

or

It Takes Money to Make

This Bunny a Honey

I know it may not be too politically correct to only discuss the Christian holidays, but I don't know enough about the other major religious holidays to give the topic justice. I know this may offend a few people, but probably not as badly as if I tried to include them. Anyway, I'll skip the religious significance and go straight to the fun stuff. After all, that's what most Christians do these days anyway.

To get ready for Easter, one of the traditions that may be dying is the coloring of Easter eggs in preparation for the Easter Rabbit. We've grown up on this, so to us, this seems like a perfectly normal thing to do. We take a breakfast food that comes from a chicken and turn it into a holiday decoration. Don't get me wrong, I think this is far more sanitary that hanging lamb chops on the wall to celebrate the holiday, but it isn't exactly what I'd call "normal behavior" either.

The history of decorating eggs dates back to at least sixty thousand years ago in Africa. Back five thousand years ago, the Sumerians used to decorate ostrich eggs with gold and silver to bury with their dead. Needless to say, these were not Easter eggs, considering Jesus didn't hit the scene for another three thousand years. Christians took over the tradition, painting eggs red like blood and using them to symbolize the tomb Jesus was buried in. Sorry, but I have a hard time with this. Just picturing yelling, "Hey, kids! Great news! Time to make little Jesus death tombs! Jimmy, grab that red paint there so we can pretend it is his blood all over it!"

We have since gotten a bit cheerier with the egg thing and now do them in a bunch of happy colors. As with nearly all traditions, if there is a way to make money from something, someone will commercialize it in a heartbeat. These days, to color eggs, you have to buy a kit. Kids can now make them psychedelic or whatever they want and even put googly eyes and costumes on them.[352]

Most unusual activities on holidays involve kids. Easter has an exception in that one of the biggies involves women, and that tradition is the Easter bonnet. For some reason on this day, women decide that fruit that you may normally find in a bowl on the kitchen table, flowers that were in the garden, and feathers that used to live happily on a bird now all belong together in some sort of haphazard fashion on top of their head. It is especially popular among elderly women, making you wonder why these large contraptions aren't snapping their poor necks.[353]

The actual day starts off with the kids waking up phenomenally early because they know the Easter Bunny has left a little present for them. This first present is usually a basket full of candy. Gracing the center of the basket is a chocolate rabbit. So here is yet another oddity—here is a rabbit getting young kids to associate "delicious" with "rabbit." Isn't that just begging some kids to turn into Elmer J. Fudd? That is like an old lady dousing herself with barbecue sauce and having her million cats lick it off her every day. Even with all the purring, at some point, they are going to turn.

---

352 Quite often, religious purists are upset at the commercialization of religious holidays. I've got to say, however, that this is an exception. If Jesus were to come back on this Earth, I think he'd far rather see cheery eggs rather than bloody reminders of him being entombed.

353 As a general rule, elderly people aren't known to exercise their necks often. They are more of a "got my eye on the road in front of me and *screw* what is behind me." This "forward thinking" may sound noble, but when they are pulling out from a side street into oncoming traffic, it can be heart pounding.

Hopefully, the kids will wake you up rather than sneak into the living room so they can eat enough chocolate that their sweat alone would be enough to put a diabetic into a coma. Let's just say that there won't be a whole lot of vitamins getting into their bodies on Easter. Don't even pretend that the amount of milk in milk chocolate will be promoting strong bones and teeth, because waving that much sugar near teeth should induce cavities.[354]

The physics of how Santa gets to all the houses with the sleigh are mind boggling. However, he has got *nothing* on the Easter Bunny. This rabbit doesn't even have $*@# arms, never mind thumbs, and yet he is able to carry baskets and eggs all over the place with a brain that is about the size of an old grape. Don't even ask how this super-human rabbit came into being or why he thought it would be a good idea to give kids candy when some of our biggest uses for rabbits are entrees in French restaurants or shooting at them with pellet guns to get them out of our gardens.

The Easter Bunny has modernized his operation over the years. In the old days, eggs were actually, well, eggs. So where did he get these eggs? Did he run chicken sweatshops where he forced chickens to pump out incredible amounts of eggs right before the holiday? These days, he usually goes with plastic eggs that he puts candy inside of. Luckily, he hasn't caught too much flak from environmentalists on the plastic thing, but at least he doesn't have to worry about the vegans breaking his kneecaps, assuming rabbits have kneecaps.

The Easter Bunny can either hide eggs inside the house or outside. These days, I think the rabbit usually has no interest bumbling outside in the dark to do anything. Ever since that wonderful invention of indoor plumbing that led to the subsequent demise of the outhouse, people have not been thrilled to leave a cozy house in the morning unless there is a fire.

Usually, the candy eggs are hidden in one room. That way, the children can obliterate just a confined area instead of destroying the

---

354 How we got from Jesus dying to chocolate bunnies and marshmallow peeps is beyond me. I'm figuring it is a dental/toothpaste company conspiracy. I don't know whether a former pope was promised a lifetime of free dentures by the dentists or what, but this is one psychedelic holiday when you think about it.

entire house. It is *very* important if you have multiple children that they are *not* allowed into the living room without parental guidance. Barricade them in their rooms if you have to—but the rule is that no one can go *near* the room or even look into it unless the parents give the nod. Otherwise, as soon as the Easter egg hunt starts, the early riser "magically" knows where all the eggs are, and the other children are left with empty baskets and full heads of vengeance.

That means that the kids know that they need to wake you before anything good is going to happen. There may be a knock on your door at 4:30 a.m. asking if it is time to go downstairs yet. Try not to swear on holidays. Order them back to bed. Sometimes, you get lucky and they go back to sleep. Most of the time, they will knock every fifteen minutes until you can't take it anymore and pry your near-lifeless body out of bed. One confounding issue is that if there is an age gap so you have a teen and a young child, you know with absolute certainty that the older kid will not only not want to be woken up early, but be physically incapable of doing so. Light a pack of fireworks and toss it into his room, throw in a few rabid raccoons, jack up one side of the bed so he is clinging to the mattress at a ninety-degree angle—if you can't sleep, you may as well get the party started.

You would think it is worse with a giant age gap. You would be wrong. When two kids are separated by a year or two, there is far more anxiety in the household. The problem here (as there always is a problem) is that there is competition between the kids, and the older child is inherently better at finding eggs than the younger child is. Personally, I was perplexed that the children could find any eggs whatsoever since they usually couldn't find their own shoes when they were on their own feet.

So you have the potential of one kid whipping around the room and the other one spinning around crying. Sometimes, the older kid will just watch the younger one's eyes, and when the younger one spots an egg and goes for it, they just outrace them to the spot. So what is a parent to do? Help the younger one cheat! When the older child isn't looking, you can point to where an undiscovered egg is. Let's say the egg is under a couch cushion. You can point to the couch. The child will get there, not see it sitting in plain view, and cry.

You then have to mime reaching under a cushion, all without attracting the attention of the older child.

The other alternative is that the kids are only allowed to find so many eggs each so that they get an equal amount. In some houses, the Easter Bunny is so sophisticated that he brings each child a particular colored egg so that the child only finds that and leaves the others. Great for being equal. Bad if one kid sucks at finding eggs. If you allow kids to eat while the other one is still hunting, they do a sort of taunting candy dance. They will sashay around the room until the kid hunting breaks down in tears or physically attacks them. If you make them all wait, they will mutter unflattering things under their breath until…well, he breaks down in tears or physically attacks them. It is up to you to keep things moving along. You can point or do the "warmer/colder" trick. If that doesn't work, you can attach strobe lights to the egg so the kid can find them.

You would think when some kids get older that the Easter Bunny should get more devious in where the eggs are hidden. Sounds like a good plan, but not when it meets the hard facts. Kids peak in their egg-hunting skills early in life, unless they are trying to steal them from a sibling, and then they are little Billy the Kids. Otherwise, not so much…Older kids wander around the room like zombies, apparently unaware that you may have to move something to find an egg or that it may not be directly at eye level. If they can find them from the vantage point of sitting on the couch, they are all set. For these kids, you can make the hunt less painful by taping all the eggs to the television screen so they can find them. Otherwise, expect a saga on par with the search for the Holy Grail for these kids to find a dozen brightly colored eggs in a fifteen-by-fifteen-foot room.

Another problem is that the kids are eating the eggs as fast as they can find them. By the time they usually have breakfast, they will have consumed their entire weight in chocolate and can't look at something healthy without vomiting. That would be fine if you had a giant hamster wheel for them to work off all this energy. However, you don't. Instead you have walls that you will be sheetrocking once the holiday is over. The children will be bouncing off of them all day long like Daffy Duck on a bad acid trip.

For some strange reason, the parents seem to know exactly how many eggs were hidden.[355] Whether they have some psychic connection to the rabbit or some other sort of intuition, it is good to let the kids know so they can either keep going or know when to stop. That is the easy part. The much harder part is that the parents *should* know where all the eggs are hidden, but by morning, that is no longer the case. Therefore, when there are only two or three eggs left, the parents often have to join in the hunt.[356]

The next question on Easter is where families gather for Easter dinner. If relatives are coming to your house, your wife is going to be phenomenally busy cooking something like a ham dinner. It is best not to have it around lunchtime as the kids won't be able to touch any additional food. The trick is that you somehow have to hide their candy midmorning so they can eventually work up some sort of legitimate appetite. You then have to run around behind them cleaning up in their wake.

In the end, it proves the axiom that holidays are for kids. For adults, it is about a whole lot more work. The Easter Bunny had best be on top of things! Things will *not* go well if you have the candy but don't have the basket. It will not be the same if the candy is presented in a plastic grocery bag. Sleep and money become a little scarce around the holiday season. Speaking of money, I'm not sure when Easter turned into Christmas Part II. When I was young, the Easter Bunny hid eggs with candy inside and gave us a basket of candy featuring a chocolate bunny. We were all quite happy with that. Now, however, there are often presents in the basket. When the hell did this happen? How does the Easter Bunny even carry these things, never mind get his paws on them in the first place? And why? When did a whole crap load of candy become not enough?

---

355 OK, so this is a *huge* tip here. There may be some "traditionalists" out there who hide actual eggs. By "traditionalist," I mean nut job. First off, if you don't at least hard-boil them, you are asking for serious trouble on par with flossing with a weed whacker. Second, if you do, you still invariably won't find at least one. You lose a candy one, no problem, but a real egg is going to stink eventually. The child will "find" the egg when he accidentally falls on it, crushing it forever into the carpet.

356 Do *not* trust your children when you ask how many eggs they have found. If they miscount, you can be looking forever for the egg that doesn't actually exist. Been there. Done that.

Mother's Day

or

For What She Does for 364 Days, She Had *Best* Have One Day!

Children get a little bit of righteous indignation when holidays come around that are "exclusive," meaning the world doesn't revolve around them for several daylight hours. They will make no bones about their belief that if there is a Mother's Day, then to have cosmic balance, there should also be Kids' Day. You then have to remind them exactly how many presents Santa left for them or how many eggs they were allowed to find. Every holiday is Kids' Day, along with nearly every weekend day. Don't try to guilt them with that fact because it will backfire and every weekend day they will proudly exclaim it Kids' Day and try to get away with doing as little as possible.[357] It's bad enough trying to get them to put their laundry in the basket without them walking around acting like they are royalty.

To a father, Mother's Day starts off several days earlier than the actual day. Why is this? Because women like sentimentality, and that is a bad thing. Sentimentality means extra work and thinking on your part, things that most men like to avoid like herpetic lesions. You see,

---

357 Technically, they don't do much on the usual weekend day, but it is much worse when they admit out loud that they shouldn't have to.

the kids need to be involved in the decision-making process. Kids can't even decide on what cartoon to watch in the morning, and now you're expected to bring them to the mall to pick something for their mother. You will have to go to the stores with them and point them in the correct directions. If you don't point them in the right direction, go look for them in the toy section.

Usually it is best if you have an idea of what she wants and then convince the kids it was their idea. How do you know what she wants? Hopefully, she convinced you somehow so you think it is your idea. Otherwise, you and the kids end up going into jewelry stores and picking out cheap jewelry that is gaudy enough to make Liberace giggle. If you turn your back, the kids may get your wife an eight-pound bag of candy gummy worms, a video game featuring hacking up mummies with chainsaws, or some other gift that would get your wife into a very, very bad mood.

Once you have a gift, you need a card. What are you doing going to the stationery store? No, you're not that lucky. Instead, the children should make the card. Why? A homemade card is more *sentimental*. Mothers want cards that they will cherish so much that they'll save them forever. She'll have a bureau of cards, art projects, drawings, etc., that you will have to cart with you every place you move till death do you part. Therefore, you've got to find a time when your wife is not around (next to never) and your kids are willing to take time out of their busy schedule of watching TV, playing computer games, and trying to kill each other (even closer to never).

Hopefully, your wife will go out shopping at some point, and you can physically threaten the children with bodily harm if they don't do something nice for their mother. You then have to supply crayons, construction paper, and scissors. Don't leave them unsupervised—it's not so much the fear of them doing anything dangerous with the scissors as them drawing fighting ninjas that is the problem. Keep them on the basic heart theme, and if they are going to accessorize, a simple arrow will do rather than fighter planes attacking it with missiles.

Mother's Day starts off with the mom being able to sleep in. While she's downstairs, the husband and children then have to estimate when she is going to get up because it is always nice to cook her breakfast in bed. If it is cooked too early, she doesn't get a chance to relax.[358] Too late, and she is going to be really ticked if she has to pretend to be asleep for most of the day because she knows breakfast is coming. Yes, it is Mother's Day, and yes, your wife is not your mother, so, technically, you don't have to help with the cooking. But when she is crunching on shells in her scrambled eggs or trying to swallow toast that is steeped with jelly to hide the fact that it is burned beyond recognition, she will eat it, but she may accidentally leave some rancid milk on your side of the bed come Father's Day. If it is really bad, the milk may be joining you in the bed.

So what does a mother want to do with her family on Mother's Day? Nothing. Actually, less than nothing. My wife didn't want to see, hear, smell, or touch the kids. After wiping their butts all year long and playing referee during brawls between the children, this is the day she takes off from being a mother. Your job is to isolate the children from her. No matter what their complaint is, you've got to get the kids hushed up before your wife has to deal with them. Gag them if need be, but keep them quiet and away from your wife. If your wife is outside, keep them inside. If she's inside, get them outside. If the kids are in that whiny type of mood, then you've got to get them out of the house even if the wind chill is near stripping the flesh off their bones.

The best way for a woman to not see the children is to not be in the house. She can go out with other mothers shopping or with her own mother since her actual mother would like this now that she isn't an annoying kid anymore. The most enjoyable day is to spend the hours forgetting the last few years of stretch marks, wiping snotty noses, and cooking for ingrates who would rather have a nuked bowl of Chef Boyardee. When the afternoon is over, it is back to semireality for the woman.

To break her back into motherhood gently after a day's reprieve, it is nice to take her out to dinner. If you haven't booked a month ahead of time, all the best restaurants will be full, and you'll be lucky

---

358 With kids under five, it is a serious problem that they will wake their mother up super early so their mothers don't miss a blessed second of their special day. For teenagers, you'd be lucky if they got up in time to make their mother lunch.

to get a pizza delivered on time. If you show up with a pizza, the topping had better be jewelry. Hopefully you'll overhear a few women in the office talking about how they had best not be disappointed yet again on Mother's Day so that it will jog your memory into doing something. You should book at a restaurant that has a hostess, menus, and nonpaper plates. Whatever you do, don't look at the prices. If she wants lobster, she can have lobster. If you look at the prices and gawk, she won't be happy. Yes, you could clearly save money by eating at home, but the labor rates go up phenomenally on Mother's Day. You may not pay with cash, but it will come out of your hide in the end.

Father's Day

or

You May Want Something Special from the Kids, but You *Really* Want Something Special from Your Wife

In your mind, Father's Day should be the same as Mother's Day with the roles reversed. Maybe you'd like to kick back while being pampered by your family. In the old days, they'd go grab your slippers and fetch you the newspaper. Well, the only time a guy is in slippers these days is if he isn't allowed sneakers because they are afraid he will try to hurt himself with the shoelaces. And newspapers have gone the way of music cassettes and the ability to drive to the corner store without a GPS. So what does your family get you? Let's just cross your fingers that they remember.

So once you do remind them of what day it is, do you get to go out and do something manly? Nope. Per the definition supplied by your wife, Father's Day is the day where you spend every last moment with your children being a father. What about doing what you want to do? As long as it is with your children, is something they want to do, and does not involve watching the television, that is fine. You'll be outside running around with them spending quality time while your poor wife has to stay in the house or go out with her friends or mother. So exactly how does Father's Day differ from Mother's Day? One is in May, while the other is in June.

One of the great inconsistencies between Mother's Day and Father's Day is that schools go crazy with projects for Mother's Day. They are making cards, writing poems, and making pottery ashtrays for their mothers even though no one in the house smokes. So what happens on Father's Day? Oh, that's right—Father's Day happens in June when either schools are out or the kids are studying for finals so there is jack squat time for arts and crafts for the dad. I smell conspiracy and it isn't pretty. My current theory is that Hallmark has something to do with it. They knew guys aren't crazy about cards, so they dumped the holiday in June where it could get lost with graduation cards—if men don't want cards, then they don't deserve anything!

You may be able to request a favorite meal from your wife or go out to a favorite restaurant. Maybe. The guy may want to go out to a sports restaurant where there are a million televisions all tuned to different sports channels all blaring so loud that no conversation is possible. Bliss. Do you need to make a reservation? The only way these restaurants are busy is if there is a playoff game. The good news is that you can get a beer without a dirty look. A second beer gets a raised eyebrow. A third is a severe clearing of the throat. A fourth, and you will best be hoping the couch isn't lumpy.

Come night, you may want to reenact what got you to be a father to begin with. That is absolutely fine! "Wanting" is no issue whatsoever. "Getting" is another thing entirely. After all, it isn't Husband's Day.

Fourth of July

or

Kids & Explosives: What Could Go Wrong?

O ne of the traditional things to eat on this day is a barbecue. It is one of the rare times where the women can sit back and let the men do the work. I should put in a quick pause here to let married women recover from the sarcastic guffawing to the downright nausea that the previous sentence produced. After all, it was the women who did all the shopping. If the meat was marinated, that was probably the woman, too. If there are shish kabobs, the woman cut the meat and veggies to do all the assembling. So what has the guy done? He turned on the barbecue[359] and then put the

---

359 In this day and age, you don't even need to make a pile of charcoal briquettes, spray it with highly volatile carcinogenic liquid, and then drop a match in, hoping that you can dive back in enough time to keep your eyebrows. Instead, gas grills have become the rage. All you need to do is open up the gas, hit the starter, and you are good to go. Well, you are good to go if you actually remembered to turn off the gas from the previous outdoor activity or you simply ran out—which is not really your fault, so your father-in-law shouldn't need to look at you like you are telling the story of the first time you and his little girl were intimate. Just because you may have run out of propane at his grandson's birthday party and had to go store to store on a Sunday desperately trying to find a place open while the hungry guests waited around does not make you a loser. OK, I still have some issues to get over here.

meat on it. All he has to do is look at it thoughtfully every now and again and turn it around so it cooks enough that people don't get food poisoning.

For this effort, the guy gets the congratulations for a job well done, and the woman gets the pleasure of cleaning up the mess. Hey, it is like at Thanksgiving where the woman does phenomenal amounts of work, but the guy is the one that carves the turkey. We can trust women with every other appliance in the kitchen, but a big knife? Nope, the guy has got to cut in and do the heavy lifting yet again before he eats and goes back to watching the football games.

The big thing about this day is the fireworks at night. Kids love them, so it is a good activity and sounds inexpensive since towns usually don't charge people to look up when they are firing them off. To get a good seat, you usually have to arrive hours ahead of time. Make that hours and hours. When you get to the field, you then need to lay a towel down to stake out your territory. Of course kids don't want to stay still for minutes, never mind hours. Therefore, they'll go trundling off, and you've got to keep one eye on them and one eye on your spot. Naturally, thousands of other people have had the same idea, so the place looks like a G-rated Woodstock with towels everywhere. If you can see a blade of grass, someone is going to try to put a towel on it and crowd the surrounding ones a bit more.

By the time the fireworks are about to start, you've got to pry the kids off the jungle gym without dislodging the surrounding several dozen children. It is like trying to pluck out a particular feather from a chicken running around the yard. Why not just call them and have the little angels run over to you? Because, angels that they are, you may believe in them, but you don't actually expect them to perform a miracle just because you ask. Now the kids usually need to go to the bathroom. Unless you want to walk a half mile or so to a restaurant and pretend you want to eat there along with the eighteen families in front of you, then you've got to head to the infamous porta-potty.

Since there are hundreds to thousands of people gathered in the same location, many of whom are adults who were or are imbibing copious amounts of alcohol, the line is going to be phenomenally long. If you've been to Disney, you are used to a line this long that ends with something like the Pirates of the Caribbean or the Haunted Mansion. In this case, you wait just as long and end up instead staring into a hole filled with bodily excrement and smelling so bad that your stomach starts going into miniretches. If nothing else, it is a great abdominal workout.

After a night like this, just looking at the toilet seat may make your skin want to leap off your body rather than make contact with it. Some men don't aim well, but the drunk ones don't even try. Once it is your turn, you have to go in with the child, as he or she is going to want to touch things in there, and after what that little plastic shack has experienced in this night alone, you'd probably cringe every time you hugged your child the rest of your life. Now, these stalls are not meant for two people, so it becomes very easy to bump into things accidentally. If this happens, just make a mental note to burn this clothing prior to entering your home.

Hopefully, your child is male and has to urinate. If he is too short, you can pick him up and aim his entire body. If it is a girl or the child has to poop, you have got to pick them up into a modified hovering position. Please be careful with this, however, as if the level in the porta-potty is high, you don't want to have the falling poop cause a splash-back on you. Once done, the necessary paper work must be finished as you'd expect. Since there is no sink, it is an ironclad guarantee that the lock on the unit has been touched by hands that are less than immaculate. Therefore, I always make it a point to try to open the door with my foot. If that can't be accomplished, an elbow or the hand wrapped in unused toilet paper are the next-best options. Once you are out, you can breathe that blessed fresh air again. Even if you are next to low tide at a beach that is a medical waste dump, it is still a step up.

After that, you've got to make your way back to the blanket. Since it is getting close to the right time, everyone else is sitting down. Afraid that your child is going to step on a dozen or so people, you've got to pick him up and do a human hopscotch. Now, if your kid had stepped on someone, that would have been considered rude. If you step on someone while carrying your kid, the added weight should be an easy lawsuit.

Eventually, you'll get back to the blanket. By now, you've got families on every border. Hopefully, the blanket wasn't "accidentally" scrunched up by other people getting a little more room for themselves and then acting nonchalant about it. If so, the kids may have to be in your lap. Either way, they may end up there in a minute anyway, for here is the moment of truth. Some kids just love the fireworks, and some kids hear those first explosions and act like they're being shelled and their lives are in imminent danger. They'll dive into your lap and try to burrow into it until they reach your pancreas.

For those kids who love it, it is a piece of cake. For those kids who don't, you've got to try to cover their ears and point their heads up so that they can get a glimpse and realize they just may like them. Just make sure the rest of their body turns with the head, or you may hear a snap, and then your extended family will be seeing you on the 11:00 news. If you refused to allow an anxious child to use the porta-potty, you may both end up looking like you had an accident as his bleeds through his shorts and onto your lap.

The evening certainly doesn't end with the grand finale. Instead, it ends with a giant throng of people trying to wind their way to the parking lots. If you thought it was difficult keeping track of your children before the fireworks started, you are in for a new level. This is like trying to grab popcorn as it is popping. You've got to grab on to them and not let go, or they will be swept out in a sea of suntanned, sweaty bodies. No, it doesn't end there either. Once you do manage to get to your car, you've then got to wait in a line of traffic you'd normally see when OJ takes his Bronco out for a drive.[360] Naturally it is at that time that your child will announce he or she needs yet another potty break.

---

360 For those with limited memories, O. J. Simpson was a famous football player accused of killing his wife and her friend. The evidence started to pile up against him, and so he was supposed to turn himself in to the police. Instead, he decided to go for a drive. When he was spotted, he ended up being followed by police cars and then helicopters. By the end, he had over twenty helicopters and 95 million people watching on television as he crept along the highway. OJ's friend called from the car claiming that OJ was suicidal. As you'd expect with most attempted suicides, they found a bag of cash and fake moustaches in the car after. In a striking bit of coincidence, he was headed for the Mexican border. Maybe he was going to do himself in by eating tainted tacos.

Halloween

or

Trick or Buckets of Treats

Here is a holiday that has become controversial in recent years. Some people believe that this holiday is teaching kids about the dark arts. No, I am not kidding. Somehow, some people believe that if a kid wears a witch costume, she will want to become an actual witch. Really? So if she dresses up like an M&M, will she want to go around and chisel holes in other children's teeth? In the history of Halloween, has there ever been a child who put on a vampire costume and then thought it was a good idea to bite someone's neck? Unless there is video evidence of Marv Albert as Dracula, I rest my case.[361]

I'm more worried that Halloween teaches them about begging and bribery than anything to do with evil. Heck, by that logic, if I dress my boys in nice shirts/pants/ties, they should automatically

---

361 One of the great sportscasters of our time was a guy named Marv Albert. He didn't play basketball, yet he is still in the Basketball Hall of Fame. He made up the amazingly innovative catch phrase "Yes!" With talent like that, how could they deny him the hall? He did get into a bit of trouble when some woman claimed that he raped and bit her on the back. As with most back bites, you normally expect that they are self-inflicted by the supposed victim. Unfortunately for Mr. Albert, apparently they found his DNA in her wounds. Maybe she was able to find a lot of letters he was writing to orphans in under-privileged countries and used the saliva he used to lick the envelopes to wipe over her body. Maybe not.

start behaving themselves because they are dressed properly. Right? And if I put a beret on their heads, that will help so much with French class. Let's face it—the people who complain have far too much time on their hands and don't want kids engaging in anything that would actually cause them to have more fun than could be had wallpapering the hall. Licking stamps may be a bit too risqué for them since it involves the tongue actually leaving the mouth.

The big decision here is what the kids want to dress up as. When I was a kid, it used to be easy. The parents would take you to a store that had a bunch of cheesy plastic masks and a cloth that you'd drape over yourself that would say what you were in case people couldn't figure it out. You'd then spend the night trying to get enough air through those little holes near your nostrils to keep you conscious. Even though the temperature may be frigid so your body was suffering from hypothermia, you found out just how much your face could sweat since none of that air was circulating. Since everyone did the same thing with these costumes, it was easy to get ready for Halloween (except for those kids who passed out during).[362] These days, the costumes are *far* more elaborate. There are now stores that specialize in fancy costumes—with fancy prices.

Therefore, you've got to get them something decent. One problem is that kids may want to be something that could be embarrassing in later years. One year, my son wanted to go as Pikachu. To those people who know him, Pikachu was a very popular cartoon character who was able to fight other monsters by shooting electric bolts. However, to other people, he looked like a giant yellow mouse. Knowing it would be difficult to explain it to my parents and, more importantly, to my son in later years when he would ask why I let him do that (as his mother showed his date embarrassing pictures), I took it upon myself to talk him out of it. Trust me, he'll thank me for it later.

---

362 For those years that you had a cold, the snot would block up the holes by the time you got to the second house. At that point, you had to wear the mask on the top of your head and then pull it back down when you got to the door, collect the goods, and then get back to the street to pull it back up before your eyes rolled back into your head.

Far worse than that are the costumes for girls. If you have a girl who goes trick-or-treating, expect to be horrified. The costumes have—I kid you not—all become "sexy." They have sexy cats with leggings, sexy witches showing more exposed thigh than the Thanksgiving turkey, princesses with cleavage, etc. Let's make this simple: young girls' costumes should *not* make girls look like they are in training to be hookers. I would absolutely love to get the manufacturers of those costumes and make it a requirement that if they aren't willing to let their own mother and spouse wear that same outfit for a week going to supermarkets, work, etc., then they aren't allowed to sell it to children.[363]

Halloween has become much bigger in recent years and now is one of those days when the house *needs* to be decorated, much like Christmas. Don't ask me why. Your wife freaks out all year long whenever she sees a spider's web, and now she is making you put up artificial ones in every doorframe so you have to crawl to get out of a room. If you go to the store, you can buy fake tombstones with little hands pretending to dig their way out of a grave, motion-activated skulls that start talking when someone walks by, and all other sorts of ghoulish gifts. The truly scary thing, though, is the price of all this crap. The real heart-stopping moment of Halloween is when you go to the checkout counter. If you go to the store the day after Halloween, you can back a truck up and throw your pocket change at them to haul the stuff away.

Here is an unusual tradition. You go down to the grocery store and try to find this large fruit. This fruit can be used to make delicious pies. Instead, however, you are going to dig it out and cut holes in it so that it can then rot on your front doorstep. Wouldn't the people in Ethiopia love to hear about that tradition? OK, it is not as scary as how that circumcision tradition must have started, but it is still a little crazy.[364]

---

363 I'm not here assuming at all that the costume executives are men. If they are women, their husbands should wear it and that will really cut down on the skimpiness (we'd hope).
364 Actually, there are good reasons for circumcisions. The first is smegma. What is smegma? It is dead skin, oil, and sweat that can collect under the foreskin. If not cleaned appropriately, it can smell and cause an infection. Now, boys are usually endlessly fas-

Whenever I opened that pumpkin up, I thought my kids would dive into it because they usually like doing things that make a mess and get their hands dirty. Instead, they wouldn't do it because they thought it was icky. Icky? These were the same kids who would pick someone else's nose on a dare. So good ol' dad had to scoop out all the pumpkin goop until they got older and realized it wasn't icky. Then, however, they were just sloths and *still* didn't want to do it.

It then comes time to carve the pumpkin. That used to be pretty simple. You just decided whether it was going to be a happy face or a scary face and then hacked away at it. Triangles are easy, so the nose and eyes were combinations of triangles. Now, they have these intricate silhouettes that you can somehow sketch onto the pumpkin. Personally, if my kids were to ask me to carve one of these new designs, I would state that it looked too commercial for me and I liked the old-school designs, but the truth is that it just looks much too involved for me to really attempt. I would almost feel like paying the neighborhood ruffians to kick in the intricately designed jack-o'-lanterns for showing the rest of us poor, lazy slobs up.

When the day arrives, the kids get all dressed up, and then there are enough pictures taken that you'd think they were off to Frankenstein's wedding. When the kids are young, one parent has to stay at home to hand out the candy to the neighborhood children, and the other has to go out with the kids. Not leaving a parent home means that there may be more tricks on your house since there aren't any treats. Dishing out the candy is pretty easy. You can watch something mindless and be interrupted every few minutes. Some guys like to get into it and dress up and scare the children that come to the door. That's considered all right for the older kids, but you've got

---

cinated with their "little buddy." However, it is another thing entirely to make sure they clean it appropriately when in the tub. By appropriately, I mean it will never ever get done unless they are forced into the matter. What has been unusual is how dramatic circumcision has been in reducing the spread of HIV. Now, here is where you need the greatest marketing people of all human history—groups like the World Health Organization have to go get grown men to agree to painfully getting the skin of their penis voluntarily cut off.

to watch out that the crowd doesn't include one or two young ones who will lose bladder control.[365]

There will be some older—much older—kids who go out trick-or-treating these days as well. Their enthusiasm for dressing in costumes is not particularly high and may consist of wearing a baseball cap backward and being a rapper or sideways and being a gangsta (correct spelling). Be guaranteed that the cap will not have the bill pointing forward. You may have a temptation to kick these kids off your lawn. If you do, you better hope there is a bus stop near your house so you can get to work the next morning because your tires will be flatter than a steamrolled pancake. It is best just to give them the candy and leave it at that. It is difficult scraping dried eggs off a breakfast plate. It is impossible getting them off your car. If you really want to stand on principles, be my guest, as long as you don't mind standing on a ladder afterward trying to get the toilet paper out of your trees.

If you get to go out with your kids, that can be fun.[366] You trundle up to the doors of the neighbors you know, and they pass out the candy. When the kids are young, sometimes they are nervous, so they may be embarrassed to knock on the door or say anything. My middle son was like that—until he realized what he was getting for his efforts. After that, you'd see that three-year-old plowing down eight-year-olds to get the goods. When the kids get older, they reach the point where they are embarrassed to have a parent along (or even to let other children know they technically have parents). Therefore, you've got to hang around near the street pretending like you just happened to be taking a late-night stroll and it is only the wildest of

---

365 One year in my younger days, I dressed up as a mad scientist (not much of a stretch for the people who know me). I made up colored solutions and plopped in dry ice so that all sorts of things were bubbling and smoking. The kids thought I was cool (yes, there is a first for everything). However, many parents flipped out and threw themselves between the kids and my door as if things were about to explode. No doubt, those parents probably tossed the candy I gave them by the time they left the apartment building.

366 There are exceptions to this. If it is a blistering cold rain or you live in a northern state that is experiencing a cold snap that will frostbite any exposed skin, the level of fun plummets enormously. It also becomes difficult for the kids to wear their costume since you've got to put warm clothes on underneath. If your child is a ballerina, then she ends up looking like someone from the former women's East German swim team in a tutu.

coincidences that your kids happened to be nearby. If people don't call the cops on "that creepy-looking guy staring at these kids," consider yourself fortunate.

When the trick-or-treating is done, the kids then try to stuff as much of the loot down their throats as they can before you stop them. Personally, I think it is OK to have them indulge a bit. However, when the candy wrappers pile up to around midshin level, it is a good idea to cut them off. Of course if you ate that much, you'd either be doing sit-ups two hours a day for the next week or be poking extra holes in your belt to make it fit, not that there is any way your pants would be coming off without a potato peeler.[367]

---

367 There is what I refer to as a "parental tax." You took your kids out and got them their costumes (OK, so your wife got them the costume), so you naturally should enjoy a smidgeon of the fruits of their labor. You start off by eating the ones you know your kid isn't fond of. However, it is a slippery slope as you then eat the ones they *may* not be fond of. Before long, you've got your head stuck in the plastic pumpkin, and you are bumping around the kitchen trying to find a knife to saw it off your own head as you *certainly* aren't going to call for help!

Thanksgiving

or

Pilgrims? What Football Team Are They the Mascot For?

T hanksgiving is a day that somewhat confuses kids. It is an actual holiday that doesn't revolve around them. Nobody is fawning over them. There is not even a reason to get themselves (and you) up at 5:00 a.m. Instead, it is just two days off from school. They may be thankful for that. However, you aren't so thankful that you've had to spend the last three nights making a Pilgrim/Native American diorama.[368] There are two choices on

---

368 What is a diorama, you may ask? Some may describe it as a 3-D model. I describe it as hell on Earth. Basically, kids take a box, put it on its side, draw pictures of things, cut them out, and then stand them up in the box to make a scene. Now, anyone who already has kids is laughing hysterically right about now. Why? Because I said the kids will be doing it. In the history of school dioramas, I don't know if one has *ever* been completed without a parent's "help." Help can range anywhere from a parent doing 100 percent of the project all the way down to 95 percent of the project. I've got my own job. It keeps me *very* busy. I really don't need to be finding pictures on the Internet that I can print, glue to cardboard, cut out, and then tape to a box and—without the ability of a magic wand—have it stand up and make it all the way to school. It is tedious. It is painful. However, the worst part is that even *if* the kid did it, I don't know what the &$#@-ing thing is supposed to teach them. If a teacher wants them to know about the first Thanksgiving, they can teach them about it, have them read it, hell, I'm sure there is a %#%#-ing video on YouTube of someone re-creating it. What does a diorama possibly teach? Maybe that

Thanksgiving: your family will be hosting the holiday meal, or you will be traveling a long distance cooped up in a car. For a man, the choice is basically whether your kids will be in a bad mood or your wife will.

It may sound like a wonderful idea to be surrounded by family and friends in your own home, but your wife would rather be surrounded in a hyena den wearing zebra-skin underwear. It is not that she doesn't like the company of everyone; it is just that she feels the pressure to prepare a meal fit for the British royal family and to step out of the kitchen looking like she just came from a shoot for *Glamour* magazine. She will fret about cooking this meal the entire month of November. What will she cook? Who will sit next to whom? If the turkey isn't properly done, does homeowner's insurance cover *Salmonella* outbreaks? It gets so bad that if you were to randomly poke her while she was sleeping, she'd bolt upright and scream something about being chased by a can of cranberry sauce.

If indeed you will be hosting the dinner, your wife will start stocking up food roughly two weeks before the event. To you, it will look like she is preparing for a nuclear winter. To her, it is nothing less than a referendum on whether she is a modern woman who can balance the demands not only of work but also of family—or if she is a failure in life, only pretending to be a proper mother and wife. If the man's mother comes and she is picky, then the pressure is really on. If the wife's mother comes over and is picky, well, that is often par for the course any day of the year.

A significant note of caution here: sometimes there is an underlying thread of competition between the woman who has taken care of the man all these years by dressing him, babying him when he is sick, cutting up his food, etc., and his mother. At no point should the man state that one of the women is a better cook than the other one

---

life is like a box of chocolates. Sometimes you get one you like, and other times you can get one with a metal filing in it that chips your tooth, but you can't go to the dentist to glue it back on because you accidentally swallowed it, so you have to wait for it to pass through your digestive tract and monitor your stool to find it, and when you do and sterilize it, it doesn't quite have the right shape when the dentist glues it back in…and *that* is how much I hate dioramas.

even if the answer is pathetically apparent. Your wife could set off the smoke alarms not only in your house but in the house next door, and you should still eat the meal like it was ambrosia sent down from the heavens by the gods themselves. If your mother is bringing over her "special potato salad" that you "loved" as a kid even though you have abdominal cramps for two days after touching it, you better put a healthy dollop on your plate.

It should also go without saying that the house should be immaculate when people are coming over for the holidays. By immaculate, I mean that everything should be shoved into the closets the night before or the morning of. Any carpets need a vacuum swept over them. If one of the kids' (all of the kids') rooms looks like a flop house for crack addicts, best to weld the door shut to prevent visitors from walking in to put their coats down somewhere. You do *not* want the topic of the dinner to be how you should be raising your children better, especially if there are wine and sharp utensils all within easy reach.

If you are traveling on the holiday, the problem here is that it is the biggest travel day of the entire year. You can expect traffic to be backed up on every single highway, street, road, and sometimes driveway. Where all these cars are hidden all year long is beyond me. It is like every community has underground bunkers of cars waiting to spring into action as soon as this holiday is rolled out.

You can also travel by plane. Contrary to popular belief, airfare tickets can still be purchased up till the last minute. However, they will cost approximately as much as the home you are going to visit. Expect to get to the airport several hours early if you have any hope at all of getting through security. It is even money that you will be behind a person who didn't know you needed to bring a valid driver's license to get on the plane. You will then be behind a person going through security who not only doesn't know about taking out liquids prior to going through the detector, but has no idea about the metal thing so at first doesn't take off anything, and then when he realizes he is not doing something right, decides to overcompensate and get down to his skivvies to make sure he's got everything that could set the alarm off. Oh, and if there is snow at any airport in the country, the flight delays will magically ripple from shore to shore.

So let's assume that everyone is together and it is Thanksgiving Day. In the morning, the kids are all looking forward to the Macy's Thanksgiving Day Parade. They'll be so excited to see all the wild parade fun. Actually—that is what you *think* will happen. The kids today couldn't give a rat's butt about parades. You may sit them down in front of the television for tradition's sake. When the parade begins, however, the kids realize that it is a bunch of boring bands and floats that are now nothing more than commercial advertisements.[369] The only things that some of the smaller kids seem to think are pretty cool are the giant balloons of cartoon animals. Unfortunately, when the Snoopy balloon comes out, you may be excited to point him out, but most of the kids don't even know who the heck he is these days. That is when you go into the next room and cry for a little while.

Usually the Thanksgiving scene premeal looks like something out of junior high: all the guys are chatting in one room, and all the women are in another. Usually the women take over the kitchen so that the ones cooking don't miss any of the juicy gossip. I know that sounds stereotypical of me to talk about the women in the kitchen, but that's the way it is in 99.99 percent of households. The women know that if men were in charge of the Thanksgiving meal, they'd be having turkey subs and, if they were lucky, some Stovetop Stuffing on the side.[370]

So what do the men talk about while the women are discussing family affairs? Anything but. Men hit topics like any new purchases with motors, sports events, and any other topic that does not really impact anyone's personal life significantly. Meanwhile, the kids, behaving in the community spirit that is Thanksgiving, are teasing the living crap out of each other because they have lost all interest whatsoever in the parade.

---

369 Sorry, but I don't need to see floats where they reenact Pocahontas giving corn to the Pilgrims and, in turn, she gets a debit card with no transaction fees. Kill me now.

370 I am *not* complaining about Stovetop Stuffing. I love the stuff. My brother and I lived off that, macaroni and cheese, and Hamburger Helper when we roomed together. When we had more than one thing on our plate at the same time, that was high gourmet for us.

So when it is dinnertime, the whole family bellies up to the table. Usually the table is not big enough to fit the whole crowd. When this happens, there is an accessory location known as the "kids' table." Personally, I didn't make it to the adult table until I was about sixteen years old. My legs would be in all sorts of contortions as I tried to squeeze them under two feet of space. On at least one side, I'd have one kid who would rather squeeze the squash in his fist than actually put it into his mouth, and the conversation wasn't particularly intellectually challenging since it often mentioned boogers. I'd look over at the adult table longingly and realize the only way to make it there was for one relative to kick off. Come to find out when I finally did make it to the adult table, the booger jokes were more entertaining than the stuff discussed there.

It is then time for a man to carve the turkey. Now, a woman usually had to get up at 4:00 a.m. to haul out the turkey and get it into the oven. For the several days previous to this, she's been baking pies and other assorted foods that can be made ahead of schedule. Now that she has finished off this masterpiece of culinary delights and the attention of everyone is focused, the guy picks up the knife and does the carving. Why shouldn't the woman get the glory? Does the guy think that by this simple act he can make claim to helping with the whole dinner? Does the woman not think herself muscular or adept enough to cut the turkey after clean and jerking it in and out of the oven? More likely after all these hours of her slaving away while the guy is relaxing, he thinks it best that she not brandish anything too sharp while he is sitting there defenselessly.

So now comes the time for people to eat. The idea here is to eat so much that you physically feel uncomfortable for the rest of the day. If you are unable to button your pants without losing the sensation in your legs, so much the better. How does this pay homage to our forefathers? The same way hiding eggs helps us remember someone rising from the dead.

After everyone is painfully full, then they bring out the pies. There will be several choices that you simply can't pick between. So what do you do? Have multiple pieces and have them throw a scoop of ice cream on top so you get that balance of hot and cold sensations.

After eating this, you should feel like you are about to act out a scene from *Alien*. You should be so tired of eating that you can't even close your mouth because your jaw muscles have given out.

So what to do after all this? Well, the women who have been spending the entire day cooking had better get back to the kitchen to clean the damn thing up! Meanwhile, the guys, who only had one of their members carve a turkey for about a minute and a half, now retire into the living room so that they can watch football games. It could be the worst two teams in the league playing, but the men are going to watch it anyway.

Why is this such a hallowed tradition? Is it because the men don't want to clean up the mess? Partly. Is it because they love the game of football? Certainly that is also a contributing factor. The big reason, however, is that men are plum out of ideas of what to talk about. Small talk is not a forte of men. It is on par with flossing one's teeth: it doesn't feel bad, and it can lead to decent results, but there are a million and one things he'd have more fun doing. Watching the game allows men to talk about the plays, the coaching decisions, the referees' calls, etc. Take the game away from men, and you've got a wax museum display on your hands.

The only thing left to do for Thanksgiving is divvy up the leftovers and head back home. Hopefully, the kids are so full that they lapse into a food coma in the car and don't give you any trouble. Unfortunately, if that is the case, your wife will fill in the gaps. Knowing that you haven't heard all the latest family news, she—come hell or high water—is going to fill you in on what you missed. You, being in the driver's seat, are a captive audience. Why does she insist on torturing you on the way home? The same reason you pee while standing up—because she can.

Christmas

or

Ho, Ho...How Much Did We Spend?

M ost people think Christmas is a holiday. It is not. It is a season. You may as well call it spring, summer, fall, Christmas, and then winter. The day after Thanksgiving is usually given as a day off by most companies. Why? It certainly has nothing to do with Thanksgiving. This is the day the Pilgrims sat around belching and getting the runs from undercooked turkey, which is nothing to celebrate.[371] We have this day off because it is the first day of the Christmas season.

So how best to celebrate the coming birthday anniversary of what many people believe is the savior of the world? Fast? Not going to happen. When "fast" is in the same sentence as food with Americans, you can bet they're talking about greasy cheeseburgers and even greasier fries. Moment of silence? That may involve something incomprehensible like turning the television off! Ain't going to happen. So what do we do? The answer is...Go shopping!

The day after Thanksgiving is *the* busiest day of the entire year for stores. In this one day alone, most stores make about the same amount they do for the entire month of July. You will find shoppers

---

371 Unless you are a supermodel.

literally fighting in the aisles with other shoppers to buy things. Nuns and senior citizens are seen giving each other headlocks and atomic knee drops as they try to grab up the last of the two-for-one sales. The stores know this. They live for this. Even though Christmas is over a month away, they've got their Christmas lights on and trees up, and they're pushing subliminal spending-spree messages on you in the Christmas carols Muzak. Unfortunately, they know this only too well and are trying to expand the season by starting with the Christmas decorations right after Halloween.

To make matters worse, it is difficult to find anyone to help you in the store, but you are nearly tripping over Santa Clauses. And then you've got to come up with some catchy excuses for your kids as to how they can be seeing a dozen Santas throughout the day. If an unlucky clerk accidentally falls out of his hiding place inside the clothes rack, then he is swarmed by customers demanding assistance. Clerks have been picked to the bone so that all that is left is their little yellow smiley button.

One of the big things stores do is have one or two amazing bargains that are "only while supplies last." That means that they have about a dozen of them ready for the thousands of shoppers. Therefore, the only way to get your hands on this bargain is to get there hours before the store actually opens. My family spent the night at my parents' house one Thanksgiving, and they actually asked me if I wanted to get up at 4:00 a.m. to go with them to the big sale. Not in this lifetime.

Of course one of the times you are out at the mall, you'll have to stop so that your kids can talk to Santa Claus. While your kid sits in Santa's lap, the "elves" will take a picture for you. With help these days, it is tough enough finding even one jolly person to deal with the public, never mind with children. That person usually gets to be Santa unless he does not have the characteristics to pull it off—i.e., too short, too liquored up, or breasts. The "elves" are people getting paid near minimum wage to have enhanced ears and enhanced attitudes. Most real elves are short in stature, so kids may be confused when they see these rather tall elves. It is up to you as to what your story is—that fresh mall air makes them grow; Santa only brings the giant, surly ones as punishment; they are elves in training who can get shrunk later if they get the job, etc. Their job is to hustle the kids through the whole process without threatening any of their lives and yank them from Santa's lap before they start peeing.

To get the picture, it costs about as much as the camera that took it. Before your kids get to see Santa, you'll have to stand in a line that is reminiscent of the old Soviet Union days when they had shortages of toilet paper. Since every child will want to tell Santa every toy that the toy companies have been deluging him with for the past six months, they are going to have to be pried off Santa's lap. Not every child is like this, though. Some ramble on and on, but when they sit in the big man's lap, they get stage fright and can't even recite their own name. Some kids don't like the whole experience and just cry...and pee.

When most kids act up for that month, the parents can say that Santa is watching and he's crossing toys off his list every time they are bad. That is usually enough to silence them for a good fifteen or twenty minutes. That may sound like a minuscule time for those people without children, but for those with, it is these periods that allow a bit of sanity to ebb back into one's life.

It goes without saying that this holiday takes a significant amount or preparation. The question is who does this work. Women, in general, like shopping, and men hate it. Men are happy to pass *all* the shopping off. Women, however, do not want all this responsibility, especially when it comes to things like getting his family presents. There is clearly a phenomenal difference between going out shopping and planning what each and every relative would possibly want/ need that somehow she has to know that they don't already have even though they would love it and couldn't imagine life without it once they had it.

The trick to who does the shopping is that men play the waiting game far easier than women do. Men just don't know that they are even playing it. By Thanksgiving, most women like to have a rough idea of who they are giving gifts to, what gifts they are giving, and how much they want to spend. They'll still go to every store in creation approximately eight times apiece to ensure themselves of the validity of their original lists, but they usually end up buying whatever they chose the first time around.

Women can do this because they have made mental notes all year long. Whenever someone remarks on something they like or need, women make a note that it would be a good gift idea. Meanwhile, men are vaguely aware that Christmas is even occurring next month. Their mental list usually consists of "If I don't get her something more thoughtful than the toaster I got her last year, I'm going to be choked with the extension cord."

So December starts off, and the woman insists to her husband that he is to get his family their gifts this year. "No problem," states the guy. A week passes, and she'll ask if he has completed his task. "Not yet." Has he even thought about it? "Not really, but there is no rush yet. Oodles of time left." Another week passes by. Another warning. Another week. The woman cracks like the Liberty Bell. She knows that he is supposed to get the gifts, but she is afraid that if he gets a boner gift, she's going to have to put her name on it, and her mother-in-law will talk about her behind her back—if she is lucky. If not, the mother-in-law can cast a smile that will wither flowers and convey the message that your wife has urinated in your family's gene pool.

The panic really starts to build, and she makes suggestions to the husband. His reply? "Sounds good. Since you know what you think best, why don't you pick it up?" She capitulates, but plans on spitting in the food she cooks him each and every day until Arbor Day. Has the man done anything wrong? Technically, no. He still had plenty of time according to his time scale to pick the stuff up. It's not his fault that the stores are so conveniently open on Christmas Eve and the Internet "guarantees" delivery on December 24! Unfortunately, that guarantee means it may leave the company, but other companies have to actually bring it to your door, and they guaranteed you no such thing.

Women especially worry about the kids' gifts. For some inexplicable reason, toy manufacturers hype at least one toy a year and then make only enough of the product to incite brawls in the stores. Anyone remember Cabbage Patch dolls? The things that were so homely that they were "cute." Mothers were literally stealing them out of other carts to get them. Their children were not going to be "deprived" of that special toy. 'Tis the season of giving as long as mothers are giving to *their* children. Some women start buying for their children in September so they'll be all set. The only thing men have ever planned out that far is putting someone on the moon.

The big present that the man really does have to watch out for is his wife's. Personally, I have absolutely no taste in clothes, jewelry, or anything else to do with what is considered fashionable. I have trouble picking clothes to wear that don't have stains. If my wife wanted clothes, I'd literally walk into the clothing store and wave money around hoping a clerk would take it and shove some articles of clothing at me. Therefore, getting something that my wife wants is pretty unlikely unless I get a hint. By hint, I mean that my wife has to tell me what she wants, the size, what store to find it at, and even the shelf it is on.

For my wife to really get the present she wants, it helps if she actually brings me to the store and pushes my face into it so that I can't possibly screw up. The only problem with this method is that I can't surprise her if she knows exactly what she is getting. Therefore, there is going to be some guilt. Better guilt, though, than her having that look on her face like you wrapped a puppy in a box and forgot to put breathing holes in it.

At some point during the month, it will be time to go pick out a Christmas tree. Again, something that sounds so simple can become an event when a wife is included. I had thought (foolishly) that to get a tree, I merely had to go to a place selling trees by the road and grab one. Now I have to pack the entire family up and go to get the tree. It is no longer a mere purchase, but an event. For a man, what he looks for in a Christmas tree is one that will fit in the corner. A woman, on the other hand, believes that there is a single perfect Christmas tree for her somewhere within a hundred-mile radius, and it is her quest to find it. Personally, I didn't even know there were different species of trees that qualified as Christmas trees. Now my wife is going over the advantages and disadvantages of spruce, Douglas fir, Scotch pine, and other nonsense. When my wife became a forest ranger, I'm not quite certain. Personally, I care about the type of tree as much as I care about the sexual life cycle of peat moss.

When your wife picks a candidate tree, your job is to hold it straight up. You wouldn't expect her to make such a critical decision with the tree at an angle! Not only must the tree be perpendicular, but your wife must then view the tree from about twenty yards' distance to ensure that it looks as good far away as it does close up. Your living room can be the size of a walk-in closet, and she'll still do this. You've then got to slowly spin the tree around to see if it has any bad spots. It can have a maximum of one, and that can be put against the wall. How can you tell if it has any bad spots since the branches haven't fallen down yet? What the heck does it matter anyway since it is going to have approximately seventy pounds of decorations that will completely obscure anything green you could possibly see on the tree? Don't bother asking or she may tell you.

So now you've got to get the tree home. Hopefully, the place has delivery or you know someone with a truck. Otherwise, you've got to get it home by strapping it to the top of your car. I'm not going to even begin giving advice on how to get a tree home this way per advice of my lawyer. Let's just say that the tree experts had better do the tying, or you'll be meeting several lawyers since you don't get special dispensation just because the object you maimed someone with represents Christmas cheer.

Once you've got the tree home, you are supposed to saw the bottom off. The reason you do this is to allow the tree to better take up water. That way, it will stay fresh longer rather than dry out. When the needles turn brown on the tree, it is a greater fire hazard than a birthday cake with Roman candles. Anyway, once you cut the bottom off, you've then got to get it into the house and into a tree stand. While you are trying to tighten the screws in the stand, that maximum of one bad spot multiplies dramatically as you've got the tree careening off every major piece of furniture, getting needles embedded so deeply that you'll be finding them through the Fourth of July.

Getting the tree straight is a project. When the kids were young and useless, they couldn't be much help. It is a minimum of a two-person job. I would have my wife hold the tree, and I'd get underneath and tighten the screws. She'd then step back (you can't judge if a tree is straight unless you are at least six feet back). Then she'd have me spin it left/right and push it back/forward until she had the best side...and then pronounce it wasn't straight. She'd have to hold it again while I unscrewed it. Then I'd have to get up and wiggle it until it did look straight. She'd hold it, and I'd go back to screwing (up). Rinse. Repeat. When the kids were older and still useless, they could hold the tree while my wife gave her critique. The problem here was that if she said it needed to go to the left, the kids wouldn't know that my wife meant her left. Even then, you aren't just supposed to push—you have to pull the tree up and set it down at the better angle. Eventually, I'd have to get out from under the tree and show them how, again proving they were actually smarter than I was as I did their work.

It now comes time to decorate the tree. First come the lights. The thing you'll notice right off the bat is that sometime during the last year, some evil being snuck into your attic and tied the lights into such knots that it would take a pack of Boy Scouts hours to untangle. Since they aren't around, the job falls to you. Once the lights are untangled, it is a good idea to check them to see if they actually work or not. The old lights they used to sell would not work if a single bulb was burned out. If you still have these sets kicking around, just toss one end around the nearest rafter and pull (making sure the other end is firmly around your neck). Trust me, this is far less painful than going through light by light—especially when one burns out when they are on the tree, and you've got to contort yourself to get to every light to find the culprit.

When you put the lights on, you go around and around the tree hoping they'll be spaced remotely evenly. Helpful hint—keep enough slack at the end so the string can reach the outlet, otherwise you will have to twist the tree, and then the bad spot is front and center and will taunt your wife until she breaks down and you have to redo it. By the time you're done, you should have about a dozen plugs in each outlet[372] and enough wire piled up to light a Las Vegas casino. Once that is done, you can then add the garland and bulbs. A guy's impulse is to throw them up randomly. Your wife will be indignant that you would take a custom so "important" as putting round things on a dead plant lightly. Therefore, put an expression of contemplation on your face and pause between each ornament before placing it randomly on the tree.

When Christmas evening arrives, the kids look like they are going through the DT's. Your job is to get them into bed at a reasonable time. This is important for two reasons: (1) they will be up no later than 5:00 a.m., and so will not only wake you up so you have no sleep, but will get so cranky later in the day that they will try to force-feed each other Legos; and (2) they will be up in eight hours, and Santa has approximately ten hours of toy assemblies to do. Kids are not going to be satisfied staring at the boxes the toys come in. They want to play with them immediately. That means that the toys have all got to be built. Your excuse to get the kids into bed is that Santa won't come while they are awake. Hopefully, they don't think it is Santa doing all the swearing in the living room.

Christmas morning arrives and, as expected, the kids will come screaming into the room to wake you and your wife. Are you the type who likes to have breakfast or a shower before you start your day? Forget it. You'll barely have enough time to be sure everything is tucked properly in your boxers before you are bodily dragged into the living room. The kids will start to open their presents. The only way to really describe it is a land version of what sharks do during a feeding frenzy. Shredded wrapping paper is flying all over the place, much like you'd expect at tobacco companies before an FDA inspection. Kids either want to open everything, barely glancing at the toys they get (which makes you feel like you are doing a bad job of parenting since they are obviously spoiled), or they examine each and

---

372 Again per the lawyer, I'm not recommending this either.

every part of the toy, including wanting to read the directions (and you become bored out of your mind).

Once the kids open up everything, they usually want to play with their favorite thing. What is that thing? Look for the most expensive thing you've purchased…and put that aside.[373] If it is a young child, their favorite will unequivocally be the biggest box that something came in. That box is a wondrous thing of magic. You come to think that you'd be a hero if, rather than spending the money you did on actual presents, you'd just hung out behind the local Sears[374] and grabbed yourself a big box.

If you have boys, chances are that they got something that you think is cool. Maybe it is a video game where you are trying to blow the heads off of Nazi zombies or a bow that shoots suction-cup darts so the cat's life will never be the same again. Basically, boys never grow up, just out. These days, more girls get cool things too. Heck, maybe *you* got some cool stuff. Regardless, it is time to play, right? Well, your wife may want the living room to look like a living room again rather than a tornado landing site. If there is company coming over, it would be easier to fight real Nazi zombies than deal with her, as the house should look like the picture on a Christmas postcard rather than a Halloween one. You've got to start recycling paper and vacuuming up pine needles.

A word of warning here—you may not have had the discipline you should have for keeping the tree watered.[375] The tree is now an

---

373 The expense of a gift *does* come into play the older a kid gets. When the kids are small, you can usually pick up a few toys at Walmart, and they will go to town with them. Give a teenager something from Walmart, and you could have quite a negative reaction, especially if it is clothing. I may not be the best person when it comes to discussing style, as I would still be buying Garanimals if they made them for adults. When kids are older, they love more electronic stuff like iPhones, iPads, and iAmgoingtobescrewedpayingvisabills. At that age, the smaller the thing, the more expensive. If you have an older kid who thinks they should have just as many gifts as the younger child even if you had to raise the money giving corpses sponge baths at the morgue to pay for what you gave them, just switch the tags on the presents and then look at their smiling face when they see their younger brother/sister using their new phone as a teething ring.

374 By the time this gets published, Sears may have gone the way of the Pony Express, Polaroid cameras, and being able to get through the day without someone Facebooking, Tweeting, and/or Skyping what they ate for lunch and thinking you actually care.

375 Like never.

electrified tinderbox. Every time anything touches the tree, pine needles rain down on the carpet. Therefore, you have to be extremely dainty vacuuming around it, or you will be picking up a never-ending supply of needles.[376]

After that, the rest of your day is spent trying to learn game rules, installing batteries, or adjusting things that Santa didn't quite put together right at 3:00 a.m. due to lack of sleep and tears of frustration blurring his vision. Of course when you look around the room and see your kids laughing and your wife smiling, you'll know that this husband/father thing ain't so bad and you wouldn't want to live life any other way.

---

376 After this is all over and it is time to take out the tree, there will be pine needles in your hair, clothes, and carpet. No matter how well you attempt to clean up, you'll be picking up needles till the Fourth of July.

Made in the USA
Lexington, KY
03 November 2016